The Story of the

BISHOP'S STORTFORD
STANSTED AND DISTRICT
FOOTBALL LEAGUE

VOLUME ONE 1922-1989

PAT BRAZZIER

**'It was said that the League's constitution was one of the
finest in the country'**

A story of grassroots football

Many thanks to Ron Hampton, Terry Ball and Andy Lines for supplying much of the official League information, without their help this project would not have been possible

Many thanks also to David Brown, Brian Curtis, Roger Brinsford, Andrew Bubien, Richard Knight, Graham Hartley and everybody else who supplied and helped with information

Many thanks also to Reach plc

A CIP catalogue record for this book is available from the British Library

ISBN 978-1-917329-16-3

Front Cover

The 'Town Ground', 3rd October 1919

Mr Charles Preston Lyall, Mr George Wilson and Mr Bill Bruty

This book is dedicated to Jeff Dallimore

(1940-2011)

'Involvement with all the local lads leading to the formation of S.J.F.C., he loved being part of that'

'A true gentleman'

Also, for Ryan Blake, Michael Dover, Bob Jerrard, John Kitchener, Ian Lambert, Neil Matthews Mick Murphy Ian Phillips, David Robinson, John Sivyer, Nick Tilstone, Bob Quinn and Kevin Gunn

All taken too soon

Also, for Mrs Margaret Perry, a true Hatfield Heath Football Club legend who served the Club for decades, always with a smile on her face

Contents

Foreword

Andy Lines, Daily Mirror Chief Reporter and former Hatfield Heath Football Club player, Bishop's Stortford, Stansted and District League Representative Team member and League Committee member.

The Bishop's Stortford, Stansted and District Football League played a major role in the lives of tens of thousands of people for more than 90 years.

For nearly a century it was often the highlight of people's weeks.

It was one of the strongest leagues in the country and so efficiently run by the volunteers who made up the League committee.

It's been disappointing there has not been some sort of book documenting its importance.

Now Pat Brazzier has finally put this right and has taken him years. He has put in thousands of hours of work and research. The whole community around the Stortford area owes him a huge debt of gratitude.

Thanks to this book the exploits of clubs from the entire North West Essex and East Herts border areas will now be recorded forever.

There will always be debate about when the League was at its strongest.

There will be those who recall the 1940s and 50s - the years after the Second World War - where village sides regularly attracted crowds of several hundred and many even charged entrance fees.

Then in the 60s, 70s, and 80s when some of the great Harlow sides like Great Parndon, Alemite, Delta, Pitney Bowes joined to make for some memorable competitive seasons.

Personally, I can still vividly recall my first ever game for Hatfield Heath Reserves in the 1979 season.

Called up on the Friday lunch-time I excitedly looked forward to my debut - only to be thrashed 6-0 soundly by North Weald Reserves!

When I played my last competitive game in the 2007 season I was able to look back with great fondness on our battles with Sheering, Hatfield Broad Oak and numerous other sides.

It's such a shame that the League doesn't exist anymore.

I would particularly like to thank all those unsung officials who worked so tirelessly over so many decades.

I was very privileged to have been asked to write the foreword to this book for an organisation that played such a major part of my life.

It's a real honour - and I do so on behalf of every single player who turned out for any club who played in the League.

Introduction

Having been away from the district for a number of years, a chance meeting with Ted Nately led me to researching and writing this story of the Bishop's Stortford, Stansted and District Football League. We spoke about our memories of local football and Ted then told me that the League had been disbanded.

Now retired and after giving it some thought, I decided to put pen to paper to record the League's history. I spent many hours travelling from my home in Crowle, North Lincolnshire to Hertford and weeks researching the Herts & Essex Observer newspapers but having to visit the Herts Archives where the copies in bound leather volumes and later copies had been transferred and kept on microfiche.

Further research was carried out at Harlow Library, Harlow Museum, Saffron Walden Library and the British Library in Boston Spa.

I am sure that there are some people who wondered whether the book would ever see the light of day. Hopefully, the books will prove to be both an accurate historical record and an enjoyable read, it's all here, in the two volumes of the Story of the Bishop's Stortford, Stansted and District Football League.

Football may well still be the beautiful game, attracting millions of viewers each week, but at grassroots level the genuine love of the game appears to have disappeared. It has become a spectator sport instead of a participation sport.

While the top of the football pyramid has prospered, the weekly slog of touring local villages has been on an alarming slide. There has been a clear move away from people being interested in playing sport at the weekend.

This has been due to many reasons including increasing costs (rising pitch fees and the cost of fuel etc), establishment of the Premier League and the Saturday lunchtime televised game and changing work patterns.

The number of 11-a-side male adult amateur football teams in England continues to decline steadily. Four out of five football pitches are provided by local authorities who must choose where to spend their ever-dwindling budgets leading to run down facilities, abject amenities and poor pitches being cited as reasons for declining participation and disincentive to attract new players.

It is not just about lack of players. Every team needs a dedicated team of people to run their team including a Chairman, Secretary, Treasurer and Manager.

Every league also needs an organising body with full responsibility for its competitions.

Last, but not least, a league needs Referees who play a crucial role in helping football take place.

Every week on football pitches across Hertfordshire and Essex footballers played real football, the grassroots game, where you had to pay to play, hoped that a referee turned up, changed in a shed, played on rain-sodden muddy pitches and took their own kit home to wash.

Just over one hundred years ago, in 1922, the League began as the Bishop's Stortford and District Junior Football League with twelve member clubs : Birchanger Reserves, Bishop's Stortford Baptists, Bishop's Stortford Congregational, Bishop's Stortford Junior Club, Bishop's Stortford Juniors, Little Hadham Juniors, Little Hallingbury Reserves, Much Hadham Villa, Sawbridgeworth Joinery Works, Sawbridgeworth Juniors, Stansted Juniors and Woodside Green.

To have a successful league they must have three things – loyalty and sportsmanship on the part of the clubs, a competent executive, and sound finance. They could congratulate themselves on having all three.

After World War II in July 1945, the Essex County Football Association made a big drive to get as many pre-war leagues as possible and clubs restarted for the following season, and to bring new clubs into being.

Their slogan was in fact: 'A football club for every village in the county.'

Between the two world wars some teams played in more than one league due to the lack of number of clubs playing in each league.

It was known in the early days for several hundred supporters to make their way to a League match and nearly 2,500 spectators at Rhodes Avenue saw Dunmow thrash Potter Street 7-1 to win the 1948/49 Premier Division Challenge Cup. Nearly 500 supporters accompanied the Dunmow team.

Junior competitive football in the area was largely dependent on 'gates' at the League's Cup Finals. In 1950, the League was very gratified that it was left in an exceptionally healthy financial position, due almost entirely to the splendid gates the League had at its finals.'

The Honorary Treasurer said : 'I have every confidence the gates will continue, because the public love to see a game of football when the whole 22 players are all out for the full 90 minutes.'

Speaking as a representative of the Essex FA, Mr A Frost said : 'the League's constitution was one of the finest in the country.'

He also told club officials that he considered the League to be on very sound footing and that its success was due in no small measure to the hard work put in by their Chairman, officers and committee members.

From its birth, the League always had good people. To name but a few : Messrs Glasscock, Tresham-Gilbey, Duchesne, Merchant, Ashford, Markwell, Baker, Lyall, Collison, Reed, Thorne, Harrison, Wilson, Banks, Brinsford and Barry.

Bill Bruty and Sugar Perry, from Hatfield Heath, were both Chairman of the Bishop's Stortford, Stansted and District League. Three of the League's annual trophies were named in honour of former Heath players, the W.A. (Bill) Bruty Memorial Cup, the W.J (Wally) Day Memorial Cup and the Sugar Perry Sportsmanship Cup.

Hatfield Heath joined the League from the Rodings (Roothings) and District League in 1934 and stayed until 2015 apart from the break for the Second World War, re-joining the League in 1947, and competed in consecutive seasons until 2014/15. The club's reserve team joined the League in 1947 and also competed in the League in consecutive seasons until the end of season 2010/11.

There were other long-standing member clubs in the League including Albury, Birchanger, Burnt Mill, Elsenham, Farnham, Great Parndon, Hatfield Broad Oak, Heath Rovers, Langley, Manuden, Newport, Potter Street, Quendon, Sheering and Thaxted.

Other clubs such as Bishop's Stortford Reserves, Bishop's Stortford Swifts, Harlow Reserves, Saffron Walden Reserves, Sawbridgeworth, Stansted and Takeley moved up to higher standards of football.

Thanks should be given to Bishop's Stortford Football Club who provided their grounds and facilities for many of the League's Cup Finals and League representative matches. Stansted, Sawbridgeworth and Saffron Walden Football Clubs also supplied their grounds and facilities.

Unfortunately, a number of young players passed away while playing in League fixtures and also a number of members of the Management Committee passed away before their time. They will never be forgotten.

Photographs play a tremendous part in football literature. The local newspaper, the Herts & Essex Observer played its part. From 1952 until 1962 the newspaper introduced wonderful team photographs with both teams posing together and sometimes with the referee. Team photographs, action shots, personalities and grounds and cartoons are depicted in this publication.

During the same period, some games were covered by the newspaper's cartoonist which must have been inspiring for the players involved. The mysterious 'JDB' created caricatures and cartoons. Previous similar cartoons had appeared in the Harlow Citizen drawn by Jimmy Brown, so it is assumed they were one and the same person.

The photos and cartoons were later replaced by single team photographs and action shots from games.

It is interesting to see the different styles of writing that local newspapermen used to report on Cup Finals over the years.

A number of seasons' programmes were heavily affected by bad weather but none as bad as 1962/63. The winter was the coldest for 200 years in Britain. It began abruptly just before Christmas in 1962.

In February 1963, the League recognised the impossibility of making up the fixture leeway caused by the freeze-up and abandoned the outstanding programme.

The Premier Division and Division I were divided into groups of six teams, the winners of each group playing off for the divisional championships.

The League cups continued, and in fact would be the only programmes for Division II teams. Promotion and relegation were suspended.

46 clubs provided teams for the League during the seventies and there was an average of 48 teams per year playing in the League during that time. There were 5,204 League games played and 25,178 League goals scored during those years. In season 1977/78 there were 1,036 player registrations, a record number.

The second half of the 1970s saw the League and its players together with the North-West Essex League battling with the East Herts District Council about the price of the hire of pitches at Grange Paddocks in Bishop's Stortford and the almost non-existent facilities there.

As can be seen from the statistics at the end of Volume II, the League had an abundance of volunteers who gave up their free time over many years who served the Hertfordshire and Essex Football Associations, the League, their clubs and officiating duties. Many of these people are long gone but we remember and thank them.

Fair play and sportsmanship, a subject close to Bill Bruty's heart, was a message promoted by all officers and visiting guests at Annual General Meetings and Dinner and Dances.

However from the 1980s the League saw a rise in the number of dismissals and cautions leading eventually to the introduction of a disciplinary code.

In 1977 the League was sponsored for the first time by Don Burlingham Associates Ltd., of Bishop's Stortford.

Further sponsorship deals were made with Brian Skingle Sports, S.C.S. Forklifts, Stansted Airport Ltd, E.J. Waterman & Son and finally Footprint.

In 1981 the League's President, George Wilson and the League's Chairman, Bill Bruty passed away and in 1982, the League's Honorary Secretary, Roger Brinsford, tendered his resignation, to become the Secretary of Bishop's Stortford Football Club.

To lose the top three League officials certainly caused some disruption.

My Story

I look back and say I'm glad I played

The earliest memory relating to football is my father, a Sheffield Wednesday supporter, showing me the Daily Newspaper, 7th February 1958, the Munich Air Crash. I have been a Manchester United fan ever since.

When I was a young boy in the 1960's, we played football every moment we could on a green at the top of Elizabeth Road where I lived in Bishop's Stortford and organised games against other streets. All we needed was a ball. Now that green has a sign 'No Ball Games.'

I attended St Joseph's Primary School and played for the school team for a couple of years which was run by a teacher, Mr Eddie Humes. I was also selected to play for the Bishop's Stortford and District Primary Schools team. Other players that I remember in that team included Paul Coombe (captain), Nicky Noakes, Roger Surrage, Stephen Fitzsimons, Mark Surridge and Stephen Andrews, all from Thorley Primary School.

At St Joseph's we had not known that Mr Humes had been a Flight Sgt Navigator during World War II and was the only survivor of a crew of seven when he was forced to parachute out of his aircraft, a Lancaster, which was shot down over Belgium after a bombing raid over Germany. He had spent the rest of the war in a prisoner of war camp. Recently I found that he was living within 50 miles of my home in North Lincolnshire and I was able to talk to him after a period of 55 years.

After leaving primary school I attended a rugby playing school, so I had to wait for a few years before becoming involved with local football.

It is interesting to note that at this time my family were frequently visited by an insurance agent, Mr Lionel Thorne, who had been a local referee and was the Honorary Appointments Secretary for the Bishop's Stortford Stansted and District League from 1953 until 1964. The position was later to be renamed Honorary Referees Secretary. He also became Vice-Chairman of the League from 1963 until 1971 and a Vice-President from 1971 until his death in 1976. Lionel was also a steward at matches held at Wembley Stadium and I still have a collection of programmes that he gave me from the matches he attended.

During this time, every month I was given copies of Charles Buchan's Football Monthly by one of my father's friends, Ted Mansfield. The magazine was the first British football magazine.

In the early sixties the boys on the Havers Estate in Bishop's Stortford formed the first team that we had been involved with and we called our team Stortford Athletic. The team photo appeared on the front page of the Classified Newspaper.

Back Row (left to right) J. Rolfe, P. Brazzier, J. Kitchener, A. Osborne, B. Nichol, M. Barry. Front Row (left to right) G. Brace, N. Matthews, G. Thurley (Captain) I. Windley. I. Macarthy.

Six of the players in the photo went on to become some of players who formed S.J.F.C. playing in the Harlow & District Sunday League and also the Bishop's Stortford, Stansted and District League.

In 1967 at the age of 15 I attended a 'trial' for local club Heath Rovers which had been formed in 1958. When I joined the club, it had three Saturday teams, the first team and the 'A' team played in the Bishop's Stortford, Stansted and District League and the reserve team played in the Hertford and District League. There was also a fourth team playing on a Sunday morning in the Harlow & District League.

I signed for the club and started playing in the 'A' team which was a mixture of 'elderly' players, younger players and other players who just enjoyed their weekend game of football.

I remember at that time playing with some great characters including Jim Hartley, Brian Doyle and John White.

Over the next four years I progressed to the first team that included players such as Peter Sokell, Bob Whitelock, Alan Cooper, Bernard Precey, Eddie Chesterman, Ernie Paul, Dennis Elms, Dave Locke, Phil Matthews, Graham Miller, Terry Wellham and Brian Simmonds who was probably the best player that I ever played with and was always the leading goal scorer for the club each year winning the 'Vic Day' trophy.

Other players and club members that I remember were Ron Underwood, Ron Hampton, John Dickinson, John Redfern, Tom Hamilton, Geoff Wynn, Eddie Wright, John Beeston, Terry Garner, Roy Newsome, John Perry, Alan Oakley and John Oakley, Dave Collins, Denis Potter, Ted Levey, John Clemmett, Roger Wickendon, Alan Langford, Alan and John Shannon, Graham and Trevor Nutter, Chris Brunning, Richard (Dick) Culpin, Bill Smith, Terry Martin and Brian Oak. Also, Tony Eaton, Denis Metson, Fred Lenton, Ron Barrett, Tony Knightley, David Reed, Dennis Kitchener, Aiden Mynott, Lawrence Ross, Cliff Bailey, Colin Broadbent, Peter Harvey, Chris Hawkes, David Vealey, Terry McCormick, Graham Hartley, Dave Thomas, Mick Pottle, John Perry, Peter Hanks, Brian Cracknell, Marshall Hinson, Steve Chipperfield and Miller Lumsden.

Some of my young friends that also joined the club included Mick Barry, John Spencer, Peter Vealey and Bob Quinn, all gifted players.

According to the weekly team sheets, when I first joined the club, the meeting place for away matches was at HRFC. I mistakenly thought at first that this was a clubhouse. However, it just meant at the junction of Heath Row and Fulton Crescent!

I was lucky enough to win a ticket through Heath Rovers for the 1970 FA Cup Final between Chelsea and Leeds and attended the match with Chris Hawkes who also won a ticket. You may remember that the Wembley stadium's pitch was in very poor condition with the Horse of the Year Show having taken place there a week previously. The match went into extra-time and ended 2-2.

I had an interesting conversation with Dick Culpin who I played with at Heath Rovers and who I had not spoken to for over 40 years.

He reminded me of the annual Heath Rovers Boxing Day match between the Tankards and Anti-Tankards. When you had played 100 matches for the club you were awarded a tankard.

Dick remembered that one year the pitch was covered by a foot of snow, but we still played. Brian Simmonds brought us all a bin bag which we used as undershirts as it was very cold. In the match Brian played in his wellies!!

During my time with Heath Rovers, I was lucky enough to play in over 100 matches for the club and therefore able to play for both the Tankards and Anti-Tankards. I also won the Bob Dyton Memorial Trophy as leading scorer of the club's Sunday team for four years in a row. Bob Dyton was a former Rovers player.

We also spoke about Heath Rovers getting through to the Herts Junior Cup Final which was played at St Albans at the same time as a club tour of the Swansea area in 1969 where we stayed at the Mumbles and played a couple of friendlies.

One of our matches on tour was refereed by Tom Reynolds, a top referee from Wales who refereed in the Football League Division I (now the Premier League) at the time. He told me to stop tying my laces in bows!

I spoke with Elsie Hartley (88) who told me that, before my time, the club's players used to get together at New Year, and everybody dressed up and over the years there were various themes. She also spoke of the tremendous camaraderie at the club.

I was a founder member of S.J.F.C. Most of the players had been friends living on the Havers Estate in Bishop's Stortford.. We wanted to play in a team together and started in the Harlow & District Sunday League in 1973 and then also joined the Bishop's Stortford, Stansted and District League in 1974. In the first two seasons in the Stortford League, we achieved two trebles scoring a total of 216 League goals in 43 games!

On Saturdays after leaving S.J.F.C. I played for other teams in the Bishop's Stortford, Stansted and District League including Sheering, Farnham and Grange Park and managing S.J.F.C. and the Telecom Dynamos boys' team for a while.

I also played for Standon and Puckeridge, Much Hadham and Tewin in the Hertford and District League, Sawbridgeworth Rangers and BP Harlow in the Harlow & District Sunday League and Sawbridgeworth in the Essex Olympian League, and lastly the Cockerills FC in the Bishop's Stortford Sunday League.

Interesting Facts

The Division I Challenge Cup was the oldest by many a long year of the Cups held by the League. It was a magnificent rose bowl, which, according to the inscription, was 'presented to the Stansted Football League by Ormond Blyth, October 15th, 1907.' The winners of this Cup are legion and included Bishop's Stortford Town 1910/11 and 1919/20, Stansted Rovers 1913/14, Saffron Walden 1907/08 and 1920/23, Much Hadham 1937/38, Rodings Utd 1948/49 to name but a few. This trophy was originally presented to the Stansted and District League Winners.

The original Challenge Cup was given to the League by Mr Tresham Gilbey.

Mr George Reed donated a Rose bowl which was used as the Division III Championship Trophy in 1988. He also donated the Division III runners-up shield.

The Division III Challenge Cup was donated by North Weald in memory of two players killed in a car crash early in the 1969/70 season.

The Inter-Divisional Cup which was originally competed for by teams from Divisions II and III was presented to the League by the President, Mr G H Wilson when the competition first began in the 1969/70 season.

The W.A. (Bill) Bruty Memorial Trophy was a superb Solid Silver Cup, which was very kindly donated by Mr Eddie Bentley, President and Chairman of Bishop's Stortford FC, in memory of the League's late Chairman of over 30 years standing.

A new Premier Division Championship Cup named the R E Baker Memorial Cup, in memory of the League's late Secretary and the A L Rushforth Memorial Cup, in memory of the League's late Vice-Chairman were introduced for the 1963/64 season.

The new Premier Division Challenge Cup was donated by the Herts & Essex Observer and was also introduced from 1963/64.

Chris Newman was the League's most decorated player and received a League Badge for representing the League team on three occasions, a League Plaque for ten appearances and the only player to receive a special Plaque for representing the League on twenty-five occasions. Chris was of course one of the players of Albury FC that was successful in the seventies and early eighties.

Annual Subscription Fees

1959 – Premier Division £1 15/-, Division I £1 1/-, Division II £15/-

1972 – Premier Division £2.50, Division I £2.25, Division II/111 £2.25

1976 – Premier Division £3.50, Division I £3.25, Division II/III £3.00

1983 – Premier Division £20.00, Division I £18.00, Division II/III £16.00

1988 – Premier Division £25.00, Division I £23.00, Division II/III £21.00

1994 – £30.00 for each first team, £25.00 for each reserve or 'A' team

2004 – £40.00 for each first team, £35.00 for each reserve or 'A' team

2014 – £40.00 per team

Match Official's fees

1938 – 3/6d, plus 3rd class rail or bus fare, whichever was the cheaper or 2d per mile cycled

1976 – referee £1.75 and linesmen £1.25

1983 – referee £5.00 and linesmen £2.50

1988 – referee £8.00 and linesmen £4.00

The Officials of the League draw attention to the following definition of a "Sportsman" and earnestly hope that ALL, whether as Players or Spectators, will keep this definition to the forefront of the League's Football.

A SPORTSMAN

1. Plays the game for the game's sake.

2. Plays for his side and not for himself.

3. Is modest in victory and generous in defeat.

4. Accepts all decisions in the proper spirit.

5. Is chivalrous towards a defeated opponent.

6. Is unselfish and always ready to help others to become proficient.

7. As a Spectator, applauds good play on both sides

8. Never interferes with Referees or Judges, no matter what the decision.

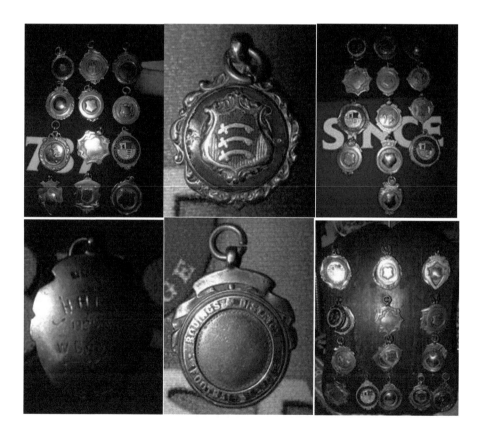

Medals belonging to Bill Bruty, Harry (Dick) Bruty, Albert Bruty and Fred Bruty from Hatfield Heath

Timeline

The Bishop's Stortford and District Junior Football League was founded in 1922.

The original member clubs of the League were :-

Birchanger Reserves, Bishop's Stortford Baptists, Bishop's Stortford Congregational, Bishop's Stortford Junior Club, Bishop's Stortford Juniors, Little Hadham Juniors, Little Hallingbury Reserves, Much Hadham Villa, Sawbridgeworth Joinery Works, Sawbridgeworth Juniors, Stansted Juniors and Woodside Green.

Bishop's Stortford Baptists were the first League champions.

In the first League Challenge Cup Final, Little Hallingbury Reserves defeated Bishop's Stortford Baptists by two goals to one.

The Bishop's Stortford and District Junior Charity Cup was introduced in 1923.

In season 1924/25, Stansted Juniors became the first team to complete the Division I League and Cup double.

The first League Handbook that I have, dated 1929, stated as its first rule: The competition shall be called the Bishop's Stortford and District Junior League and shall be open to Junior Clubs within a radius of eight miles of the Chequers Hotel, Bishop's Stortford.

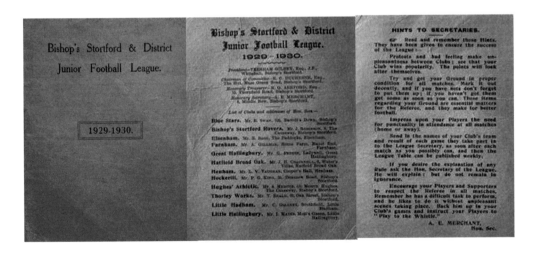

The 1928 final of the Challenge Cup between Little Hallingbury and Blue Star was drawn and was the first replayed final.

In season 1932/33 Hatfield Broad Oak won the League's Challenge Cup for the third season in a row.

In these early years, a member of each club was expected to attend each League Council meeting. At the 1933/34 Annual General Meeting it was proposed that any club not represented at a meeting should be fined 2s 6d (half a crown) and the proposal was carried.

In 1936, the death was announced of Mr 'Freddie' Markwell the League's Honorary Secretary at the very young age of 31.

The League was first increased to two divisions for the season 1936/37 when the League amalgamated with the Stansted and District League and became The Bishop's Stortford, Stansted and District Junior Football League

In season 1938/39 Abbess Roding scored 172 League goals in 28 games and were Division I Champions.

It was first noted in the minutes of the League's 1938/39 Annual General Meeting that there had been 735 registrations.

The 1938/39 League Handbook stated as its first rule: This combination of Amateur Clubs shall be called the Bishop's Stortford, Stansted and District Junior Football League and Challenge Cup, and shall consist of not less than five and not more than 32 Amateur Clubs within a radius of 12 miles of the Corn Exchange, Bishop's Stortford, all of which shall be affiliated to a recognised association, and whose names are returned on Form D to the Essex County Football Association on or before August 1st in each year.

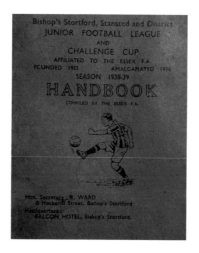

The 1939/40 season was disrupted by the start of the Second World War. However, the League was formed for the season in two sections, North and South.

After the Second World War, the League had only one division for a season but returned to two divisions for the season 1947/48 and three divisions for the season 1948/49.

In March 1949, the death was announced of Mr E C Duchesne a well-known personality in Bishop's Stortford and a former Chairman and President of the Bishop's Stortford, Stansted and District Junior League.

Nearly 2,500 spectators at Rhodes Avenue saw Dunmow thrash Potter Street 7-1 to win the 1948/49 Premier Division Challenge Cup. Nearly 500 supporters accompanied the Dunmow team.

In 1950 Dunmow became the first team to complete the double by winning both the Premier Division championship and retaining the Premier Division Cup.

Green Tye defeated Takeley Reserves 3-1 in the Division II Challenge Cup Final, after two replays in 1950. This was the first Challenge Cup Final to go to a second replay.

In August 1950, the death was announced of Mr Arthur Collison, Chairman of the League. He was succeeded by Mr Bill Bruty.

The Bishop's Stortford Charity Cup was reintroduced in 1950 and the final was played on boxing day at Rhodes Avenue, the home of Bishop's Stortford FC.

The League's first known headquarters was the Falcon Hotel, Bishop's Stortford. By season 1951/52 the headquarters had changed to the Reindeer Hotel, Bishop's Stortford.

The League returned to a two division format for the 1954/55 season.

In 1954 Rhodes Avenue and Birchanger drew their Division II Challenge Cup Final 2-2 and it was reported that each club would hold the cup for 6 months. I believe this was the only occasion that this had happened. However, at the start of the 1954/55 season the 1953/54 season Division II Challenge Cup Final went to a second replay with Birchanger eventually beating Rhodes Avenue 1-0. This was only the second Challenge Cup Final to go to a second replay.

In January 1955 Mr Hayward, the League's Honorary Press and Match Secretary was asked to resign.

The 1954/55 Premier Division Challenge Cup Final between Burnt Mill and Great Parndon was abandoned during extra-time with the score standing at 1-1. This was the first Challenge Cup Final to be abandoned.

The name of the League was amended in 1956/57 to the Bishop's Stortford, Stansted and District Football League.

The death of League President, Mr C W P Lyall was reported in December 1956. He was succeeded by Mr George Wilson.

In 1957 the League's representative team won the West Essex Inter-League Competition for the first time.

In season 1956/57 Rhodes Avenue scored 170 League goals in 26 games.

The League increased to a three division format for the season 1958/59.

Month to month fixture lists were introduced for the first time for the 1959/60 season.

From 1961, the League's clubs no longer had to attend the monthly League Council meetings. The League was now run by its officers and a committee.

In season 1961/62 High Laver won the Premier Division for the third season in a row and for the fifth time in six seasons.

In 1962 Takeley Football Club was disbanded but reformed in 1963.

The League changed its headquarters once again at the start of season 1961/62 to The British Legion Club, Windhill, Bishop's Stortford.

The winter of 1962/63 was the coldest for 200 years in Britain. It began abruptly just before Christmas in 1962. The weeks before had been changeable and stormy, but then on 22 December a high-pressure system moved to the north-east of the British Isles, dragging bitterly cold winds across the country. After Boxing Day snow swept across the nation. Blizzards and icy fogs froze the country. Temperatures plummeted to -22 degrees centigrade. It was the coldest winter since 1740. The elements did not relent until March. Rivers and lakes froze over. Snow drifts reached 20 feet deep. Food prices soared. Power Cuts became commonplace and fuel was in short supply. Football stood no chance. This situation was to last much of the winter. Sporting events all over the country were severely disrupted including the Bishop's Stortford, Stansted and District Football League. The seasons matches were abandoned, and an emergency competition set up.

In April 1963, 16 years-old Michael Dover, the Albury goalkeeper, was fatally injured in a match against Elsenham.

In 1963, the death Mr A L Rushforth was announced. At the time of his death he was Vice-President of the Newport Football Club and Vice-Chairman of the League. For some years he was Chairman of Newport.

The League was originally affiliated to The Essex FA and to the Hertfordshire Football Association from the 1963/64 season.

Bishop's Stortford Swifts were runners-up in the Herts Junior Cup in season 1963/64 and were the first team from the League to reach the final.

In season 1963/64 Takeley scored 178 League goals in 22 games, the highest amount of League goals scored by a team in any season.

Mr Bob Baker B.E.M., the League's Honorary Secretary, passed away aged just 47 in 1963. He was succeeded by Mr R C Harrison.

In 1964 Potter Street won the new Premier Division Cup, known as The Herts & Essex Observer Cup.

In 1964 Bishop's Stortford Swifts were awarded the new Premier Division Championship Cup named the R E Baker Memorial Cup, in memory of the League's late Honorary Secretary. Rhodes Avenue were awarded the new Division I Championship Cup named the A L Rushforth Memorial Cup, in memory of the League's late Vice-Chairman.

In 1964 cups were also given to the Divisional League runners-up for the first time.

The League's Management Committee introduced the Sportsmanship Cup for the season 1964/65. Hatfield Heath were the first winners.

At the end of the 1964/65 season Bishop's Stortford Swifts withdrew from the League to play higher level football.

1965/66 saw the introduction of the Linesman's Trophy presented by the North-West Essex Referees' Society. The first winner was Hatfield Heath's Mr F C Bruty.

In 1967 a young Bishop's Stortford sportsman who lived for football died playing the game he loved. Birchanger's David Robinson was buried still wearing the football kit in which he died.

In season 1967/68 Potter Street won the League's Premier Division for the fourth season in a row.

Substitutions during matches in the League were first permitted in the 1968/69 season.

In April 1969, The first 'David Robinson' Memorial Cup was played at Rhodes Avenue, Bishop's Stortford FC when the League beat the Harlow & District League by two goals to one.

In season 1968/69 Albury scored 175 League goals in 26 games.

In 1969 the League expanded to include a fourth division as well as the Inter-Divisional Cup contested by clubs in Divisions II and III.

1970 saw the League's first lady secretary, Mrs D Trott from Hatfield Broad Oak.

On 20th May 1971, the League's Representative team won the West Essex Inter-League Cup Competition at the Epping Town FC ground beating the Eastern Suburban Football Combination by 2 goals to 1.

The sudden deaths of Mr W J Day, the Honorary Registration Secretary and a Vice-President, Mr A C Harris were announced during 1971.

The League changed its headquarters again at the start of season 1971/72 to the Bishop's Stortford Working Men's Club, South Street, Bishop's Stortford.

1972 marked the 50th anniversary of the League and it was presented with a pennant marking the anniversary from the Harlow League by Chairman Arthur Dimond.

In season 1972/73 Albury won the League's Premier Division for the third season in a row.

In 1973 Brian Bayford, who was at that time the Bishop's Stortford Football Club Secretary and member of Hertfordshire FA, was elected as a Vice-President.

Individual divisional sportsmanship awards were introduced for the 1973/74 season.

Great Parndon left the League in 1974 to play in the South Essex League until 1976.

The Jack Cottrill Memorial Cup for the 'Secretary of the Year' was introduced in 1974.

In 1975 Takeley became the first team from the League to win the Essex Junior Cup.

The death of a Vice-President Lionel Thorne was announced in March 1976. Lionel served the League as Honorary Referees' Secretary (1953-66) and Vice Chairman (1963-71).

Albury became the only club from the League to win the Herts Junior Cup in 1976.

In season 1975/76, S.J.F.C. completed the second of two treble wins, having retained the Inter-Divisional Cup and won the Division I and II Division Championships and Challenge Cups.

S.J.F.C. also competed in a game rare to the League in 1976 – a second replay in a Cup Final, only the third occasion this had happened.

A further change to the League's headquarters was made for the season 1976/77 to the Birchanger Working Men's Club.

In season 1976/77 Takeley won the League's Premier Division for the third season in a row.

In 1977 Don Burlingham Associates (Commercial) Ltd became the first sponsor of the League. The company sponsored the League for 3 seasons from 1977/78 until the end of season 1979/80.

The first W.J. (Wally) Day Memorial Cup was played in 1977.

Takeley's teams withdrew from the League at the end of the 1977/78 season to compete in higher level football.

It was announced that Roy Harrison, who had served as the League's Vice-Chairman, Honorary Secretary, Honorary Press and Match Secretary and Honorary Fixtures Secretary, passed away in 1978.

Season 1978/79 saw a record 69 referees registered with the League.

On 1st April 1980, the League's Representative team won the West Essex Inter-League Cup Competition for the second time at the Epping Town FC ground beating the Romford & District League by 2 goals to 1.

In 1980 Great Parndon completed the quadruple by taking the Essex Junior Cup, the Premier Division Championship and Cup and the West Essex Border Charity Cup.

In 1980 the League was delighted that they were able to find sponsors for all Cup Finals. This was the first occasion that it had ventured into this particular field and it proved highly successful. The first sponsor was the Herts & Essex Observer Group.

In 1981 Brian Skingle Sports agreed to sponsor the League for 3 seasons but in fact sponsored the League from 1981/82 until 1987/88.

The deaths of the Vice-President and Chairman W A (Bill) Bruty and President of the League, G H Wilson and were announced in 1981. Following the death of Mr Bruty, the League introduced The W A (Bill) Bruty Memorial Trophy.

Mr Wilson was succeeded by Mr J E Barry and Mr Bruty was succeeded by Mr L G Banks.

At a special general meeting of the League in November 1982 Pelham Rangers FC were expelled.

Players were required to wear numbered shirts (1 to 13) from the 1982/83 season.

In season 1982/83 Great Parndon won the League's Premier Division for the fourth time in a row and for the fifth time in six seasons.

The first W.A. (Bill) Bruty Memorial Cup Final was played in 1983.

In 1984 the death of Mr Les Frost, a Vice-President of the League was announced. In addition, as well as being a Vice-President of the League, Mr Frost had been associated with

Takeley FC for over 50 years and the club offered to donate a trophy for a competition between Takeley FC and the League Representative side to be played as a pre-season match every year.

In season 1983/84 Great Parndon won the Premier League Challenge Cup for the third time in a row.

A long service certificate from the Essex FA was awarded to Mr J E Gransden (Quendon Athletic).

In season 1987/88 Sheering Reserves won the Inter-Divisional Cup for the third season in a row.

Also, in season 1987/88 Hatfield Broad Oak won the W.A. (Bill) Bruty Memorial Cup for the fifth season in a row.

In 1988 S.C.S. Forklifts became the new sponsors of the League and remained sponsors until the end of 1993/94 season.

In October 1988, the death was announced of Bob Jerrard of Hatfield Heath. The officers and League Management Committee paid tribute to the ex-League representative player who was the perfect example for players to follow being a one club man and matching up over 1,200 games without ever being cautioned or sent off.

Essex FA long service certificates were awarded to Mr K H French and Mr J Rushforth (Newport).

The tragic death of ex N.A.L.G.O. and League Representative goalkeeper John Sivyer was announced in 1989.

The death of Mr Len Reed of Farnham FC was announced during 1989.

The death was announced of former referee and local football official Mr Tom Gee in December 1989.

Hartspur Writes

Reproduced from the Bishop's Stortford Football Club Handbook 1969/70.

Despite the lack of facilities in some areas, and this is one of them, the younger generation, I am afraid, do not realise just how fortunate they are in regard to amenities for playing or watching sport.

This is not an attempt to knock the modern youngster who is often heard complaining that there isn't this or that available, but a plain statement.

Way back in the 1920's and even later there was little or no organisation of sport for the teenager and as far as football was concerned, what few pitches were provided by the local authorities were even more primitive than they are now.

If you had the good fortune to be allocated a pitch, it was up to you to provide the posts, erect them and under-take the weekly marking out.

But we managed to enjoy ourselves and like to think that through our own efforts sowed the seeds of the youth and junior organisations which exist today.

Let me give you an example of how we went about breaking in on the soccer scene,

It was an August evening that several of us were wandering through the churchyard of a town not many miles from Stortford when someone suddenly thought it might be a good idea to form a football club.

The idea immediately caught on and within an incredibly short space of time things were on the move. Primarily because his father was verger at the church and we thought that the stokehole would be as good as a place as anywhere to hold our committee meetings, one of the gang was appointed secretary.

Money obviously presented a problem, but one of our associates was not only a pretty useful player but came from a family somewhat better off financially than most of us. From him we borrowed enough to purchase some nets and a ball, made our own goal posts and, of course, purchased our own kit.

Because there was little organised football for those in our age group, arranging friendly matches presented no particular problem, I think we played around 30 in the first season.

Incidentally, we had no knowledge of the need to become affiliated to the county FA and played our last game at Letchworth in the middle of June!

Transport to away games presented something of a problem, but my father had a car, an Austin Seven, in which, three of my team-mates travelled with me on a rota basis with the remainder happily cycling 20 or 30 miles for a game.

To meet running costs, we each paid fourpence into the kitty at home games and two pence when playing away.

The club, I am happy to say, prospered until Hitler decided to have a punch-up. Several players graduated to senior status, at least two of them playing for Stortford.

For me anyway. The 'good old days,' so often derided, had something to offer.

Football In The Area Before 1922

On the 30th of September 1882, members of several local football clubs discussed the formation of a 'Football Association' at the White Hart Hotel. The name 'Essex County Football Association' was proposed and seconded.

Football had been played in Hertfordshire from around 1860. The Hertfordshire County Football Association was founded in 1885 after the existing teams (then numbering around 20) agreed to hold a meeting to discuss their position and ended up affiliating.

Some well-known clubs had teams playing in the Bishop's Stortford League at one time, and advanced to more senior football.

Saffron Walden Town was established in Saffron Walden in 1872 and are the oldest senior football club and were a founder member of the Essex County Football Association.

Bishop's Stortford Football Club was established at the Chequers Hotel on 28th January 1874. In 1885 the club were founder members of the Hertfordshire County Football Association

Bishop's Stortford won the last FA Amateur Cup Final in 1974, the club's 100th anniversary and also the FA Trophy in 1981. Both these finals were played at the old Wembley Stadium.

There are references to Stansted Football Club existing in 1892 but the founding date is put at the date the club moved to Green Meadow in 1902. The club won the FA Vase in 1984 and this final was played at the old Wembley Stadium.

The Sawbridgeworth Football Club was formed in 1897 by members of Sawbridgeworth Cricket Club. Sawbridgeworth were the first winners of the West Essex Border Cup in 1922 and were the first team from the district to win the Herts Junior Cup in 1927.

In 1879 at a meeting at the Coach and Horses Inn it was unanimously decided to form a football club in conjunction with the Hockerill cricket club, and the following were elected to act with the present committee of the Hockerill cricket club, Messrs Clarabutt, F Glasscock, W Glasscock, Green, Spanner, Tuck and A O Watkins. Mr E L Swift was also elected captain for the season.

Playing members' subscription for the season was fixed at 2s 6d.

It was reported in the local press that the Hockerill Cricket and Football Club played a scratch match by 'torchlight.' The club ground was situated on the corner of Dunmow Road, opposite the Nags Head and as the highway runs along two sides of the field and at somewhat higher elevation, the spectators had a good opportunity of seeing what took place.

The preparations for 'throwing a light upon the subject' were at one varied and unique. The game commenced at 8 o'clock – a gun being discharged to set the ball rolling – and by that time half-a-dozen large bonfires fed by faggots and tar barrels were in full blaze, and from a dozen stands 10 feet high, – placed at suitable distances apart – on which were tin vessels containing a combination of combustibles – improved 'cressets' so to speak – there leaped forth fiery flames, while dotted about the field were a number of Chinese lanterns, and now and again coloured fires and fireworks, added effectiveness to, as remarkable scene as has been witnessed in Stortford during the present generations.

The number of persons present was estimated at 2,000 and viewed by the changing shades of light, they formed a striking back ground to the weird picture of which the club in their tight fitting costumes, were the central figures as, lithely and agilely they coursed after the ball. Play continued for an hour and a half, with a shortened interval at half-time and was kept up with much spirit.

Sides were chosen by Mr Swift the captain and Mr F Glasscock, the vice-captain. The latter was considered to be the stronger team but the former scored a goal. The services of the band of the Sixth Rifle Volunteers were engaged for the occasion.

Albury were founded in 1888.

The East Herts and District League was formed in 1896 and its first season included Burnt Mill & Netteswell who became champions and Bishop's Stortford Wanderers (Bishop's Stortford FC).

Hockerill Athletic Football Club was formed in the 1896.

The Herts County League was formed in 1898.

Takeley Football Club was established in 1900.

Hatfield Heath were re-formed in 1901 but anecdotal village folklore puts it in 1898 but could be earlier.

The Stansted and District League was formed in 1907 with four teams entering in its first season, Saffron Walden Town (champions), Harlow Town, Bishop's Stortford and Stansted Rovers.

The Hertford and District League was formed in 1910.

The Saffron Walden and District League was formed in 1911 and included Bishop's Stortford (champions), Stansted Rovers and Saffron Walden Town.

The Roothings and District League was formed in 1920.

The Dunmow and District League was formed in 1921.

Source : Fred Maslen / Herts & Essex Observer

HOCKERILL ATHLETIC 1921/22

The Herts County League folded in 1925 but the Herts & Essex Border League was formed in the same year and included Saffron Walden Town, Harlow Town, Sawbridgeworth and Stansted. This League ran until 1934/35.

Source : Fred Maslen / Herts & Essex Observer

HOCKERILL ATHLETIC 1925/26

The local leagues that existed in the season before the Bishop's Stortford and District Junior Football League was formed included the Rodings and District League which had been renamed at the start of the 1921/22 season. The League had originally been called the Roothing's and District League. Member clubs of the League at that time were :- Fyfield, Good Easter, Hallingbury, Hatfield Broad Oak, Hatfield Heath, Matching Green, Moreton, Rodings United, Sheering and Willingale.

Bishop's Stortford, Burnt Mill, Harlow, Sawbridgeworth and Stansted Rovers were playing in the East Herts and District League.

Division I of the Stansted and District League included Bishop's Stortford, Burnt Mill, Harlow, Saffron Walden, Sawbridgeworth and Stansted Rovers.

Division II of that Stansted and District League included the following clubs :- Birchanger, Burnt Mill Reserves, Dunmow, Harlow Reserves, Hockerill Athletic, Manuden, Saffron Walden Reserves, Sawbridgeworth Reserves, Stansted Rovers Reserves, Takeley, Thaxted and Wendon.

The Saffron Walden and District League Division II member clubs were :- Debden, Great Chesterford, Ickleton, Little Chesterford, Newport, Saffron Walden Ramblers and Saffron Walden 3rd XI. In 1921 the Saffron Walden and District League had invited applications from clubs to form a second division.

The Dunmow League member clubs were :- Bannister Green Rovers, Dunmow Reserves, Felstead Rovers, Great Waltham, Stebbing, The Eastons and Thaxted Reserves.

The Albury and District League was also set up in 1921 and the founder member clubs were :- Albury, Braughing, Brent Pelham, the Baptist Guild (Bishop's Stortford), Farnham, Furneux Pelham and Little Hadham. Interestingly Mr Walter Bayford, of Furneux Pelham, was the Honorary Secretary. Walter was Brian Bayford's father.

The Clavering League was also mentioned in the Herts & Essex Observer which included Brent Pelham, Clavering, Langley, Manuden Reserves and Stansted Juniors.

Many other teams were regularly playing friendly matches.

The players in local football in the days just after World War I were amateurs in the true sense of the word. They had to pay a membership fee to belong to their club, and usually a shilling or more each time they played to help towards the travelling and tea expenses. They provided all their own kit except the jerseys and the goalkeeper usually had to supply even that. Travelling to a match was not done in the comfortable luxurious manner of the present day. Admittedly, most of the journeys were within a 30-mile radius and Cliff Jeary remembers, when playing for Stansted, travelling to away matches in an open lorry, with a 'tilt' over it supported by a wooden frame. The players sat on wooden forms placed around the inside.

The Early Years

The Bishop's Stortford and District Junior Football League was formed in 1922.

Unfortunately, many of the final League tables and results of some Cup Finals were not recorded in the Herts & Essex Observer in the earlier years of the League but where possible information has been acquired and recorded.

Records of the formation of the League appear to be practically non-existent and the only record that Roy Harrison, Honorary Secretary, writing in 1968, could find was on the plinth of a Stansted & District League trophy (which was being used as the League's Division I Challenge Cup) and that it was won by Saffron Walden Town in 1907/08. This was the original Stansted & District League Division I League Winners trophy.

However, it is known now that it was a flimsy organisation. It was reported in August 1922, in the Chelmsford Chronicle, a junior competition, limited to players who were aged up to the age of 21, was formed at Bishop's Stortford, with Mr P H Glasscock as Honorary Secretary. Mr Glasscock, in his youth was a very keen footballer, and played for Bishop's Stortford Casuals. He was a keen Tennis and Billiards player and was also a football referee.

The League was started largely through the influence of Mr Duchesne and Mr H S Tee, to provide competitive football for young teams.

Charles Lyall, who served later as Chairman and also President of the League, was one of the men who also had helped to establish the League, together with Mr R G Ashford and Mr R Ward.

The original twelve member clubs of the Bishop's Stortford and District Junior Football League for the **1922/23** season were :- Birchanger Reserves, Bishop's Stortford Baptists, Bishop's Stortford Congregational, Bishop's Stortford Junior Club, Bishop's Stortford Juniors, Little Hadham Juniors, Hallingbury Reserves, Much Hadham Villa, Sawbridgeworth Joinery Works, Sawbridgeworth Juniors, Stansted Juniors and Woodside Green.

In that season there were still other local leagues including the Rodings and District League :- Bush End, Good Easter, Hallingbury, Hatfield Heath, Magdalen Laver, Matching Green, Moreton, Roxwell, Rodings United, Sheering and Willingale & Fyfield.

The Saffron Walden and District League :- Arkesdon, Debden, Ickleton, Little Chesterford, Newport, Saffron Walden 3rd XI, Saffron Walden Ramblers and Wenden.

The Albury and District League :- Albury, Bishop's Stortford Baptist Young Men's Guild, Brent Pelham, Farnham, Furneux Pelham and Green Tye.

The Dunmow and District League :- Bannister Green Rovers, Braintree St Michael, Dunmow, Felstead Rovers, Great Leighs, Great Waltham Roothings & Canfield, Stebbing. and Thaxted.

Burnt Mill, who were to join the Bishop's Stortford and District Junior League later were playing in the Stansted and District League Division I. Takeley, who would also join later, were playing in the Stansted and District League Division II.

The first mention of the League in the Herts and Essex was on the 20th September 1922. The fixtures, Hallingbury Reserves vs Sawbridgeworth Joinery Works and Sawbridgeworth Juniors vs Bishop's Stortford Juniors were announced. Reports of these matches appeared in the following week's issue. At Hallingbury, the visitors winning by 2-1. Sawbridgeworth Juniors beat Bishop's Stortford Juniors by 3-2. Little Hadham Juniors also played their first match entertaining Bishop's Stortford Baptists with the visiting team winning 1-0.

In the first season of the Bishop's Stortford and District Junior Football League it had seemed that Sawbridgeworth Joinery Works would be champions, but in March 1923 they were deducted ten points for playing illegal players.

A large company of spectators assembled on the Bishop's Stortford Town Ground to witness the meeting of Hallingbury Reserves and Bishop's Stortford Baptist Young Men's Guild in the first Junior League Cup Final.

The game was very fast and even with both teams going all out from start to finish. The Baptists were the first to score, the ball being rushed into the net from a scramble in the goal mouth. This put Hallingbury on their mettle and they attacked strongly. R Bayford secured, and after a fine elusive run passed to H Gunn, who was well placed to equalise.

H Bayford then put Hallingbury ahead with a spinning shot and at half-time they were leading 2-1.

In the second half play was principally in the Hallingbury territory but the Baptists could not score and the numerous corners they were awarded all failed to materialise. An interesting game ended with the interval score unchanged. The cup and medals, together with those for the winners of the League, would be presented at a smoking concert in the near future.

The match between Bishop's Stortford Baptist Young Men's Guild and Bishop's Stortford Juniors decided the championship of the Junior League, the Baptists winning 3-0, after a fast and exciting game watched by a fair company of enthusiasts. The Juniors were unfortunate in having their left-back off the field for three parts of the game, but the Baptists were in good fettle and scored through D Edwards (2) in the first half and A Thurley in the second.

The Juniors pressed in the latter stages of the game but were unable to beat the goalie, who amongst other shots saved a penalty.

1922 also saw the first West Essex Border Cup Final. The trophy, a handsome silver cup was donated and presented by Mr H Sowerbutts from Sheering. The object of the cup was to raise funds for local hospitals and others by means of a competition between the junior clubs along the Hertfordshire and Essex borders.

Mr Sowerbutts was President with Messrs H P Morley and B T R Pyle as Vice-Presidents and Mr C W P Lyall (Sawbridgeworth) as Honorary Secretary. Sawbridgeworth defeated Burnt Mill in the final at Bishop's Stortford Football Club by two goals to one.

There were twelve member clubs for the **1923/24** season of the League. However, Bishop's Stortford Junior Club and Standon Villa withdrew from the League during the season.

Mr E C Duchesne, who was later to become President of the League, felt that he should write to local footballers, via the local press about the 'offside' Law.

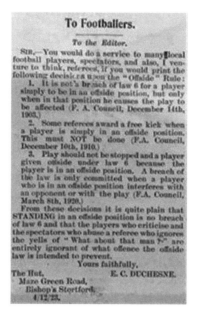

To Footballers.

To the Editor.

SIR,—You would do a service to many local football players, spectators, and also, I venture to think, referees, if you would print the following decisions upon the "Offside" Rule:

1. It is not a breach of law 6 for a player simply to be in an offside position, but only when in that position he causes the play to be affected (F. A. Council, December 14th, 1903.)

2. Some referees award a free kick when a player is simply in an offside position. This must NOT be done (F.A. Council, December 10th, 1910.)

3. Play should not be stopped and a player given offside under law 6 because the player is in an offside position. A breach of the law is only committed when a player who is in an offside position interferes with an opponent or with the play (F.A. Council, March 8th, 1920.)

From these decisions it is quite plain that STANDING in an offside position is no breach of law 6 and that the players who criticise and the spectators who abuse a referee who ignores the yells of " What about that man ?" are entirely ignorant of what offence the offside law is intended to prevent.

Yours faithfully,
E. C. DUCHESNE.

The Hut,
Maze Green Road,
Bishop's Stortford,
4/12/23.

Source : Herts & Essex Observer)

Hadham Villa were Champions.

In the second Challenge Cup Final Little Hallingbury Reserves retained the cup by beating ten-man Bishop's Stortford Juniors by three goals to one.

Several hundred supporters were present on the Town Ground when the final round for the silver cup presented by Tresham Gilbey for competition among the junior clubs in the League was played, the finalists being Little Hallingbury, who secured the trophy last season, and Bishop's Stortford Juniors. The event provided a fast and exciting game. The outcome of the match was the proof that in the ranks of the present day 'juniors' in the district, there are several who give promise of being well able to hold their own next season among those attached to some senior or reserve teams.

The homesters won the toss won the toss and Hallingbury kicked off uphill with the sun and wind in their faces. From the start the visitors, who were the heavier team, forced the game, and within a few minutes the exchanges became fast and exciting. It was some time, however before R Bayford and Trundle tried a promising run down on the right but the ball was easily cleared by E C Clark, who commenced and continued by punting the ball well up the field. H Gunn put in a shot which was saved at the expense of a corner, and which Akers cleared. For a time, the holders had slightly the best of things. The wingers on both sides failed to keep well up forward to receive from the half-backs, while most of the players found difficulty in controlling the ball correctly owing to its resiliency and the hard state of the ground. Parkes made one or two commendable attempts to open the scoring but received meagre support.

Shortly afterwards Sheldrake shot wide and just before half-time Parkes netted the ball, but the offside rule was applied. At half-time there was no score.

The second half opened with the homesters forcing a corner, which was cleared. After a pretty run Parkes put in a shot which only missed by inches. The visitors then took up the running for a time and Akers was forced out of goal to clear. After Clark at back had, with a huge kick, transferred the play to the Hallingbury half, H Eldred was forced to kick the ball out. Turvey however trapped it with a first-time effort sent it speedily along the ground into the net, the Hallingbury goalkeeper not having a chance to save. The holders made big efforts to get on equal times and once or twice were nearly successful, Akers effecting a good save by tipping the ball over the crossbar. Parkes again netted but was given offside and almost immediately afterwards E J Clark sent in a shot. H Eldred got to it, but in endeavouring to clear he failed saw it roll into the net. With a clear two goals advantage the homesters forced matters and to the end had the best of the exchanges. A good combined on the part of the home forwards resulted in Parkes reaping his reward for an all round excellent display; with by far the best shot of the game he easily beat the Hallingbury goalkeeper. Shortly afterwards Robinson scored the fourth goal for his team. To the end the visitors were outplayed, and when the final whistle was sounded the Juniors had won by four goals to nil. The winners deserved their success but on the run of play were not quite so superior as the score might suggest.

At the close of the game the winners were greeted by a large crowd at the entrance to the pavilion to witness the presentation of the cup and medals. Mr A S Barrett explained that he was deputising for Mr Tresham Gilbey, who was unable to be present. Mr Barrett handed the cup to J Robinson, captain of the winning team, and also silver medals to the players.

Hockerill Juniors and Stansted Juniors were the finalists in the Junior Charity Cup Final.

There were nine member clubs for the **1924/25** season of the League.

There was a play-off for the Championship between Hockerill Juniors and Stansted Juniors who had similar records. Both teams had won 13 matches, drawn three and lost one. However, had goal difference been in place at that time, Stansted Juniors would have automatically become champions as they had a superior goal difference of 32 against 20 for Hockerill Guild. Stansted Juniors won the play off to secure the Championship.

Stansted Juniors defeated Woodside Green in the Challenge Cup Final.

Hockerill Juniors and Stansted Juniors were the finalists in the Junior Charity Cup.

STANSTED JUNIORS

LEAGUE AND CHALLENGE CUP WINNERS 1924/25

The player sitting with the ball is Kenneth C Turner (1904-1994) who played for Stansted for a number of years.

There were eight member clubs for the **1925/26** season.

The Championship was again won by Stansted Juniors. At Havers Farm, Hockerill Guild and Stansted Juniors met and in a good game, Stansted Juniors won by two goals to nil and secured the League Championship for the second year in succession.

The Challenge Cup Final was won by Green Tye who defeated Bush End by two goals to one.

Between three and four hundred spectators watched a fast and exciting game in the Junior Charity Cup Final on the Bishop's Stortford Town Ground. The Bishop's Stortford Congregational were soon one up through a Bush End player accidentally putting though his own goal, and throughout the first half had somewhat the better of the game, hitting the framework of the gaol several times and keeping their opponents' goalkeeper busy. Midway through the second half Bush End drew level and almost immediately made the score 2-1.

The Congregational made great efforts to equalise but could not beat the Bush End goalkeeper who at the end of the game was carried shoulder high from the field.

Mr Knight of Dunmow was referee. The 'gate' was sent to the Hospital. After the game, the cup and medals were presented to the winning team by Mr A Carruthers.

At the end of the 1925/26 season the Albury and District League was disbanded.

More clubs joined the League for the **1926/27** season increasing the number of clubs to thirteen.

The Championship was won by Hockerill Guild.

The Challenge Cup was also won by Hockerill Guild who defeated Green Tye by six goals to one. An interesting game was witnessed by a large number of spectators on the Bishop's Stortford Town Ground. The game was very-fast throughout. Hockerill scored the first goal though Thurgood with a great shot. Play was very even, but Hockerill got away on the right for Alderton to centre accurately in front of goal. Thurgood met it with his head and notched a second goal. Soon after the restart, Green Tye scored. Hockerill then had much more of the play and Vaughan scored another goal. Further goals were added through Webb, Miller and Warwick and the game ended in a victory for Hockerill by 6-1. Mr H Cox presented the cup to the winners and also congratulated the losers on their display, especially the Green Tye goalkeeper.

At the end of the season, Hockerill Guild, the champions, played a team selected from the rest of the League teams on the Hockerill ground. The game resulted in the defeat of the champions by 6 goals to three. It was a good and sporting game and at its conclusion Mr H Cox presented the League Challenge Cup to Hockerill. He congratulated the League and Cup winners upon their success and wished them similar success in the next season. A vote of thanks to Mr Cox was accorded, on the preposition of Mr A F Sadd.

Green Tye beat Little Hadham in the Junior Charity Cup Final.

There were fifteen member clubs for the **1927/28** season but Bishop's Stortford Congregational, Takeley Reserves and Thorley Works Reserves withdrew during the season.

FOOTBALL JOTTINGS

General sympathy will be felt with Hallingbury's popular captain, E Bayford, who sustained a dislocated elbow in the recent game with Blue Star, in the Charity Cup competition, and all wish him a speedy recovery.

AN INTERESTNG SUGGESTION

Mr P Brewster, Honorary Secretary of the Little Hallingbury Football Club, raises an interesting point in the following letter :-

Re the recent accident to E Bayford, Hallingbury's captain I am writing to you to ask if you will please try and find room to put in the following in your football jottings. I would make a suggestion to the effect that a Benevolent Fund be started amongst all Football Clubs in the district, say at the nominal sum of three pence (3d) per week : this is to be collected by the Club Secretaries each week and handed to a Treasurer to be appointed in Bishop's Stortford, which is central. There are quite a lot of clubs running now in the district and funds would soon be obtained to be able to pay out a weekly benefit to anyone unfortunate enough to have an accident in the future. I know this idea is carried out amongst clubs round the outskirts of London, so why not here.

A FOOTBALL INSURANCE SCHEME

The Herts & Essex Observer replied to the suggestion of the Benevolent Fund.

Unfortunately, there are always a certain number of accidents every season, and unless the player concerned is covered by some form of insurance his injuries are likely to prove a real hardship if they keep him from his occupation for a lengthy period. The scheme is a sound one and we see no reason why it should not be worked if taken up by the various leagues and made compulsory – a voluntary scheme would, we fear, be of little avail. The suggested payment of a weekly contribution would entail a great deal of work, and a better method would probably be for every registered player to pay a small sum at the beginning of each season, and for every club to annually contribute from their funds. This would form a useful nucleus and there should not be much difficulty in augmenting the fund by an occasional whist drive or even a summer fete – supported by all the clubs in the district. If this scheme were adopted every player would have the security of knowing that should be unfortunate enough to be injured he would have some source of income during the time he was laid up.

Mr G M Boxall, the Honorary Secretary of Bishop's Stortford Football Club also commented :- We agree that it is a fine idea and should if possible be started without delay. If a gentleman who is interested in the scheme would come forward and act as Treasurer perhaps a meeting could be arranged, when all clubs in the district could be represented and air their views, as it appears to us that it is only a question of how much a club should contribute each week.

LEAGUE IS A VALUABLE ASSET

Beyond a few additions to the football fixtures and an occasional report of a match one hears very little of the League, yet it is proving a most valuable asset to the smaller clubs in the neighbourhood. It was started in 1922 and since then it has ceased to be a 'Junior League' as age is concerned and the majority of its twelve members are village teams, several of which play a surprisingly good game of football. Besides the League competition there is a Challenge Cup and a Hospital Cup – which is the means of raising a substantial amount for our local Hospital each season – so that each club has a fixture nearly every Saturday. Lovers of the game will appreciate the fact that the League is thus providing each Saturday afternoon a strenuous match for some 132 players, many of whom would otherwise never take an interest in organised sport.

In Mr Merchant, the League is fortunate to have a capable and energetic Secretary, but it has one great need – more referees. None of the clubs are able to take a 'gate' and travelling expenses absorb such a large proportion of their small revenues that voluntary referees are essential. The unfortunate result seems to be that the Secretary is unable to provide each match with an efficient referee and several good games are thereby spoilt. There must be a number of old players in the district who still care for the game enough to be willing to help these smaller clubs by taking charge of an occasional game, and if by chance these notes come before them they should contact Mr Merchant.

The Championship was won by Bishop's Stortford Congregational.

There was an attendance of about 500 on the Town Ground to witness the meeting of Little Hallingbury and Blue Star in the Challenge Cup Final. The game was played at a fast pace and in the earlier stages Hallingbury had the better of the exchanges, but weakness in front of goal lost them several good opportunities. Hallingbury then took the lead from a penalty and this was the extent of the scoring in the first half. Soon after the interval, R Bayford put Hallingbury further ahead with a splendid shot. Blue Star then rallied and attacked strongly, gaining one goal from a penalty and the equaliser from a scramble in the goalmouth. Blue Star were now much the fresher team and for the last few minutes had practically all the play but could not score further, the game ending in a 2-2 draw.

The replay was held, as usual, on the Town Ground. There was a again a large attendance, most of the teams in the League, being represented on the touch line. In the first half play was fast and even, but neither side could gain an advantage. Just after the interval Reg Bayford gave Little Hallingbury the lead and soon after his brother Ralph scored the second goal. The second goal made Blue Star pull themselves together and they pressed with determination and scored from a penalty. For the rest of the game Hallingbury were mostly on the defensive but the play was rather spoilt with too much kicking the ball out of touch. There was no more scoring and Hallingbury ran out winners by 2-1. Mr Legerton of Saffron Walden was the referee. After the match, the trophy and medals were presented by Mr H S Tee.

Green Tye, the holders, and Bishop's Stortford Congregational met on the Bishop's Stortford Town Ground in the final of the Junior Charity Cup. At the interval, the score was 2-2 but in the second half Green Tye had most of the game and ran out winners by 6-3.

There were twelve member clubs for the **1928/29** season.

The Championship was won by Bishop's Stortford Congregational.

On May 4, 1929, a report appeared in the Herts & Essex Observer regarding the 1928/29 Challenge Cup Final.

(FROM 'THE FOOTBALL FAN')

Hatfield Broad Oak 1 Little Hallingbury 0

On Saturday at the Town Ground, Bishop's Stortford, Little Hallingbury (holders) met Hatfield Broad Oak in the final of the Challenge Cup.

From the kick off Hatfield Broad Oak started a very-fast game indeed and quickly scored the only goal of the game. This was a very-fine shot Raymond Hockley from the right-wing. The fast pace set at the start was maintained by both teams right up to the finish of the game. Although Hatfield Broad Oak won, and on the run of play deserved to win, Little Hallingbury played a magnificent game. Their defence was good, and they showed some fine passing movements. Their centre-forward, Ralph Bayford, is a very- dangerous shot. The Hatfield

Broad Oak strength lay particularly with its two backs and goalkeeper W. Warner (Bill). Shot after shot was made at the Hatfield Broad Oak goal but Bill – cool as a cucumber – caught each shot cleanly and kicked it up the field cleanly again. Hatfield Broad Oak's J. Cook (Jimmy) was undoubtedly the best player on the field. Jimmy, by the way, is Hatfield Broad Oak's captain, and his sound judgement and sure tackling and the distance he sends the ball back up the field must have been very wearing to the Little Hallingbury forwards. All the players in both teams were excellent and it seems invidious to mention some but nevertheless Hatfield Broad Oak owe much to their centre-forward and left-half Sylvester and F. Potter. Both these players have worked very hard right through the season and on Saturday they did particularly well.

The Challenge Cup was presented to Hatfield Broad Oak on this occasion by Mr Percy Cox, a Vice-President of the League and one of its keenest supporters.

Anyone watching this game who had not seen a Junior League team play before could not have failed to have been struck by the very- high standard of football that had been played in the Essex villages and by the sportsmanship shown by all. As in the past the villages were still the backbone of the nation. Their football certainly deserved all the support it could get.

This Junior Challenge Cup Final was played on the Town Ground between Little Hallingbury and Blue Star, an exceedingly well contested game resulting in a win for Little Hallingbury, 3-1.

Good football was exhibited by both sides and the crowd had a good display for their money. At the conclusion of the game the Cup was presented to the captain and medals to the team, by the Reverend F W Lane, who thanked the teams for giving such a good display for such a deserving cause. He called for three cheers from the victors to the vanquished, who had put up a very plucky fight. Mr J Bennett (club captain), in reply, said his team had achieved their ambition, as they had set out at the start of the season with the Charity Cup as their objective.

At the end of the season an interesting match was played between Bishop's Stortford Congregational, the champions, and a team representing the Rest of the League. Early on it looked as though the powerful League forward line would dominate the game and it was not long before they scored three goals, a lead they held at the interval. During the second half the Congregational recovered the form which took them to the top of the League and, but for brilliant goalkeeping by Johnson, would have run up a very large score. Amid much excitement the final whistle blew with the Congregational leading by 5-4.

The team chosen for the Rest of the League was: Johnson (Hockerill Guild), Law (Elsenham), Goodson (Little Hadham), Willett (Albury), Trundle (Green Tye), Treacher (Henham), Bayford (Little Hallingbury), Haylock (New Town Albion), Cook (Hatfield Broad Oak), Field (Bush End), Miller (Blue Star).

Trundle was unable to play and Webb (Blue Star) filled the centre- half position.

There were twelve member clubs for the **1929/30** season of the League.

The Bishop's Stortford and District Junior League opened the season's programme with six matches in the town and district. The League, which was entering its eighth season, although 'junior' in the football sense, had developed a high standard of football. That it supplied a real need and was very-popular was shown by the fact that in 1929 upwards of 500 spectators witnessed the Junior Charity Cup Final on the Bishop's Stortford Town Ground. It was interesting to note that there were three 'works' clubs in Bishop's Stortford. Blue Star (Messrs Ernest Lake Ltd) had been members of the League for some time, but Thorley Works and Hughes Athletic (Mr W Hughes, the Causeway) registered for the season.

The League's 12 clubs did not charge for admission to matches but relied entirely on their members' subscriptions and the generosity of the public.

FOOTBALL JOTTINGS

As one who has seen Junior match every season, I cannot help thinking that our own Town Club has some valuable talent on its own doorstep; we have players in the Junior League who are worthy of a place in the senior team, and I feel sure the local football club would profit by signing on some of our juniors – giving the local lads a chance – instead of going so far afield for their players.

The Championship was won by Little Hallingbury.

The Challenge Cup was once again played on the Bishop's Stortford Town Ground between Little Hallingbury and Henham.

Henham were making their first appearance in the final but were worthy opponents to Little Hallingbury who were in the habit of collecting silver at that time of the season. The two clubs had already met once previously in the League and on that occasion Little Hallingbury had triumphed by the odd goal in five. But past records are very often misleading and as the style of play adopted by the clubs concerned was somewhat different it may have been that the final score be rather surprising.

In the final, Little Hallingbury defeated Henham by five goals to nil completing a League and cup double.

In 1982, Roland Bayford wrote to the Herts & Essex Observer about the Little Hallingbury team who played at Barsteads Farm. He said that he was 20 at the time and recalled there were five Bayfords in the team, his elder brother Ralph and younger brother Reginald and two other Bayford brothers from another family, goalkeeper William and Ernie.

Source : Roland Bayford

LITTLE HALLINGBURY

'We were all local boys,' said Roland Bayford. 'I still keep in touch with my brothers and Donald Sandford.'

Four of the players were gardeners. They also had a carpenter, a ploughman and a joiner among their number. Roland was a van boy for Shell at the time and his friend Donald Sandford worked for Handscombs.

The Junior Charity Cup Final was competed for by Henham and Little Hadham at Stansted Football Club.

There were eleven member clubs for the **1930/31** season.

Very little is known about the season as there were no League tables published at all during the season, and only a few fixtures published. From these it is known that Burton End, Dunmow Reserves, Farnham, Great Hallingbury, Hatfield Broad Oak, Hatfield Heath Reserves, Little Hadham, Little Hallingbury and Thorley Works entered the League.

At the Blue Star Annual Dinner in September 1930, the club was wished every success and it was mentioned that the club had kindly been lent a pitch at Plaw Hatch Close. It appears that the Henham and Elsenham United clubs joined forces for the season.

The final of the Challenge Cup between Hatfield Broad Oak and Little Hadham was left drawn after two hours play on the previous Saturday was replayed on the Bishop's Stortford Town Ground. Hatfield Broad Oak won by 5 goals to 2, a score which hardly did justice to the play of the losers. Despite the very bad conditions, play was extraordinarily good and was marked by an excellent spirit between the teams. Hatfield Broad Oak scored twice in the first half and Little Hadham once from the penalty. In the second half, Hatfield Broad Oak scored three times and Little Hadham once. Both teams missed chances of scoring when a goal seemed inevitable, but the greasy ball and wet ground were responsible for several failures. Hatfield Broad Oak won because their half-backs were definitely superior and also, they were able to keep on their feet better. Their forwards, too, played a more skilful game and in their outside wings had a couple of and clever players. Both goalkeepers did well and with the exception of possibly the first goal, the Hadham keeper was not responsible for the heavy score against his team. Both sets of backs did well under the circumstances but had Little Hadham taken advantage of the bad habit of running across to the right which the Hatfield Broad Oak left-back continually displayed, the score might have been different.

Mr Chapman was the referee.

In presenting the cup and medals to the winners, Mr Duchesne expressed the sincere gratitude of the Junior League to Bishop's Stortford Football Club for their kindness and courtesy in granting the use of their ground.

THORLEY WORKS

The photo above was identified by the Herts & Essex Observer as Millars Sports. However, Thorley Works were in fact the representatives of Millars Machinery Co.

The final tie in the Junior Charity Cup was played at the Bishop's Stortford FC ground between Thorley Works and Great Hallingbury with Thorley Works winning by three goals to two. Great Hallingbury won the toss and chose to play from the north end having the advantage of the slight slope and little wind. The start was exciting as within a minute Thorley Works scored their first goal. The lead was not held for long as Great Hallingbury equalised in four minutes. Thorley Works took the lead again in ten minutes and added a third before half-time. During the second half both goals had narrow escapes but there were no further goals until twenty minutes from time when a mistake by one of the Thorley Works backs gave Great Hallingbury a chance which they took. In an endeavour to at least make a draw of it brought one of their full-backs into the forward line with the result that their forwards were overcrowded and got in each-others way. And their defence was weakened so that had not Thorley Works missed several chances by over eagerness and the Great Hallingbury goalkeeper given a remarkable performance, Thorley Works would have added to their score. Thorley Works were able against a weakened defence to keep the ball away from their own half more than they would otherwise have been and so relieve the pressure on their own defence. However, the Thorley Works goalkeeper managed to bring off a couple of extraordinary saves and his side ran out winners.

The match was well attended, and Hospital funds benefited by £10 2s 0d.

Mr Legerton of Saffron Walden was the referee.

Mr H S Tee presented the cup and the medals to the winners and congratulated both teams on the display they had given.

ANNUAL GENERAL MEETING

The League's Annual Meeting was held at the Institute, Water Lane. Chairman, Mr E C Duchesne presided.

The annual report, presented by Mr A E Merchant, Honorary Secretary, stated that the League had comprised of 11 teams (Elsenham withdrew during the season). The Honorary Secretary expressed the thanks of the League to Bishop's Stortford for their generosity in allowing the League in allowing the use of their ground for the final ties and added that the League committee were grateful to the public for their support on each occasion the matches were played. The interest shown by the public warranted that the League is popular and deserving of encourage.

The financial position of the League for the coming season was reported to be very sound, as for the first time since its formation, a satisfactory balance was carried forward.

The report concluded with thanks to Mr E C Duchesne, whose interest and support were so valuable to the League. Thanks were also given to the Honorary Treasurer, Mr R G Ashford, whose work not only in connection with the League's finance, but in many other ways was always well done.

TAKELEY MEETING

A meeting of the newly revived Football Club was held at the Green Man, Mr Collison presided and others present included the Treasurer, Mr J Webb and the Honorary Secretary, Mr J Dobson, The Chairman gave a report of the meeting of the Bishop's Stortford and District Junior League and intimated that the Club had been accepted as members of the League for the coming season. The name of Mr Frost was added to the committee. The Club will play on the Forest Ground and the members agreed to do the necessary work to put the playing pitch in order.

There were ten member clubs for the **1931/32** season.

By beating Thorley Works at Twyford, Little Hallingbury became champions. Great Hallingbury finished as runners-up.

Hatfield Broad Oak and Little Hadham contested the Challenge Cup Final at the Bishop's Stortford Town Ground resulting in a win for Hatfield Broad Oak by 6-3.

Little Hadham won the toss and defended the Thorley end goal, Holdgate kicking off before a large crowd, both teams having a big following. Little Hadham lost a player early on when Prentice had to be assisted from the ground owing to knee trouble. Following a corner, the referee awarded a penalty to Hatfield Broad Oak from which Hockley scored. Hatfield Broad Oak quickly scored a second, Bayford went through with the ball and got his shot, which Watts turned through his own goal.

Changing over, Hockley went close with a good effort. Little Hadham pegged away and Squires tested Hasler with a smart drive which the goalkeeper failed to clear and the ball was rushed through. It appeared that Chalkley was the last to touch the ball before it crossed the line. Moore increased the lead with another good shot. Moore scored again for Hatfield Broad Oak and Holgate added a sixth. With still fifteen minutes to go, the players were drenched to the skin, Little Hadham stuck at it and Squires centred for Watts to reduce the lead. Although defeated Little Hadham were by no means disgraced and they had in Squires the best player on the field. After the game, the cup and medals were presented to the winners by Mr H Cox. Mr J W Hockley of Forest Gate was the referee.

The Junior Charity Cup was also won by Hatfield Broad Oak who beat Thorley by four goals to one.

There were 11 member clubs for the **1932/33** season.

The Championship was won by Hatfield Broad Oak.

For the third year in succession Hatfield Broad Oak won the Challenge Cup by beating Albury by 3-1. The game was played at the Bishop's Stortford Town Ground and there was a large attendance who saw a very good game. The teams were very even, but Hatfield Broad Oak were the more finished side. After the match, the winning team were presented with the cup and medals by Mr Tresham Gilbey who complimented the players.

It is said that Hatfield Broad Oak kept the Challenge Cup trophy after winning the competition for the third year in a row. The trophy can also be seen in the earlier photo of Stansted Juniors.

Here is the cup, pictured with the man who now looks after the cup, Mr John Hoare.

Source : Harlow Observer

Hatfield Broad Oak joined the Stansted and District League and the Herts & Essex Border League for the 1933/34 season.

In addition to the first Herts Senior Cup victory in 1932-33, Bishop's Stortford "A" team won the Bishop's Stortford and District Junior Charity Cup.

Source : Bishop's Stortford FC

BISHOP'S STORTFORD 'A'

Bishop's Stortford 'A' won the Junior Charity Cup by beating Sheering 4-0.

RECORD BALANCE ANNOUNCED

The Honorary Treasurer reported on his balance sheet which showed a record balance after very heavy expenses.

The election of a Referees' Secretary was left over until the first League Council meeting to see how the appointment would work.

Takeley proposed that Club colours and Dressing Rooms/Ground details were added to the League handbook.

Great Hallingbury proposed that medals should be given to the runners-up in the League and not to the League Challenge Cup runners-up if the funds were strong enough to stand it.

There were 13 member clubs for the **1933/34** season.

The League Championship was won by Little Hallingbury.

After a goalless draw Matching Green beat Little Hallingbury in the final of the Challenge Cup played on the Bishop's Stortford Town Ground. The score was 4-2 and about 900 spectators witnessed a good game of cup-tie football.

Matching Green won the toss and defended the Thorley end. Little Hallingbury kicked off at full pace but were checked by Matching Green's backs who were sound. After ten minutes H Peacock gave Matching Green the lead. Little Hallingbury equalised through R J Bayford. Corner after corner proved fruitless to Matching Green until D Sandford made a fine run to the other end and put a centre across the Matching Green goalmouth only to see a team mate miss an open goal. A corner for Little Hallingbury taken by D Sandford gave them the lead.

After seven minutes of the second half S Whitbread equalised for Matching Green, the ball hitting one of the Little Hallingbury's backs as it went into the net. Matching Green played faster football and after ten minutes C Holgate gave them the lead. After 20 minutes play B Perry scored Matching Green's fourth and final goal.

The referee was Mr G F Rouse of the Herts FA.

At the conclusion of the game the cup and medals were presented to the winners by Captain C W Randall, Vice-President of the League. The losing team and the referee were also given medals.

Mr Rouse thanked both teams and said he would always think of the three hours hard football he had refereed in the final and replay.

After the Matching Green captain had led cheers for Little Hallingbury, Mr A Collison, the League Vice-Chairman thanked all for their support and the Bishop's Stortford Club for the use of the ground.

The final of the Junior Charity Cup between Hatfield Broad Oak and Thorley Works was held on the Bishop's Stortford Town Ground before 800 spectators who saw a good game which ended in a draw after extra-time had been played. The match, however, was somewhat marred, by a certain amount of fouling.

Thorley Works won the toss and defended the Town end and after five minutes Haylock scored for the Works which was his 50th goal in his 20 matches for the season. Shortly after the same player netted again. A misunderstanding by the Works backs led to Moore scoring for Broad Oak. After Haylock hit the post with a first-time shot Broad Oak then made raids on the Works' goal and Moore equalised. Four minutes later the same player scored again completing his hat-trick. A further foul led to led to the Works equalising, E Fuller scoring from the free kick from 40 yards out.

In the second half Haylock scored again, completing his hat-trick but after 20 minutes play the Works had to pay for a big mistake by giving Broad Oak a penalty from which Cook scored. No more scoring took place before full time or during the extra-time played and the game ended in a 4-4 draw.

As a result of the gate Bishop's Stortford Hospital would benefit by £19 18s, bringing the total for the season handed over for the competition to around £24.

The replay would have to delayed until the start of the following season.

There was a large crowd of supporters of both teams at the Town Ground. The Works heavily took the lead after ten minutes when Crameri put the ball past Hanley.

In the second half Silvester obtained the equaliser after a centre from the right. Fifteen minutes from the end Moore put his side ahead with an excellent effort. Milton was again beaten by Silvester, following good work by Moore. With a few minutes to go, Holdgate concluding the scoring, Moore again providing the opportunity.

ANOTHER RECORD BALANCE ANNOUNCED

Another record balance for the League was announced by the Honorary Treasurer.

In these early years, a member of each club was expected to attend each League Council meeting. At a Special General Meeting it was proposed that any club not represented at a League meeting should be fined 2s 6d (half- a-crown) and the proposal was carried.

There were fourteen member clubs for the **1934/35** season.

Matching Green were Junior League Champions by ten points. The team won 24 of their 26 matches, losing just one match and drawing the other. They scored 119 goals with just 22 against. Great Hallingbury finished as runners-up.

Matching Green as Champions played the Rest of the Junior League on the Bishop's Stortford Town Ground. The match was arranged in aid of the King George's Jubilee Trust Fund and there was a fair number present.

Matching soon attacked and Perry ran in and scored from close range. The Rest then took up the running and went near to scoring. Nichol opened the account for the Rest and at half-time the score remained 1-1.

After the restart, the Rest went away and pressed until Lund headed in a fine goal. Matching were getting weak and shot after shot was well saved by their goalkeeper. L Wood made no mistake when he scored the Rest's third goal from the penalty spot. At the other end Perry sent in a fine shot, only to see Patmore tip the ball over for a corner which proved fruitless. The end came with the Rest winning 3-1.

Mr Gee of Bishop's Stortford was the referee.

Mr E C Duchesne, League Chairman, thanked the supporters, the Town Club and all who had helped.

Vice-Chairman, Mr A Collison handed the cup and the medals to Matching Green, the League Champions.

Matching Green : E Steward, C Binder, H Gooday, H Peacock, B Perry Captain, H Holgate, J Blowes, W Perry, A Haylock, J Whitbread, C Holgate.

The Rest : A Patmore Captain (Burton End), R Day (Great Hallingbury), L Lewis (Burnt Mill), R Warden (Hatfield Heath), E Dellow (Farnham), L Wood (Burnt Mill), A Rayment (Stansted), E Lund (Burton End), J Nichol (Burnt Mill), J Reynold (Little Hadham), A Smith (Henham).

Matching Green retained the Challenge Cup and completed a League double when they beat Hatfield Heath in the final played on the Bishop's Stortford Town Ground. Both teams played at much too fast a pace during the first half with the result that the second half was rather slow and uninteresting.

Matching undoubtedly deserved their win, but if they had taken advantage of all their chances, they would have won by a larger margin. Hatfield Heath would also have fared better if they had been more certain in front of goal.

From the kick off the Matching forwards broke through and S Whitfield netted, but he was adjudged offside. From a breakaway the Heath scored through Storey, who sent in a good

44

shot which had the goalkeeper beaten. The equalise was scored by S Whitbread, and, after a period of give and take play, Haylock gave Matching the lead. The Heath goalkeeper pushed a shot out and Haylock got hold of the ball and netted with a stinging shot. Both goalkeepers were called upon to save, and Haylock scored the Green's third goal with a shot which the goalkeeper mishandled.

Soon after the restart the Heath were awarded a penalty and Bruty netted. The game now opened out a little, but both teams lacked finish in front of goal. The game ended in a win for Matching Green by 3-2. Day, Bruty and Warden played well for the Heath as did Haylock and S Whitbread for Matching.

Mr H E Edwards from the Herts FA was the referee.

At the conclusion of the match, Mr E C Duchesne, League Chairman, said that it had been a good match and the winning team deserved their win.

Mr J Brazier, Chairman of Bishop's Stortford Urban Council, handed the cup to the captain of the Matching Green team and medals to the members of both teams and the referee. Mr Duchesne led cheers for Mr Brazier.

STANSTED FC

Stansted Reserves won the Junior Charity Cup by beating Little Hadham 2-1 in a replay following a 0-0 draw.

Mr C W P Lyall, of Sawbridgeworth was co-opted by the Executive Council of the Essex County Football Association as representative for Group 5 in place of Mr F Dearch of Stansted who had resigned, and would serve on the Junior Selection, Referees and the League's Sanction sub-committees. Mr Lyall had spent a great part of his life in the cause of Junior Football in Essex and his reward was richly deserved. He had many local interests in addition to his county work, including that of Chairman of the Stansted and District League, Herts & Essex Border League and also of the Bishop's Stortford and District Branch of the Referees' Association and had also been Secretary of the West Essex Border Charity Cup for 15 years.

At a League Council meeting on 1ˢᵗ May 1935 the Honorary Secretary raised the question if it was possible to join with the Stansted and District League. The thought was that it would stop unplayed games and make more sport and therefore it was left to the Honorary Secretary to write to the Stansted and District League.

ANOTHER RECORD BALANCE SHEET

A record balance sheet was presented at the League's Annual Meeting held at the Institute, Water Lane.

Mr A Collison, Vice-Chairman, presided and with him were Mr R G Ashford, Honorary Treasurer, Mr E C Duchesne, Chairman, Mr S F Markwell, Honorary Secretary, Mr R Ward, Honorary Assistant-Secretary, Mr A Crameri and Club delegates.

The Treasurer presented the statement of accounts, which showed receipts of £38 3s 6d, totalled £82 10s 7d. Expenditure amounted to £23 17s 2d, leaving a balance in hand of £38 13s 4d.

Mr Crameri proposed, that subject to the permission of the Essex Football Association, an honorarium be given to Mr Markwell.

Replying, the Secretary thanked Mr Crameri, and said he was pleased to do all he could for the League.

It was decided to approach the Stansted and District League, with a view to amalgamating the two leagues to make one good league out of the two, with two divisions.

There had been fourteen member clubs for the **1935/36** season.

Sawbridgeworth Reserves were accepted into the League but withdrew after the fixtures had been produced. Bishop's Stortford 'A' were accepted in their place.

Mr Adam, from the Bishop's Stortford club invited any club's players to the Bishop's Stortford Town Ground for training under their new coach.

At the December League Council meeting Mr Crameri proposed that the League should hold a dinner. Arrangements were left to the Sub-committee. The County Football Association gave their permission if funds will allow it.

Following the death of King George V the Honorary Secretary confirmed that games would be played on January 25ᵗʰ but clubs must bear in mind that black arm bands must be worn and a silence of 2 minutes before the kick-off.

Stansted Reserves were Champions.

The outstanding team in local football had been Much Hadham, although they lost the Championship after appearing certain winners all season, they had been the soundest team in the League and most of the points dropped had been when they had to field insufficient substitutes for regular players. Stansted Reserves and Bishop's Stortford 'A' had had a slight advantage in that Stansted Reserves had the assistance of one or two first team players on occasions and the 'A's' the help of one or two reserve players occasionally. Although

Stansted Reserves had won the League, they were rather fortunate in that Great Hallingbury and Matching Green both withdrew from the League after having beaten them. Great Hallingbury also had a moral victory over Bishop's Stortford 'A,' although the game was abandoned, there was not long to go, with Hallingbury leading.

Hatfield Broad Oak, but for a bad slip, could have won the League, they lost a number of points early on and they lost to a lowly Thorley team. At the time, it appeared that Broad Oak had little chance of resisting the challenge of Much Hadham, but a few of these points saved would have left them as champions. Broad Oak proved themselves a good sporting teams and had a name for sportsmanship second to none in the League.

By defeating Bishop's Stortford Territorials 5-1 on the Town Ground, Much Hadham won the final of the Challenge Cup. Much of their success was due to the excellent shooting of Dewey who netted four of the best goals seen on the ground but at times they were hard put to defend their goal.

The crowd was a record for junior trophy finals, between 1,200 and 1,300 spectators attending. Before the start of the game the Drums of the Ist Herts Regiment beat the Retreat and also played at the interval.

Hadham at once took up the attack and Dewey found the net within two minutes. Play went to the other end and the Territorials forced a corner. Then against the run of play, Dewey forced his way through to score with another first-class shot.

The Territorials put on pressure to try and make up leeway, and after being awarded a penalty for hand ball, S Dellow shot straight at Ruff who brought off a good save.

Even exchanges followed, Watts being noticeable in the Territorials defence, while Abslom, who had played for Bishop's Stortford, was prominent among the Hadham team. Just before the interval, Dewey completed his hat-trick to give his team a 3-0 lead.

After the change-over, Vest missed an opportunity or reducing the Territorials arrears. The soldiers, however, kept up pressure and eventually, Hayward took advantage of a misunderstanding to net a simple goal.

The Hadham defence was all out to defend their goal, and Ruff had plenty of work and did it well. Abslom was also prominent. They successfully held the Territorials attack, and just before the end scored two more goals from Dewey and Squires.

After the game, the cup and medals were presented by Mr H S Tee, one of the founders of the League 14 years before.

Bill Pells Medal

Source : Sue Stracey

The finalists of the Junior Charity Cup were Stansted Reserves and Potter Street. Stansted Reserves put up one of their best performances of the season at the Town Ground, Potter Street won by a goal scored in the last minute of extra-time, but Potter Street had the assistance of some first team players, and it was only after a great fight that they managed to win. It had been pleasing to note that that there was a good attendance.

Mr E Devoil of Dunmow was the referee.

Mr T Ward, Chairman of the Council, presented the cup and the medals. The gate money went to Bishop's Stortford Hospital.

At a sub-committee meeting in May it was decided that Mr Duchesne, Mr Crameri and Mr Ward should attend the Stansted League meeting in regard to the amalgamation of the two leagues.

JUNIOR FOOTBALL LEAGUE'S FIRST ANNUAL DINNER

The first Annual Dinner of the League was held at the Chequers Hotel, Bishop's Stortford, Mr E C Duchesne (Chairman) presiding. With him at the top table were Messrs, A Collison (Vice-Chairman), S F Markwell (Secretary), C W P Lyall, R T Crameri, C de Bolts (Secretary of the Bishop's Stortford Football Club) and C Oakley.

Before the Loyal Toast, one minute's silence was observed as a tribute to the memory of King George.

The toast to the King having been proposed by the Chairman, and duly honoured. Mr Collison proposed the toast to the Essex Football Association and said that when just over 30 years ago he played for an Essex club, that Association had no more than 100 clubs under its jurisdiction, now the number was over 600. In those days players often cycled 20 miles for a game. The County Association had made Junior Football what it is today. With the toast he coupled the name of Mr Lyall whom they congratulated upon his appointment as a member of the County Association.

Replying to the toast, Mr Lyall said the members of the Association were all good sportsmen and gave a lot of time to the work. Speaking of football in the old days, he said that in those days referees 'had to mind what they did' –'I am not saying that they do not do that today,' he continued, amid a good deal of laughter.

He appealed to footballers to keep their tempers as all sportsmen should. However, referees had to report incidents or football would not be clean, healthy game it is today and the finest in the world. He was sure that those now connected with football would go on watching it until they could do no longer. In conclusion Mr Lyall said, 'I hope in the future you will go on playing football in the same fine sporting spirit as you have done in the past.'

'The Bishop's Stortford and District Junior League' was proposed by Mr Lyall, who said their present Chairman had been connected with the organisation since its formation in 1922. They were still going strong, with sixteen clubs, better still they had a substantial balance in the bank, which showed that the League had been run on correct lines by such good sportsmen as Mr Duchesne and Mr Markwell. He was sure that the League had fulfilled its object in providing competitive for local juniors.

The Chairman, replying they had got past the unlucky thirteenth year and he felt that they could congratulate themselves on the comparatively small amount of trouble they had experienced since the League was formed. He acted as a referee until five years ago, and only on one occasion did he have to send a man off the field, and that was because he had had a little more than he could quietly carry! A Chairman often got credit for the work done by his Secretary and they owed a great deal to Mr Maxwell and those he succeeded. Concluding, Mr Duchesne said the time was coming when he would have to a back seat, but in Mr Collison they had one who was quite ready to succeed him. His fourteen years in the chair had been most pleasant.

Proposing 'The Secretaries of Clubs in the League,' Mr Collison spoke of the difficulties which confronted them and appealed to those who were not secretaries to give them their support.

Mr de Bolte, responding, said that there had been a feeling that the Bishop's Stortford Football Club was top dog and looked down on smaller clubs. He wished to make it clear that this was not the case, neither did they wish to crush any club. Their object was to provide senior football, which those who came into the town from the villages could witness.

Mr Markwell also replied, saying that, with the help of club Secretaries, he endeavoured to make the League a success. That end could only be achieved by mixing as much as possible with clubs, players and secretaries.

At a League Council meeting in June, Mr Collison in the chair, was supported by Mr Lyall and the following club delegates, Stansted League, Stansted, Sawbridgeworth, Harlow and the Eastons.

The League was represented by Birchanger, Burnt Mill, Thorley, Potter Street and Hatfield Broad Ok.

The meeting was called to discuss the proposed amalgamation of the two leagues.

After considerable discussion it was proposed by Burnt Mill and seconded by Thorley that the Stansted League should be invited to a special meeting, after the Annual General meeting to decide whether there should be an amalgamation or not.

Amalgamation And The Pre-War Years

LEAGUE TO AMALGAMATE WITH THE STANSTED LEAGUE

At the League's Annual Meeting held at the Institute, Water Lane, it was agreed to amalgamate with the Stansted and District League for the **1936/37** season.

The Honorary Secretary had little to report, other than the fact that the League had had a most successful season, from almost every point of view.

The Honorary Treasurer, on the other hand, was able to report another record balance in hand of £37 19s 3d. Subscriptions from Vice-Presidents totalled £5 14s, while 'gates; for the semi-finals and final of the Challenge Cup Competition had brought in a total of £16 1s 11d, these together with other items, bringing the total receipts to £68 14s 1d.

On the expenditure side there were two new items, an honorarium to the Honorary Secretary (£5) and the dinner (£6 12s 10d). Other items included the printing of handbooks (£3 0s 6d) and the cost of medals and engraving (£7 10s 6d).

The Treasurer suggested that the League should send a donation of £1 1s to the Bishop's Stortford Football Club in appreciation of the loan of the ground.

Introducing the question of the proposed amalgamation with the Stansted and District League, the Chairman reminded the meeting

:- That at a special meeting held last year to consider the matter, the representation of the League had been so small that it had been impossible to come to any decision. The representatives of the Stansted League had, however, shown their compete approval of the proposal, and it now remained only for the League to come to a decision.

Me R Crameri remarked that the amalgamation would bring the total number of clubs in the new League to about 20. If all the games were to be played it would be necessary to divide the League into two divisions.

The Chairman said that at the moment we are dealing with question of amalgamation.

It was agreed that the representatives of the League should meet with the representatives of the Stansted and District League to go into details.

On behalf of those present, Mr Ward was thanked for carrying out the work of the Honorary Secretary, Mr Markwell, during his illness, and also the Chairman for presiding.

By 1936 the Stansted and District League had dwindled to just five clubs, Easton and Duton Hill, Stansted, Harlow Reserves, Bishop's Stortford 'A' and Sawbridgeworth, and it was at the beginning of the 1936/37 season that the amalgamation of the two leagues took place to form the Bishop's Stortford, Stansted and District Junior League.

The renamed League had two divisions for the first time.

There were 7 teams in Division I and 10 teams in Division II but Northmet withdrew during the season and as they had not completed 75% of their fixtures their record was expunged.

BENEFIT MATCH FOR 'FREDDIE' MARKWELL

Arranged for a benefit match for F C Markwell, a great worker for local junior football, who has been seriously ill for some time, an interesting game was staged on the Bishop's Stortford Town Ground between a team of Essex Referees and London Referees.

The London 'refs' proved far too good for the Essex men and won 6-1.

The crowd were quite delighted when Referee Bloxham blew his whistle for an infringement of rules by men who are given the task of calling attention to similar infringements when they are the 'knights of the whistle.'

The Essex Referees :- T Gee, F Spearman, J Yardley, W Bayford, W Haw, W G Snow, F T Crameri, W Gleeson, C G Oakley, F Finch, R Ward.

Mr A Bloxham (trainer-coach to Bishop's Stortford Football Club) was the referee.

RULE AMENDED REGARDING SENIOR PLAYERS

A Special General Meeting was held in October to discuss a proposed alteration of Rule 8D.

In the chair, Mr Duchesne, supported by all club delegates and secretaries.

At a previous meeting, Hatfield Heath asked if permission could be given to play N Cunningham, who had played for Harlow this season. The Chairman remarked that nothing could be done until it was decided about Rule 8D. After a ballot was made it was decided to call a Special Meeting to discuss the alteration of the Rule.

Proposed by Henham and seconded by Hatfield Heath that the words 'or in any matches of the Spartan League,' be withdrawn. The Chairman then called a ballot, and the result was 14 for and 1 against.

The rule now reads (subject to approval by the Essex County Football Association) – All players shall not be eligible to play in the League, who has taken part during the current or previous season in three or more senior competition matches, unless a period of six months has elapsed since he so played. '

DEATH OF MR S F MARKWELL ANNOUNCED

After an illness lasting a year Mr Stanley Frederick Markwell passed away.

Mr Markwell, who was 31 years of age, was very well known in the local football world where he was affectionately as 'Freddie.' For three years he was Honorary Secretary of the League and also refereed local matches, being a member of the local Referees' Association. He was a member of the Hockerill Athletic Club, for which he played cricket. Mr Markwell left his wife and three young children.

It was noted in the Football Jottings Column 'By Linesman' in the Herts & Essex Observer : I would like to pay tribute of 'Freddie' Markwell, who gave such splendid service to the League as Honorary Secretary. A football enthusiast, a thorough good fellow, he was deservedly popular, not only with his associates in the sport which he loved, but all those with whom he came into contact in his daily work. He leaves behind a memory of work well done – duty faithfully performed. Much sympathy is felt for the young wife and three small children left behind.

In March at a League Council meeting, it was proposed that the League should grant £5 towards the F C Markwell Benevolent Fund if funds allowed and permission granted by the Essex Football Association.

Hatfield Heath became Division I Champions while Hatfield Broad Oak were runners-up.

A large crowd were present at Rhodes Avenue to watch the Division I League Challenge Cup. Although the margin of victory was wide, the Broad Oak team won by 6-1, the football witnessed was always good, the game being played at a very fast pace throughout.

At the opening, Hatfield Broad Oak, appeared to be the better balanced side, and despite of good work by the Heath defence, in which Cunningham was outstanding, they led at the interval by three clear goals. H Moore netted the first, and after G Roff had scored, the same player scored the third.

Early in the second half, Hatfield Heath pressed hotly, and it appeared that they might wipe off the deficit. The Broad Oak also had a sound defence, however, Cook their captain, playing well at left-back. Pyle missed one or two chances, and midway through the half the issue was settled when P Moore left Jackson helpless with a terrific drive. Shortly after Roff netted the fifth goal, and then got the sixth with a slow shot which should have been saved. Eleven minutes from time Pyle scored Hatfield Heath's solitary goal.

Takeley were Division II Champions while Henham were runners-up.

Another large crowd gathered to watch the final of the Division II Challenge Cup.

After a very hard-fought game, Takeley ran out winners by 3-2, but it was not unfair to say that the result was scarcely consistent with the run of play. Henham were on the offensive for three-quarters of the time, and it was only by packing their goal that Takeley prevented their opponents from scoring. Milton, in the Takeley goal, put in some hard work. When play reached midfield, however, Henham were by far the more impressive of the two teams, and the Takeley goals were mainly the result of breakaways.

Takeley opened the game by a fairly early goal from R Skingle, which was the result of a period of pressure, during which Takeley were better than at any stage of the game. From that time, Henham swept into the attack and were difficult to hold. During a breakaway, Takeley secured a corner which C Wright pushed into the net. Henham's first goal came from a penalty taken by P Snow .

Soon after the resumption, Lindsell put on the equaliser for Henham, and thereafter followed a terrific tussle with Henham pressing hard. Only a few minutes before the end, Takeley swept up the field once more for Bolden to net the winning goal.

The cup and medals were afterwards presented by Mr F Goacher.

Hatfield Heath became the holders of the Junior Charity Cup when the defeated Much Hadham by 2-1 in the final.

The game, which was played at Rhodes Avenue, was played at a steady pace throughout and the teams were exceptionally well matched. During the first half Hadham seemed rather superior to their opponents and they were leading by the only goal at half-time. Following the resumption, however, the Heath fought back in grand style, and were on their performance, worthy winners.

Hadham started strongly and soon carried play to their opponents' goalmouth. Jackson made a few saves but was rather too inclined to rush out of his goal for absolute safety. He did well, however, to save a penalty shot, after a foul close to the goal. Hadham scored their goal through Briscoe.

In the second half Hatfield Heath were just slightly superior, and Pyle and H Newman managed to score on their behalf. Hadham never lost heart and were struggling gamely at the end of a game that had been far more interesting and exciting than any of the preceding cup games.

In presenting the cup to the winning captain, Mr A Collison (League Vice-Chairman) said that the competition had raised around £20 for Bishop's Stortford Hospital.

ELSENHAM ROVERS FIRST ANNUAL GENERAL MEETING

The first Annual General Meeting of Elsenham Rovers was held at the Village Hall. The Chairman, Mr C P Chalk presided over a fairly representative attendance.

In the course of his report, the Honorary Secretary remarked that although they had only finished eighth out of ten teams in the second division of the League, the fact that they had fielded a team on 29 occasions during their first season, showed that the club was no failure.

The balance sheet showed a balance in hand of £13 2s 10d, which for a new club was highly creditable to all who had worked to raise the sum.

A SUCCESSFUL SEASON CELEBRATED

One of Takeley Football Club's most successful seasons was celebrated by a dinner at the Silver Jubilee Hall.

Chairman, Mr A Collison presided and with him were Mrs Dobson, Reverend D Mears, Brigadier-General Charlton, Mr F Ward, Honorary League Secretary, Mr A G Cox and Mr E J Truck.

Following the honouring of the Loyal toast, the two cups won by the club, the Second Division Championship and the Second Division Challenge Cup were presented to the captain, Mr C Wright, by the Chairman.

In making the presentation, Mr Collison said that as Vice-Chairman of the League, he was in the unique position of making the presentation to his own club. He congratulated the club on their success and went on to remark upon the great hold which football had gained on the British Public. It taught young men to take hard knocks, and also the value of team-work, and it was a game in which there was no snobbery. The Takeley club had a fine reputation for sportsmanship in their League. There might come a time when such young means were, who were the flower of the countryside, might be called upon to defend their country. He prayed that such a time would never come, but if it should, he felt confident that they would do so in the same great spirit as they were now showing.

In proposing the toast of 'The Takeley Football Club,' Mr E J Tuck spoke of its great recovery over the past five years. It was a great delight to see the young men of the village coming forward and doing so well, and he knew there was fresh talent in the school which would be of assistance to the club in the future.

In reply, Mr R Skingle, Honorary Secretary, said the club had had a most successful season. Of their 16 League matches, they had won 13, drawn 2 and lost one, so that they finished the season with 28 points. The highest goal-scorers were C Wright (31), R Skingle (26), L A Frost (13) and S Gunn (9).

In proposing 'The League,' Mr A L Frost paid tribute to the work of the officials. The League provided for about 250 players and that in these days a very fine thing. From the amount of support football received, there seemed to be a danger of our developing into a nation of supporters, but in his opinion it was better to play in a fourth rate game than to watch the Arsenal or Spurs (Applause). The standard of both play and refereeing in the League was good, and its present successful position was largely due to the work of Mr Ward.

Replying, the Chairman also said that much of the success of the League was due to Mr Ward, who was a worthy successor to the late Mr F Markwell, who rendered the League so many years' service.

The Chairman proposed the toast to the Vice-Presidents.

Mr Cox proposed the toast to the visitors, to which Mr E J Tuck and the Reverend D Mears responded.

Thanks to the Chairman were voiced by Mr A L Frost, and in replying, Mr Collison said that this would be his last official appearance in connection with the club. He was pleased to be leaving it at its peak.

FIRST ANNUAL MEETING

The first Annual Meeting of the Bishop's Stortford, Stansted and District Junior Football League which came into being a year ago as the result of an amalgamation between the Bishop's Stortford and District Junior League and Stansted and District League was held at the Falcon Hotel, Bishop's Stortford. An encouraging statement of accounts was submitted by the Honorary Treasurer, Mr A J Ashford. In view, however, of the fact that one of the League's main sources of income, 'gates' at final games, was dependent upon the weather, he asked the delegates to consider cutting down one of the main items of expenses, the large number of medals at present provided,

Mr R C Duchesne, Chairman, presided, and with him were Mr A Collison (Vice-Chairman), Mr R Ward, Honorary Secretary, and Mr A J Ashford, Honorary Treasurer.

An expression in the minutes of the last Annual Meeting that the late Mr F Markwell might be able to resume his duties as Honorary Secretary of the League during last season, caused the Chairman to remark that Mr Markwell's fatal illness had prevented this. Regret had already been expressed to Mrs Markwell, and at that meeting they could but repeat that expression.

The Honorary Treasurer then presented his statement of accounts. The Bishop's Stortford carried forward to the new League a balance from the 1936/36 season 0f £37 19s 3d and after making certain donations, had carried forward to the new League a balance of £31 5s 4d. The Stansted and District League carried forward a balance of £2 1s 1d, so that the new League commenced with the sum of £33 6s 5d. Subscriptions from Vice-Presidents totalled £2 1s and receipts from clubs £11 4s. Net gate receipts were £23 18s 5d making total income £70 6s 2d.

The main item of expenditure was the cost of medals. The fee for affiliation to the Essex FA was £1 10s, an increase of 10s, being occasioned by the fact they had two divisions. The total credit balance was £33 2s 10d. There were contingent liabilities for the use of the ground for Cup Finals, engraving of cups and to the Referees' Association.

Mr Ashford said that the main contingent liability was to the Bishop's Stortford Football Club. He had written to them explaining that junior competitive football in this area was largely dependent on 'gates' at their Cup Finals and asking for some reduction in the charge for the ground, namely £3 3s per game. He had received a reply that the committee had decided to adhere to this charge but were willing to make a donation to the League of £1 1s. A balance of £5 is services during the year. was therefore payable.

Mr Ashford went on to express thanks to Mr Ward for his services during the year. He wanted to point out that whereas the League began with a balance of nearly £40, this would now drop to a little over £26. There had been an item of £10 10s which would not recur, but wet weather might cause a drop in receipts in finals, and if the Bishop's Stortford Football Club were to continue their charge, it might be necessary to affect some economies. The only way in which they could reasonably economise was in the number of medals issued.

The Honorary Secretary gave a brief verbal report, thanking Mr Duchesne and the committee members for the help they had given him, and the local press for their assistance to the League. He congratulated Hatfield Heath and Takeley upon winning the cups and wished success in the second division to Little Parndon, a team which had played sportingly through the season , in which they had not won a match.

In view of the fact that some of the clubs had not yet held their annual meetings, it was agreed to defer the formation of the League to a special meeting, which it was decided to hold on July 1st, at which certain alterations to the rules will also be considered.

An application by Abbess Roding for membership to the League was rejected, as they would not accept election to the first division.

Mr Tresham-Gilbey was re-elected President and the Vice-Presidents were re-elected en bloc.

Mr Duchesne regretted that he could not accept nomination for re-election as Chairman, a position which he held for 15 years . He wished to propose Mr C W Lyall.

Mr Collison was also proposed, but, as the result of a ballot, Mr Lyall was elected by 9 votes to 6.

Mr Collison declined to accept re-election as Vice-Chairman, in spite of the Chairman's appeal for him to do so. The matter was, however, left until the special meeting in the hope that he would re-consider this decision.

Owing to pressure of business, Mr Ashford wished to resign from the Honorary Treasurership. The Chairman made what he described the 'cheeky' proposition that Mr Ashford and himself should be elected jointly to the position, and this was agreed to. Mr Ward was re-elected Honorary Secretary, with Mr A J Bilney as his assistant. Mr F Goacher and Mr C Olney were re-elected Honorary Auditors.

Messrs Bilney, Duchesne, Harris, Lyall and Ward were elected to form the sub-Committee.

`

Hatfield Heath became Division I Champions for the season **1937/38** but were defeated 1-0 in the final of the Challenge Cup by Much Hadham.

Sheering were Division II Champions but Abbess Rhoding beat Sheering in the final of the Division II Challenge Cup by 4 goals to 2 after a replay.

Eastons and Duton Hill defeated Hatfield Heath in the final of the Junior Charity Cup 5-0. L Jacques (2), W Perry, J Barker scored together with an own goal.

When Prime Minister Neville Chamberlain returned from Munich on 30th September 1938 to give the frail, futile flutter for appeasement in our time, it signalled just one more complete season of normal football before the advent of the strangely still September Sunday nearly a year ahead.

ENCOURAGING PROGRESS REPORTED AT ANNUAL MEETING

A really encouraging year all round was reported at the Annual General Meeting of the League held at the Falcon Hotel, Bishop's Stortford. A very good illustration of the good sportsmanship of the players was shown by the fact that although 400 matches were played only six men were ordered off the field. It was decided to recognise the excellent work put in by the Secretary, by giving him an honorarium.

Mr C W P Lyall (Chairman) presided, and with him were Mr E C Duchesne (Vice-Chairman), Mr R Ward (Honorary Secretary) and Mr R J Ashford (Honorary Treasurer). There was a large attendance.

In his report, the Secretary thanked the officers for what they had done for the League, and for their help to him. He also thanked the local press, who had been a very great help.

Mr Ward referred to the sportsmanship of the League clubs generally. Although only six men had been sent off he expressed hope that next season no player would be ordered off. When the League was first formed in 1922, they had seven clubs and now they had 22 and it was proposed to alter that number that evening to 32. The report was adopted.

The Treasurer presented the statement of accounts which showed that receipts, with a balance of £33 2s 10d, totalled £101 1s 5d and included £46 7s 0d, net gate receipts £13 5s 6d, club receipts and £7 5s subscriptions. Expenditure amounted £48 4s 10d including £11 1s 6d ground expenses, leaving an increased balance in hand of £52 16s 7d.

Continuing, the Treasurer said he was struck by the difference in the size of the meeting and the first meeting of the League in 1922, which was also attended Mr Duchesne, the Secretary and one of their Vice-Presidents (Mr H S Tee). He said that he was proud to be one of the of the players in the first match under the League. To have a successful League they must have three things – loyalty and sportsmanship on the part of the clubs, a competent executive, and sound finance. They could congratulate themselves on having all three. When he took over as Treasurer in 1928 he found that no proper accounts had been kept. They started in 1928 with nothing in hand, at the end of the next year they had a deficit, but from then on their financial position became consolidated, so that they now had a record balance in hand. To a large extent the generosity of their Vice-Presidents, and the takings at the finals had made this possible.

The Chairman said it was a very good report and they could congratulate themselves on being in such a sound financial position.

Mr Duchesne proposed the adoption of the statement of accounts and expressed thanks to Mr Ashford.

This was seconded and carried.

Mr Duchesne moved a vote of thanks to the officers. It demanded, he said, a great deal of time and tact to run a league of that type, and he was sure they could not have chosen a better set of officers. Their Chairman had had a great deal of experience, and the other officers had also played their part as well. Mr Ward had proved a worthy successor to their late friend, Mr S F Markwell. He had done a tremendous amount of work and during the past season had carried on in spite of having had an accident. As a mark of appreciation and goodwill to Mr Ward, Mr Duchesne proposed he be given an honorarium.

The Thaxted representative seconded the vote of thanks and said that as a new club they were delighted with the way they had been treated.

Mr Ashford seconded the motion that Mr Ward be given an honorarium, remarking that he knew the tremendous amount of work the Secretary did. He had often sacrificed his work in order to attend a League business. Mr Ashford mentioned that last season the Secretary wrote about 800 letters.

The Chairman endorsed what had been said about Mr Ward.

The proposition was unanimously carried and the Secretary suitably replied.

It was decided to alter the rules in order to make the number of clubs admissible, 32 instead of 22 and to increase the radius from 10 miles of Bishop's Stortford to 12 miles. Another alteration was that a player of six matches or more in the first division should be deemed a first division player and that no club should be allowed to play more than four first division players in a reserve match. The rule relating to the Challenge Cup – that in the event of a drawn final, the League should pay the travelling expenses of 13 players of both teams was approved.

Abbess Roding FC, promoted from Division II last season, were the winners of Division I in **1938/39**. The team was strengthened at the beginning of the season by the inclusion of Bert Perry and the brothers S and H Whitbread (former players of Harlow Town) and the return of former player Bretton at centre-forward. Bretton scored over 90 goals in League and cup games.

Bill Pells Medal

Source : Sue Stracey

Bishop's Stortford Rovers crowned the success of their first playing season in the League by winning the Division I Challenge Cup. Their victory by the odd goal of three over Hatfield Heath was undoubtedly deserved, though the close score was an accurate indication of the play.

The game was played on the Bishop's Stortford Town Ground.

A stiff wind blowing down the field from the Rhodes Avenue end, added considerably to the difficulties of a hard ground. Hatfield Heath won the toss and elected to play with their backs to the wind but found it not always in their favour. They had the better of the opening exchanges, but finishing was difficult and twice in succession Mascall was unable to overtake the ball sufficiently to gain control and send in an accurate shot. After about ten minutes the Rovers began to make brief raids on their opponents' goal and the game settled down to a succession of end-to-end play, which was to continue until the final whistle. Rovers attack might well have been successful at this and at later stages, but for the presence of Cunningham whose work in the Heath defence singled him out as the best player on the field.

There was no score in the first half, although each side was awarded a penalty. When the game was 20 minutes old when Hatfield Heath were awarded a penalty when S Hayward touched a dropping ball just outside the goal. Claxton, however, shot a yard wide of the upright. Play swung straight to the other end and within a matter of five minutes the Rovers were also awarded a spot kick. Selves' shot was punched out by Newman. The ball rebounded into play and suddenly came rolling towards a bunch of players, a goal being narrowly averted when Hatfield Heath defenders scraped the ball away literally off the goal line.

Towards the end of the half, it seemed almost inevitable that one side or the other, though there was nothing to indicate which team it might be. H Newman, who was running rather too many risks in leaving his goal, twice saved in splendid style by diving to lift the ball straight from the feet of the attackers. At the other end R Dellow, fumbled the ball when it was passed back to him by Hayward but fortunately for the Rovers, Pyle was unable to overtake it before it had trickled wide of the goal.

In the second half the Rovers forwards were able to settle down seriously to business. After having had to depend mainly on Selves during the first half, they were now receiving strong support from the wing halves and with Veremiglio to turn Lund's passes to good effect they began to appear a dangerous combination. After Brown's shot had struck the bar, the Rovers swept down to the other end, where Vest made no mistake with a pass from Hayward. After Humphreys had hooked a sitter over the bar from a couple of yards out, Monk added the second goal when he met the ball as it rebounded after W Hayward had struck the crossbar.

Two minutes later Hatfield Heath managed to reduce the deficit. H Mascall struck the bar with his shot and the ball dropped to the feet of Anthony, who had changed positions with Brown at the beginning of the half and was now standing by the upright. Somehow, he managed to slip the ball past Dellow and back into the opposite corner of the net. The Heath never looked like scoring again and Rovers dominated the remainder of the game. Hesitancy between Veremiglio and Monk probably robbed Rovers of a third goal.

At the end of the game the cup and medals were presented by Mr J Brazier.

It was reported that Hatfield Heath's inside-left, Anthony, had given a number of fine displays and he had all the makings of a good player and more should be heard of him in the future.

Butterfields United were champions of Division II. However, runners-up, Horneybrookes were deducted two points, which proved costly, as they could have forced a playoff if they had not been penalised.

Farnham beat Butterfields 1-0 in the final of Division II Challenge Cup.

Played at Sawbridgeworth, Sheering lost to Burnt Mill by 2 goals to 1 in the final of the Bishop's Stortford Charity Cup. Sheering were first to score after 15 minutes when White scored with a good shot. After this the game was more even and in an attack by Burnt Mill, a free kick was awarded for an infringement against Prior, just outside the penalty area and as a result the Burnt Mill right-winger scored. Four minutes from time the Burnt Mill left-back scored the winning goal.

The Saffron Walden Rotary Cup was introduced and in the final Saffron Walden defeated Stansted 3-2.

EXCELLENT RECORD OF FIRST SEASON BACK

The Annual Meeting of the Bishop's Stortford Rovers Football Club was held at the Old Bull's Head.

The Honorary Secretary reported that the playing record of the Club in the League and also the Challenge Cup had been an achievement for each and every member of the Club to be proud of.

In presenting his report, the Honorary Secretary said it gave him much pleasure to see such a large gathering of members and players at their Annual Meeting. The Club had been formed solely for the purpose of bringing back local interest in the League, and they undoubtedly had achieved it. 'Some few years ago,' said the Secretary, 'Bishop's Stortford was represented in the League by two or three teams, but one by one each club had dropped out, until for the last three years it has had no representative at all. I hope that, through our lead, more local clubs will be formed, and greater interest will be shown.'

The Secretary reported that all members of the last year had notified him of their intention of re-signing on, and he had, therefore, after consultation with members of the committee, entered a second team in Division II of the League.

JUNIOR CHARITY CUP

It was reported at the Bishop's Stortford Rovers Annual Meeting that in the semi-final of the Bishop's Stortford Charity Cup they went down 4-2 to Hatfield Broad Oak at Sawbridgeworth. However it was also reported that a Charity match, in aid of Bishop's Stortford Hospital, had been staged at the end of the season on the Bishop's Stortford Town Ground between Bishop's Stortford Rovers and Burnt Mill, who had beaten Sheering in the semi-final of the Charity Cup. Before an excellent crowd, the Rovers defeated their opponents by 5-2, after being down at half-time. For this win they had been presented with a silver Challenge Cup, and each team a set of medals. One has to assume that, for some reason, Hatfield Broad Oak were not able to play in the final.

CLUBS URGED TO ARRANGE MORE EARLY FIXTURES

APPEAL FOR MORE REFEREES

Clubs represented at the Annual General Meeting of the League, Mr C W P Lyall, League Chairman, were urged by the Chairman and others to arrange as many matches as possible to be played in the early part of the season. Last season the congestion of fixtures due to postponed games having to be played in the final weeks caused considerable trouble and to the referees.

The Honorary Secretary, Mr R Ward, opened his annual report by thanking all the League officers and club secretaries for their services during the past season, and also the local Press for their assistance.

Play throughout the League last season had been of a high standard and appeared to be on the upgrade. The total number of goals scored by all clubs was 2,087. The number of players registered with the League was 735, and of these, only four had been ordered from the field.

In the coming season it was expected the League would be at its full strength of 32 clubs. At the end of last season, there were several matches which had not been played, and unless they arranged to play evening matches at the end of August and in September, they would have still more trouble in the coming season.

Commenting on the report, the Chairman said it gave him much pleasure to know that in all the games played in the League, only four cases had been reported to the county.

The Honorary Treasurer, Mr R Ashford, then presented a statement of accounts for the past year. This showed that the credit balance had been increased from £52 16s 7d, to £58 15s 2d.

Total receipts during the year, including the balance brought forward, were £105 1s 7d, subscriptions amounting to £9 5s, receipts from clubs to £18 7s 10d, and gate receipts from the two Cup Finals to £24 12s 2d. One of the principal items of expenditure was the cost of medals and engraving cups, which amounted to £15 1s.

Mr Ashford mentioned that the Secretary's postage box had shown that Mr Ward sent out no fewer than 768 communications last season.

The report and financial statement were then adopted, thanks being expressed to the officers and to Mr H A Bilney, the referees' appointments secretary.

The Chairman read a letter from the Bishop's Stortford branch of the North-West Essex Referees Society Association, appealing for more referees, and suggesting the formation of a committee of representatives of the referees and the clubs to consider the fixtures with a view to securing the appointment of referees for every match and of avoiding any congestion.

World War II broke out early into the **1939/40** season and the threat of air attack and the introduction of conscription made it impossible for football to continue as before.

On 8th September 1939, the Football Association declared that all football except that organised by the armed forces was suspended 'until official notice to the contrary.'

However, the amateur game survived, its aim to provide recreation for the participants and onlookers whatever obstacles presented themselves.

A natural sequence to the outbreak of war was the immediate suspension of club football but hopes were being entertained in many quarters that the great winter game could be resumed in a modified degree in the not too distant future.

If experience shows that large assemblies in day-time are not subject to undue danger, then the ban on football may be lifted, at least in some districts. In times such as this, it is desirable that the public should have something to divert their minds from the anxiety and horror of war, and nothing could most meet the need better than football.

Earliest casualties among the ranks of the amateur leagues in the south of England were the top competitions like the Isthmian and Athenian Leagues. These ground to a halt as soon as war was declared.

Minor amateur games were hit but it would appear that the Bishop's Stortford, Stansted and District Junior League did in fact continue to play some games with the League splitting into North and South sections.

In October 1939 Bishop's Stortford FC played the first of their matches under the 'emergency' programme which they had arranged. The visitors to Rhodes Avenue were local League side, Bishop's Stortford Rovers, who were defeated by 7-3.

A few weeks later Bishop's Stortford Rovers paid a further visit to Rhodes Avenue and again lost, this time by 8-2.

At the November League Council meeting it was reported that several clubs were unable to take part in League football. It was proposed by Hatfield Heath and seconded by Hatfield Broad Oak that the League should be divided into two divisions, North and South.

The following clubs were elected :- North – Albury, Bishop's Stortford Rovers, Eastons, Farnham, Stansted, Takeley, Thaxted and Widdington. South – Burnt Mill, Hatfield Broad Oak, Hatfield Heath, Little Hallingbury, Potter Street, Sawbridgeworth and Sheering.

Bishop's Stortford and Harlow were invited into the League but Bishop's Stortford refused. Harlow accepted and were invited into the South division.

It was suggested by the Chairman that medals should not be awarded this season and that the fixtures should start on November 25th.

At the League's Council meeting in early December it was proposed by Sheering and seconded by Hatfield Broad Oak that Challenge Cups should be run.

The Chairman proposed that the Honorary Secretary inquire if medals should be got if necessary for both League and Challenge Cups.

The first mention of the League in the Herts & Essex Observer for the season 1939/40 was on December 23, 1939.

The fixtures for December 23rd, 1939, were:

North – Hatfield Broad Oak v Little Hallingbury, Sawbridgeworth v Sheering, Thornwood v Potter Street, Harlow v Hatfield Heath

South – Farnham v Stansted, Albury v Bishop's Stortford Rovers

December 25th, 1939:

North – Hatfield Broad Oak v Potter Street

December 26th, 1939:

North – Thaxted v Easton & Duton Hill

Results of the matches played on December 16th, 1939:

North – Bishop's Stortford Rovers 3 Easton and Duton Hill 2, Farnham 3 Widdington 2, Albury 0 Stansted 6

South – Burnt Mill 1 Sawbridgeworth 6, Hatfield Heath 6 Thornwood United 1, Sheering 1 Potter Street 2

At the next League Council meeting in early January it was proposed by Sawbridgeworth and seconded by Bishop's Stortford Rovers that medals be given to the League winners and Challenge Cup winners.

At the same meeting, a letter was received from Potter Street who wished to withdraw from the League owing to players being called up for the Army.

The next mention in the Herts & Essex Observer was on January 13th, 1940, which included the draws for the Challenge Cups.

North – Easton & Duton Hill v Albury, Stansted v Widdington, Takeley v Thaxted, Farnham v Bishop's Stortford Rovers

South – Little Hallingbury v Thornwood United, Hatfield Broad Oak v Burnt Mill, Sheering v Sawbridgeworth, Hatfield Heath (Bye)

Ties to be played by February 10th, 1940.

At the February League Council meeting Farnham and Takeley withdrew from the League.

Result of match played on January 10th, 1940:

South – Sawbridgeworth 2 Thornwood United 0

Fixtures for January 13th, 1940:

North – Hatfield Heath v Harlow, Sheering v Sawbridgeworth, Thornwood v Little Hallingbury

South – Bishop's Stortford Rovers v Albury

Further mentions continued in the Herts & Essex Observer

Results of matches played February 24th,1940:

North – Stansted 7 Easton & Duton Hill 3, Albury 6 Widdington 0

Fixtures for March 2nd, 1940:

North – Stansted v Widdington, Challenge Cup, 2nd Round

South – Hatfield Heath v Thornwood United, Little Hallingbury v Burnt Mill (at Burnt Mill)

A Special Meeting was held in early March to decide whether or not medals should be given for the Challenge Cup and League this season.

The Chairman stated at commencement of this season he received a leaflet from the Essex Football Association recommending that all leagues not to give medals this season. He then introduced Mr Duchesne who stated it was his firm conviction that medals should not be given this season and explained his reason. Firstly he thought the money the League has in hand should be put aside so as to give the League a good start after the war. Secondly it was his, and some other Vice-Presidents opinions, that medals not to be given as more than half of the clubs have had to withdraw from the League, through no fault of their own and it was only right these clubs should have the money when the League starts again.

After discussion it was proposed by Bishop's Stortford Rovers that medals should be given to the League champions only. This was seconded by Little Hallingbury and the motion was carried.

At the next League Council meeting letters were received from Sawbridgeworth, Thaxted and Sheering withdrawing from the League.

A further letter was received from Eastons stating the League was out to kill local football. It was proposed by Thornwood and seconded by Burnt Mill that a letter be sent to Eastons, strongly resenting this allegation and asking for a full explanation.

Results of matches played March 31st, 1940

North – Stansted 3 Widdington 4

South – Harlow 9 Little Hallingbury 0

Fixtures for April 6th, 1940

North – Stansted v Albury, Challenge Cup, Semi-Final

South – Little Hallingbury v Thornwood United, Challenge Cup, 1st Round

League matches

Harlow v Hatfield Broad Oak, Hatfield Heath v Burnt Mill

Results for matches for April 6th, 1940

North – Stansted 5 Albury 0, Challenge Cup, Semi-Final

South – Little Hallingbury 2 Thornwood United 0, Challenge Cup, 1st Round

League matches

Harlow 0 Hatfield Broad Oak 3, Hatfield Heath 3 Burnt Mill 5

Results for matches for April 10th, 1940

South – Hatfield Broad Oak 4 Hatfield Heath 1

Fixtures for April 13th, 1940

South – Little Hallingbury v Hatfield Heath, Challenge Cup Semi-Final at Harlow

League Match

Burnt Mill v Hatfield Broad Oak

Fixture for April 20th, 1940

North – Bishop's Stortford Rovers V Stansted, Challenge Cup, Final at the Bishop's Stortford Town Ground. Referee – Mr F Harriman, Linesmen – Messrs F French and W.G.Snow. Challenge Cup to be presented by Mr C W P Lyall, Chairman of the League.

Results for matches for April 13th, 1940

League Match

Burnt Mill 3 Hatfield Broad Oak 4

South – Little Hallingbury 0 Hatfield Heath 5, Challenge Cup Semi-Final

Results of matches for April 20th, 1940

South – Harlow 3 Hatfield Heath 4, Hatfield Broad Oak 4 Burnt Mill 0

North – Bishop's Stortford Rovers 0 Stansted 5, Challenge Cup, Final

The final of the Bishop's Stortford, Stansted and District Junior League Cup Northern Section was played on the Bishop's Stortford Town ground. The match resulted in a comfortable win for Stansted, who defeated Bishop's Stortford Rovers 5-0. The game was played at a fast pace. And while Stansted showed some superiority throughout, it was only in the closing stages that they completely dominated the game. Stansted only scored once in the first half and this goal came a minute after the kick off. Encouraged by it, the Stansted forwards heavy pressure to the Rovers' defence, but Dellow in goal dealt capably with a number of shots. Play was fairly even during the remainder of the half, and with better finishing, Rovers might have equalised.

Early in the second half Stansted were awarded a penalty but Dellow saved the shot. It was in the final quarter of an hour that Stansted scored four very quick goals.

After the match, the cup was presented by Mr Lyall.

Fixture for April 27th, 1940

South – Hatfield Broad Oak v Hatfield Heath, Challenge Cup Final South at the Bishop's Stortford Town Ground. This game was won by Hatfield Broad Oak.

Fixture for May 1st, 1940

South – Hatfield Heath v Harlow

Fixture for May 4th, 1940

Hatfield Broad Oak v Burnt Mill, Junior Charity Cup Final

On May 11th, 1940, it was reported that Stansted had almost come to the end of their fixture list in the League and where they had had very-little opposition and were still top of the League table.

Stansted and Hatfield Broad Oak, the winners of the two sections of the Bishop's Stortford, Stansted and District Junior League, met in a friendly at Rhodes Avenue in May 1940. The match was arranged by the League committee in aid of two players (from Easton & Duton Hill and Hatfield Broad Oak) who were injured during the season.

Stansted brought their football season to an end when they defeated Hatfield Broad Oak by two goals to one and afterwards the cups were presented. Unfortunately, there was only a small attendance. Ken Little scored both Stansted goals and Hatfield Broad Oak's only reply came in the last minute of the game and was scored by the centre-forward.

Due to World War II the League was eventually abandoned from 1940 until 1945.

In a flyer inserted into the Essex FA Handbook the President, J B Slade stated, 'Almost all of our operations in the Football world will be suspended. I trust, however that we may all look forward to, and hope for, an early termination to the struggle, and in the near future to see our members return to the game which we have so much at heart.'

THE BOXING DAY DEMOLITION OF HATFIELD HEATH BY THE POWS FROM CAMP 116 IN 1946

Identified players in the photo below:

Back Row – F Bruty, W Bruty Front Row – B Nicholls, H Peacock, J Want, R Jones, L Wilkins, W Day, E Gunn, G Brown and R Howard.

On boxing day 1945, Hatfield Heath Football Club played against the POWS from POW Camp 116 which was built in 1941 in Mill Lane in the village. The 100s of people imprisoned there weren't Nazis but ordinary decent German, Italian, Austrian guys conscripted by their respective governments to fight.

It is said that the match was watched by an estimated 750 people, POW 'fans' on one side of the pitch and villagers on the other side. The Heath were beaten by a then record score against them, 11-0. The POW team included a former Under-23 international.

During, and after, the war many worked on the farms around Hatfield Heath, many produced art work given as gifts to local families, some stayed after being released.

Source : David Brown / Hatfield Heath FC

HATFIELD HEATH v POW TEAM, HATFIELD HEATH

Bill Bruty was a great believer in peace and friendship. He organised the 1946 game as a conciliatory gesture. The club remembered Bill for his bravery and kindness in organising that match which was never forgotten for many decades but now is the most iconic game in the club's history.

It is interesting to note that on 28th August 1943, Bishop's Stortford Football Club took on a team of Polish Army POWs and went down 4-2 in an exciting game at Rhodes Avenue. The POWs were based in a camp at Much Hadham, and the large crowd gave a warm reception to the Poles fluent style of football.

The Post War Years To 1949

'A FOOTBALL CLUB FOR EVERY VILLAGE IN THE COUNTY'

In July 1945, the Essex County Football Association made a big drive to get as many pre-war leagues as possible and clubs restarted for the following season, and to bring new clubs into being.

Their slogan was in fact: 'A football club for every village in the county.'

However, this was by no means easy because of the dearth of suitable playing pitches, to say nothing of paucity of players.

Still, a start had to be made, hence the Association circulated every civic authority in the county, requesting co-operation in its efforts to restore Essex football to its pre-war position by providing facilities for football pitches for teams in parks, etc.

Further, the Association was prepared to send, if desired, speakers to any football gathering with a view to promoting the interests of the game. To ensure this, competitions would have to make known their requirements to the Honorary Secretary of the Association, Mr J T Clark.

It was probably not known generally that until a club was dually affiliated to the County Association it could not be in a position to function, matches with unaffiliated teams being forbidden by the governing body of football.

Another point was that there were, no doubt, many pre-war players who, after six years abstention from football, would now be unable to 'go the pace,' but would still like to be associated with the game in the capacity of referee or linesman. To enable them to do this, the Association held examinations in different parts of the county as required, and also arranged, where possible, instruction and coaching classes for candidates.

Here again, they only had to contact Mr Clark, who after thirty-seven years as Honorary Secretary, was as anxious as ever to see Essex loom large again in the amateur soccer world.

INITIAL MEETING HELD

A meeting was called by the Chairman, Mr Lyall, and held at the Bell Hotel, Stansted, on December 18th, 1945.

The following clubs were represented :- Bishop's Stortford, Newport, Saffron Walden Town and Stansted.

In opening the meeting, Mr Lyall stated he had hoped to have at least 5 clubs to restart with but Saffron Walden Wanderers and the Glider Pilot RAF club clubs had since decided not to participate. After discussion it was decided to restart with the four clubs represented.

The Chairman stated he had been unable to get any of the League's books or other matter appertaining to the League owing to the last Secretary, Mr Ward, being still abroad, and not being able to get in touch with Mr Ward although he had called on several occasions at the Ward's house.

In the absence of books of rules it was decided to run through one the Chairman had and agree in principle to those deemed to be applicable to the present circumstances. It was pointed out by the Chairman that these would have to be submitted to the County Football Association Sanction Committee before matches could be played.

It was agreed the entrance fee and subscription remain the same as hitherto, 5s, and entrance fee for a new club, 2s 6d.

The following rule as to players was agreed. A member of a club who has played for that club in the League during the current season shall not be allowed to play for another club without a transfer and no player shall be eligible who has played in three senior games after 31/12/1945.

Five clear days notification by the home club shall be given in writing giving full particulars of ground and time of kick-off to the referee and Secretary of the visiting club.

The referee's fee to be 5s plus 3rd class railway fare, bus fare or 1d per mile cycle.

There would be no medals to players, only the League Cup to the winning club.

Result of all ties to be sent to the Secretary within 2 days, these not to include Sunday.

It was decided to call another meeting shortly as soon as sanction was obtained from the Essex Football Association.

A further meeting was held on 15th January 1946. The clubs represented together with Mr Lyall were :- Bishop's Stortford, Stansted, Newport, Saffron Walden and the following who desired to enter the League, Duddenhoe End, Hadham United and R.A.F. Stansted.

The Chairman stated that the League had been affiliated to the Essex County Football Association and sanction applied for, which would probably come along shortly, an abbreviated copy of rules sent. Clubs could now go ahead.

It was agreed that all protests be sent to the acting Secretary within three days of the match.

Mr Lyall warned the clubs that there was a dearth of registered referees in the district and consequently clubs would in a good many cases have to find a referee themselves. But he would appoint registered referees where and when it was possible.

Fixtures were then made and it was agreed that the times of the kick-off be for January 2.30, February 3.00 and March and April 2.30.

The League was therefore reformed in January and saw 7 clubs enter – Bishop's Stortford Reserves, Duddenhoe End, Much Hadham, Newport, R.A.F. Stansted, Saffron Walden Reserves and Stansted.

Saffron Walden Town Reserves were able to win the competition after dropping five points in their first three matches. Two wins in a week gave Saffron Walden Town Reserves the Bishop's Stortford, Stansted and District Junior League Championship. The Reserve team received special praise from the club's Honorary Secretary, George E Moore in his Annual Report at the Annual General Meeting when he commented: 'Who will forget the leg-weariness of the Reserves on the last Saturday of the season' he continued, 'Beating Duddenhoe End on Tuesday, and R.A.F. Stansted on Thursday, they drew 3-3 with Saffron

Walden Wanderers after extra-time on Friday to become joint holders of the Saffron Walden Junior Charity Cup, and then beat Much Hadham defeating on Saturday them by five goals to one to win the League – a truly great performance.'

The Reserves team had a final fixture when they were at home to the R.A.F. (Samford). Proceeds of the game were for the Essex FA Benevolent Fund.

Newport Football Club were actively preparing for the forthcoming season.

Training for all those interested was given by Mr H Palmer every Wednesday on Newport Common which started on July 24th. Any footballers who were eager to play were invited to communicate with the Club Committee and particularly the Honorary Secretary Mr K C Hampson.

A meeting was held on 12th June at the Bell Hotel, Stansted chaired by Mr Lyall. Correspondence had been received from Bishop's Stortford Football Club who advised they were withdrawing from the League. A card was also received from Hatfield Broad Oak hoping to again enter the League. A letter was also received from Newport, asking for information on matters relating to the League.

DISTRICT LEAGUE'S PLANS FOR THE COMING SEASON

The League, which was forced to suspend its activities for the majority of the war-time seasons and was recommended on a limited scale during the latter scale of last season, would resume a full programme under normal conditions in the season ahead. Fourteen clubs entered the League, which, for the **1946/47** season comprised of one division only. This was stated at the League's Annual General Meeting which was held at the Falcon Hotel on 10th July..

Mr E C Duchesne, who presided at the meeting, said he did not think the coming season would be an easy one for the League and he appealed to the clubs to do all they could to help its smooth running and to avoid any differences of opinion which might increase its difficulties.

A short report on the competition organised by the League in the latter part of last season, in which seven clubs participated, was given by Mr C W P Lyall, and a statement of accounts, showing a balance in hand of £40 7s 11d, was presented by Mr R Ashford, who said that, so far as finance was concerned, the League would be able to restart in a very sound condition. It was agreed that the League competition should be confined to one division.

The meeting agreed to an increase in payment to referees from 5s to 7s 6d per match and it was also decided the rule under which a player who had taken part in more than a limited number of senior matches is debarred from playing in the League's games for a period of 6 months should be waived for the first month of the coming season.

It was pointed out that the enforcement of the rule during the period would cause difficulties to clubs in the selection of teams and hardships to players who had turned to senior teams for a game during the past season, at a time when many of the village clubs were not in operation.

Twelve teams entered the League for season 1946/47 with five teams withdrawing.

THE DEATH OF MR TRESHAM GILBEY ANNOUNCED

The death was announced of Mr Tresham Gilbey, 84, who had been President of the League from 1933 to 1937. Mr Gilbey presented the original Challenge Cup to the League. For many years Mr Gilbey was known as one of Bishop's Stortford's best-known residents.

Manuden withdrew from the League during the season.

Harlow Reserves were champions.

The Challenge Cup was won by R.A.F. Stansted who defeated Hatfield Heath by two goals to one.

In 1972 Harlow Town life member Ernie Ellis, who had been connected with the club at that time for 50 years, said : 'They were all local boys in those days – there was a lot of local talent. They didn't do too badly then.'

He remembered vividly the club's training sessions on the playing field behind the Green Man pub at Mulberry Green.

Source : Paul Cox

HARLOW TOWN FC

(Including Reserve team members that won the Bishop's Stortford and District Junior League)

At a League Council meeting in May it was proposed by Sawbridgeworth and seconded by Hatfield Heath, that medals should be awarded to League winners.

It was also proposed by Sheering and seconded by Harlow that medals should be awarded to League runners-up.

It was decided that the Champions versus the Rest of the League fixture should take place on May 31st. The League team would be selected by Mr French, Mr Bruty and Mr Elliott.

Harlow defeated the Rest of the League team 4-2.

At a League Council meeting in June, Harlow's Mr Parish, regretted that his club would be withdrawing from the League, as they had been accepted into the Herts County League. Sawbridgeworth would be withdrawing from the League, also as they had been accepted into the Herts County League.

The League winners, Harlow, were asked to choose their medals for the Honorary Secretary to place the order, this was done and two sets of the same medals would be ordered for the winners and runners-up.

TWO DIVISIONS FOR STORTFORD JUNIOR LEAGUE

At the Annual General Meeting held at the Falcon Hotel, 15 clubs were elected to form Division I. Ten teams, including reserve teams from some of the Division I clubs, were elected to Division II and any further applications before the fixture meeting would be considered for admission to that division. In the latter category R.A.F. Stansted, one of the strongest teams in the League in the previous season, had not, at the time of the meeting, notified their wish to compete.

Harlow Reserves, the previous season's champions withdrew from the League together with Sawbridgeworth Reserves who were accepted into the Herts County League.

New clubs (i.e., clubs not members of the League in 1946/47) admitted at the meeting were : Burnt Mill, Great Parndon, Saffron Walden Wanderers Reserves, Potter Street, Black Lion (Bishop's Stortford), Great Hallingbury, Stansted Reserves, Butterfield's United (Nazeing), Hockerill Athletic, Much Hadham, London Aero and Motor Services (L.A.M.S. – Stansted).

Clubs elected to Division I were Albury, Hatfield Broad Oak, Hatfield Heath, Newport, Post Office Engineers (Bishop's Stortford), Sheering, Takeley, Rodings United, Burnt Mill, Saffron Walden Wanderers Reserves, Potter Street, Stansted Reserves and Hockerill Athletic.

Manuden also took their place in Division I.

The composition of Division II (subject to any further admissions) would be Farnham, Little Hadham, Great Hallingbury, Butterfield's United, Black Lion, Much Hadham, and (probably) Hatfield Heath Reserves, Takeley Reserves, L.A.M.S. and Rodings United Reserves.

Much Hadham would also continue to compete in the Hertford and District League.

Rodings United Reserves did not take their place in Division II, however, Easton & Duton Hill Reserves, Elsenham Rovers and Birchanger also joined the League.

Mr C W P Lyall, who presided at the meeting, said the fact that some of the clubs had been unable to complete their fixtures for the previous season would not affect the position at the top of the League table.

In presenting his statement of accounts, Mr R Ashford (Honorary Treasurer), expressed the opinion that the financial position of the League was as strong as it ever had been. They had a credit balance of £83, compared to a balance brought forward of £40, their total receipts of £101 6s 3d having included a record 'gate' of over £29 from the Challenge Cup Finals. There were, however, some expenses still to be met, ass it had been necessary to close the accounts before the end of the extended season.

It was mentioned that among expenses outstanding was the cost of four sets of medals, expected to be between £40 and £45. The clubs concerned had offered to make a substantial contribution towards the expenditure.

The following officers were elected : Mr E C Duchesne – President, Mr C W P Lyall (Vice-President and Chairman), Mr A Collison (Vice-Chairman), Mr R E Baker (Honorary Secretary), Mr R Ashford (Honorary Treasurer) and Mr M Connolly (Honorary Assistant-Secretary).

BISHOP'S STORTFORD FOOTBALL CLUB CRITICISED

Criticism that Bishop's Stortford Football Club failed in the 1946/47 season to make sufficient use of local players were answered at the Annual General Meeting held at the Thorley Works.

Major L A Leech, who presided and was elected President of the club, said it should be clearly understood that every effort had been made in the previous season to use local players, provided they had the necessary ability. 'But we are not thought readers,' he added, 'and prospective players must come forward and make themselves known to us. Surely in a town of this size, there must be plenty of hidden talent.'

In his annual report, Mr R A Dent, Honorary Secretary, said that in the coming season, as in the past, the Club would concentrate as much as possible on local players, provided they were of sufficient ability.

The Rhodes Avenue Ground used for the League's Cup Finals

HOCKERILL ATHLETIC CLUB

At an extraordinary general meeting of the Hockerill Athletic Club held at the Falcon Hotel, Bishop's Stortford, it was decided to form a football section.

Mr P G King, who presided, said that the club had been entered into the Bishop's Stortford, Stansted and District Junior League and elected to Division I. They had about 20 players available, the majority already being members of the ricket or tennis sections.

Mr S Thurgood was elected Secretary, Mr F Herrington Assistant-Secretary, Mr R Day Captain and Mr R W Camp Trainer. A committee was also elected.

It was decided that subscription should be 10s (5s under 21).

1947 – 1948 SEASON		
League Competition	Winners	Runners up
Division I	Hatfield Heath	Hockerill Athletic
Division II	Easton and Duton Hill Res	Great Parndon
League Cup		
Division I	Newport	Takeley
Division II	Great Parndon	Farnham

Junior football in the district was almost back to its pre-war position for the 1947/48 season. The Bishop's Stortford, Stansted and District Junior League – now covering an area extending from Potter Street to Saffron Walden – was organised into two divisions, with promotion and relegation under the usual rules.

In their first game of the season , Hockerill Athletic beat Takeley by 3 goals to 2 at Takeley. In the home goal, Sullivan, brother of the Bishop's Stortford Football Club goalkeeper, played an excellent game and for the visitors, Skerritt, Turner and Herrington, did good work.

In the first half, play was fairly even, and the teams crossed over with the score 2-2. D Camp and F Herrington scoring for Hockerill. In the second half Hockerill had more of the play, and H Skerritt increased the score from a penalty. Hockerill had signed R Halls, a former Isthmian League player, and also had the services of former Bishop's Stortford players R Day, H Skerritt, G Dougan, B Perry, J Kimber and H Kimber.

At the October League Council meeting Rodings United Reserves asked for withdrawal from Division II and after some discussion on how the club could be helped to carry on it was proposed by Takeley and seconded by Hatfield Heath that Rodings United Reserves be withdrawn from the League.

In November, Butterfield's United inquired at a League Council meeting as to POW's playing in the League. The Chairman said this was not permissible and he would inquire about how aliens were placed for playing in the League.

At an informal social gathering in November 1947, Colonel F C Drake, President of Harlow, handed medals to members of the Harlow Reserve team as the previous season's champions of the League. The players who received medals : S Baker, F Cakebread, W Savage, A Moore, J Canty, L Baker, L Crisp, F Brown, R Fish, K Fish, K Byford and W J Lambert.

● TEAM OF LIONS: Back row(l to r) Mr Greenley, Mr Chapman, Geoff Fuller, Tony Luff, Dick Kitchener, Douglas Axton. Front row (l to r) Len Emerson, unknown, John Clarke, Eric Neville, Fred Wright

Source: Herts & Essex Observer

BLACK LION

THOSE GLORY DAYS (Source : Toby Allanson/Herts & Essex Observer)

The 1947 Black Lion team, those were the days of real footballing legends, when Stanley Matthews dazzled defences with his quick feet and delivered crosses of such accuracy that players like Stan Mortensen and Nat Lofthouse were able to avoid heading the painful laces of the ludicrously heavy ball.

The team before you are fit to be mentioned in the same breath as those heroes of the beautiful game.

Who could forget the tricky wing wizardry of Geoff Fuller, or the safe hands of goalkeeper, Tony Luff, whose imposing bulk meant few shots ever nestled in the back of his net. These were players who brought glory to their favourite Bishop's Stortford pub, once called Scruffy Mac's, and hours of entertainment to the faithful who turned out to watch them week after week.

'They didn't do too badly and had a good time,' Mrs Fuller, from Piggotts Way, said modestly. 'They had all been abroad fighting for their country and it was a relaxation after they got home.'

As well as the vital creative role Mr Fuller played on the flanks, he would also drift inside and notched several times for the Bridge Street based side.

His heading prowess was hampered by an injury picked up during the Second World War, but as Mrs Fuller admitted, this did not detract massively from his all-round game because he was regularly the smallest player on the pitch.

As such, you would expect to see Mr Fuller, seated in the front row of the photo rather than standing, third from the left, next to the keeper.

Mrs Fuller explained, 'I asked him what on earth he was doing at the back next to the biggest man in the team. He told me that he had remembered his shirt, his socks and his boots, but had forgotten his shorts. I think he was too eager to go and have a drink!'

Mrs Fuller believed all the team had served during the Second World War. Douglas Axton and Tony Luff were in the Navy, and all the others, apart from her husband, were in the Army.

Mr Fuller fought in an airborne regiment and was taken prisoner on D-Day. He returned to Bishop's Stortford in 1946 and shortly after the team was formed.

The Fullers' son, Stuart, followed in his father's footballing footsteps playing in goal for Bishop's Stortford Swifts. Mrs Fuller said. 'When you compare the boots that my son wears with what my husband used to wear, well it's a different ball game altogether.'

Mrs Fuller is right, but I don't doubt who would have emerged victorious had the two faced each other on the pitch.

Indeed, the only uncertainty surrounds just how many times Mr Fuller senior would have slammed the ball past his son, fancy dan boots and all.

In March, Elsenham Rovers withdrew from Division II of the League.

In April L.A.M.S. withdrew from Division I of the League.

In April, at Rhodes Avenue, Hockerill Athletic entertained Takeley in a League match and it was watched by a crowd of around 700 spectators comparable in size with some Spartan League games. Takeley were in the lead after five minutes but Camp equalised and put Hockerill in the lead before half-time. On resumption of play Shuttlewood had bad luck with several good shots and at the other end Sullivan brought off a point blank save from Skerritt. Camp completed his hat-trick from a well-placed centre by Kitchener, and soon after Shuttlewood headed Takeley's second goal. Camp was always a thorn in Takeley's side, and he scored again just before the end.

In spite of heavy rain there was another big crowd at Rhodes Avenue to see the final of the Albury Cup between Hockerill Athletic and P.O. Engineers. Hockerill won 4-1 in extra-time. Hockerill scorers were Thurgood, Kitchener and Camp (2).

Over a period of months, following a complaint from Butterfield's United regarding an allegation that Elsenham Rovers played a POW in a number of games, the matter was discussed at length in League Council meetings.

It was decided that Elsenham Rovers had in fact broken the rules and were fined and deducted points. However, Mr Day the Elsenham Secretary was not convinced that his club were guilty and was convinced the player was eligible to play and would pursue the matter to the Football Association at Lancaster Gate.

DIVISION I CHALLENGE CUP FINAL

NEWPORT 2 TAKELEY 0

Before a crowd of well over a thousand spectators at Rhodes Avenue, Newport beat Takeley 2-0 in the final of the Division I Challenge Cup.

Takeley took the initiative from the kick off and Holgate's shot was blocked by Newport's centre-half. At the other end Sullivan saved well from Westwood.

In midfield Takeley were superior, but their finishing was poor, In an attack by Takeley, one of Newport's players, J Westwood, collided with his inside-left and had to be taken to hospital, where he was detained for treatment.

Playing with ten men Newport were on the defensive until half-time when there was no score.

On resumption Takeley attacked vigorously, but a stubborn defence held their forwards in check. Against the run of play Newport opened the scoring when their outside-right beat Sullivan with a good cross-shot.

From then on Takeley dominated the game, Shuttlewood, their centre-forward, just missing the goal several times. Corners by Takeley were frequent but Newport held out, and after defending almost continually in the second half, a breakaway ten minutes from the end gave them a further goal.

After the match, the cup and medals were distributed my Mr A Collison, Vice-Chairman of the League.

Source : Mike Connoly

POST OFFICE ENGINEERS

The Post Office Engineers team reached the final of the Albury Cup where they lost 4-2 to Hockerill Athletic. The team's home ground was at Plaw Hatch Close.

Their colours were red and white striped shirts which they scrounged from an army unit, and black shorts made from black-out curtains.

JUNIOR CHARITY CUP FINAL

MUCH HADHAM 4 HOCKERILL ATHLETIC 1

Well over a thousand spectators saw the final of the Junior Charity Cup at Rhodes Avenue. Hadham attacked from the kick off and Blyth tested Baker with a fast ground shot which was cleared only with difficulty. Hockerill failed to settle down quickly on the rain-soaked pitch, and early in the game Hadham were one up when J Mumford scored with a good cross-shot. Frequent corners were forced by Hockerill, but Briscoe, playing extremely well in Hadham's defence, cleared every time. Play in midfield showed up the strength of Hadham's include men and their forward passes were always a menace to Hockerill's defence.

After the interval Hadham scored again through their outside-left. Kimber broke away several times for Hockerill, but his shots were well held, and two more goals came quickly for Hadham, the first from Crowe and the second deflected by Hockerill's left-back, Pope.

Two penalties against Hadham were taken by Day but the first hit the post and was cleared and the second was saved by the goalkeeper.

Dr R P Gammie presented the cup to the Hadham captain. Gate receipts were over £40.

DIVISION II CHALLENGE CUP FINAL

GREAT PARNDON 4 FARNHAM 4 (AFTER EXTRA-TIME)

Source : Barbara Hudgell

FARNHAM

The game was replayed at the start of following season with Great Parndon winning 3-0.

Hatfield Heath finished as Division I champions and Hockerill Athletic were runners-up.

Easton and Duton Hill Reserves finished as Division II champions and Great Parndon were runners-up.

In his report to the Annual meeting of the North-West Essex Border Branch of Referees, held at the Falcon Hotel, the Honorary Secretary Mr T S Gee said that the branch had increased membership from nine to twenty-eight. Coaching classes had been held and all fifteen candidates coached had passed the examinations.

An appointments scheme had been operated on behalf of the Bishop's Stortford, Stansted and District Junior League, the Dunmow League and other local competitions by Mr F T Harryman, but it was apparent that more co-operation must be forthcoming from club secretaries and referees alike if this were to prove a success.

TAKELEY DINNER REVIVED AFTER TEN YEARS

The growing popularity of junior football in the district was stressed by speakers at the Takeley Football Club Dinner. Chairman Mr H L Frost, in proposing the toast of the Bishop's Stortford, Stansted and District Junior League, pointed out that the League catered for 25 clubs in two divisions. Junior football was undoubtedly gaining popularity with the public, as was shown by the fact that 1,500 people watched the Division I Challenge Cup Final, and two days later a League match in which Takeley met Hockerill Athletic attracted a crowd of 700.

Mr A Collison presided at the dinner, which was the first to be held by the club for ten years, He was supported by Mr Frost, Mr D W Pallett (Captain and Honorary Secretary) and Mr L Swallow (Honorary Treasurer). Among the guests were Mr R E Baker (League Honorary Secretary) and Mr S Sullivan (Bishop's Stortford and Hertfordshire goalkeeper).

Proposing the toast to the club, Mr E Ellis paid tribute to the officials, players and supporters. Replying, Mr Pallett said the first team had finished the season in third place in Division I and had reached the Challenge Cup Final. Top goal scorers were J Shuttlewood (42) and R Bradley (21) and it was a credit to the goalkeeper, B Sullivan, that their goals against column showed the lowest figure in the League.

JUNIOR FOOTBALL BACK TO PRE-WAR STRENGTH

At the Annual General Meeting fifteen teams were elected to the Premier Division, twelve to Division I and thirteen to Division II. The composition of those divisions was subject to further applications. New teams (not members of the League during 1947/48) elected were : Bishop's Stortford 'A', Rochford Sports, Green Tye, Millars Sports, Little Hallingbury, Netteswell and Burnt Mill Reserves, White Roding Social and Sports, Roydon, Potter Street Reserves, Saffron Walden Athletic, Hatfield Broad Oak Reserves, Great Parndon Reserves, Hockerill Athletic Reserves, Dunmow and Dunmow Reserves.

Clubs elected to the Premier Division : Albury, Bishop's Stortford 'A,' Dunmow, Great Parndon, Hatfield Broad Oak, Hatfield Heath, Hockerill Athletic, Netteswell and Burnt Mill, Newport, P.O. Engineers, Potter Street, Sawbridgeworth, Stansted Reserves, Sheering and Takeley.

Division I : Birchanger, Black Lion, Dunmow Reserves, Eastons & Duton Hill, Farnham, Great Hallingbury, Little Hadham, Little Hallingbury, Manuden, Millars Sports, Rodings United and Saffron Walden Athletic.

Division II : Butterfield's United, Great Parndon Reserves, Green Tye, Hatfield Broad Oak Reserves, Hatfield Heath Reserves, Hockerill Athletic Reserves, Much Hadham, Rochford Sports, Netteswell and Burnt Mill Reserves, Potter Street Reserves, Roydon and White Roding.

Sawbridgeworth withdrew before the start of the season and were replaced in the Premier Division by Saffron Walden Wanderers. 21 V.R.D. joined before the start of the season and were placed in the Division I. Hatfield Broad Oak Reserves withdrew before the start of the season while Sheering Reserves, Takeley Reserves and Thaxted joined and were placed in Division II.

In presenting his statement of accounts Mr R Ashford, Honorary Treasurer, said the £44 11s paid for the previous season's medals had caused a serious set-back on the League's financial position. The balance in hand of £33 7s 2d showed a loss on the year's working of £14 12s 11d. Mr Ashford pointed out that the League really finished 'all square' there were proceeds to come from two drawn games outstanding from the season which would be played early in the new season. He warned the meeting, however, that they must increase their balance 'in readiness for a rainy day.'

1948 – 1949 SEASON		
League Competition	**Winners**	**Runners up**
Premier Division	Takeley	Dunmow
Division I	Rodings United	Dunmow Reserves
Division II	Hatfield Heath Reserves	Buttersfield United
League Cup		
Premier Division	Dunmow	Potter Street
Division I	Rodings United	Dunmow Reserves
Division II	Much Hadham	Green Tye

Junior football in the district surpassed its pre-war strength for the 1948/49 season and the League was organised in three divisions instead of the previous season's two.

Boyd Gibbons Sports joined the League and were placed in Division I. However the club withdrew before the season started.

At the start of the season Elsenham Rovers paid their fines and withdrew their protest regarding the complaint made by Butterfield's United.

1947/48 DIVISION II CHALLENGE CUP FINAL REPLAY

GREAT PARNDON 3 FARNHAM 0

REPORT OF A SENDING OFF

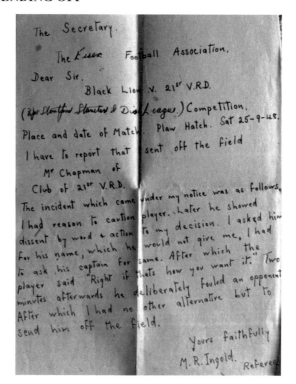

Source : Graham Ingold

In January 1949 Birchanger withdrew from Division I.

THE DEATH OF MR E C DUCHESNE ANNOUNCED

In March 1949, the death was announced of Mr Ernest Collier Duchesne a well-known personality in Bishop's Stortford and a former Chairman and the President of the Bishop's Stortford, Stansted and District League.

Brought up in Bishop's Stortford, he was an all-round sportsman, but football appears to have been his main game having started at Bishop's Stortford FC.

In 1880 Mr Duchesne moved to Bournemouth and in 1890 he was listed as playing for Bournemouth FC.

After retirement he moved to Harlow and then finally to Bishop's Stortford where at the start of World War II, he was a preacher at Bishop's Stortford Non-Conformist Church and a town councillor.

Mr Duchesne's son Richard Ernest was listed as killed in action on 8th October 1916 and is featured on the Bishop's Stortford War Memorial in the Town Park.

Source : Helen Smith

GREEN TYE FC

The player standing second in the back row was called Jack Kellor who was a German Prisoner of War. It is presumed that he had been an inmate at the Wynches POW camp at Much Hadham.

In March, a decision was made to purchase the new Cups for the Division II League and Cup winners for the price of £10 10s each. It was agreed that clubs pay 10s and the remainder be met by a Champions v Rest of the League match. All winners medals were to be purchased for 10s 6d and the cost of the engraving to be met by the winners.

A letter was received by the League from the Referees Association asking if the referees appointed to Cup Finals could be awarded a medal instead of the fee. It was proposed by

Burnt Mill and seconded by Takeley that the referees appointed to Cup Finals be presented with a medal, which was carried. The Honorary Secretary then asked if the Referees Association Rules and Referees details could be inserted in the League Handbook. This was proposed by Burnt Mill and seconded by Roydon and carried.

PREMIER DIVISION CHALLENGE CUP FINAL

DUNMOW 7 POTTER STREET 1

Nearly 2,500 spectators at Rhodes Avenue saw Dunmow thrash Potter Street 7-1 to win the Premier Division Challenge Cup. Nearly 500 supporters accompanied the Dunmow team.

Source : Herts & Essex Observer

At the kick off both teams were affected by nerves and several chances were missed on either side. Dunmow went ahead after 28 minutes through Groves and half-time arrived without further score.

Early in the second half Potter Street attacked strongly but Dunmow's defence held out. As the result of a corner, well taken by Copping, Dunmow increased their lead, Groves scoring again. Dunmow had settled down by this time and were playing good football and from then-on they scored a succession of goals. It was no surprise when Copping scored two, and shortly afterwards Groves completed his hat-trick. Beattie's clever headwork often had Potter Street's defence running the wrong way and he was rewarded when he put Dunmow further ahead.

Potter Street, rallying gallantly, scored their only goal when Taylor, Dunmow's goalkeeper, in attempting to clear, kicked the ball against Phillips and saw it rebound into the net. Dunmow then attacked again and Wyper put Copping through to complete the second hat-trick of the match.

Mr C W P Lyall the new Chairman of the League, handed the cup and medals to the winners.

TAKELEY ANNUAL DINNER

'I think the more facilities that are given to young people to play sport, the better it is for the sport' said Club President Mr E Ellis at the Annual Dinner at Takeley Football Club, held at the Silver Jubilee Hall.

He continued, 'By sport I mean good, clean sport, not at the dogs and so on. I think sport is the birth right of the English people. We have set an example to the world on how to play the game in a sporting manner.'

The toast of 'The Club' was proposed by Mr C W P Lyall, the Chairman of the League, who was referred to by Mr Ellis as 'the grand old man of the sport.' Mr Lyall said he had been connected with the League for over 25 years and had always found Takeley players to be the keenest and finest of sportsmen. He handed the championship trophy and medals to members of the first team, who were League champions for the 1948/49 season, and said the team would be successful in the next season.

Source : Herts & Essex Observer

TAKELEY

Takeley players and officials with the league championship cup. Back row ; V. Shuttlewood (linesman), S. Metson, E. C. Whitting, R. W. Sullivan, W. Rhaney, R. A. J. Tebbit, A. L. Frost (chairman); front row ; S. Brighten, F. Campbell, S. C. Holdgate, D. W. Pallett (captain), M. J. Shuttlewood, R. A. Bradley, D. A. Brown.

Mr D W Pallett (Captain and Honorary Secretary), replying to the toast, said the club started the season with two objectives – the League Championship and the Challenge Cup. They had been successful in the former and were only 'pipped at the post' in the latter.

He thanked the players for their support and said it had been a privilege to captain them.

The toast of 'The League' was proposed by Mr A L Frost (the Takeley Chairman) who said the League was a leading one in Essex.

The Honorary Secretary of the League, Mr R E Baker, replying said the past season had been 'most outstanding.' Over £140 had been realised from Cup Finals and other games, and they would commence the following season free from any financial worries.

Members of the Dunmow Football Club were welcomed by Mr H J Piper when he proposed the toast of 'The Visitors' who finished as runners-up in the Premier Division.

The Honorary Secretary of the Dunmow Football Club, Mr J Knowler, congratulated Takeley on winning the Championship trophy. 'I wish you the best of luck next season,' he added.

Mr Armstrong, who was President of the club about 20 years ago, spoke of the feats of the old team, and said, 'They played football very squarely and although I have heard a lot about the present club is doing, I would like to remind you young players you have not come up to the standard of the old 'uns.'

Rodings United were Division I champions and Dunmow Reserves finished as Division I runners-up.

DIVISION I CHALLENGE CUP FINAL

RODINGS UNITED 1 DUNMOW RESERVES 0

Dunmow Reserves were defeated 1-0 by Rodings United after a hard game.. Dunmow should have equalised when Crow hit the crossbar. Rodings were the heavier and more experienced side, but were fully extended by the young Dunmow team, for whom Sewell in goal was outstanding.

DIVISION II CHALLENGE CUP FINAL

MUCH HADHAM 2 GREEN TYE 1

Source : Hatfield Heath FC

HATFIELD HEATH RESERVES

JUNIOR LEAGUE'S STRONG POSITION

Due to what the Honorary Treasurer, Mr R Ashford, described as 'phenomenal' gate receipts, the League was in a strong financial position, it was reported at the Annual General Meeting. Mr Ashford said, 'The receipts at the finals and cup matches were phenomenal, being a record for each division. As a League we are in a strong financial position and are also strong in membership and administration. We have a balance behind us which puts us out of any anxiety for the future.'

He reported that the balance brought forward of £33 7s 2d had been increased to £124 2s and receipts had amounted to £220 14s 8d. The record receipts from the Premier Division Final had been £66 15s, and the first and second division finals had brought in £39 15s and £37 13s 3d, respectively. The highest item of expenditure had been £40 0s 3d for the medals.

Mr R E Baker, Honorary Secretary said that, as shown by the balance sheet, the past season had been very successful. The League was becoming one of the best in the country and it was important that they should try to make it even more successful.

The Saffron Walden and Saffron Walden Wanderers clubs amalgamated.

Mr C W P Lyall, the League Chairman, who presided, thanked the officials and said the League were looking forward to the coming season.

Election of officers resulted : President, Mr C W P Lyall (succeeding the late Mr E C Duchesne); Chairman Mr A Collison; Vice-Chairman, Mr W Bruty; Treasurer. Mr R G Ashford; Secretary, Mr R E Baker; Assistant-Secretary, Mr M J Connolly.

1949 – 1950 SEASON		
League Competition	Winners	Runners Up
Premier Division	Dunmow	Takeley
Division I	Rodings United	Manuden
Division II	Green Tye	Hockerill Athletic Reserves
League Cup		
Premier Division	Dunmow	Sheering
Division I	Manuden	Rodings United
Division II	Green Tye	Takeley

National Service was a standardised form of peacetime conscription. All able-bodied men between the ages of 18 and 30 were called up. They initially served for 18 months, but in 1950, during the Korean War (1950-53) this was increased to two years.

Between 1949 – when the National Service Act came into force – and 1963 – when the last National Serviceman was demobbed – more than 2 million men were conscripted into the Royal Army, Royal Navy or the Royal Air Force.

Many local footballers completed their National Service during this time including Archie Warwick, Richard 'Dick' Barker (see below), Bert Search, Jack Greenley, Bryan Atkinson, Roy Wacey, Peter Baker, John Sewell, John Hancock, Derek Smith and John Robinson.

Source : Richard Knight

PRESENTATION TO MR C W P LYALL

A presentation to the district's 'grand old man of football' – 76 year-old Mr C W P Lyall – who has been associated with the game for nearly 60 years, was made at a dinner held by the North-West Essex Border branch of the Essex Society of Association Football Referees in December. Handing Mr Lyall a silver cigarette box, on behalf of the branch, Chairman, Mr T S Gee, said : 'All the years that I have known our President, Mr Lyall, I have always found him very helpful and very willing. He has always found time to assist us. There is no reason for him being a member of the Branch other than the effect he is genuinely fond of football.'

Replying, Mr Lyall said : 'I joined a football club when I was 17 and played for several years before I had an accident which finished my playing days. I then took up refereeing, which I carried on for a number of years. When I became too old for that, I gave my services in other ways – helping referees and football clubs.'

'It has always been very enjoyable following this game of football. Played in the proper spirit, there is not a finer game in the world.'

It was reported, for the first time in many years the outcome of the championship of the League for season 1949/50 was anybody's guess. At the period of time usually it would be possible to pin-point the prospective champions but on this any one of six or seven could end the season at the head of the table.

Takeley, the previous champions were only the only undefeated side and based on form would be there fighting it out at the season's end.

Dunmow, whose forward was the best on the League at that time, but who had just suffered their first League defeat at the hands of lowly-placed Bishop's Stortford 'A' also had a sporting chance.

Next perhaps, Hockerill Athletic, who, on paper, had the strongest team in the League. They were trounced recently by Stansted Reserves, their only defeat of the season, although previously Sheering had defeated them 6-1 at home in the League Challenge Cup.

Gallant Hatfield Heath, unpredictable Saffron Walden Reserves and equally erratic Potter Street, had chances but perhaps they had already dropped too many points.

Junior League football had a great following in the villages and the season had proved to be one of the keenest ever. The standard of play had improved greatly, interest was keen, and the sportsmanship shown by players and officials alike had been a credit to their clubs.

The Fifties

In 1950 Dunmow became the first team to complete the double by winning both the Premier Division championship and retaining the Premier Division Cup.

In 1950 Green Tye defeated Takeley Reserves 3-1 in the Division II Challenge Cup Final, after two replays. This was the first League Cup Final to go to a second replay.

Hatfield Heath were Premier Division champions three time in the 1950s and also runners-up on a further three occasions. The club were also winners of the Premier Division Challenge Cup on four occasions as well as finishing as runners-up on a further occasion.

The Bishop's Stortford Charity Cup was reintroduced in 1950 and the final was played at Rhodes Avenue, the home of Bishop's Stortford FC on boxing day.

In 1957 the League's representative team won the West Essex Inter-League Competition for the first time.

Alan Springham played for the Bishop's Stortford Army Cadets team in the Saffron Walden and Dunmow Youth Service League. The Army Cadets side won the League Cup in 1947 and the League Championship in 1948. He also represented the 3rd Battalion, Bishop's Stortford. He played for Bishop's Stortford 'A' before spending time in the army. In 1950 he played for Rhodes Avenue together with his brother Alan, David and Dick Barker and Dick Cracknell. Many of the members of the team had been in the Army Cadets team.

Source : Elsa Springham

BISHOP'S STORTFORD ARMY CADETS 1947

Initially it was only the boys and men of Rhodes Avenue who were allowed to play for the team but as time went on others were allowed to join like Brian King.

Tony played right-back, and he said that Rhodes Avenue were one of the best sides in local football. They won League Cups regularly and the final was always at the home ground.

Tony told his grand-daughter Elsa a story about the Italian Prisoner of War Camp which was at Silver Leys and Rhodes Avenue played them on a Sunday and 400 people went to watch. The Italian side had not lost a match until they played Rhodes Avenue. Sadly, Tony passed away in August 2021.

At a League Council meeting in March it was proposed by Burnt Mill and seconded by Rodings United that 12 sets of medals be purchased and the expense be born by the League. It was proposed by Takeley and seconded by Burnt Mill that the clubs involved pay for the engraving. Both these motions were carried. It was also agreed that the sub-committee would select the medals.

At the same meeting it was agreed that Farnham would be allowed to withdraw from the League.

PREMIER DIVISION CHALLENGE CUP FINAL

DUNMOW 4 SHEERING 2

In April 1950, the large crowd who thronged the Rhodes Avenue ground to see Dunmow, the holders, and Sheering, contend the Premier Division Challenge Cup, saw a game that was a credit to both teams and to the standard of local junior football. Play was keen, vigorous and fast, and there were combined moves that one expects, sometimes in vain, to see in senior football.

The Dunmow team had strong, hard tackling defenders, and a forward line possessing both punch and football skill. Copping was a forceful leader, Beattie and Wyper, the insides, were both capable of engineering openings, while both Attridge and Groves on the wings were potential match-winners.

Dunmow Retain Junior League Cup

Source : Herts & Essex Observer

Dunmow's Captain, J Beattie, receives the 1949/50 Premier Challenge Cup from League President, Mr Lyall.

Sheering, a much lighter side were handicapped by a lack of inches, particularly in goal and at forward where only C L Farr on the left-wing, measured up to the size of the Dunmow defenders. They had however in G Hockley, a constructive inside-left, who made good use of the open spaces in midfield to initiate attacking movements. C Farr, their right-back, was a steady and strong kicking defender, and had much the better of his duels with Groves. Unfortunately for Sheering, Farr was injured in the second half and finished the game, a gallant trier at outside-right.

The game sprang into life right from the first whistle and both goalkeepers were soon in action. After 17 minutes Shuttlewood the Dunmow centre-half, put in a terrific rising shot from 45 yards, which hit the angle of the crossbar with Canty hopelessly beaten.

Five minutes later Attridge drove across a long high centre from the right touchline which Canty, lacking height, failed to reach and the ball dropped just under the bar.

Encouraged by this rather lucky goal, Dunmow pressed hard and after 40 minutes Copping, unmarked in the centre, scored with a hard and rising shot which sailed above the goalkeeper's outstretched hands into the net.

Two goals down, Sheering fought back, and just before half-time, C L Farr, moving in from the left-wing, missed a good chance, firing high over the bar from close in. After seven minutes of the second half, Hext of Dunmow, was penalised but from the spot Eady shot wide, and it appeared Sheering had thrown away their last chance of saving the game.

This opinion seemed to be confirmed when, three minutes later, Beattie scored Dunmow's third goal from close in. Ten minutes later from a Groves' corner, Beattie headed in with Farr's frantic efforts to retrieve the ball only helping the ball it into the net.

Dunmow were four goals up and the game seemed over But in the gathering gloom of the chill April evening, Sheering to their great credit mounted their longest and strongest counter attack, and after clever midfield passing Eady scored Sheering's first goal. Shortly after

Sheering were awarded a penalty and from the spot G Hockley scored Sheering's second goal.

The cup and medals were presented by Mr C W P Lyall, President of the League, who was introduced by the League's Chairman, Mr A Collison.

Dunmow had to win their last two remaining games to be certain of winning the Premier Division Championship. This was accomplished after a hard struggle, and Dunmow became the first to complete the League double, as they had previously won the Challenge Cup by defeating Sheering in the final.

DIVISION I CHALLENGE CUP FINAL

MANUDEN 4 RODINGS UNITED 3

Source : Janice Keyte

MANUDEN

DIVISION II CHALLENGE CUP FINAL

GREEN TYE 1 TAKELEY RESERVES 1 (AFTER EXTRA-TIME)

DIVISION II CHALLENGE CUP FINAL REPLAY

GREEN TYE 1 TAKELEY RESERVES 1 (AFTER EXTRA-TIME)

Four hours football failed to decide who would hold the Division II Challenge Cup. After drawing 1-1 after extra-time, the teams met again four days later and the result was the same. Green Tye were definitely the better combination and only strong defensive play by the Takeley rear-guard deprived them of the trophy. Takeley forwards were weak on the wings and only Smith, at centre-forward and French, at inside-left, were really effective.

The first half was fairly even and at the interval Green Tye led by a goal scored after 30 minutes scored by D Brace, after Pallett, in the Takeley goal had mishandled the ball. In the second half Green Tye were definitely on top and Pallett atoned for his previous lapse by some saves.

It was against the run of play when, after 35 minutes Takeley equalised. There was momentary hesitation between the Green Tye backs and Flowers the goalkeeper, and Croll nipped in to score from close range. The full time came with score 1-1.

During the first period of extra-time, Takeley lost their captain, Smith with a badly cut eye, and the last stages of the game were dour contest between the Green Tye attack and the Takeley defence.

The final was replayed at the start of the 1950/51 season with Green Tye beating Takeley Reserves by three goals to one in a second replay. By winning the cup Green Tye achieved the Division II double.

Source : Helen Smith

GREEN TYE

By a unanimous vote, Sawbridgeworth Football Club decided at their annual meeting to take over the town's Youth Football Club. The decision was made after it had been stated that probably half the junior team were now ready to play with the reserves, while two or three were even up to first team standard.

DUNMOW FOOTBALL CLUB MAY SEEK ENTRY TO HGHER STANDARD

Dunmow Football Club, who achieved a 1949/50 100 per cent record by winning all three competitions which they entered, could seek entry to a higher standard of football in the 1951/52 season.

The Club's Honorary Secretary Mr J A Knowler, addressing the annual meeting said, 'When we commenced last season, it seemed that we should do extremely well if we could repeat the previous season's successes. Not only was this accomplished, but we achieved a 100 per cent record by winning the three competitions entered, the Bishop's Stortford, Stansted and District Junior League Premier Division and Challenge Cup, and the Waltham Cup.'

TREASURER REPORTS RECORD BALANCE

Two years ago expenditure by the League exceeded their income. But at the League's Annual Meeting at the Falcon Hotel, Mr R G Ashford, Honorary Treasurer, told members that there was now a record balance in hand of £200 1s 5d.

This, said Mr Ashford, was due almost entirely to gate receipts from four finals, which had brought in a total of £140. He pointed out that included in the £200 was a sum of £40 representing a £1 deposit from each club. 'Thus,' he added, we have £40 which really does not belong to us. It is only held by the League on behalf of the clubs.'

Congratulating the League on the 'very satisfactory financial position,' Mr Ashford remarked : 'Your Chairman and myself were recalling just before presenting the accounts. Then, but for the generous response of the Vice-Presidents, we would not have been able to exist.'

'It is just two years ago,' he continued, 'that I told you our expenditure exceeded income. Last year we had an exceptionally good season and we got our balance up to £124. Now we have a record balance.'

'We feel very gratified that our League is in this exceptionally healthy financial position. It is due almost entirely to the splendid gates we had at our finals.'

'I have every confidence the gates will continue, because the public love to see a game of football when the whole 22 players are all out for the full 90 minutes.'

Mr Ashford added that an interesting item of the receipts was a donation of £1 1s 4d, representing the balance of the Old Boys' League. About 20 years ago, he reported, several people endeavoured – unfortunately without success – to form this League for old boys from local schools.

The Honorary Secretary, Mr R E Baker, reported a very successful season. He referred particularly to the record of Mole Hill Green. They had played 26 games, won none, drawn one game and finished with one point. 'But they carried on and were not, disheartened,' he said.

Mole Hill Green announced their withdrawal from the League. It was stated that the club were withdrawing not because their record last season, but because half their players would not be available in the coming season.

It was agreed to increase the honorarium to the secretaries from £10 10s to £15 15s. 'They heartily deserve it,' commented the Chairman, Mr A Collison, who presided.

Officers elected : Mr C W P Lyall, President; Mr A Collison, Vice-President; Mr W Bruty, Chairman; Mr W Fisher, Vice-Chairman; Mr R E Baker, Honorary Secretary; Mr R G Ashford, Honorary Treasurer; Mr J F Lofts and Mr N J Davies, Auditors; Mr M J Connolly, Assistant-Secretary and Registration Secretary; General Purpose Committee, Mr L E Hayward, Mr W R Waterman, Mr R P Melbourne and Mr A E Goate.

Mr A L Frost said that the Executive Council of the Essex Football Association, of which he was a member, were seriously concerned the number of cases of misconduct by players, which was a reflection on the game as a whole. It was hoped the clubs would elect as captain men who would also set an example of good sportsmanship, on and off the field.

Mr C W P Lyall thanked the retiring Chairman, Mr A Collison, who, in reply, mentioned that he had been connected with the League since 1930.

1950 – 1951 SEASON		
League Competition	Winners	Runners up
Premier Division	Dunmow	Hatfield Heath
Division I	Green Tye	Hatfield Broad Oak
Division II	Albury	Rochford Sports
League Cup		
Premier Division	Bishop's Stortford 'A'	Hatfield Heath
Division I	Green Tye	Hatfield Heath Reserves
Division II	Quendon and Rickling	Takeley Reserves

THE DEATH OF ARTHUR COLLISON ANNOUNCED

In August 1950, the death was announced of Mr Arthur Collison, aged 78. He began work with Messrs D A Fyfe & Co of Takeley and he rose to become manager of the chaff factory and a Director of the firm. Keenly interested in the British Legion, he was for many years a member of the Essex County Executive and Chairman of the of the Takeley branch. He was also Treasurer of the Silver Jubilee Hall, and past Chairman of the Bishop's Stortford Coal Merchants' Association, and a former school manager.

For many years Mr Collison took an active interest in local sport. Chairman of Takeley Football Club until 1939, he was connected with the old Stansted Junior League and later with the Bishop's Stortford, Stansted and District Junior League, of which, after retiring as Chairman was made an Honorary Vice-President.

The first League Council meeting of the season in September opened with a silence for Mr Collison.

At this meeting, My Lyall spoke and said this was the first full meeting that the Chairman, Mr Bruty, had had as the Chairman and appealed to all delegates to give him all their support during the season and to help him by keeping order throughout the meetings.

The Honorary Treasurer, Mr Ashford, then pointed out a scheme he had in mind for the League's surplus cash. He said Mr Lyall and himself had done into the matter and the suggestions that they had drawn were as follows:-

Suggestion I

Give better medals to winners of the Premier Division, League and Challenge Cup and slightly better to Division I.

Suggestion 2

Handbooks and Result Books to be free, except in the case of the Handbook where some charge must be made as Rule 2 says, Each club shall be required to purchase 3 copies of the Handbook. As it does not say the amount we would be within the rule if we charged the clubs a very nominal fee of 2d each.

Suggestion 3

Give a donation to both the Essex and Hertfordshire Football Associations Benevolent Funds, say £10 to Essex and £5 to Hertfordshire, as Hertfordshire have only about half the number of clubs.

Suggestion 4

Have a League dinner in the Autumn, towards the end of October, with a few good artists. The cost to members , half-price, complimentary tickets to the County Officials and also to Club Secretaries of the League (the cost of this would amount roughly to £45 and would have the effect of bringing together our League delegates to a more friendly and sporting spirit in the League.

Suggestion 5

Cost of engraving medals be borne by the League.

In addition Saffron Walden suggested that Challenge Cup finalists be awarded expenses.

The Chairman then asked the clubs to decide if the suggestions be adopted. Mr Rushforth suggested that the five suggestions be adopted with the addition of Saffron Walden's suggestion and this was seconded by Stansted Reserves and was carried by 33 votes to nil.

1949/50 DIVISION II CHALLENGE CUP FINAL REPLAY

GREEN TYE 3 TAKELEY RESERVES 1

The 1950/51 League handbook is the first that I have that has details including club colours :

Newport – Navy and White Quarters, Hatfield Broad Oak – Green and White Quarters, Netteswell and Burnt Mill   Black & White Quarters, Henham – Green and White Quarters, Great Hallingbury – Scarlet and White Quarters, Black Lion – Black and White Quarters, Little Hadham – Light and Dark Quarters while Hatfield Heaths colours were described as Amber and Black but were in fact also Quarters.

Saffron Walden Town Reserves colours were described as Red and Black Quarters and Blue Knickers!

It was not until the 1960s that 'shorts' became the preferred term.

SELECTION OF VICE-CHAIRMAN

It was proposed by Mr Baker that Mr Jack Webb of Takeley be nominated, this was seconded by Great Hallingbury. Mr Melbourne proposed Mr George Wilson and this was seconded by P.O. Telephones. Voting took place and Mr George Wilson was successful.

A Hatfield Heath FC dance was held in October in the Trinity Hall when Mr D H Banner (Chairman of the Committee) introduced Mr B T R Pyle (President), who made a presentation to the retiring Secretary, Mr W A Bruty. Mr Bruty thanked everyone, and said he hoped that they would all support his successor, Mr W Day in the same encouraging manner.

Mr Bruty had been appointed Chairman of the League, succeeding Mr A Collison.

BISHOP'S STORTFORD, STANSTED AND DISTRICT JUNIOR FOOTBALL LEAGUE ANNUAL DINNER

In November 1950, Mr C W P Lyall, who at 78, was still President of the Bishop's Stortford, Stansted and District Junior Football League, was presented at the League's Annual Dinner held at Long's Restaurant with an inscribed wristwatch in recognition of his services to local football.

Making the presentation, Mr W (Bill) Bruty, Chairmen of the League, told the 200 members present, 'Mr Lyall was one of the founders of the old Stansted League, which was amalgamated with the Stortford League in 1936, and was a member of the Essex FA from

1935 to 1949. He has done a wonderful lot of work for football in the District, and we all hope he will continue to take an active interest for many years to come.'

Mr Lyall referred to the happy times he had had during his association with the League and from the time he started playing football when he was about 17. 'Due to the work of your officers and the help they have given me, we have been able to form one of the finest junior football leagues in Essex, or in any county round about,' he added.

Proposing the toast of the League, Mr A R Pegg, a member of the Herts FA, told members, 'I have watched your progress with great interest, and if anyone is at all uncertain as regards the enthusiasm and the progress of your League, he would lose all doubts if he saw you here tonight. I am very much surprised at the size of the gathering and it proves that that you have a lot of enthusiasm and interest.'

Mr Pegg also referred to the services of Mr Lyall and said the position which the League held in the district at the present time was due to largely to his work and leadership.

He congratulated members on the size of the League, three divisions comprising 42 clubs, and said that the standard of football was very high.

Mr Pegg added, 'It is pleasing, as a County Official, to note that on very, very few occasions, it is necessary for the FA to admonish a player for contravening the rules. We like to see football conducted as it should be conducted. There are only 17 rules of the game and we don't want any more rules made.'

Continuing, he said he wished that many more footballers would become referees when their playing days were over.

He pointed out that at that time the County Officials were concerned about minor football. It had to be remembered that junior footballers of today were the senior players of the future and he continued. 'Years ago, when a boy left school, he could not hope to become a member of a club until he was at least 17 years of age. But now we are asking leagues to make provision for boys aged 14 or so.'

He asked the members to consider forming two or more divisions consisting of players aged between 14 and 16, and 16 and 18.

Mr Pegg added, 'The Bishop's Stortford club try to foster junior football in this League by allowing you to play your finals on their ground. You should be grateful to that for looking after you like that.'

Proposing a toast to the guests, Mr R Ashford, the League's Honorary Treasurer, said the League should be very gratified that the County Associations were behind them. He also welcomed representatives of the Referee's Association and remarked that when he took his referee's examination, the examiner was Mr Lyall.

Speaking as a representative of the Essex FA, Mr A Frost said the League's constitution was one of the finest in the country.'

Mr T S Gee, one of the oldest members of the Referee's Association appealed for more referees. 'We are very, very short of referees, but if every club could provide one, the position would be rectified,' he added.

In December P.O. Telephones were allowed to withdraw from the League.

The Bishop's Stortford Charity Cup was re-introduced in 1950 with the final tie being played on boxing day. The Bishop's Stortford St John Ambulance division, Herts FA and Essex FA Benevolent Funds received support from funds raised by the competition.

Source : Glyn Warwick

BRITISH ROAD SERVICES

Dunmow Football Club won the Premier Division championship in 1949/50 and again in 1950/51. However, Hatfield Heath were the team of the decade. The team won the Premier Division Championship on three occasions and were also runners-up also on three occasions.

As a result of the two semi-finals of the Premier Division Challenge Cup Bishop's Stortford 'A' and Hatfield Heath were to meet in the final. There was a total of 20 goals scored in the semi-finals. Bishop's Stortford 'A' beat Manuden 13-2 and Hatfield Heath beat Saffron Walden Reserves 5-0.

HOCKERILL ATHLETIC DISCONTINUE FOOTBALL SECTION

In April 1951 it was announced that because of running expenses exceeding income, and enthusiasm lacking, members of Hockerill Athletic Club, at their annual meeting, voted unanimously to discontinue the football section at the end of the season.

Reporting a deficit of £54 3s 9d, the Honorary Treasurer Mr P G King pointed out that the football section's expenditure totalled £69 4s 5d, towards which members raised only £12. He continued, 'I do not know why it is that we never seem to raise sufficient money from the footballers. They raised only a third of their expenses, whereas the cricket raised over two-thirds to meet their expenses.' Mr King explained that if the football section was discontinued only a very small sum in subscriptions would be lost. A footballer at the meeting told the meeting. 'The way the section is running at the present, I do not think there is any enthusiasm. Only about five players turn up for practices and they are all members of the cricket section.'

In April 1951 Little Hadham were allowed to withdraw from the League.

Following P.O Telephones withdrawal, the League purchased their yellow shirts to be used in Inter-League matches. A purchase price of £5 was agreed.

PREMIER DIVISION CHALLENGE CUP FINAL

BISHOP'S STORTFORD 'A' 5 HATFIELD HEATH 2

The Premier Division Cup Final saw Bishop's Stortford 'A' beat Hatfield Heath 5 goals to 2. Eight times Hatfield Heath had reached the Premier Division Challenge Cup Final and for the eighth time they were the losing team, when they were outclassed by Bishop's Stortford 'A.'

Bishop's Stortford 'A' were always on top, although plenty of passes went astray and there were periods of aimless kicking. Atkinson, their 16-year-old centre-forward, played well and earned his hat-trick, his fourth in the last five games. He was supported by his co-forwards, particularly inside-right Perry and right-winger Gates.

In direct contrast to the Heath, Stortford's defence was never really worried, and Curran put in a lot of effective work.

Atkinson gave Stortford the lead about five minutes after the kick off, and shortly afterwards inside-left Haggerwood put them further ahead with a grand shot.

STORTFORD'S CUP-WINNERS: (Below) Bishop's Stortford "A" team photographed with the Bishop's Stortford, Stansted and District Junior League (Premier Division) challenge cup, which they won on Saturday evening. With them are (left) Mr. G. Wilson (chairman of the club) and (right) Mr. G. Wrigglesworth (trainer-coach).

Source : Herts & Essex Observer

BISHOP'S STORTFORD 'A'

Stortford were combining well and had the Heath's defence worried. But the Heath were always dangerous in brisk breakaways, and after they had forced three corners centre-forward Nicholls rammed the ball into the net through a mass of players.

Both teams were settling down, but both were trying to walk the ball into the net. Stortford were in trouble when the ball was punted upfield into the goal area, and while goalkeeper Banks was unsighted Moore crashed the ball only inches outside the post.

Stortford should have scored just after the interval, when Gates placed the ball cleverly in the Heath's goalmouth, but an over eager forward missed. Atkinson got his second goal when he shot from close range and the ball glanced off the post into the net, giving goalkeeper Barker no chance.

Shortly after Nicholls again decreased the lead with a good shot following a movement started by outside-right Newman.

About this time Stortford nearly got themselves into a lot of trouble by appearing content to defend, and the Heath were quick to take advantage of this lapse. Had they pulled out a little extra at this stage they might have forced a draw. Stortford's defence was combining well and kept their lead intact, breaking up several dangerous moves and putting their forwards through with grand passes, but the forwards failed to take their chances. Then Atkinson made the mistake of the match – with the ball at his feet and an open goal he shot wide.

After about 25 minutes Perry was carried off injured but returned five minutes later. Soon afterwards he again went off, returned after three minutes – and then off he went again. Before he returned five minutes later Stortford increased their lead with the goal of the match. Outside-left Gilbey put a good pass across the Heath goal from a narrow angle and Gates scored with a grand drive into the corner of the net.

Just before time Stortford were awarded a very debatable corner, and Atkinson completed his hat-trick with a good header.

DIVISION I CHALLENGE CUP FINAL

GREEN TYE 1 HATFIELD HEATH RESERVES 0

In May Manuden were allowed to withdraw from the League.

DIVISION II CHALLENGE CUP FINAL

QUENDON AND RICKLING 3 TAKELEY RESERVES 2

Hockerill Athletic and Black Lion could not play a number of fixtures at the end of the season and all points were awarded to their opponents.

JUNIOR LEAGUE'S STRONG FINANCIAL POSITION

Three years previously the League had a balance in hand of £33. Two years before there was a balance of £124, and last year this rose to £209.

Mr R G Ashford, Honorary Treasurer, told members of the League at the Annual General Meeting that this 'remarkable' increase was due to the stringent watch kept on expenditure by the officers and the large gates at the League's Cup Finals.

Reporting there was now a balance of £92 12s 1d, which included the membership deposits of the clubs, he explained that last year it was felt the League did not need a large balance and thought they would be justified in liquidating some of it, The League held their first dinner which cost £57 and grants totalling £15 were made to the benevolent funds of the Herts & Essex Football Associations. The clubs had benefitted from further expenditure incurred by the League.

Referring to a decrease of £20 in last season's Cup Final receipts, Mr Ashford thought the committee should aim next season at making income balance expenditure. He pointed out that the cost of 12 sets of medals had risen very sharply to £116 4s 8d and said the League Council would have to consider whether as many or as good medals could be given next season.

Mr Ashford announced his retirement as Honorary Treasurer. He had been associated with the League since 1922 and he was elected an Honorary Vice-President in recognition of his services.

The past season had been a great success, said Mr R E Baker, Honorary Secretary. Highlights were representative matches against the North Essex and Hertford and District Leagues.

The League were thanked for their 'magnificent help' to the Essex F A Benevolent Fund by Mr H Frost (district representative).

Appealing to players to improve their knowledge of the rules of football, Mr Frost said the number of cases of misconduct by players showed no sign of decreasing. He pointed out that the referee was the appointed official of the F A and his decision had to be accepted.

'Many players do not know the rules of football and even more spectators do not,' he added.

Officers elected : Mr C W P Lyall, President; Mr G H Wilson, Vice-President; Mr W Bruty, Chairman; Mr W Fisher, Vice-Chairman; Mr M J Connolly, Honorary Treasurer, Registration Secretary and Assistant-Secretary; Mr R E Baker, Honorary Secretary.

1951-52 SEASON

29 Clubs (37 Teams) competed in the League and League Cup Competitions for the 1951-52 season.

League Competition	Winners	Runners-up
Premier Div.	Hatfield Heath	Takeley
Division 1	Braughing	Manuden
Division 2	Farnham	Thorley
League Cup		
Premier Div.	Hatfield Heath	Rodings United
Division 1	Clavering	Manuden
Division 2	Thorley	Farnham

In January Burnt Mill Reserves were allowed to withdraw from the League.

In February Hatfield Broad Oak were allowed to withdraw from the League.

On February 1952 the King, George VI passed away. It was decided that two minutes silence should be observed at the next matches and black arm bands worn.

WHY REFEREES ARE NOT ALWAYS AVAILABLE

'Enjoy your game' was the theme of a talk given to players and officials of local football clubs by Mr T S Gee, Chairman of the North-West Essex branch of the Referees' Association. He dealt with the laws that chiefly worried players, especially the offside law and afterwards answered a number of questions.

Mr W A Bruty, Chairman of the BSSDL asked why it was not possible for all their matches to be covered by an official referee, and whether a referee benefitted by taking Spartan League 'lines' in preference to refereeing junior games.

Mr Gee replied that while there were as many referees in the district now as ever there had been there was greater competition for their services. The only answer was more referees, and he appealed to clubs to urge at least one member to take up refereeing. If all local clubs would do this, the shortage would disappear overnight.

He added that referees wishing to progress to senior leagues had to take a percentage of 'line' appointments.

Mr W J Day, Honorary Secretary of Hatfield Heath Football Club, thanked the speaker for a very interesting and enlightening talk.

Source : Herts & Essex Observer

HARLOW UNITED

DIVISION I CHALLENGE CUP FINAL

CLAVERING 1 MANUDEN 0

It was reported that over 700 spectators saw the League Division I Challenge Cup Final at Rhodes Avenue.

The match was played under ideal conditions, although the football was not of the usual standard seen in the finals, a keen game resulted.

Source : Herts & Essex Observer

The **CLAVERING** and **MANUDEN** teams together before the kick off.

Defending the Thorley end in the first half, Manuden were constantly on the defensive in the first 15 minutes, only spasmodic breakaways initiated by B Clark, causing Clavering any trouble. In defence Manuden were well served by Hutchings, who played well throughout.

In the 24th minute Clavering were awarded a penalty, but brilliant anticipation by Middleditch, who saved magnificently, spoiled their chance of taking the lead.

After this escape Manuden attacked vigorously, but the ball appeared difficult to control and many passes went astray. There was no score at half-time.

Clavering were the more balanced team, and Rushant and Fayers, their left-wing pair, were always dangerous. It was Fayers who scored the all-important goal. Receiving a good pass from Rushant, he cut in to beat Middleditch, with a well-placed low shot which hit the post before going into the net.

Manuden tried hard to equalise, but the Clavering goal led a charmed life, Clark shot over from six yards, and Harrington, with only Camp to beat, missed the opportunity. The Clavering defence played well and held out to the end.

PREMIER DIVISION CHALLENGE CUP FINAL

HATFIELD HEATH 3 RODINGS UNITED 2

HATFIELD HEATH WIN LEAGUE CUP AT NINTH ATTEMPT

At their ninth appearance in the final, Hatfield Heath were successful in winning the Premier Division Challenge Cup. The final at Rhodes Avenue was an exciting struggle, with both sides going full out.

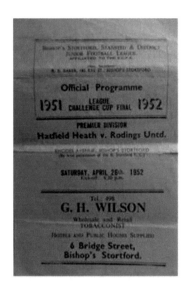

From a corner the ball was only partially cleared, and Moore put it back into the goalmouth for Roy Nicholls to score.

There was still little to choose between the two teams and although both forward lines worked hard, the defences remained on top until half-time. With the start of the second half, the Heath attacked and Roy Nicholls, after shooting high over the bar, put the ball only inches wide with Mann out of position.

Rodings fought back and forced a corner which was perfectly placed by Fogg. Goalkeeper W Bruty failed to hold the ball and Byford scrambled it over the line. Rodings nearly went further ahead when a bad clearance when a bad clearance by H Search let them through, but Clark's shot was well held by W Bruty who was almost bundled over the line.

The Heath equalised after some fine approach work. Bob Nicholls cleverly beat his man and pushed the ball through to R Search who rounded a defender and put into the bottom corner of the net, Mann diving too late.

The Heath began to press after this. One shot was missed by Mann, but Peacock kicked the ball off the line. The Heath took the lead when D Search put the ball into the goalmouth, the ball beat Mann and the ball hit the crossbar and came out for Roy Nicholls to score from the rebound.

DIVISION II CHALLENGE CUP FINAL

THORLEY 2 FARNHAM 1

Thorley gained an early lead when Dellow beat Hampton and raced through. Although Warwick, in the Farnham goal, stopped the powerful drive which followed, he could not hold it and the ball trickled over the line.

Thorley's finishing was better than that of Farnham, and Barker's long through passes proved dangerous. Dellow's experience was evident, and he was well supported by Kimber, although the latter was at times inclined to hold the ball too long.

There was no further score in the first half, but after the interval Thorley were pressing most of the time, and after 20 minutes Kimber made a magnificent run through, beating five men, to score their second goal.

Farnham managed to force three corners, and W Knott scored their goal, a few minutes before the end, with a lob which went over Dupe's head.

DRAMA OF CUP FINAL HEARTACHE (**Source** : Alasdair Gold/Herts & Essex Observer)

The rain lashing down, the grass becoming mud beneath your feet and the thwack of a wet ball against your cold head, there is nothing like amateur football. As unappealing as that may sound to some, to most football lovers, there's very little in life which is better. The euphoria of the ball hitting the back of the net, the perfectly timed leap of a goalkeeper and the inch perfect crunching sliding tackle, it's not called the beautiful game for nothing.

Former footballer, Archie Warwick, was in complete agreement. One special season that he would forever hold close to his heart was 1951/52, when he starred up front for Farnham FC. The club were dreaming of capturing the Bishop's Stortford, Stansted and District Junior Football League Division Two championship as well as the Challenge Cup Final. By mid-April, the team had the League in the bag, with more than 100 goals scored and only 26 against. The 16-year-old inside-right, Archie Warwick had weighed in with a quarter of that century of strikes while his brother, Stanley, was the all-action goalkeeper.

Then came the evening of Wednesday April 30, 1952. It was the day of the Cup Final at Rhodes Avenue and the team were to face a Thorley side that had pushed all the way in the League. Despite Farnham's ton of goals, a tight match was expected, although hopes were still high of a magical double.

Disaster struck early on when a young Stanley Warwick struggled to hold on to a powerful Thorley drive and the ball trickled agonisingly over the line. A shocked Farnham side held on to half-time, but after 20 minutes of the second half, a magnificent solo effort from one of the Thorley players saw him beat five men and slot the ball past Warwick. It was a killer blow. A late lob from a Farnham winger was merely a consolation for the League winners and the Cup Final was lost. The players were dejected, but looking back, Mr Warwick would always treasure that that trophy-lifting season.

National Service played a part in stopping the striker from furthering his football career, but had age dulled his appetite for the sport.

'Not at all.' He said, 'I still love the game and watch all the games on the television. There is far too much shirt pulling these days and players diving all over the place. They're supposed to be grown men. I'm always telling my wife they must be off their heads to keep falling over all the time. Why would you want to keep on the floor when there's football to be played?'

Source : Janice Keyte

FARNHAM

Source : Herts & Essex Observer

HATFIELD HEATH

The photo above, shows members of Hatfield Heath Football Club with four cups which they held at that time (Season 1951/52), The Premier Division, The Premier Division Cup, the West Essex Border Charity Cup and the Bishop's Stortford Charity Cup.

Back Row – J Gunn, E Halls, E Gunn, J Want, S Newman, R Jones and W Austin

Second Row – E Long, F Mercer, H Long, B Eldred, W Bruty, J Gunn, E Clanford, H Maskell and F Jackson

Third Row – R Griffiths (Trainer), R Howard, Bob Nicholls, Mr W A Bruty (Chairman), H Search, Mr D Banner (President), F Bruty, Mr W J Day (Secretary), Roy Nicholls, R Dedman and Mr H Pyle (Treasurer)

Front Row – D Search, C Moore, L J Trott, M Jackson, S Barker, L Wilkins, R Search and A Wilinson

NEWPORT ANNUAL DINNER

Newport Football Club held their Annual Dinner at the Coach and Horses Inn which was attended by eighty members and guests.

Proposing the toast to the club the President, Dr A Salaman, said they had started well last year but their fortunes had deteriorated later in the season. They had, however, met with some bad luck in the tremendous number of injuries suffered during the season, at one time having as many as fourteen players crippled.

He went on to thank all those who had helped the club during the season, and said he understood the club Chairman, Mr C M Fiddian, had approached the Council to see if something could be done about draining the field, which, as all club members knew, was frequently unfit for play.

Mr Fiddian spoke appreciatively of the work done by the club Secretary, Mr A L Rushforth. Also referring to the number of injuries suffered during the season, he said that if they were to field two teams the following season, they must have more playing members.

On the question of the ground, he said he could make no promises. He had approached the Council on the subject, but it appeared there was a natural spring near the field and that might be the cause of the trouble.

Mr Rushforth proposed a toast to the visitors to which Mr A L Frost, the area representative of the Essex FA replied.

Mr Frost said that Essex was one of the largest county associations in the country, having over 800 clubs affiliated. There had been fewer cases of misconduct in North-West Essex than for many years and he thought that said much for the for the sportsmanship of the players.

Mr W Bruty, Chairman of the League proposed a toast to the players and Mr S Richardson responded.

HATFIELD HEATH CELEBRATE WINNING THE PREMIER LEAGUE DOUBLE

A social and dance to celebrate the winning of the Premier Division double of the League was held by Hatfield Heath Football Club in Trinity Hall.

Congratulating the first team on the achievement, Mr W J Day (Honorary Secretary) said the reserves had also played their part. A fine club spirit had been created. He pointed out that although the club had won the League championship before, it was the first time in nine appearances in the final that they had won the League Challenge Cup.

The cup and League medals were presented by Mr D H Banner (Chairman) in the absence of the President, Mr B T R Pyle. He presented county colours to Mr C Moore, the third player from the club to receive the honour.

Mr F Bruty, (first XI Captain), thanked the players for their support, and said the club's successes would not have been possible without the backing of the reserves.

Mr W Bruty, (League Chairman), congratulated the club on their successes and the players who had represented the county in the match with Hertfordshire.

SENIOR STATUS FOR LOCAL LEAGUE SUGGESTED

A suggestion that at some time in the future the League should consider applying for senior status, in order to attract local senior clubs, was made by Mr C F Wells (Stansted) at the 1952 Annual General Meeting of the League.

Mr Wells said that there were a number of senior clubs in the area competing in Division I of the Spartan League. There was not a local league of senior status, and there never had been in his time. In his opinion the Spartan League had been gradually 'falling through' in recent years. The League wanted to compete with such leagues as the Athenian, Isthmian, Corinthian and the new Delphian League.

Mr Wells continued, at the Annual General Meeting, the Premier Division was extended 'rather significantly' to 16 teams and Division I reduced to 13 teams. He added , 'My inference is that next season, or the season following that, the League will be formed in much the same way as the other senior leagues – one division and a reserve section. In a year or two I visualise Division I no longer in existence and local senior clubs looking for a league in which to play.'

'Here we have the machinery, and I do earnestly suggest that the League bear in mind the possibility of applying for senior status and inviting the local senior clubs to play in a local senior league. It would improve the status of the League and bring better football.'

After League Chairman, Mr W Bruty, had commented that there was a lot of feeling against it and he personally, thought they were 'doing it right,' Mr Wells added, 'If it is not done within the framework of this League, it will be done outside of the League by the clubs themselves.'

In his report, Mr R E Baker, Honorary Secretary, said the work of the League had gone very smoothly and congratulated the League and cup winners.

In his financial statement, Mr M Connolly, Honorary Treasurer, reported that, due largely to the good gates of the Cup Finals, the League's position was a very good one. Receipts for the Premier Division final were £48, a record in the history of the League compared with £38 for the previous season, which included the sale of programmes.

With the aid of Mr R Ashford, Vice-President and former Honorary Treasurer, a considerable saving had been made in the cost of medals and engraving. The cost for the season was £54 compared with £116 for the previous season.

Mr Connolly pointed out that the League relied upon the gate receipts from the finals for their balance, and he stressed the need to safeguard themselves against bad attendance. He felt that about £10 or £15 should be put aside each year for this purpose.

1952 - 3 Season

League	Winners	Runners-up
Premier	Harlow Untd.	Hatfield Heath
Division I	Gt. Parndon	Stansted Airport
Division II	Northmet	Quendon & Rickling
League Cup		
Premier	Hatfield Heath	Rodings Utd
Division I	Gt. Parndon	Stansted Airport
Division II	Northmet	High Roding

SHORTAGE OF PLAYERS IS FORCING CLUBS OUT OF LEAGUE

At the annual meeting of Manuden Football Club, Mr W A Anderson emphasised the importance of contacting prospective junior players in view of the more difficult games that could be anticipated as a result of their promotion to the Premier Division of the League.

It was reported that before the season began, Hatfield Broad Oak had to withdraw from the League because they were unable to field a team, while Rochford Sports and British Road Services Reserves also withdrew, for the same reason.

It was also reported that Farnham, who were Division II champions and League Cup Finalists in 1951/52 were desperately in need of players. They had 13 signed players but only 10 were able to play regularly. If the position did not improve, they too, would have to also withdraw.

It also looked likely that British Road Services first team would have to also withdraw from the League.

Northmet, who only just missed promotion to Division I strengthened their team for the forthcoming season with the signing of several Farnham players including their leading goal scorer, Len Emerson. Jack Hanratty, the old Sawbridgeworth, Bishop's Stortford and Stansted player, would again captain the side.

At the first League Council meeting of the season the Chairman asked all present to stand in silence in memory of committee member Mr Waterhouse.

In October Farnham were allowed to withdraw from the League.

Source : David Brown

JUNIOR CHARITY CUP FINAL (1951/52 FINAL)

HATFIELD HEATH 6 SHEERING 2

Wilkinson's thrust in the middle had a great effect on the Sheering defence, which was over-run, while Moore's skill had more scope at left-half.

Hatfield Heath almost met disaster in the first half by giving outside-right C L Farr too much room. He was Sheering's danger man, and his runs down the wing and his accurate centres were always threatening. He neutralised Hatfield Heath's sixth minute goal after 22 minutes when he beat Wilkins and his shot dropped into the top corner of the net.

He had a hand also in the second, a really grand effort. Law sprung the ball out to Clark, and the latter centred for Farr to push it through again to Law, who scored on the run.

Hatfield Heath's goal came in the early stages when they were pressing hard. A blocked clearance and the ball went to Jackson, who centred for R Search to score from close in.

Sheering owed much to Prior for helping to keep out the Heath at this stage. He gave a sterling performance at centre-half, in which he was ably supported by Harrington, who despite his slender build and the heavy going, got through an amazing amount of work.

After an initial attack by Sheering in the second half, Hatfield Heath settled down to take control of the of the game. Their forward line over-ran the Sheering defence.

The two Search brothers combined well on the left-wing and Wilkinson supplied the thrust in the middle. Trott and Moore gave sound support.

R Search equalised after 11 minutes and Wilkinson followed with another good goal two minutes later. D Search added another after 15 minutes with a shot that was intended to be a centre.

R Search completed his hat trick after 20 minutes and made his final contribution for minutes before the final whistle.

The season saw Hatfield Heath complete a Premier Division League and Challenge Cup double as well as winning the Charity Cup.

In March Newport Reserves were allowed to withdraw from the League.

In April Henham were allowed to withdraw from the League.

PREMIER DIVISION CHALLENGE CUP FINAL

HATFIELD HEATH 5 RODINGS UNITED 1

For the second year running Hatfield Heath and Rodings United met in the final of the Premier Division Challenge Cup at Rhodes Avenue and saw the holders, Hatfield Heath celebrate their tenth Cup Final appearance with a decisive victory by 5 goals to 1.

In the 35th minute Hatfield Heath went ahead. Gurnett collected a long pass, moved upfield and centred from almost the corner flag. Goalkeeper Mann leapt for the ball, but in trying to punch clear turned it into his own goal.

Soon after the interval, Roy Nicholls scored the Heath's second goal and H Search made it 3-0 from the penalty spot.

In the 65th minute R Search drew the Rodings defence hopelessly out of position and slipped the ball to Gurnett, who took his time in scoring.

Rodings were awarded a penalty from which Gooday reduced the lead, but after Mann had made several fine saves in the following minutes, R Search again managed to confuse the Rodings defence, and good passing via Roy Nicholls enabled Gurnett to complete his hat-trick.

DIVISION I CHALLENGE CUP FINAL

GREAT PARNDON 4 STANSTED AIRPORT 2

A Cup Final true to tradition, was fought out between Great Parndon and Stansted Airport at Rhodes Avenue. Not only was the match entertaining, fast and clean, but with it went all the enthusiasm and high spirits of supporters that go to make up such occasions. Coach loads of supporters arrived sporting paper hats, whistles, rattles and gaily coloured scarves, with groups chanting in unison a rallying song: 'Two, four, six, eight.....who do we appreciate.....'

Great Parndon were worthy winners of the Division I Challenge Cup, but their 4-2 win was no easy victory. Good passing by both teams in the opening minutes took the ball from goalmouth to goalmouth, with Parndon having slightly more of the game and forcing two corners. A powerful clearance upfield in the tenth minute sent the Airport forwards into the opposing half, but Tucker's high lob, beating oncoming goalkeeper Peacock, dropped a yard from the empty goal and bounced over the bar.

Parndon resumed the attack and a misunderstanding between the Airport's hard-pressed defenders led to an own goal by Childs. The Airport, however, took the misfortune as a signal for a great offensive which took the game into the Parndon half for most of the time until the interval.

Their centre-half, Murdock, dominated this period. It was usually he who put an end to Parndon's attacks and started the moves of his own side. Close shots by Scraggs, Abbott, Matthews and Tucker gave the Parndon supporters many anxious moments before a good pass from Osborne found Tucker's feet, and he equalised with a fine shot after beating two men.

After the interval both goals escaped some close shots, and a great dribble by Matthews and Tucker, who beat three defenders, gave the latter the opportunity to put his side ahead. They maintained the pressure with Tucker always dangerous, but Parndon managed to hold, thanks to Harknett, James and Lewin, who played a great game.

Several fast raids by their right-wing sent the Airport defence hurrying back, but they could not prevent Pointer from heading into the net after a pass from Wood. Soon afterwards Hale managed to score again after a scramble in the goalmouth.

Parndon were definitely on top by this time, and the Airport feeling the effect of the pace, the play remained mainly in their half. About 15 minutes from the end, Wood again moved the ball upfield and gave a perfect pass to Jacobs, who, with only the goalkeeper to beat, made the score 4-2.

Once again, the Airport took the initiative, but despite their great efforts could not change the final score. In a thrilling game in which neither team let up until the final whistle, special credit must go to the goalkeepers, whose task was made the easier by the fading light.

Source : Lorraine Burton   Source : Jamie Fowler

GREAT PARNDON DIVISION I LEAGUE AND CHALLENGE CUP WINNERS

DIVISION II CHALLENGE CUP FINAL

NORTHMET 4 HIGH RODING 2

In the last match of the season at Rhodes Avenue, the Division II Challenge Cup Final, Northmet defeated High Roding 4-2.

A large crowd watched Northmet, who were the Division II champions, bring off the double after a 1-1 score at the interval. Roding, playing with the wind, opened the scoring through Crow in the 12th minute, but Northmet's fast tackling halves held the pressing Roding forwards and after half an hour Hanratty equalised from the penalty spot.

After the interval Northmet took command of the game but missed several times with close shots. J Smith, Emerson, and Reed were prominent, and Emerson succeeded to put Northmet ahead after beating Whitting and Dann. Five minutes later he again found the mark with a well-placed shot.

Little narrowed the margin after receiving a pass from Crow, but the excitement had scarcely died before J Smith lobbed the ball into the Roding net to make the final score 4-2.

BISHOP'S STORTFORD FC DROP THEIR 'A' TEAM

Mr E H Melbourne, Secretary of the Bishop's Stortford 'A' team, reported that the past season had been the poorest for that team since it was formed, and that he was on occasions hard to field an eleven. This was mainly due to call up of players or their appearance for the other teams of the club if they showed good form and promise.

These difficulties made it impossible to fulfil the purpose for which the 'A' team had been formed, namely, to develop young players for inclusion in the first team, and the committee had therefore decided not to run the team in the following season.

NEW CLUB FOR LOCAL PLAYERS ONLY

'If you live in our street you can play for us' was the only stipulation Stortford's youngest football club – Rhodes Avenue FC – was making before signing on a player.

At their formation meeting Mr M Barker, who was elected Secretary, said it had always been one of his ambitions to form a football club which picked its players from local talent – 'right from our own street' in fact.

Members were informed that they would have their own pitch in the town in October, and that regular Saturday night whist drives were to be run to build up the slender financial resources at their disposal.

All players on the books of Rhodes Avenue had local junior football or Spartan League experience, and after the club's recent election to Division II of the League the club looked forward with confidence to their first season in competitive football. Club colours would be pink and black. Players who moved from Rhodes Avenue during the playing season would be allowed to finish the season with the club.

Officers of the club were named as : Mr J Boswell, President; Mr A Harlow, Chairman; Mr P Steward, Deputy Chairman; Mr M Barker, Secretary and Treasurer; Mr J Cracknell, Captain and Mr D J Barker, Vice-Captain.

Harlow United withdrew its team from the League at the end of the season to play in the Northern Suburban League.

LEAGUE ON SOUND FOOTING DUE TO HARD WORKING OFFICIALS

At the League's Annual General Meeting, Mr A L Frost, Essex County Football Association representative, told club officials that he considered their League to be on very sound footing and that its success was due in no small measure to the hard work put in by their Chairman, officers and committee members.

Mr L H J Thorne, it was reported, would continue with his referees' appointments scheme, but would do this within the framework of the League. He was thanked for his efficient handling of the scheme, which was run formerly by the West Essex Border Branch of Referees.

Mr C W P Lyall was re-elected President, and Mr R G Ashford and Mr G Wilson as Vice-Presidents. Mr W Bruty was re-elected as Chairman with Mr A L Rushforth, Newport, Vice-Chairman. Mr R E Baker, Honorary Secretary, Mr M J Connolly, Honorary Treasurer, Mr L E Hayward, Press and Match Secretary, and the Auditors Messrs N J Davies and J H Hills were all re-elected en bloc.

1953 – 1954 SEASON		
League Competition	Winners	Runners up
Premier Division	Hatfield Heath	Takeley
Division I	Millars Sports	Hatfield Heath Reserves
Division II	Rhodes Avenue	Birchanger
League Cup		
Premier Division	Burnt Mill	Potter Street
Division I	Hatfield Heath Reserves	Millars Sports
Division II	Birchanger	Rhodes Avenue

HARLOW & DISTRICT LEAGUE FORMED The Harlow & District League was formed in 1953 and included teams from Sheering, Potter Street and Netteswell and Burnt Mill who also fielded teams in the Bishop's Stortford, Stansted and District Junior League.

Harlow United Reserves and Holbrooks United who had withdrawn from the Stortford League at the end of the previous season also joined the Harlow League.

OLD PLAYERS RETURN

Thorley, having been relegated to Division II saw a number of players from their cup winning team return including Joe Kimber and George Clarke.

Secretary Ken Cook reported that Ron Oxborrow, Phil Akers, and Jim Robinson all signed again, and it was hoped that Gordon Barker and Ron Money would be available frequently.

Les College was elected as skipper of the team with Ron Oxborrow vice-captain. Mr A F Knight, a former Bishop's Stortford goalkeeper joined the selection committee.

Although his job was to keep fires under control, Fireman W Nott was well aglow with enthusiasm as his club, Farnham, Division II champions in 1951/52, would again be taking the field after a year's inactivity and competing in Division I. The club already had around twenty players signed up.

Mr Nott the club Secretary said that most of the players come from Bishop's Stortford, but he, his brother Ron and R Warwick were all Farnham residents and would provide the local touch for the side.

Their captain and left-half, E Scraggs, wore the colours of Stansted Airport previously, and centre-forward and vice-captain, Len Emerson, played for Northmet. They had two good goalkeepers in Stanley Warwick and Tony Luff, the former was no stranger to the side, for which he turned out since the war.

Fred Maslen, Doug Axton, a former Hockerill player, and Cyril Clarke who had played with Bishop's Stortford 'A' and British Road Services were also signed up.

Northmet, who won promotion to Division I expected to find competition more exacting and would have a youthful look when their League programme got off the marks.

A friendly against Stansted Reserves, which they won 2-1, gave them the opportunity to try out several of their new players. A young Roy Wacey, a familiar name in local cricket circles, would enter his first year in competitive football with the club, and his performance at left-half was highly praised. The club regarded him as their 'find of the season.'

Their goalkeeper, Brian Seaber, came from the Cambridge area. A Potter, formerly with Bishop's Stortford Reserves, would don his football boots again after a few seasons' inactivity.

After twenty playing seasons with Newport, B Harvey, 'Pop' to the younger generation of players, decided to retire from the game. His experience would be missed, but not lost altogether, as his interest in club affairs remained as lively as ever. He would still be seen on the field running the line at club matches.

Club Secretary, A L Rushforth had sufficient football experience to realise when changes were stirring, and he thought that the fighting spirit of old had returned among the playing members of Newport Football Club.

Several young footballers were added to the club's books and included D Revell (inside-right) and M Bunten (outside-right), were definitely bright prospects, who, it was hoped, would aid the team to regain its Premier Division place in local junior football.

Newport were to lose the services of several players. J Start and C Eves returned to Saffron Walden, while A Gilder and R Westwood would don Debden colours in the Saffron Walden and District League.

Mr B Rand, who completed 25 years' service to the club at that time, would carry on as club Treasurer and S Richardson would again captain the side.

Unless there was a repetition of the previous season's weather the Junior Charity Cup competition would be making football history in 1953/54 by having its Cup Final twice played off in the same season. Five clubs were still in the running, Saffron Walden, Stansted, Takeley had qualified, while Harlow United and Hatfield Heath had yet to meet in order in order to supply the fourth semi-finalist.

When Hatfield Heath and Harlow United failed to play off the Junior Charity cup tie by the due date the competition's committee met to investigate the matter. They decided to award the game to Hatfield Heath.

Hatfield Heath's Derek Search's football career had come to a premature close. Specialists told him that he must never kick a ball again. Derek had all the makings of an outstanding footballer and was widely regarded as the best player produced by Hatfield Heath for many a season.

Little Hallingbury were surviving but it was touch and go for they nearly missed affiliation to the FA and the League.

Matters began to drift after the close of last season, but the love for the game won the day, and with help from newly elected officers and League Secretary Mr R E Baker, forms were hurriedly dispatched with the result that the club was re-instated.

Mr R V Rattey, the club's new Secretary, said : 'We simply could not let the club fade out. After all, there was a time when junior cups were regarded as the property of Little Hallingbury. So, we got together and ironed things out.'

The club had over 20 players on their books, including Keith Harris, who had joined from Northmet, R Barker (from P.O. Engineers), Dick Hardy (who was also Hallingbury's fast bowler during the cricket season), R Sibley (centre-forward, who played for Herts Army Cadets) and V Eldred. F Eldred was making a comeback in goal and Ken Whitten was skipper of the side.

Other players included Bill Bradford, winger E Eldred and Teddy Flatt, a very promising inside forward entering his second season with the club. Secretary Rattey was coming out of retirement after a couple of years absence and hoped to make the grade in his half-back position.

In October Standard Telephones applied to join and were allowed to join the League.

TAKELEY OPEN NEW GROUND

Takeley's new ground at Stane Street was opened officially by Commander Cory-Wright, a member of the Hatfield Forest Committee of the National Trust in 1952. He was introduced by Mr A Frost, Chairman of the club and a member of the Essex FA who commented that it was only through the help and co-operation of the Forest Committee. And the hard work of members, that the club were able to have the ground. He went on to say that club members had started clearing the ground 6 months previously, when it was scrubland with two bomb craters in it. Now they had a good ground – apart from the 'eternal rabbit' which was causing some concern.

Commander Cory-Wright also commented that the club started with a 'bomb site' but now had a presentable ground with an adequate pavilion.

Mr Frost said that the materials for the pavilion, which contained a kitchen and storeroom, had cost about £100. The building had been erected by club members.

After the opening ceremony, at which Mr C R Hockley, the club's President and Mr B Robinson, the club Secretary, also spoke. Takeley played Saffron Walden Youth Centre in the first round of the Essex Junior Cup competition. Takeley previously played their home games at Station Field and Bonnington's Farm, Takeley.

Source : Herts & Essex Observer

TAKELEY

Source : Harlow Citizen

POTTER STREET

FOOTBALL UNDER THE MICROSCOPE

Hungary's great soccer performance at Wembley in November 1953 when they beat the England team by 6 goals to 3 provided one of the main topics in football circles.

Mr A L Frost, Chairman of Takeley, told the Herts & Essex Observer in a letter, that the lessons to be learnt from the Hungary match were discussed by the club committee reviewing the matter from the small amateur club's point of view. 'We feel,' writes Mr Frost, that we should get back to the fundamental skill of the game. Note that it is called football, not air ball or head ball, and this implies skill with the feet in the control of the ball. Players should practice with both feet. Further, the ball should generally be kept on the ground.

Another point stressed by the Takeley committee was positional play. 'Ground passes are easily intercepted, and to avoid this, players not in possession of the ball should constantly be on the move, seeking the empty space.'

'The third point is physical fitness. Training for the short, sharp burst of speed to carry the player past an opponent is all important. Unfortunately, the small junior club seldom has any facility for training during the winter evenings. Perhaps some senior club having such facilities might invite junior players in this area to train with them.'

Mr H Search of Hatfield Heath FC, and Mr S A Sewell of Dunmow FC, also stressed the importance of fitness, Both would have liked to see more blackboard instructions and tactical talks, but as Mr Sewell wrote, 'I feel that the small amateur club does not get enough training. Some of the teams do not see each other from one Saturday to the next.'

Mr Search also made an interesting suggestion of forming a coaching scheme which had been inaugurated at Harlow, 'This,' he concluded, 'would greatly improve local football and eventually the country's soccer standard in general.'

In contrast with these opinions, which admitted the master can learn from his pupil, came a forthright stand in defence of English football as it was. The writer was Mr L Mason, Secretary of Albury FC.

'Having seen the continental way of training at first hand, I hope that English soccer will never employ such systems, which turns a man into soccer machine, where a player's day is a time-table and where constant supervision is the rule,' he says.

'Don't let the game become your master. The aim of English sport should be to play the game for the game's sake.'

DIFFICULT TIME FOR TAKELEY

From Takeley came news of a difficult time for the club.

The team had missed the support of Holgate, who is suffering from rheumatism, while Harris and Pallett are available only available every other week.

The club had, however, a number of promising youngsters, of whom Terry Bull deputised at inside-left against Hatfield Heath. Though he found the going hard on a heavy ground against players much bigger than himself, he showed both pluck and coolness. The filled-in bomb crater was proving quite a menace to defenders playing in that half of the field. In wet weather its surface is coated with thick, muddy clay, making the task of kicking a stationary ball far from easy.

In April Rodings United and Avia Sports were allowed to withdraw from the League.

JUNIOR CHARITY CUP FINAL (1952/53 FINAL)

TAKELEY 1 HATFIELD HEATH 1

Old rivals met in the final of the 1952/53 Bishop's Stortford and District Charity Cup Final at Stansted. The competition was heavily delayed due to bad weather.

Due to bad light extra-time was not played and the two clubs remain joint holders of the trophy.

After a rather slow start, the game suddenly sprang to life when a movement on the Takeley right, initiated by Camp, was carried forward by Ball, from whose centre Thurgood scored with a fine shot. The cheers had scarcely died down when Hatfield Heath equalised, a mistake by the Takeley defence giving Roy Nicholls an easy chance.

Hatfield Heath played the better football in the second half, and only some fine defence work by King, Scraggs and goalkeeper Sullivan kept the score level. Takeley made several fierce counter attacks, but the Heath defence was very sound, with Moore, Search and goalkeeper Barker outstanding.

In April High Roding and Avia Sports were allowed to withdraw from the League.

PREMIER DIVISION CHALLENGE CUP FINAL

BURNT MILL 0 POTTER STREET 0 (AFTER EXTRA-TIME)

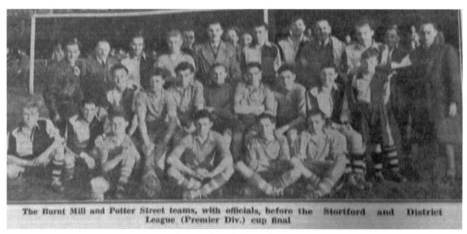

The Burnt Mill and Potter Street teams, with officials, before the Stortford and District League (Premier Div.) cup final

Source : Herts & Essex Observer

The **BURNT MILL** and **POTTER STREET** teams together before kick-off.

After 30 minutes of extra-time there was still no score in the Premier Division Challenge Cup Final. Both sides missed many opportunities often after some good approach work, and it was due mainly to bad shooting that neither side scored.

Potter Street in the first half kept Burnt Mill on the defensive for long periods and shortly after the start, Walters, leading the attack, saw his shot beat the Burnt Mill goalkeeper Tymonds, only to strike the post and go behind for a goal kick. It was Tymonds, who, during these Potter Street attacks saved his side more than once.

Woods played well on the Potter Street wing, but was not sufficiently employed, while in defence, wing halves Snell and Taylor always supplied their forwards well. Burnt Mill's defence, with Rowlands, Hale and Marshall outstanding, must be congratulated on keeping a clean sheet during this period.

True to Cup Final form, the second half saw play unexpectedly swing into the Potter Street half, with Burnt Mill attacking strongly. Reed and Patmore, their right-wing pair, produced some good movements, but found the opposing defence steady, Bayford being supported by a very experienced player in Calver.

Shortly after the interval, a free kick was headed away from the Potter Street line. Extra-time saw more opportunities of scoring missed by both sides.

Source :
David Brown

Source : Herts & Essex Observer

MILLARS SPORTS and **HATFIELD HEATH RESERVES** players together before the Division I Challenge Cup Final. My father, Reg Brazzier, is the first player on the left in the back row. 'Sugar' Perry directly in front of him.

DIVISION I CHALLENGE CUP FINAL

HATFIELD HEATH RESERVES 2 MILLARS SPORTS 1

Millars played in copy-book style while the Heath adopted typical cut-and-thrust opportunist cup-tie football, with the youngest members of the team, 18-year-old outside-right 'Sugar' Perry and inside-left Gunn outstanding.

Of the losers, Trigg and Corbett, left-half and centre-half, added coolness and steadiness to a generally safe Millars defence. Wild shooting, often terribly wild of the mark ended Millars scoring chances after some excellent approach work.

Jones handled in the second minute of play but, R Bradford missed from the spot but Millars went ahead in the 20th minute when Bidwell deflected R Bradford's shot into the net.

Heath quickly replied, Pyle tapping the ball into the goal after Gurnett's header had rebounded from the post and a minute later, from a breakaway, they scored their winning goal.

Millars were off to fast start after the interval and never surrendered their grip on the match, but although they forced corner after corner, the Heath, with the whole team defending, held their one-goal lead to win a match which never lacked excitement, good spirit and sportsmanship.

DIVISION II CHALLENGE CUP FINAL

RHODES AVENUE 2 BIRCHANGER 2 (AFTER EXTRA-TIME)

Source : Herts & Essex Observer

RHODES AVENUE (black collars) and **BIRCHANGER** players together before the match.
Holding the ball is Rhodes Avenue mascot, Billy Boswell.

Third and last of the League Challenge Cup Finals ended in a draw when the Division II finalists Rhodes Avenue and Birchanger, left the field all square at 2-2 after two hours play. At the time it was decided that each team would hold the trophy for 6 months, which I believe, had never happened before. However, the two teams in fact, replayed the final at the start of the 1954/55 season.

Only three minutes after the kick off, centre-forward George Banks put Birchanger in the lead, but before half-time, the Avenue equalised from a penalty, which had to be taken twice. Goalkeeper E Banks saved D Barker's first shot, but Harris made no mistake with the second kick ordered by the referee.

Fifteen minutes after half-time Birchanger were in the lead once more, Banks again being the scorer. The Avenue drew level for the second time when R Barker headed home the rebound after a shot by Gawthorn had hit the bar.

Another shot by Gawthorn hit the bar during extra-time when the Avenue were by far the more aggressive side.

PREMIER DIVISION CHALLENGE CUP FINAL REPLAY

BURNT MILL 4 POTTER STREET 2

The Premier Division Challenge Cup Final replay was won by Burnt Mill, who beat Potter Street 4-2.

BIRCHANGER DINNER TO CELEBRATE SUCCESSES

Birchanger Football Club, joint holders of the Division II Challenge Cup and Division II Runners-Up for the 1953/54 season, held a dinner and social evening at the Birchanger Village Hall to celebrate their successes.

Source : Herts & Essex Observer

The club had only been reformed the previous season. The Chairman, Major J P Godwin, presided and announced that because of donations and gifts the dinner cost the club nothing and in fact a profit was made. The League was represented by its Honorary Secretary, Mr R E Baker and the medals were distributed by Mrs Godwin. There was an attendance of about 200.

Defeat of Millars Sports in the Division I Challenge Cup Final was a double disappointment for the club since it destroyed their chances of winning the cup and securing promotion in the same season. It had been some years since Millars had a team who had gained a place in the local football spotlight and this would have been a grand finish to their season.

Three years previously they finished only third from the bottom of the League table. Their revival started last season when they rose from fourth to top. Their selection is confined to members of Millars Sports Club and it should not be forgotten that there were several good footballers who worked at Millars but played for other clubs.

Early in the season things did not go too well for the club. They lost the services of Jimmy Rolph to the town side and although they gained a clever forward in Reg Bradford from Little Hallingbury and a promising left-winger in Arthur Bidwell from Stansted, it was some weeks before the team was welded into a winning combination. Only perseverance by a grand committee, including Bob Humphreys, a former centre-forward, enabled them to overcome all the difficulties.

Meanwhile, Avia Sports took four League points from the side. It is interesting to recall that Avia were the only team to beat Millars in League matches, yet they themselves had to withdraw from the League later in the season because they could no longer field a team.

Apart from defeats in the Herts Junior Cup and West Essex Border Charity Cup, the Division I Challenge Cup Final was the first time Millars had been beaten since the early part of the season and their League record was: Played 19, won 17, lost 2, goals for 89, goals against 17.

They were fortunate in having several good players, Alec Ballard, George Williams and Barry Shepherd, to mention a few, who had stood by the club although unable to get a regular game. Vic Cogan was in charge of the team as trainer and they owed a good deal also to their captain, Dave Corbett whose experience with senior clubs in the district was reflected in his skilful leadership.

In November 1953, young Grenville Jeary, whose father played for both Stansted and Bishop's Stortford, some 25 years before, made his first appearance in Millars goal, releasing Reg Brazzier to play on the field. It was about that time that Reg Bradford persuaded his brother Ben not to hang up his boots and when Ben was converted to inside-forward he promptly scored four goals at Newport. John Warwick, who incidentally, headed the team's list with 40 of their total 116 goals during the season.

MILLARS SPORTS REWARD

The players, committee and a few supporters of Millars Sports held an informal get together and Mr Maclaurin, Chairman, attended. Their reward for winning the Division I championship and being Cup Finalists will be numbered shirts for next season.

INTER-LEAGUE COMPETITION PLANS

In 1954 plans for an Inter-League competition went ahead and the chances of it succeeding were quite bright. Such a competition would have been welcome as it could have increased the chances of representative honours for local players leading to an improvement in the standard of play.

The Harlow & District League announced it would play in gold shirts with black collars and cuffs. The Bishop's Stortford, Stansted and District Junior League had at that time not decided on their colours.

It was understood the idea was for the leagues in the area – Harlow & District, Bishop's Stortford, Stansted and District and Ongar and District – to form one part of the competition and three leagues in the Ilford area to form the other and the top teams of both sections would play each other to decide the championship.

A member of one the local junior teams expressed their concern over the failure of some clubs to provide a first-aid kit. The member explained that on two occasions a member of an opposing team had been injured and they had to come to the rescue. Items in a first-aid kit were expensive and it was unfair to the opposing team to look after both teams.

SAWBRIDGEWORTH REVERT TO JUNIOR FOOTBALL

Sawbridgeworth Football Club, who achieved senior amateur football status many seasons ago, but have had several unsuccessful seasons since the war, decided after one year in the intermediate Herts County League, that they must revert to junior status. This was announced at the club's Annual General Meeting.

The Secretary, Mr F D Lloyd, said the decision had been taken in fairness to the Supporters Club, the players, supporters and the club itself and application had been made to the Bishop's Stortford, Stansted and District Junior League for the admission of both Sawbridgeworth teams. It was felt, he went on, that this was the only way to keep football in the town, as it was quite obvious that under present conditions that they were in no position to compete with Harlow or Bishop's Stortford in senior football. It was hoped that supporters would give greater encouragement and more support to the players.

MOVE TO TIGHTEN JUNIOR LEAGUE RULES FAILS AT LEAGUE AGM

Great Parndon FC were out to improve the rules of the League at its Annual General Meeting. Their most important proposal concerned the cancellation of fixtures. In the last season, especially in Division II, many clubs suffered from a shortage of matches because fixtures were continually being cancelled.

To prevent this happening in future Great Parndon suggested the following amendment to the rules : 'A club cancelling their fixture shall be fined 5 shillings. A club failing to keep an engagement without giving a satisfactory explanation and notice to their opponents shall for the first offence be fined £1 and pay the expenses incurred by their opponents. For a second offence of the same nature a club shall be £2, pay expenses incurred by their opponents and be given a warning as to the future conduct towards other clubs. For a third offence of the same nature a club shall be fined £5, pay expenses incurred by their opponents and be expelled from the League.'

However, when the amendment was put to the vote it was defeated by a small margin.

At the meeting it was decided that there would only be two Divisions for the 1954/55 season when it was found that the constitution of the League would leave only seven clubs in Division II, of which only three could say for certain that they would take part in the season's fixtures.

The Chairman, Mr W A Bruty, said that during the last season several Division II clubs had complained to him about the lack of fixtures, and he thought it would be a good idea to run only two Divisions. The meeting agreed to the proposal.

RHODES AVENUE

Division II Championship Winning Medal

R Barker and D Barker

1954 – 1955 SEASON		
League Competition	**Winners**	**Runners up**
Premier Division	Great Parndon	Hatfield Heath
Division I	Newport	Hatfield Broad Oak
League Cup		
Premier Division	Great Parndon	Burnt Mill
Division I	Hatfield Broad Oak	Hatfield Heath Res

At the end of the 1953/54 season Thorley and Standard Telephones withdrew from the League and joined the Harlow & District League for the 1954/55 season. The reason that the Thorley team changed leagues was to save on travelling expenses. Nearly all the teams in the Harlow League could be reached by public transport, while in the Stortford League there are many villages which it is impossible to get to without hiring cars or a coach.

1953/54 DIVISION II CHALLENGE CUP FINAL REPLAY

BIRCHANGER 1 RHODES AVENUE 1 (AFTER EXTRA-TIME)

The League Division II Cup Final marathon, started last season, was continued at Rhodes Avenue and although there had been 240 minutes of football, there was still no result.

The replay was scrappy and produced few thrills. The one exciting moment came two minutes from full time when Rhodes Avenue were winning 1-0 and appeared to have the game safely won, but Gilbey, Birchanger's left-half capped a fine performance by scoring with a grand drive from 30 yards.

The first goal came nine minutes after the interval when a throw-in found Robinson unmarked and from midway inside the Birchanger half he netted with a shot that went in off the post.

Birchanger had the better of the exchanges in extra-time, but when the final whistle went there had been no further score and 22 weary players walked off the field in semi-darkness.

1953/54 DIVISION II CHALLENGE CUP FINAL SECOND REPLAY

BIRCHANGER 1 RHODES AVENUE 0

After five and a half-hours of football the Division II Cup Final was decided at Rhodes Avenue with Birchanger winning by the only goal of the match.

Rhodes Avenue were without Dick Barker and his place was taken by King. Play swung from end to end in the first half, with Birchanger slightly superior. Higgs was outstanding at centre-half for Birchanger and completely closed the middle of the field.

Birchanger took the lead about half way through the second half when G Banks gave John Cracknell no chance with a fierce drive. This stung the Avenue into action, but they failed to take advantage of their opportunities.

JUNIOR CHARITY CUP FINAL (1953/54 FINAL)

HATFIELD HEATH BEAT RODINGS UNITED

A result or report could not be traced for this match but David Brown told me that he thought that he was at this match and he would have been 8. His recollection is that the Heath won and that the Rodings side had a goalkeeper called Gunn who got knocked out but later returned to the pitch.

At a League Council meeting in October the Honorary Secretary outlined a meeting which was called by the Ilford and District League for the purpose of forming an Inter-League competition. It would, he said, be on a North and South basis, the North would be comprised of the Ongar League, Harlow League and this League, which meant two matches and if we were successful three games and it would be on a points system and not knock out basis, The Chairman then spoke on the matter and said he would like this League to enter and would like the clubs whole hearted support in the matter if we did enter. The initial cost to the League would be approximately £1 1s, perhaps more but he felt sure that that it would be a very small sum.

It was proposed by Mr French and seconded by Rhodes Avenue that the League enter the competition. This was carried.

At the November League Council meeting, after discussion, it was proposed by Burnt Mill and seconded by Potter Street that the League purchase shirts, shorts and socks to be worn by the League's representative side. The meeting in January of the League Council was informed by the Chairman that the committee had agreed that the colours were to be emerald-green with white collars, black shorts and green and white hooped socks.

At the same meeting, the future of Mr Hayward, the Honorary Press and Match Secretary was discussed following problems with the League's clubs. The committee thought that he should be asked to resign. It was proposed by Rhodes Avenue and seconded by Takeley that he be asked to resign and this was carried.

The Chairman then asked for nominees to fill the vacancy but no nominations were made. Mr Barker then said he would volunteer for the job, this was accepted and agreed that Mr Barker take over the duties of Mr Haywood. The Chairman then asked all Premier Division clubs to send result cards to Mr Barker and would all clubs please send a list of fixtures played and to be played to Mr Barker.

Stansted Airport were allowed to withdraw from the League.

Source : Herts & Essex Observer

SAWBRIDGEWORTH   **HATFIELD HEATH**

Source : Herts & Essex Observer

NEWPORT

Source : Herts & Essex Observer

LITTLE HALLINGBURY

RHODES AVENUE: Top row—M. Bell (trainer), T. Springham, A. Popplewell, P. Steward, S. Cracknell, P. Baker, B. King, B. Harlow (linesman); bottom row—B. Robinson, Dave Barker, Dick Barker, W. Pratt, A. Springham.

Source : Herts & Essex Observer

RHODES AVENUE

NORTHMET: Top row—D. Reynolds, D. Griggs, M. Reed, A. Porter, J. Hanratty, G. Matthews, P. Last, L. Emerson (linesman); bottom row—D. Last, D. Axton, B. Mollinson.

Source : Herts & Essex Observer

NORTHMET

DIVISION I - NORTHMET 0 RHODES AVENUE 10

With a convincing win of ten goals to nil over Northmet, Rhodes Avenue put themselves in a strong position for the Division I championship. Their performance, although against a depleted Northmet team, who played throughout with only 10 players, was no mean achievement, and great credit went to Dave Barker, the Avenue inside-right, as well as scoring two goals, had a hand in all the other goals, and played brilliantly throughout.

Source : Herts & Essex Observer

Sawbridgeworth's Ray Holgate beats Les Trott, Hatfield Broad Oak while Reg Walters anxiously watches the outcome.

HATFIELD BROAD OAK 2 SAWBRIDGEWORTH 3

DIVISION I

DIVISION I CHALLENGE CUP FINAL

HATFIELD BROAD OAK 6 HATFIELD HEATH RES 0

Five goals by centre-forward A Felton, and one by skipper Les Trott gave Hatfield Broad Oak the League Division I Cup at Rhodes Avenue.

Broad Oak deserved their victory because of their more direct methods and their better finishing. Some of their goals, however, were due to the bad covering of the Heath defence as on several occasions Felton and outside-left Field were left unmarked.

After 10 minutes Dawson, the Broad Oak right-winger, crossed the ball to Field, who hit the crossbar, From the resulting scramble Felton netted. Broad Oak were on top and eight minutes later Trott headed home a corner taken by Field.

Broad Oak's third goal was the best of the match. Field broke through on the left and Felton neatly turned the ball into the net.

In the 60th minute Felton completed his hat trick from a centre by Field. He added a further goal after good work by L Cook and Field.

Broad Oak completed the scoring when Field broke away and centred to Felton, who appeared to be standing offside, but the referee allowed play to continue and the centre-forward ran through and scored.

PREMIER DIVISION CHALLENGE CUP FINAL

BURNT MILL 1 GREAT PARNDON 1

(ABANDONED DURING EXTRA-TIME)

Great Parndon played more attractive football and deservedly took the lead after five minutes when Burton pushed the ball through to Hunt, who netted with a shot that went into the net off a post.

Kennedy scored a surprise goal to equalise when he secured the ball mid-way inside the Parndon half out on the left-wing and scored with shot that sailed into the far corner of the net.

In the second half Parndon produced some of their earlier form, but they found Fox in grand form.

Extra-time was started in the fast failing light and it came as no surprise when the referee abandoned the game two minutes after the start of extra-time.

PREMIER DIVISION CHALLENGE CUP FINAL REPLAY

BURNT MILL 2 GREAT PARNDON 3 (AFTER EXTRA-TIME)

The Mill were on top from the start and after 19 minutes took the lead from a penalty after a Parndon defender had handled the ball, Cox making no mistake from the spot. Within two minutes they increased their lead when, with the Parndon defence in a tangle, the ball was pushed out to Hale, who shot into the far corner of the net.

The second half saw a different Parndon. After four minutes Cardy pushed the ball forward for Wood to run on to and net. From this point they went all out for an equaliser and were rewarded when Hunt scored after receiving the ball from Burton.

In the second half of extra-time the winning goal came in dramatic fashion Pointer managed to meet it and drive the ball home. In doing so he injured himself and took no further part in the game but he had won the cup for Parndon.

Source : Eddie Hunt

GREAT PARNDON

PREMIER DIVISION LEAGUE AND CHALLENGE CUP WINNERS

JUNIOR CHARITY CUP FINAL

HATFIELD HEATH 2 STANSTED RESERVES 4

Once again Rhodes Avenue proved an unlucky ground for Hatfield Heath when, in the final of the Charity Cup, they were defeated 4-2 after leading 1-0 at the interval.

The Heath went ahead after 18 minutes when Jackson pushed the ball out to the to the outside-left and the centre-forward was on hand to head home the winger's accurate cross.

Stansted soon established their superiority in the second half and equalised through outside-right Tucker. The Heath defended stubbornly, but could not hold out the eager Stansted forwards, and centre-forward Enoch gave his team the lead. Stansted went further ahead with another lead with another goal scored by Enoch, and shortly after Tucker made the game safe. The Heath's second goal was scored by Moore, following an indirect free kick.

Source : Herts & Essex Observer

STANSTED RESERVES   **HATFIELD HEATH**

One of the black spots during the season was the decline of Sawbridgeworth. From senior, to intermediate, to junior football in successive seasons was a quick slide, but their decision to revert to junior football was welcomed in many quarters because it was felt that the slide would be halted, and they would have a chance to build up again. This was not to be, however, and they finished one from the bottom of the Premier Division of the League. Much reorganising would be necessary before the start of the season.

The Premier Division League and Challenge Cup double of Great Parndon was the outstanding achievement in local junior football. They proved themselves a good footballing side. As usual, Hatfield Heath were amongst the honours. They were Premier Division runners-up and defeated finalists in the Junior Charity Cup. Their Reserve team suffered a similar fate in the final of the Division I Cup.

Hatfield Broad Oak had a successful season by winning the Division I Cup and also promotion to the Premier Division, pipping Rhodes Avenue at the post. Newport put up a grand performance in heading Division I, dropping only seven points in 26 games and had a goal average of 153 for and 34 against.

WHERE ARE THE YOUNG PLAYERS?

Speaking at the Annual Dinner of Newport Football Club, Mr A L Frost area representative of the Essex FA, raised a question of considerable interest to all small football clubs – the failure of youngsters to take the place of the older members.

He said that many clubs who formerly ran two teams now only ran one, and others who ran only one were now defunct. He added , 'Whatever the reasons maybe I think it is lamentable thing that it is difficult to get young boys to join the social activities organised in their own village. It has become a serious problem.'

It was indeed a problem and one that had grown over the years. Some 20 years previously most villages and small towns could field teams of local players, who provided a better standard of football than that on many grounds in 1955. The decline in local talent, was due, it seemed, to the growth of 'canned entertainment,' and the ease with which people can get to the big professional games. Many youngsters became content to watch sport rather than participate.

On the brighter side, however, greater interest in sport appeared to be taken at the secondary modern schools and in the following years it was hoped there would be an improvement in the situation,

The dinner was a great success and lived up to its reputation of being one of the most popular functions of its kind. There was a very friendly atmosphere, and a club that had such a grand social side was well on the way to success. Everyone admired the club for their decision not to apply for re-election to the Premier Division, but to fight their way back when they were relegated three years previously, this was the true sporting spirit.

JUNIOR FOOTBALLERS DINNER AND DANCE

Tributes to the importance of junior football and to the part played by the Secretaries of the junior clubs were paid at the League's annual presentation dinner and dance.

Mr A C Harris of the Hertfordshire Football Association replying to a toast to the Herts & Essex Football Associations, said the friendship between the two counties was very great, and if this were so between countries it would be a wonderful world in which to live. Emphasising the important part football played in international relations. Mr Harris said it would be better if there were more football jerseys and less khaki.

This country had gone all over the world to play football and had been ambassadors. They had shown the world how to play football, and now the world were coming back to show us how to improve our game and that 'Jack was as good as his master.' Recently we had shown them that the master was older and a little more experienced.

The county associations, said Mr Harris, were the controlling body and the people who did the bulk of the work were the club Secretaries in the villages, people who were often forgotten. He thanked them for their work.

In proposing the toast Mr C French said it was due to the work in the past by Mr A R Pegg of Herts, and Mr C W P Lyall of Essex, that the annual junior county game was played.

A toast to the League was proposed by Mr J A Carr, Chairman of the Hertford and District League who spoke of the enjoyable games had a clean, sporting game. The players had always upheld the spirit of the game – the finest in the world.

Speaking of the difficulty in replacing league officials, he appealed to players to ensure that, when their playing days are over , those offices were always filled and the good work carried on.

In reply, Mr A James said that despite the formation of the new League at Harlow, the Stortford League continued to grow and next season there would be even more clubs competing.

A toast to the visitors, proposed by Mr B K Wigg, was replied to by Mr E Hardy of the Bishop's Stortford Football Club who said he felt that junior clubs were the backbone of football and without them there would be no senior sides.

A vote of thanks to the Chairman, Mr W Bruty, was proposed by Mr T S Gee, Chairman of the local Referees' Society. He said that Mr Bruty, in his playing days, had played for Hatfield Heath for many years and had been selected for Essex. Since then he had held numerous posts which included Essex County Football Association area representative, Chairman of the Stortford League, Honorary Treasurer of the West Essex Inter-League Competition, and he was an Honorary Life Member of Hatfield Heath Football Club, of which he had been Honorary Secretary for 35 years.

In reply, Mr Bruty regretted that their President, Mr Lyall, who was 83, was unable to be present. He had worked hard for the League, helping to found it in 1922, and was one of the chief organisers when it was amalgamated with the Stansted League in 1936, He was the 'Grand Old Man' of football. Mr Bruty paid tribute to the work of his officials and the club secretaries, the backbone of football.

MR A L FROST RESIGNS

Mr A L Frost, of Takeley, resigned as area representative of the Essex FA, a position he had held for six years. The area was very scattered one, stretching from Harlow to the Cambridgeshire border and out to Dunmow and Matching Green, and he had found it impossible to carry on as he did not own a car. In addition to visiting each of the 40 clubs at least once a year, he also had to assess referees for promotion. Mr Frost was Chairman of Takeley FC and continued his association with the club. He had been connected with football for about 35 years as a player and an official. He played for Takeley for 10 years and hung up his boots in 1948. He had been Chairman since the end of the war.

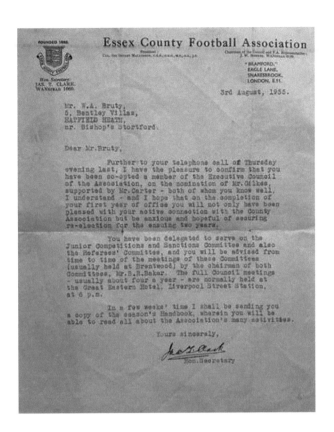

1955 – 1956 SEASON		
League Competition	Winners	Runners up
Premier Division	Hatfield Heath	High Laver
Division I	Little Hallingbury	Northmet
League Cup		
Premier Division	Hatfield Heath	High Laver
Division I	Little Hallingbury	Northmet

At the first League Council meeting in September, the Chairman opened the meeting by presenting a plaque to referee, Mr Reed, for his services to the Inter-League competition in refereeing the Final at Epping.

The October League Council meeting was informed that correspondence had been received from Mr Frost accepting to be a Vice-President of the League, he said he was very pleased to attend some of the League Council meetings.

Source : Herts & Essex Observer

RHODES AVENUE

A storming finish by Rhodes Avenue snatched victory from almost certain defeat in the Division I game at Silver Leys against Thornwood.. They were 3-1 in arrears but fought back in the closing stages to win 5-4 and regain their unbeaten record.

Source : Herts & Essex Observer

BIRCHANGER

Source : Herts & Essex Observer

SHEERING

Source : Herts & Essex Observer

SAWBRIDGEWORTH 2 HATFIELD HEATH 6

PREMIER DIVISION CHALLENGE CUP

Sawbridgeworth line up for our cameraman before the start of their Bishop's Stortford League (Premier Division) match against Epping Town Reserves on Saturday. From left to right are: back row—L. Puncher (trainer), G. Puncher, P. Roberts, I. Stacey, K. Godden, J. Godden, D. Lloyd (Club secretary); front row —G. Brown, W. Churchill, A. Baker, D. Brown, J. Rix, P. Cook.   (M.0032)

Source : Harlow Citizen

SAWBRIDGEWORTH

Sawbridgeworth had little difficulty in collecting both Premier Division points from their visitors, Epping Town Reserves, at the Cambridge Road ground. The Sawbridgeworth goals were scored by G Brown, K Godden, W Churchill and J Rix.

Source : Herts & Essex Observer

TAKELEY RESERVES   **NORTHMET**

Apart from the opening stages of each half, Northmet's superiority was seldom in doubt in the Division I game at Silver Leys. This was in spite of the fact that right-half Cooper damaged his knee soon after the start and was a 'passenger' for the rest of the game. The game was a personal triumph for Len Emerson, who scored four of his team's goals in their victory of eight goals to two.

PREMIER DIVISION CHALLENGE CUP SEMI-FINAL

GREAT PARNDON 1 HATFIELD HEATH 11

There can have been few cup semi-finals that have produced such an overwhelming victory as the Premier Division Cup semi-final at Sheering. The secret of Hatfield Heath's eleven goals to one victory was team work. Although Great Parndon paid more visits to the Heath's goal area than the score suggests, they never looked like scoring against the sound defence of their opponents.

The Hatfield Heath club took its football seriously and they met on Friday nights to discuss tactics, one of these meetings was attended by Eric Hardy the Bishop's Stortford Football Club skipper and Mr 'Jock' Elliott, the former Stortford team manager.

HIGH LAVER 8 POTTER STREET 3

PREMIER DIVISION CHALLENGE CUP SEMI-FINAL

It was a very disgruntled Potter Street team who left the field at North Weald, having been beaten in extra-time by High Laver 8-3. If the referee had allowed what appeared to be a perfectly good goal minutes before time, there would have been no necessity for extra-time, and they would have moved into the final.

High Laver, who reached the final of the Bishop's Stortford League (Premier Division) Challenge Cup by beating Potter Street after extra time, at North Weald on Saturday, pose for our photographer. (M.0032)

Source : Harlow Citizen

HIGH LAVER   **POTTER STREET**

RHODES AVENUE 0 LITTLE HALLINGBURY 7 - DIVISION I

With both teams having previously conceded only two points during the season this game may well have decided the Division I championship. As the two teams were so closely matched a hard-fought game was expected, but the spectators were disappointed as Rhodes Avenue were seldom in the picture as Little Hallingbury ran out 7-0 winners.

Source : Herts & Essex Observer

Outstanding footballer of the year

Source : Herts & Essex Observer

His performance in the game against Great Parndon, in which he scored, a few hours before, clinched 17-year old Desmond Brown's selection as Sawbridgeworth FC's outstanding player of the season.

Source : Herts & Essex Observer

MANUDEN 1 NORTHMET 6

DIVISION I CUP SEMI-FINAL

All the seven goals in this Division I Challenge Cup Semi-Final at Birchanger were scored in the first half. Northmet deserved their victory by virtue of their better team work, but some of the goals were 'gifts.' Manuden, although having some accomplished players, lacked cohesion. The result was in doubt for only the opening stages. Northmet scored and Manuden quickly equalised, but when Northmet regained the lead the result was certain. Northmet added a further four goals winning by 6 goals to 1.

Source : Herts & Essex Observer

STANSTED RESERVES 2 HIGH LAVER 6

PREMIER DIVISION

High Laver improved their bid for second position in the Premier Division, with a 6-2 victory over Stansted Reserves at Hargrave Park. Although a four-goal margin flattered the visitors a little, they were good value for their win.

DIVISION 1 CHALLENGE CUP FINAL

LITTLE HALLINGBURY 2 NORTHMET 1

All three goals in the Division I Challenge Cup Final at Rhodes Avenue were scored from the penalty spot. The deciding goal came three minutes from the end and was an extremely harsh decision. The football was not of a particularly high standard, the game being a typical Cup Final. Little Hallingbury perhaps just deserved their win by the way they had fought back in the second half, despite the fact that Nevin Clarke, their right-back had been injured and had moved to centre-forward.

Emerson scored Northmet's penalty while Ben Bradford scored both of Little Hallingbury's spot kicks. The result meant that Little Hallingbury had brought off the Division I League and Cup double. It had been many years since Hallingbury had had won the cup and the season had been their most successful for some time.

Source : Herts & Essex Observer

MEMORIES OF THE BEAUTIFUL GAME (**Source** : Toby Allanson/ Herts & Essex Observer)

In 1951, the directors of the North Metropolitan Electricity Board, now defunct, ran a cup competition for all its offices and depots in North London, Herts & Essex area.

That year, 17-year-old Tony Dellow, who was the youngest player in the squad and his ten teammates represented the Bishop's Stortford Depot. They travelled the length and breadth of the South East in pursuit of glory.

It was a strong side, and five teams were no match for the likes of inside-right Bob Nichols and inside-left Mike Reed who both plundered a hatful of goals as the boys from North Street continued their seemingly irresistible march towards the trophy.

According to Mr Dellow, the stars of the side were Bob Lambert who also played for Bishop's Stortford and left-back Bryan Atkinson. He said, 'He went on to play professionally for Watford, I would think in the mid-fifties. Then he came back to local football and took up the pub trade at the White Horse in Hatfield Heath.

With rocks like these two at the back, the lads had a solid base on which to build their attacks which Mr Dellow, who played right-half, admitted lacked something in subtlety. He said., 'We always tried to get it to the left-winger Ronnie Holland. He was pretty quick and could deliver a decent cross for Bob (Nicholls) who was big and burly or Mike (Reed) who was quite tall.'

'We didn't play football then like they do now – one or two passes and that was it.'

But on the day of the big match disaster struck the youthful Mr Dellow, and the Stortford boys went down 2-1. Clearly blotting out the painful memories, Mr Dellow could not recall who the victorious opponents were (Little Hallingbury) nor put his finger on where it all went wrong preferring instead to remember rather happier days.

He said, 'I tend to think the best teams I played for were the ones which had the best results and the years with Manuden were the most successful.'

Mr Dellow saw out his football career proudly wearing the village's shirt and when Manuden beat Hatfield Heath Reserves to secure the League cup he was at last able to exorcise those final day demons.

Source : Herts & Essex Observer

PREMIER DIVISION CHALLENGE CUP FINAL

HATFIELD HEATH 2 HIGH LAVER 0

Hatfield Heath completed the Premier League and Cup double by defeating High Laver at Rhodes Avenue. Once again, the standard of play was not particularly high and standing out above all the others were Bert Search and Cliff Moore. Reg Howard also deserved special mention for his gallant display in goal in the first half while goalkeeper Stan Barker was having an injury attended to.

The Heath's first goal came in the sixth minute of the second half. Gunn laid on a pass for Jackson whose long shot come centre dropped into the far corner of the net.

It was Roy Howard who made the second goal. Roy Search had moved in from the wing and Howard seeing him unmarked, sent over a perfect pass. The winger delayed his shot but netted as he was tackled.

NEWPORT ANNUAL DINNER

Source : Herts & Essex Observer

The cheerful, friendly atmosphere was always a feature of the Newport Football Club's Annual Dinner. Arthur Rushton (right) with four of the guests, all officers of the Bishop's Stortford, Stansted and District Football League, Mr R E Baker (Honorary Secretary), Mr M J Connolly (Honorary Treasurer and Registration Secretary), Mr L H J Thorne (Honorary Referees' Secretary) and Mr W Bruty (Chairman and Essex FA representative).

Ernie Pavitt, the 'star' of the Stansted team announced that he would not be playing for them in the following season but would be turning out for Newport, his own village team. Dr A G Saalman, Newport President, gave a hint at the club's Annual Dinner when he said he thought the club's shooting would improve as a distinguished Newport resident was leaving Stansted to play for the club.

Ernie felt that the time had come for him to turn to junior football and added, 'I am satisfied as I have had a good run.' Ernie played a lot of football in the Army and afterwards for Saffron Walden before going to Stansted. Ernie was no stranger to the Newport team as he previously played for them whenever Stansted had an open date.

LEAGUE ANNUAL DINNER

Tribute to the work of the club Secretaries was paid by Mr A C Harris, a member of the Herts County Football Association and Secretary and Treasurer of the Hertford and District Football League, at the 1956 Annual Dinner of the Bishop's Stortford and District League at Long's Restaurant.

They were the people who did who did the work in football, but they were often forgotten. 'I am quite sure that some of the players, from what I have seen and heard at different times, forget them,' he said. 'They think they are just unpaid servants or even out-of-pocket, unpaid servants.'

Junior footballers' dinner and dance

Source : Herts & Essex Observer

'If the Secretary tells them on Friday that a match is cancelled, and he can't fix up another in ten minutes, off they go and play for some other club, and when the same thing happens there, back they go to their first club.'

'It is the Secretaries who do the work for the various leagues and I sincerely thank them for the work they have done in the past year. I think the Secretaries we have at the moment are the best you can get in any football organization.' He said that the friendship between Herts and Essex was wonderful. 'If only this friendship was continued between countries, we should have a much happier world to live in' he said. 'Football, I am certain, is the making of a good world and if we could only use jerseys with coloured stripes instead of khaki, then we should do much better.'

Mr Harris was responding to the toast to the Essex and Herts Football Associations, which had been proposed by Mr Charlie French, Secretary of Sheering Football Club and Secretary of the West Essex Border Charity Cup competition.

The toast to the Bishop's Stortford, Stansted and District Football League was proposed by Mr A J Cox, chairman of the Hertford and District League, who said that the two leagues had played each other and had some good games together. What the result was did not matter – the players had upheld the finest game in the world. The spirit of sportsmanship in Bishop's Stortford, Stansted and District League would, he was sure, continue for many years to come. Paying tribute to the League's officers, he said they had always done their best to look after the interests of the players and when they retired it appealed to the present players to fill their places and continue the good work they were doing for the League.

Replying, Mr A James, a member of the League Committee and a member of the Great Parndon Football Club said the League had had a fairly good season though they had been beaten in the West Essex Inter-League competition by the Harlow & District League. 'We are keeping the strength of the League up quite well, even with the new League in Harlow' he said. 'There will be more teams playing in the League next season than there were, last season, which is a very, very good sign.'

The toast to the visitors was proposed by Mr B K Wigg, for 18 years Secretary of High Laver Football Club and a member of the League Committee. Mr E Hardy, last season's captain of Bishop's Stortford Football Club replied, saying he thought junior clubs were the backbone of amateur football. If it were not for them, senior sides would not exist.

A toast to the League Chairman Mr W A Bruty was proposed by Mr T S Gee, Chairman of the North-West Essex Referees' Society, who said that Mr Bruty had taken on jobs for football almost too numerous to mention. He was area representative on the Essex FA, he was treasurer of the West Essex Border Charity Cup competition, Vice-Chairman of the West Essex Inter-League competition, a Vice-President of the North-West Essex Referees' Society and a life member of Hatfield Heath Football Club., of which was he was Secretary for 25 years.

Replying, Mr Bruty thanked all the officers of the League for their hard work and expressed regret that their 83-year-old President, Mr C W Lyall, could not be present. He was one of the men who founded the Bishop's Stortford and District Junior League in 1922 and was one of the organizers when it was amalgamated with the Stansted and District League in 1936.

Toastmaster was Mr L H J Thorne, the League's Referees' Secretary and the Division 1 Secretary, who also acted as M.C. at the dance which followed. During the interval Mr Bruty presented trophies and medals to the League champions and runners-up. Mr Bruty also presented League badges to D Thurgood (Northmet), J Roberts (Hatfield Heath) and J Webber (High Laver), an Essex County junior badge to Roy Hawkins (High Laver) and an Essex County junior cap to Bert Search (Hatfield Heath).

Source : Herts & Essex Observer

LEAGUE REVERTS TO THREE DIVISIONS

The League are to run three divisions again and will revert to the constitution that existed three years ago. There will be 10 teams in each division.

The meeting discussed whether there should be two divisions of 15 clubs each or three of ten teams. Mr W J Day (Hatfield Heath), who was supported by Mr A James (Great Parndon) and Mr B K Wigg (High Laver), felt that ten teams would not be enough and 12 would be a good number.

Mr L H J Thorne Referees' Secretary, and Division I Secretary, said there were 15 teams in Division I last year and that was too many. If there were two Saturdays when play was not possible it meant trouble. The Premier League had only 13 clubs and their fixtures were not 'too many.' He thought ten teams were enough bearing in mind the county cups.

Mr T Knight (Rodings United) thought that there might be some danger of players 'straying' if they did not have a full fixture list.

When Mr W Nott (Hartam Rovers) said that some clubs had had to play four or five games a week at the end of the season to get their fixtures completed, Mr R E Baker (General Secretary) said it could lose a club the championship. (Mr W T Pratt, Rhodes Avenue – 'hear, hear').

The voting was 15 in favour of three divisions and eight in favour of two.

Commenting that the past season had been a successful one, Mr Thorne said : 'When the Harlow League started I was a little apprehensive as to what would happen to the League, but things have already started to take shape. Our League is going from strength to strength and with the sporting spirit we have shown continuing, we shall go on doing so. Taking the League as a whole and striking an average, the standard was as good and in many cases, better than most leagues of the same classification.'

Mr Thorne spoke of the very friendly relations which existed with the Harlow and Hertford Leagues, and said they had a mutual aid system on the question of referees so that they tried to help each other if an official was needed at the last moment.

Referees had been anxious to obtain matches in the League. Mr Thorne was proud to say and during the season only four or five matches had not had an official referee for being . Two of the matches had been due to the fact that he had not been notified of the games.

Mr Thorne congratulated Little Hallingbury on winning the Division I Cup and League and Northmet for being runners-up in each case. He sympathised with Rhodes Avenue on just failing in the Division I championship fight after being in the battle from the start.

Mr R E Baker, Honorary Secretary, in his report, said the season had been a great success. Two clubs, Hatfield Heath and Little Hallingbury, had been particularly successful, winning the Premier Division and Division I Cups and Leagues, respectively. The runners-up position in each case had also been doubles – High Laver in the Premier Division and Northmet in Division I. Mr Baker expressed the 'hope that the League would run three divisions next year.'

Mr M J Connolly, Honorary Treasurer, reported a balance in hand of £30 6s 9d on the year's working, compared with £105 9s 9d last year. Fines were down by £14 and this was due, either to the clubs behaving themselves or the committee not doing so. Gate receipts from the finals amounted to £70 13s 9d, a decrease of £50 because replays last year brought the total number of games to five. On the expenditure side medals and badges showed a slight increase, and telephone expenses had risen from £2 13s 3d to £20 15s 4d due to the fact that all three secretaries were now on the telephone. Postage was down about £2.

On the social account there was a debit balance of £26 10s.

Mr Connolly said he did not think they need worry about the future although the balance was considerably lower than the £100 or more they usually had. Although they were not aiming to make money it was good to have a 'healthy' bank balance.

In his remarks the Chairman, Mr W A Bruty, thanked the officers, members of the sub-committees and the clubs for their assistance. Thanking the club Secretaries he said without them there would be no League and no Football Association. It was the village clubs that provided the basis for the game.

Mr Bruty thanked the Press and in particular the 'Herts and Essex Observer,' who had done a lot for football, not only from the League's point of view, but also the county.

Prior to 1956 all fixtures were arranged by the clubs themselves at an Annual Fixture meeting held in July. However, from 1956 onwards fixtures were made by the Fixture Secretary, Mr R C Harrison, firstly on a seasonal basis, and latterly on a monthly basis. The League were the first Junior Competition in the area to venture the monthly basis, and it proved so successful not only from the League's point of view, but also from the clubs themselves, that it was followed by other neighbouring Competitions.

A special General Meeting was held in July before the fixtures were made, this was for the purpose of altering the League constitution.

The Chairman announced that Rodings United had withdrawn from the League and the constitution adopted at the Annual General Meeting was now unworkable and he suggested that instead of 10 teams in 3 divisions, the League revert to 2 divisions, 15 teams in the Premier Division and 14 teams in Division 1 and this was carried.

RHODES AVENUE 3 BISHOP'S STORTFORD SWIFTS 5

DIVISION I

The local derby gave the Swifts their best victory of the season. The game was keenly contested but was played in a sporting manner. It was a personal triumph for Miller, the Swifts centre-forward, who scored a hat-trick.

NEWPORT 3 POTTER STREET 7

PREMIER DIVISION

Nine of the goals in the Premier Division game between Newport and Potter Street were scored in the second half with Potter Street winning by 7-3.

Source : Herts & Essex Observer

KINGS RANGERS 4 SAFFRON WALDEN RESERVES 1

PREMIER DIVISION

Playing their first home game, King's Rangers deservedly took both Premier Division points. The game was played at a fast pace with the Rangers having the better of the exchanges from the start. King's Rangers eventually defeating Saffron Walden Reserves.

Source : Herts & Essex Observer

ELSENHAM 4
BIRCHANGER 3

DIVISION I

THE DEATH OF MR CHARLES WILLIAM PRESTON LYALL ANNOUNCED

In December 1956, local sportsmen were grieved to hear of the death of Mr Charles William Preston Lyall, of Cambridge Road, Sawbridgeworth, who was 83, had a lifelong connection with football, first as a player, then as a referee and in administrative posts. Although poor health had prevented him from taking active part in football administration for a few years, he

151

was, at the time of his death, President of the Bishop's Stortford, Stansted and District Junior League and also President of the North-West Essex Referees Society.

Mr Lyall joined a football club when he was 17 and played for several years before he had an accident which finished his playing days. became a referee as far back as 1890 and was a founder member of the North-West Essex Society of which he was Chairman from 1932 to 1949. When he retired as Chairman, he was elected President and was presented with a silver cigarette box. In 1954, he received a long-service plaque from the Essex County Society of Referees.

Mr Lyall, who was born in Singapore on 5th July 1873 and had lived in Sawbridgeworth for over 45 years, served on the Council of the Essex County FA from 1935 to 1949 and received a long-service medal. He was also for many years Secretary of the West Essex Border Charity Cup competition, and had a long association with Sawbridgeworth F.C.

Mr Lyall left a widow and three children.

At the League Council meeting following the announcement of the death of Mr Lyall, the Chairman called for a few moments silence.

Source : Herts & Essex Observer

SHEERING 4 NEWPORT 1

PREMIER DIVISION

HIGH LAVER 6 NEWPORT 0

PREMIER DIVISION

Four goals by High Laver centre-forward Ken 'Kipper' Hawkins helped his team to a 6-0 Premier Division victory over Newport at High Laver and took his personal goal tally to 52 for the season, putting him way ahead of any other goal-getter in local football.

Source : Herts & Essex Observer

SAWBRIDGEWORTH 0 TAKELEY 0

PREMIER DIVISION

If ever a team deserved to share the points it was Takeley when they visited Sawbridgeworth. Midway through the first half they lost Yeoman with a leg injury and shortly afterwards they were reduced to nine men when Read was injured. For the rest of the game Takeley fought gallantly to hold their opponents and to their amazement they succeeded.

Source : Herts & Essex Observer

BIRCHANGER 0 RHODES AVENUE 7

DIVISION I CHALLENGE CUP

At this time, Birchanger and Rhodes Avenue had both been in existence for four years as far as their post-war history was concerned. During that time, they had drawn each other three times in the Bishop's Stortford Challenge Cups. Two seasons previously they met in the final and this had to be played three times before a result was obtained. The latest when the Avenue visited Birchanger in the Division 1 Cup saw them come away with a comfortable margin of 7-0.

HIGH LAVER 10 HATFIELD BROAD OAK 0

PREMIER DIVISION

In one of the best displays of the season, High Laver beat Hatfield Broad Oak by ten goals to nil in their Premier Division match with High Laver centre-forward Ken Hawkins registering a double hat-trick.

Source : Herts & Essex Observer

LITTLE HALLINGBURY 3 HATFIELD BROAD OAK 2

PREMIER DIVISION

Source : Herts & Essex Observer

ELSENHAM - DIVISION 1

Elsenham visited Rhodes Avenue with the home club winning 6-0.

Source : Herts & Essex Observer

TAKELEY 0 HIGH LAVER 3

PREMIER DIVISION

Takeley put up a brilliant fight against High Laver, the Premier League leaders and did well to hold them to 3-0. For this they had to thank a sound defence. Had they had more thrust and ideas in attack they might have produced a shock result

DIVISION I CHALLENGE CUP FINAL

ELSENHAM 1 RHODES AVENUE 3

The game opened with a thrill, Barker hitting the crossbar and P Suckling saving Peter Warwick's shot from the rebound. Avenue continued to attack, and Pratt was prominent with some accurate centres. He went close when he headed over a centre from Perry just over the bar.

The Avenue took the lead after 26 minutes. Barker and Robinson combined well, sent the ball out to Pratt and the winger with Haylett on the ground, provided the pass from which Peter Warwick pushed the ball into the empty net.

Source : Herts & Essex Observer

RHODES AVENUE

In the 55th minute the game really sprang into life. Huggins broke away on the right, beat Murdoch and shot for goal. Steward moved across, the ball struck his foot and shot into the net.

Play swung from end to end, but gradually the Avenue began to get on top and eight minutes later Barker put Warwick through, the centre-forward hit the crossbar and Barker scored from the rebound.

The Avenue put the result beyond doubt in the 76th minute. Warwick put the ball out to Robinson, Haylett failed to hold the winger's shot, the ball ran loose to Perry, who drove the ball into the net.

During the season, the limelight among the junior clubs was stolen by Rhodes Avenue who brought off the Division I League and Challenge Cup double. So often in the past the Avenue had been among the top teams but just failed to win honours, but they had more than made up for it in 1956/57.

PREMIER DIVISION CHALLENGE CUP FINAL

HATFIELD HEATH 5 HIGH LAVER 2

The captains of the teams toss before the 1956/57 Premier Division Challenge Cup Final. Left to right – D Palmer (High Laver), Mr R Fyfe (Referee) and R Dedman (Hatfield Heath).

Source : Herts & Essex Observer

In the fifth minute the Heath went ahead. Chalk was slow in clearing and Graham Thomas raced through and netted with a fast-rising shot. Shortly afterwards Search beat Chalk and pushed the ball through for Howard to force it over the line from close in.

The Heath had an amazing escape when Ken Hawkins missed his kick and the ball bobbled about the goalmouth before being cleared. Laver were finally rewarded when Roberts, making a rare mistake, failed to clear and Ken Hawkins seized the opportunity to score a great goal.

The second half began with the Heath on the attack and Graham Thomas, receiving the ball from Howard, just scraped the crossbar. It was not until the 67th minute, however, that the Heath scored again. Search sent Graham Thomas away and he hit the crossbar, but Howard was on hand to score from the rebound.

High Laver fought back with determination and Ken Hawkins headed just over the bar. Chalk went close from Calver's pass and then nine minutes from the end Dick Thomas was unable to hold a centre from the left-wing and Ken Hawkins netted.

A minute later Heath hit back. Jackson sent the ball to Search who squared it across the goal to Howard, who made no mistake. A minute from the end the Heath put the result beyond doubt when Howard and Thomas combined well to put Jackson through, and the winger's shot slipped through Knapp's legs into the net.

High Lavers' Ken Hawkins had scored 102 goals during the season.

SAWBRIDGEWORTH FC CELEBRATES DIAMOND JUBILEE

Sawbridgeworth Football Club celebrated their diamond jubilee with their first dinner for 44 years.

Proposing the toast to the club, Councillor Col W B Sykes, President of the Supporters Club, said the present season was the most successful since 1947, when they were still in Senior football. The club owed a debt of gratitude to its President, Mr A D Bonham-Carter, and its Chairman, Councillor P M Pyle.

Replying to the toast, Mr Bonham-Carter said it was 44 years since the club held a dinner. It was in 1912/13 season when they won the East Herts and District League for the second time having won it previously in 1910/11.

Source : Herts & Essex Observer

Mr Ivor MacKechnie presents the Player of the Year to Desmond Brown at the Sawbridgeworth Football Club Jubilee Dinner.

EXTRA DIVISION FOR STORTFORD LEAGUE

At the League's Annual General Meeting, it was decided that it was to run three divisions.

Among the new teams entering the League were High Laver Reserves and Potter Street Reserves who played in the Harlow League in the previous season.

Mr R E Baker, the League Secretary, reviewing the previous season, said the League won the West Essex Inter-League by beating the Harlow League in the final and several players gained representative honours.

Mr L H J Thorne, the Referees' Secretary, said the referees were of the opinion that the standard of football in the League and the sportsmanship of the players was 'second to none.' During last season officials were appointed for all but six of the matches in the League.

The financial statement, presented by Mr M J Connolly, the Treasurer, showed a credit balance of £29 15s 9d.

The League rules were amended to provide that the League had first call on players selected for representative matches.

It was first noted in the minutes of the League's 1958 Annual General Meeting that for the 1956/57 season there had been 600 registrations.

Source : Herts & Essex Observer

Members and guests at the Annual Dinner of the Newport Football Club, held at the Studio.

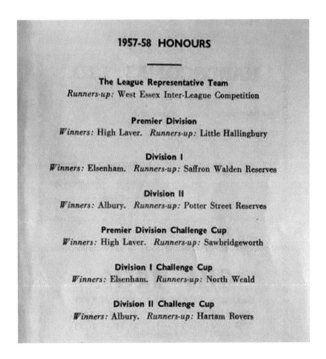

1957-58 HONOURS

The League Representative Team
Runners-up: West Essex Inter-League Competition

Premier Division
Winners: High Laver. *Runners-up:* Little Hallingbury

Division I
Winners: Elsenham. *Runners-up:* Saffron Walden Reserves

Division II
Winners: Albury. *Runners-up:* Potter Street Reserves

Premier Division Challenge Cup
Winners: High Laver. *Runners-up:* Sawbridgeworth

Division I Challenge Cup
Winners: Elsenham. *Runners-up:* North Weald

Division II Challenge Cup
Winners: Albury. *Runners-up:* Hartam Rovers

Potter Street got off to good start in their 1957/58 Premier Division programme when they beat their visitors, Takeley by eight goals to nil. Centre-forward Geoff Howe was in good form, notching five of the Street's goals.

High Laver, the previous year's Premier Division champions, took the first step towards winning the championship again with a 4-2 home win over Great Parndon.

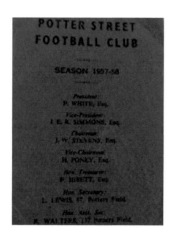

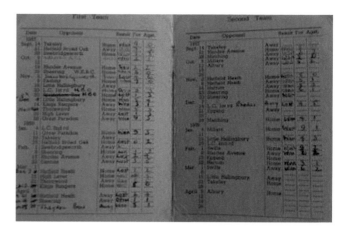

Source : Dave Wood

Source : Herts & Essex Observer

MILLARS SPORTS 1 HATFIELD HEATH 7

PREMIER DIVISION

Source : Herts & Essex Observer

SAWBRIDGEWORTH 6 SHEERING 0

PREMIER DIVISION CHALLENGE CUP

Potter Street F.C., pictured before their Bishop's Stortford League (Premier Division) match against Sheering on Saturday.
(M.0009)

Source : Harlow Citizen

POTTER STREET

Source : Herts & Essex Observer

HARTAM ROVERS

DIVISION II

Hartam Rovers fully deserved their 4-0 victory over Matching United at Silver Leys. They were quicker on the ball and in centre-forward Hutchins they had a sharp shooting leader willing to shoot at every opportunity.

SOCCER COMMENTARY

REFEREES ARE IMPORTANT PEOPLE

Source : Herts & Essex Observer

Undoubtedly the most criticised people in soccer are the referees. They have an unenviable job and are unlikely to please everyone. Often the criticism levelled at them is justified, but one thing cannot be disputed – they are also the most important people in the game.

This was amply illustrated at Silver Leys. Because several referees were on the sick list the Hartam Rovers v Matching United and Rhodes Avenue Reserves v Sheering Reserves were without official referees. Two volunteers sportingly took on the job and carried out the task quite well, but as one of the club officials said : 'It makes all the difference if you have an official referee.'

Next time you have serious allegation to make about the referee's optician stop and think what the game would be like without a referee in charge. If you are dissatisfied with the standard of refereeing why not improve it by becoming a referee yourself?

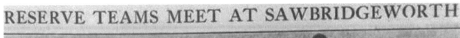

RESERVE TEAMS MEET AT SAWBRIDGEWORTH

Source : Herts & Essex Observer

SAWBRIDGEWORTH RESERVES AND HIGH LAVER RESERVES
WITH REFEREE MR R FYFE - DIVISION I

Source : Herts & Essex Observer

SHEERING 3 HATFIELD HEATH 6
PREMIER DIVISION

After leading 3-1 at the interval in a Premier League local derby with Hatfield Heath, Sheering crashed in the second half losing the game 6-3.

SPORTS COMMENTARY

HATFIELD HEATH ONLY PLAY LOCAL PLAYERS

Source : Herts & Essex Observer

Many people applauded Hatfield Heath's policy at the time to play only men living in or connected to the village. Although it limited selection they still had sufficient talent to remain as a power in the League.

It was a praiseworthy decision. Senior clubs such as Bishop's Stortford had to import players to fill positions for which there was no local talent available. They had a duty to the football fans of the town to provide entertaining football. A village team was in a somewhat different position. Their task primarily was to provide football for the young men of the village.

The Heath had their own reward because Geoff Maskell, the Much Hadham inside forward, moved to the village and played three games for the club.

Source : Herts & Essex Observer

RHODES AVENUE 4 POTTER STREET 2

PREMIER DIVISION

Rhodes Avenue gained two valuable Premier Division points at Silver Leys when they defeated Potter Street by 4 goals to 2. With both Dennis Perry and Bunny Warwick unable to play, the latter getting married, Pratt and Porter were brought in.

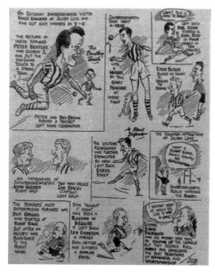

Source : Herts & Essex Observer

KINGS RANGERS 0

SAWBRIDGEWORTH 7

PREMIER DIVISION

REFEREES DINE AT BISHOP'S STORTFORD

'I have had more commissions for bad boys this year than I have had before. Is it because football is getting worse or because referees are getting better? I leave it to you to decide,' said Mr W A Bruty of the Essex Football Association and Chairman of the Bishop's Stortford, Stansted and District League, at the Annual Dinner of the North-West Essex District Society of Referees, held at the Chequers Hotel, Bishop's Stortford.

Mr Bruty, who was replying to the toast to the Hertfordshire and Essex County Football Associations, said he sometimes heard North-West described as 'the forgotten corner of Essex,' but no part of the county was forgotten by the County FA.

He could also say the same about Hertfordshire, because with representatives like Mr George Wilson and Mr Artur Harris the area was well looked after.

Mr Bruty thanked Messrs LHJ Thorne, E Hemmings and EJ Swan for their work in coaching candidates. On the shortage of referees, Mr Bruty said the games were fairly well covered, but they could be covered better. Many senior referees did not like taking junior games, others liked to watch Tottenham play. They were two reasons for the shortage of referees.

Mr Bruty, on behalf of the Stortford League, thanked the referees for making the League a success. Without them it would be 'a shambles.' He thanked the referees for what they were doing for football in the district.

MOVE TO FORM INTERMEDIATE LEAGUE

Sawbridgeworth Football Club were making great efforts to form a local intermediate competition, but there had been little response which had not been very encouraging. The idea was to call a meeting of interested clubs and if there had been sufficient support then one of the local Leagues would be asked to take it within their framework.

The clubs circulated were Stanstead Abbotts, Stansted, High Laver, Little Hallingbury, Rhodes Avenue, Hatfield Heath, Burnt Mill, Dunmow, Saffron Walden, Harlow United, Much Hadham and British Mathews. Replies were received from High Laver who were interested, Hatfield Heath, team building for the next two years and not in a position to consider higher grade football, Saffron Walden asked for a list of interested clubs and Burnt Mill were also interested but were of the opinion the following season would be too soon.

Sawbridgeworth considered whether to call a meeting of the interested clubs, but as time was running short and there were still several clubs who had not replied. Sawbridgeworth also invited other interested clubs to contact them.

Source : Herts & Essex Observer

DIVISION II CHALLENGE CUP FINAL

ALBURY 2 HARTAM ROVERS 1

The Division II Cup Final will be one game that Hartam Rovers centre-half and skipper Ron Nott would want to forget. After dominating the centre of the field for most of the game he had the misfortune to head Albury's winning goal into his own net. Albury deserved to win by virtue of the fact that they took what chances were given and twice hit the woodwork in the first half. Hartam Rovers on the other hand, although they played the more constructive football, faded out in front of goal.

The first half was goal less but only four minutes after the change of ends Wheatley, the Albury right-winger, netted with a centre which Cyril Whiffin misjudged. Shortly afterwards the Rovers goalmouth was the scene of terrific melee before Abrahams came away to clear. Hutchin was presented with a glorious chance which he failed to take.

With the paly still in the Albury penalty area the Rovers forced a corner which C Chipperfield scrambled off the goal line only to concede another corner. This time Geoff Nott beat Woollard in the air to head the equaliser. Shots from Last and Eden were cleared and in the 34th minute a scramble in the Hartam Rovers goalmouth resulted in Orwin's header being headed into his own net by Ron Nott.

In the closing minutes the Rovers fought gamely, but never really looked like saving the game.

DIVISION I CHALLENGE CUP FINAL

ELSENHAM 3 NORTH WEALD 1

Elsenham won the Division I Cup Final at Rhodes Avenue by their second half performance, but the talking point after the game was whether the referee, Mr R Reed of Sawbridgeworth, was correct in awarding the penalty to Elsenham in the first half.

Sewell, the Elsenham outside-left, was going through when he was tackled by Beattie, the North Weald right-back. Sewell fell in the penalty area and the referee had no hesitation in awarding a spot kick from which Tucker scored. Opinion among the spectators was divided over whether it was a foul or not, but it was unanimous that Sewell was tackled outside the penalty area. From the stand it appeared to be just outside. Sewell's fall also appeared to become more dramatic when he realised the penalty area was adjoining . He repeated the performance with less success in the second half.

The first goal came in the 19th minute and was the best of the match. Cheese pushed the ball through and Major hit it on the run. The ball was in the net before A Powter, the Elsenham goalkeeper, had a chance to move.

In the 37th minute there was the penalty decision and Tucker made no mistake from the spot. From then until half-time North Weald tried hard to regain the lead but without success.

In the second half both teams were battling for mastery and then in the 74th minute the game was decided. Tucker received the ball, beat off a challenge from Major and placed the ball wide of Lloyd. From that point there was no doubt that it was Elsenham's game and five minutes from the end P Suckling made the game safe with a grand drive from 30 yards.

Source : Herts & Essex Observer

Arthur Rushforth, Vice-Chairman of the League, presents the 1957/58 Division I Challenge Cup to the Elsenham captain

PREMIER DIVISION CHALLENGE CUP

HIGH LAVER 10 SAWBRIDGEWORTH 4

Source : Herts & Essex Observer

If spectators like plenty of goals they had their money's worth in the Premier Division Cup Final. Fourteen goals in 90 minutes should be sufficient to satisfy anyone. In addition, they were treated to a display of football by High Laver that did credit to a junior team.

It was a game that Sawbridgeworth will have wanted to forget. They did not play as a team and their defence was torn to shreds time after time. Their marking had to be seen to be believed especially when it came to Ken Hawkins, Laver's free scoring centre-forward.

The game was decided in the eighth minute when Sawbridgeworth handed a goal to Laver on a plate. The ball came through the middle, three defenders stood around, one attempted a half-hearted back-pass and Byford raced through to give the keeper no chance.

In the 13th minute Calver pushed the ball through Cook's legs and found Ken Hawkins. The centre-forward sliced the ball and it went to Calver who banged it into the net. Ken Hawkins and Cyril Hawkins made it 4-0 and then Laver were unlucky not to score a fifth when a fierce drive hit the underside of the bar and came out.

In the 34th minute Sawbridgeworth's Rix pushed the ball to Tony Cooke, who was deputising for the injured Puncher, and he beat Edwards before centring for Butler to head just inside the post.

Before half-time Byford and Ken Hawkins (2) made the score 7-1.

High Laver added three more goals through Byford (2) and Calver.

Sawbridgeworth, who at least kept trying, staged a late rally and scored through Cooke, Butler and Bentley.

Source : Herts & Essex Observer

Elsenham Football Club Annual Dinner celebrating winning the Division I League and Cup double.

Source : Herts & Essex Observer

Members and guests at the Takeley FC Annual Dinner

'We have had a jolly good season, but I feel that our next one will be an even better one' remarked Mr W Simpson, Captain of Takeley Football Club, at the club's Annual Dinner. He was replying to a toast to the club proposed by Mr W Bruty, Chairman of the League.

'Several young members from the village have joined us recently,' continued Mr Simpson,' and I feel that once they have a little more experience, they will be very useful.' He congratulated Mr R C Harrison, the Match Secretary of the League, on the good work he had done during the season.

Mr A L Frost, Chairman, thanked Mr Simpson, and also offered his congratulations to Mr Harrison. He proposed a toast to the League.

In his reply, Mr Lionel Thorne, Referees' Secretary , remarked that those who worked for the League worked for the love of the game, not for what they got out of it for themselves. 'Please don't think we get paid for it,' he added.

Concluding, he said the members of the Takeley club were full of fight on the field, but once they had finished their football, they were the best of pals.

Mr Frost thanked Mr Thorne and asked Mr Bruty to present a wrought iron clock to Mr B Robinson, who had recently retired as Secretary.

Thanking the club, Mr Robinson mentioned how friendly everyone had been when he first arrived in Takeley and how swiftly he had been accepted by the members of the club.

Mr Frost commented that Mr Robinson always minded the club's business and had been instrumental in getting many of the facilities at present at their disposal.

Mr H Rushden, a committee member, proposed a toast to the guests.

Replying, Mr A Rushforth, Chairman of Newport Football Club, remarked on the friendly manner of the Takeley members and thanked them for their hospitality.

LOCAL LEAGUE HOLDS PRESENTATION DANCE AT SAWBRIDGEWORTH

Source : Herts & Essex Observer

At the League's Annual Presentation Evening, Roy Hawkins, High Laver, receives his county cap from Mr W Gooch (Essex FA) while Ben Bradford (Little Hallingbury) and Denis Cook (Hatfield Broad Oak) received County Badges.

Source : Herts & Essex Observer

Mr George Wilson presents the League's Premier Division Championship and Challenge Cups to the same player.

STORTFORD FOOTBALL LEAGUE HAD A SUCCESSFUL SEASON

At its Annual General Meeting, the League reported a successful season. It was also reported that there would be six new teams competing in the League while Kings Rangers had to withdraw due to difficulties over a ground.

The new clubs, Netteswell and Burnt Mill, Harlow United, Thorley and Clavering had all competed in the League before. The other two new teams were Elsenham Reserves and Eastons & Duton Hill Reserves.

Netteswell and Burnt Mill decided to enter a team in the 'super' Premier Division of the Stortford League which was thought to be strengthening for the 1958/59 season with a view to forming an intermediate league the following year.

The decision to enter the Stortford League was taken after the Secretary, Mr L G Menhinick, had outlined the proposals made for forming an intermediate league.

At the time of the application from Harlow United, Mr A J Archer said his club were old members of the League. They had been playing in the Northern Suburban League and they wished to return to the Bishop's Stortford, Stansted and District League because there were moves to form a local intermediate competition. They had been assured by officers of the League that they would almost certainly be admitted to the Premier Division.

Mr R C Harrison, Press and Match Secretary, said he had to accept some responsibility. There had been moves to form an intermediate competition as a separate league or as part of the Stortford or the Harlow League. A special meeting for that purpose had been convened about a month before. He feared that there was a possibility of the standard of football in the Stortford League deteriorating as a result as there was a possibility of losing several Premier Division clubs.

The intermediate competition could not start the following season as it was too late, but he and the Chairman thought the best thing would be to get the clubs interested in starting the intermediate competition into the Stortford League first. They had not guaranteed to the clubs that they would go into the Premier Division because they could not, but they had said they would do their utmost to get them in so that they could see what was to happen in season 1959/60.

Mr Harrison said he was very keen to get the standard of the League higher and higher. They should have no hesitation in inviting Harlow United and Netteswell and Burnt Mill into the Premier Division. He felt that if this were turned down, he would be unable to continue in office.

Mr A L Frost, Vice-President said that having accepted the two clubs they should place them in the division most suited to their playing ability.

Mr L G Menhinick, the Netteswell and Burnt Mill Secretary, said he did not want to sing his club's praises, but they were Harlow League Premier League champions and cup holders and holders of the West Essex Border Charity Cup. He had fought 'tooth and nail' to get his club into the League and he could not go back to them and say they were entered into Division II.

As one of the relegated teams were Kings Rangers who had withdrawn, Mr Gilbert proposed that Great Parndon and the next highest team in Division I be admitted to the Premier Division. The proposal was not seconded.

The original proposal that Harlow United and Netteswell and Burnt Mill should be admitted to the Premier Division was carried by twenty-one votes to two.

However, Harlow United and Thorley did not join the League, but Albury did enter a Reserve team.

Thornwood United also withdrew their team.

In his report, Mr R E Baker, said it was the most successful in his 12 years as Secretary. Thanks to Mr Harrison, all fixtures had been fulfilled for the first time.

The financial report was presented by Mr M J Connolly, the Treasurer, who stated that there was a balance of £67 18s 8d. When the liabilities were deducted including the club's deposits, there were total assets of £39 9s 8d.

Cup and League fixtures were all completed, said Mr Harrison in his report, thanks to the co-operation of the clubs. Of the 398 fixtures which constituted the League programme, 132 were rearranged. He warned that with more teams competing he could not be so tolerant in rearranging games so that charity games could be played. He was very much in favour of the charity competition, but he had to put the League first.

Mr L H J Thorne, the Referees' Secretary, said that apart from 4 January and 11 January, when referees had been hit by the influenza epidemic, few games had been without referees. He was pleased with the general standard of refereeing. The referees reported that the standard of sportsmanship in the League was very, very high. Mr Thorne added, 'Our League is second to none. Let's keep it like it. Please convey my thanks to your players.' Mr Thorne, as Social Secretary and Treasurer, reported a credit balance of £31 11s 3d in the social fund.

HIGH LAVER CELEBRATION DINNER AND DANCE

High Laver F.C. who won the Bishop's Stortford, Stansted and District League Premier Division Championship and Challenge Cup held a celebration dinner and dance.

Proposing the toast to the Club, Mr L H J Thorne, Referees' Secretary of the League, recalled that the Club had joined the League only three years previously.

In the first season they were runners-up in the League and Cup, in the second season they won the League and now they did the 'double,' winning both the League Championship and Cup, he said.

'It seems to me they have been a very, very successful Club,' Mr Thorne went on 'Success, of course, is not everything. Success in silver, on the field does not count for all that, but when I am told that from a small Club like High Laver over 100 people should been at this dinner it proves they are a successful Club.'

All the time he had known High Laver he could not remember one of their players being in trouble and he thought that was a wonderful record.

Mr W A Bruty, Area Representative on the Essex Football Association, spoke of the two High Laver brothers who were valued highly by the County – the Hawkins brothers, Roy and Ken. Last year, Roy had won his County Cap for playing four games and Ken had played three games. He hoped that they would go on to play ten games and win their honours badge.

The tremendous amount of hard work put in for High Laver Football Club by Mr Berrill K Wigg, its Secretary for the past 19 years and before that as a player was recognised at the Club's celebration dinner and dance.

He was presented with a tankard inscribed 'Berrill K Wigg, from High Laver Football Club, August 22nd, 1958.'

The presentation was made on behalf of the Club by the President, MR C T Higgins, and the assembled company – there were nearly 100 members and guests   sang 'For He's a Jolly Good Fellow.'

Source : Harlow Citizen

Some of the guests at High Laver F.C.'s celebration dinner.

During the evening many of the speakers paid tribute to Mr Wigg's untiring work for High Laver and local football generally.

His interest in the game was perhaps most aptly summed up by Mr L G Beake, a Vice-President of the Club, who described him as 'the great little man in the football world' and said of him, 'He has for many years been a staunch friend of the Club. I think he has got football in his heart and in his blood.'

Loud laughter greeted his remark, 'It is some months ago when he was confined to his house. Rumour had it that he had given birth to a football.'

Mr Thorne, Referees' spoke of the debt that the Club and the League owed to Mr Wigg. 'You must realise what the Stortford League think of Mr Wigg. Having been in the League for only three seasons, he has been on the Committee for two' he said.

And finally, Mr W A Bruty, added his tribute, mentioning at one point, about ten years ago, as well as being Secretary of High Laver, Mr Wigg had also been secretary of High Easter F.C. for a season.'

There were 794 registrations for the 1957/58 season.

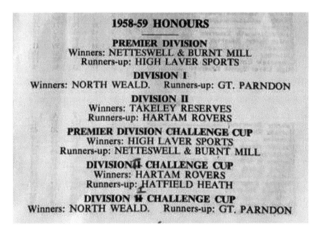

1958-59 HONOURS

PREMIER DIVISION
Winners: NETTESWELL & BURNT MILL
Runners-up: HIGH LAVER SPORTS

DIVISION I
Winners: NORTH WEALD.   Runners-up: GT. PARNDON

DIVISION II
Winners: TAKELEY RESERVES
Runners-up: HARTAM ROVERS

PREMIER DIVISION CHALLENGE CUP
Winners: HIGH LAVER SPORTS
Runners-up: NETTESWELL & BURNT MILL

DIVISION II CHALLENGE CUP
Winners: HARTAM ROVERS
Runners-up: HATFIELD HEATH

DIVISION II CHALLENGE CUP
Winners: NORTH WEALD.   Runners-up: GT. PARNDON

Source : Herts & Essex Observer

SAWBRIDGEWORTH 1 HIGH LAVER 1

PREMIER DIVISION

Sawbridgeworth and High Laver, who met in the final of the Premier Division Cup last season met again at the Cambridge Road ground in a League match and a closely contested game ended in a 1-1 draw.

Source : Herts & Essex Observer

HARTAM ROVERS 7 BIRCHANGER 1

DIVISION II

In beating Birchanger 7-1 at Silver Leys, Hartam Rovers accomplished their best performance of the season. The club went on to finish as runners-up in Division II.

In October Thornwood United were allowed to withdraw from the League.

Source : Herts & Essex Observer

BISHOP'S STORTFORD SWIFTS 3

NORTH WEALD 6

PREMIER LEAGUE

Source : Herts & Essex Observer

HATFIELD HEATH 1 TAKELEY 4

REFEREE MR LUND PREMIER DIVISION

A REFEREES' SOCIETY OFFICER FOR 28 YEARS

Source : Herts & Essex Observer

Mr G H Wilson presenting a bookcase to Mr T S Gee

'If we had a little more football rivalry in the world, it would be a far better place,' said Mr A C Harris, of the Hertfordshire Football Association, replying to a toast to the Herts and Essex County Football Associations at the 27th anniversary dinner of the North-West Essex District of Association Football Referees.

Mr Harris referred to the friendly rivalry that existed between himself and Mr W A Bruty of the Essex FA, adding : 'but we always shake hands at the beginning and at the end. We thoroughly enjoy it.'

Mr Harris thanked Mr Lionel Thorne for his work in training referees.

In proposing a toast to the two county Football Associations, Mr C G Watts, Honorary Secretary of the Society, spoke of the 'tremendous amount of work' that Mr Harris and Mr Bruty did for football in the district.

The toasts were followed by the most important item of the evening, the presentation of a bookcase to Mr T S Gee, a Vice-President.

Making the presentation Mr G H Wilson, President, said, 'I have for many years been a keen admirer of Tom Gee. When one realises that the Society was formed 28 years-ago and that Tom was one of the founder members and has been in office all that time – Chairman, Secretary, Treasurer and now a Vice-President – it is obvious that he must have spent a considerable amount of his time for the Society.'

Concluding, Mr Wilson said : 'The presentation is a token of the friendship and esteem of his many friends and an expression of gratitude for the services rendered over a good-many-years. We hope it will bring back many happy memories.'

Paying tribute to the work of other members of the society, he said that when he had to retire from an executive post, he knew the Society was in good hands.

He recalled the difficult times they had in reforming after the war and said that much of the secretarial work had been done by his wife.

Mr Arthur Lavendar, Chairman of the Essex County Referees' Association, said he had known Mr Gee for 25 years and at one time he was the North-West Essex Border Branch, as it was then. Without Tom Gee the Referees' Association would not function. They were lucky to have him in this part of the county and it was good to know he would be available to give advice.

Mr Bruty thanked Mr Gee for his work for the League.

Mr A Dimond, Chairman of the Harlow Referees' Society, said that when they elected Mr Gee President of their Society, he was the only man they had in mind. He was a sportsman and a gentleman and when they thought of him, they thought of the Referees' motto, 'Service, not self.'

Mr R Harrison announced that the gift had been oversubscribed and it was Mr Gee's wish that the balance should be used to purchase a trophy for school football.

Source : Herts & Essex Observer

DIVISION II CHALLENGE CUP FINAL

HARTAM ROVERS 3 HATFIELD HEATH RESERVES 1

Rhodes Avenue had never been a lucky ground for Hatfield Heath and the Division II Cup Final was no exception. Hatfield Heath Reserves had most of the game, but it was Hartam Rovers who scored the goals winning 3-1. It was the Rovers' second successive Cup Final having previously lost 2-1 to Albury.

Rovers made occasional raids on the Heath's goal, but it began to look as if neither team could score until the 32nd minute when Martin sliced a goal kick to Emerson who promptly banged the ball into the empty net. The goal was against the run of play.

This stung the Heath to greater efforts, but without success.

The second half was 16 minutes old when the Rovers scored again. Along through ball found Geoff Nott who beat Bruty and pushed the ball on Emerson to race through and net.

Still the Heath fought back and were rewarded in the 73rd minute when Brown sent Faulkner away on the right-wing and he centred for Search to head a brilliant goal.

The Heath saw a chance to save the game and fought desperately, but their last hope went five minutes from time when Bill Nott received the ball in an unmarked position and calmly placed it in the net.

DIVISION I CHALLENGE CUP FINAL

NORTH WEALD 3 GREAT PARNDON 1

After a keenly fought match, North Weald finally overcame Great Parndon in the Division I Challenge Cup Final. North Weald just deserved their 3-1 victory.

PREMIER DIVISION CHALLENGE CUP FINAL

HIGH LAVER 2 NETTESWELL AND BURNT MILL 1

Burnt Mill, who had the lion's share of the exchanges, could have clinched the issue in the opening half-hour when they repeatedly attacked the Laver goal, but they committed the cardinal error of making one pass too many when the situation demanded first time shooting.

Laver's first real attack brought them their first goal, Cox deflecting a harmless-looking shot past goalkeeper Wadman. They retained their one goal advantage at the interval.

Burnt Mill were still reluctant to shoot in the second half but were eventually rewarded when Ken Fish netted. Laver fought back and scored the winning goal when a free kick taken by Ken Hawkins was deflected into the net.

Source : Herts & Essex Observer

Mr G H Wilson presenting a smoking cabinet to Mr A L Frost, retiring Chairman of Takeley Football Club

Mr A L Frost was presented with a polished wooden smoking cabinet in appreciation of 21 years of service to the club at the club's Annual Dinner.

Presenting the gift on behalf of the club, Mr G H Wilson, President of the League, said it was a token of favour and esteem to a person who had long been associated with the club.

Proposing a toast to the club, Mr Wilson went on to say that a football club was only as good as the men who ran it, and in this respect Takeley were extremely fortunate. Many of their members had been with them a very long time. They had always had a good time and always played good football.

Source : Harlow Citizen

In May 1959, Netteswell and Burnt Mill President, Bill Fisher, drinks a toast to members of the Club who were presented with the League's Premier Division trophy, held by Bill Skudder, at the League's annual presentation dinner and dance.

STORTFORD LEAGUE CUPS PRESENTED

Source : Herts & Essex Observer

Mr G H Wilson, President, presented the cups and medals to the winners of the three divisions of the League at the Annual Dance held at the Memorial Hall, Sawbridgeworth. Mr Wilson was introduced by Mr W A Bruty, Chairman. Mr W A Gooch, of the Essex FA, presented an Essex Junior cap to Ken Hawkins of High Laver.

1958/59 HAD BEEN A VERY SUCCESSFUL SEASON

At the League's Annual General Meeting, League Secretary Mr R E Baker said that said that the 1958/59 season had been a very successful one from his point of view. He said, 'We ran very smoothly, and the football was second to none. Our Inter-League side were very unlucky in not reaching the final but its goals that count and I'm afraid they eluded us.'

Mr Baker thanked all his fellow officers for their assistance and also the Committee members. He also thanked all the club secretaries with most clubs answering his correspondence promptly. He also mentioned one club, - that badly let him down – that club being Elsenham. A number of letters were not answered, and Mr Baker said, 'I think that they could if they had paid more attention to League matters, saved me a lot of wasted time.'

The Treasurer, Mr G Reed, commented that the League had assets of £3 9s 4d and £32 11s 10d in the bank. He further commented that the Social Account stood at £56 0s 9d.

Mr Harrison, the Press and Match Secretary and Fixtures Secretary said, 'You all know that despite the terrible weather the fixtures were completed including 242 rearranged games, the clue to this was a maximum of thirteen clubs to a division.'

Mr Harrison went on to say that his job would not have been possible if it wasn't for the cooperation of club Secretaries.

Mr Thorne, the Referees' Secretary reported the last season was not very successful owing to a shortage of referees. He had endeavoured to get more referees but was not successful. He praised the high standard of football and said there was no better League for miles around.

New clubs entering the League for the following season were Blue Star and Heath Rovers while Clavering, Elsenham Reserves and Skyways withdrew.

Mr Harrison stood down as Honorary Press and Match Secretary and was succeeded by Mr Kime.

After a discussion, it was decided to introduce month to month fixture lists for the first time for the 1959/60 season.

1959-60 HONOURS

PREMIER DIVISION
Winners : HIGH LAVER
Runners-up : HATFIELD HEATH

DIVISION I
Winners : DEBDEN
Runners-up : BISHOP'S STORTFORD SWIFTS

DIVISION II
Winners : HEATH ROVERS
Runners-up : SHEERING RESERVES

PREMIER DIVISION CHALLENGE CUP
Winners : SAWBRIDGEWORTH
Runners-up : POTTER STREET

DIVISION I CHALLENGE CUP
Winners : BISHOP'S STORTFORD SWIFTS
Runners-up : SAFFRON WALDEN RESERVES

DIVISION II CHALLENGE CUP
Winners : MANUDEN
Runners-up : HATFIELD HEATH RESERVES

Source : Harlow Citizen

POTTER STREET

PREMIER DIVISION

Before their match against Netteswell and Burnt Mill which ended in a 2-2 draw.

LITTLE HALLINGBURY'S NEW PAVILLION OPENED

Source : Herts & Essex Observer

Source : Herts & Essex Observer

HATFIELD HEATH 1 SAWBRIDGEWORTH 0

PREMIER DIVISION

Bottom Left – Malcolm Wylie stops a fierce drive from Ron Bonney.

Bottom Right – Bonney tries to go through but is tackled by Roy Search.

SPORTS COMMENTARY

Do Forwards Lack Shooting Power

Source : Herts & Essex Observer

Was there a lack of shooting power in forward lines at this time? This interesting point was raised by Howard Pyle, of Hatfield Heath while watching on the touchline at the game between Hatfield Heath and Sawbridgeworth.

The point he made was that a forward's job was to get goals, either score them or make them. It was important, in his opinion, that every member of a forward line should have the ability to shoot. In the pre-war forward lines in which he played, they could all shoot.

Source : Herts & Essex Observer

TAKELEY 2 NETTESWELL AND BURNT MILL 7

PREMIER DIVISION

Fish, the Takeley goalkeeper, punches clear during a Netteswell and Burnt Mill attack.

Playing stylish, powerful football, Netteswell and Burnt Mill completely outplayed Takeley in the Premier League game at Takeley. The visitors were superior in all departments, but they eased up in the second half and although they had the game well in hand it could have been dangerous against a stronger team. Although outclassed, Takeley were to be congratulated on never giving up and they were trying as hard at the end as they were at the kick off. The game finished in a win for Netteswell and Burnt Mill by 7 goals to 2. Mr C G Wells of Stansted ably controlled the game.

STANSTED RESERVES 7 BISHOP'S STORTFORD SWIFTS 0

REFEREE MR L F CLANFORD DIVISION I

HATFIELD BROAD OAK 4 COOPERSALE UNITED 1

DIVISION I CHALLENGE CUP

Giving a display of hard, fast football, Hatfield Broad Oak had an easy passage to the second round of the Division I Challenge Cup when they defeated Coopersale by 4 goals to 1. Had they not missed a number of chances in the second half the margin of victory would have been greater. Centre-forward Ernie Felton had a successful day, scoring a hat-trick.

Hatfield Broad Oak played well, and it was obvious that they had considerably improved since the start of the season. Their forward line was particularly impressive, and it was thought that the team would be amongst the honours at the end of the season.

After being demobbed in February 1952, Jack Greenley signed for Thorley. He signed for Sawbridgeworth in 1953 together with Dave Rawlinson. Jack told me that he used to catch the bus outside Millars Machinery to get to Sawbridgeworth for home matches. Jack had to retire in 1959, while playing for Birchanger, due to injury.

The Sixties

42 clubs provided teams for the League during the sixties and there was an average of 39 teams per year playing in the League (not including season 1962/63).

There were 4,224 League games played and 24,183 League goals scored.

High Laver featuring the Hawkins brothers started the decade with a hat-trick of Premier Division titles in 1960, 1961 and 1962, losing only 5 League matches during that time. Bishop's Stortford Swifts with the Thurley brothers won back-to-back titles in 1963 and 1964. Harlow based Potter Street won four titles back-to-back later in the decade from 1964/65 to 1967/68. Takeley were the only other winners of the Premier Division in the decade and were also runners-up in the Premier League on two occasions.

It was surprising that no team achieved a Premier Division League and Cup double in the sixties.

Hatfield Heath and Elsenham were consistent performers in the Premier division and both clubs finished as runners-up on two occasions. During the sixties there were eight different winners of the Premier League Cup.

After transferring from their original Cricketfield Lane home to Silver Leys via Grange Paddocks, Bishop's Stortford Swifts were runners-up in the Herts Junior Cup in season 1963/64 becoming the first team from the League to reach the final but won the Premier Division. The club were unbeaten winning 23 of their 26 League games scoring 120 goals. The club left the League to play higher level league football at the end of the 1964/65 season and joined the Mid-Essex League and then the Essex Olympian League although the Reserve side continued in the League.

Source : Herts & Essex Observer

RHODES AVENUE 1 LITTLE HALLINGBURY 6

DIVISION 1

Source : Herts & Essex Observer

BIRCHANGER 1 HEATH ROVERS 4

DIVISION II

Failure to take their chances and lack of finish cost Birchanger their Division II game with Heath Rovers at Birchanger although they had slightly more of the game territorially. With the score at 2-1 Birchanger had a great chance to equalise when they were awarded a penalty, but they failed to convert, and this was probably the turning point. Heath Rovers were also guilty of missing a penalty but still won the game by four goals to one.

Source : Herts & Essex Observer

SAWBRIDGEWORTH 3 LITTLE HALLINGBURY 1

PREMIER DIVISION CUP

All the goals came in the first half. Des Brown put Sawbridgeworth ahead and almost immediately scored again. Fields reduced the arrears but Peter Kirby scored Sawbridgeworth's third goal.

In March Netteswell and Burnt Mill announced that the club would be leaving the League at the end of the season.

Source : Herts & Essex Observer

SAWBRIDGEWORTH 4 ELSENHAM 0

PREMIER DIVISION CHALLENGE CUP SEMI-FINAL

Beating Elsenham 4-0 at Birchanger, Sawbridgeworth, for whom Peter Kirby scored a hat-trick, qualified to meet Potter Street in the final of the Premier Division Cup. Sawbridgeworth were well on top for the greater part of the game and had no fewer than four goals disallowed. Sawbridgeworth's other goal was scored by Des Brown.

Source : Herts & Essex Observer

DIVISION II CHALLENGE CUP FINAL

MANUDEN 3 HATFIELD HEATH RESERVES 2

Manuden gave their supporters a fright before beating Hatfield Heath Reserves 3-2 in the final of the Division II Cup at Rhodes Avenue. After establishing a 2-0 lead in the first 20 minutes they allowed the Heath to draw level in the last few seconds of ordinary time and even after Manuden had re-established the lead in the fifth minute of extra-time it was anyone's game right up until the final whistle. Manuden won mainly because they were fortunate enough to have in their team the experienced Ted Dellow, a former Bishop's

Stortford player, who time and again stepped in to negative likely moves by the Heath forwards.

DIVISION I CHALLENGE CUP FINAL

BISHOP'S STORTFORD SWIFTS 1 SAFFRON WALDEN RESERVES 0

Appearing in their first Division I League Cup final, Swifts beat Saffron Walden Reserves 1-0, but they should have won by a more comfortable margin. In midfield they showed the better constructive ideas, only to keep their supporters in suspense until the final whistle through the lack of finishing power.

It was mainly in defence that Swifts had the players who caught the eye of senior club officials watching the match. John 'Chopper' Challis was a tower of strength at centre-half, receiving excellent support from Gilbey, a right-back of exceptional promise and Ric Gregory at left-half. Although not exactly over-worked Mollison showed that he has what it takes to make a first-class goalkeeper.

His opposite number, Webb, took the main honours for Saffron Walden with a faultless display although his task was made easier by the Swifts forwards shot shyness.

Most of the threats to the Walden goal came from the Swifts left-wing pair and early in the game J Gregory lost a chance through bad positioning when Mascall centred accurately. With Challis playing strongly Walden met with little success in their attempts to break through the middle although on one occasion Clarke went close with a quickly taken shot. In another Walden attack Mollison showed good anticipation in beating Weston to a through ball.

Swifts continued to play the better football only to miss at least a couple of chances of going in front and to find Webb in good form. It was Walden who came who came nearest to scoring, Skingley, a former Swifts player, having his header punched over the bar by Mollison just before the interval.

The Walden goal was under pressure immediately the game was resumed, but Swifts were still slow to take their chances and trying to walk the ball in. The game developed into a defensive tussle with the two centre-halves, Challis and Luckings, outstanding.

There was no scoring until 15 minutes from time when Thurley ran on to a short pass and netted with a fine angled shot. Mollison had to receive the trainer's attention after a desperate dive at a forward's feet and Stock missed a chance before danger to the Swifts' goal passed. Late in the game there were exciting incidents at both ends. Webb prevented an almost certain goal by taking the ball from Thurley's feet and Swifts had a let-off when Coe lobbed the ball against a post with Mollison out of position.

The cup and plaques were presented by Mr Howard Pyle a Vice-President of the League.

Source : Bishop's Stortford Swifts

BISHOP'S STORTFORD SWIFTS

PREMIER DIVISION CHALLENGE CUP FINAL

SAWBRIDGEWORTH 3 POTTER STREET 1

By defeating Potter Street in the final of the Premier Division Cup at Rhodes Avenue Sawbridgeworth not only gained a trophy, but also helped to erase the memory of their last final appearance when they lost 10-4 to High Laver.

The game produced little good football and there were long periods of dull, uninteresting play. There were flashes of constructive play, but they were few and far between. Potter Street had the misfortune to lose outside-right Wood with a shoulder injury at the latter half of end of the first half, but Sawbridgeworth would probably have won without the advantage of having an extra man. They looked more dangerous in front of goal while the Street failed to take advantage of their opportunities.

Source : Herts & Essex Observer

Source : Herts & Essex Observer

Presenting the cups and medals at the Annual Presentation Evening in 1960, Mr George Wilson, President, spoke of the important place filled by young players in football. He said they were the senior players and possibly the 'big names' of the future.

STORTFORD LEAGUE FINALS WERE BETTER SUPPORTED

At the League's Annual General Meeting, Mr Bruty introduced Mr Wilson who said he was pleased to see such a large gathering and that the interest in junior football was great and that junior players start off in junior leagues leading to senior football.

The League Secretary, Mr Baker, said that the past season had been very successful. The League's Cup Finals had also been more of a success last season, the weather being more kind. He said, 'the Cup Final gates are our lifeline, and we are very grateful to Bishop's Stortford Football Club for the loan of their ground.'

Mr Baker went on to say that the League was not successful in the Inter-League competition. Mr Reed reported that the Social Account was growing each year and stood at £81 7s 0d.

At the meeting there was a proposal from the Saffron Walden club to a new rule – 'In the Final Tie, the League will refund to the two competing teams the second-class railway or bus fares, whichever is the cheapest, at return rates for 13 players. This would be in addition to the present rule regarding a replayed tie.' It was pointed out the League's finances would suffer, and the proposal was defeated.

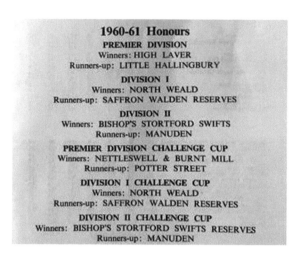

Source : Herts & Essex Observer

SAWBRIDGEWORTH 7 TAKELEY 0

PREMIER DIVISION

BISHOP'S STORTFORD SWIFTS 10 TAKELEY 0

PREMIER DIVISION

Bottom-of-the-table Takeley proved no match for Bishop's Stortford Swifts at Cricketfield Lane with the hometown taking the points by ten clear goals.

Source : Herts & Essex Observer

HATFIELD HEATH 0 EASTON & DUTON HILL 2

PREMIER DIVISION

Source : Herts & Essex Observer

Source : Herts & Essex Observer

DIVISION II CHALLENGE CUP FINAL

BISHOP'S STORTFORD SWIFTS RESERVES 5 MANUDEN 0

Winning the Division II Cup in a manner which left no doubt as to their superiority, Bishop's Stortford Swifts Reserves played some of the best football seen at Rhodes Avenue that season. They were in a completely different class to Manuden, the holders of the trophy, who never gave up trying but were rarely in the game.

Source : Herts & Essex Observer

DIVISION I CHALLENGE CUP FINAL

NORTH WEALD 5 NEWPORT 1

There was never any doubt about the ultimate result of the Division I Challenge Cup final between North Weald and Newport. Better equipped all round, North Weald had much the greater share of the game and gained an easy 5-1 win. Long before the end Newport were a well beaten team although to their credit they tried hard right up until the final whistle.

The Cup and medals were presented by Mr H Pyle.

PREMIER DIVISION CHALLENGE CUP FINAL

NETTESWELL & BURNT MILL 4 POTTER STREET 0

After enjoying territorial advantage for a major part of the first half at Rhodes Avenue, Potter Street allowed Netteswell and Burnt Mill to take the initiative and win by four clear goals.

There was little danger to either goal until Burnt Mill took the lead, against the run of play, in the 35th minute Fox made progress down the right-wing and his centre was pushed out to Cox who netted with neat shot.

At the start of the second half Potter Street were forced back on the defensive, falling further in arrears when Barnard completely misjudged Kurley's centre-come-shot in the 55th minute. Two minutes later Driver took advantage of another error by Barnard, who fumbled a harmless looking shot and allowed the ball to run loose.

Although Bentley once made a splendid interception to prevent a goal Burnt Mill were in complete control and it came as no surprise when Cox put them further in front a quarter of an hour from time.

The cup and medals were presented by Mr G H Wilson.

Source : Harlow Citizen

Holding the 1961 Premier Division Challenge Cup Netteswell and Burnt Mill skipper Frank Kurley chaired by Peter Bentley and Alec Reid after they had won the trophy.

Source : Herts & Essex Observer

Presentations were made at the League's Annual Dinner in 1961 to two of its officers who had outstanding records of voluntary service. The Honorary Secretary for the past fifteen years, Mr R E Baker, the recipient of a cigarette lighter, had only been absent from only one League meeting during that time. Mr W A Bruty, to whom a silver cigarette case was presented, had an almost equally impressive record, having missed only three meetings during the thirteen years he had been Chairman. The presentations were made by Mr George Wilson, President of the League, who presided over a gathering of about 250.

Proposing the toast to 'the League,' Mr Howard Pyle, Vice-President, said that he had enjoyed 'roughly 25 years' playing experience in the competition, referred to the formation of the Bishop's Stortford and District Junior League in 1922 and its amalgamation with the Stansted and District League fourteen years later. They were fortunate to have had the competition to provide continuous football over that period, Mr Pyle remarked, 'It is one of the best leagues to be found locally.'

Speaking appreciatively of the support received from Mr George Wilson, who was also President of Bishop's Stortford Football Club, Mr Pyle expressed the view that Bishop's Stortford had done more for junior players than any other local senior club.

Mr Pyle also praised the work of the officers of the League, particularly that of Mr Bruty, who was a former Hatfield Heath player and Secretary, and was now the area representative on the Essex FA. 'Where he goes from there, your guess is as good as mine.'

Mr Bruty, who replied, spoke of the rivalry between the Bishop's Stortford, Hertford and Harlow Leagues and of its value in fostering friendship between players and officials. Thanking his fellow officers and associating Mrs A J H Kime, wife of the Press and Results Secretary, with his remarks, Mr Bruty said that ensuring 490 fixtures being played, the Fixture Secretary Mr R C Harrison, arranged a total of 681 games.

Adding his thanks to Bishop's Stortford FC, Mr Bruty said, 'I know they pinch a number of our good players, but we must not grumble – it's a good thing for junior football.' Mr Bruty thanked the referees and appealed to them to ease the shortage by taking more junior matches.

This Annual presentation was the first to be followed by dancing rather than just a dinner.

SMOOTH RUNNING OF LOCAL JUNIOR FOOTBALL LEAGUE

At the League's Annual General Meeting, Honorary Secretary, Mr R E Baker said in his report on the past season, it had been a great success and the League had run very smoothly.

The Treasurer, Mr G Reed, said that they finished last season with £48 8s 1d cash at the bank in their general account. The social account was in a very healthy state with a balance of £82 13s 10d.

During recent years, the Bishop's Stortford Football Club have looked more and more to the League for recruits for senior football.

They have not been disappointed, for on a recent Saturday no fewer than no fewer than 15 of the 22 players wearing Stortford's colours came from clubs competing in the League.

I believe that actually 21 players from the League appeared for Bishop's Stortford Football Club during the season.

1961-62 Honours

PREMIER DIVISION
Winners: HIGH LAVER
Runners-up: BISHOP'S STORTFORD SWIFTS

DIVISION I
Winners: HEATH ROVERS
Runners-up: HATFIELD BROAD OAK

DIVISION II
Winners: POTTER STREET RESERVES
Runners-up: BIRCHANGER

PREMIER DIVISION CHALLENGE CUP
Winners: POTTER STREET
Runners-up: SAWBRIDGEWORTH

DIVISION I CHALLENGE CUP
Winners: ELSENHAM
Runners-up: HATFIELD BROAD OAK

DIVISION II CHALLENGE CUP
Winners: BIRCHANGER
Runners-up: HIGH LAVER RESERVES

The affairs of the League were managed up to season 1960/61 by the League Council, which consisted of the Officers and one elected delegate from each competing club. However, from season 1961/62 it decided to conduct its affairs by a Management Committee. This Committee consisted of the Officers and two members from any two clubs in each division. By this latter method the meetings, held on the first Thursday in each month were reduced from approximately 35 to 40 delegates to 13.

At the October Management Committee meeting, the Chairman said he was very pleased to inform the meeting of a very great pleasure he had at the County Association meeting to hear of Mr Harvey of Langley Football Club standing as Honorary Secretary for 33 years and he would be honoured at a later date.

RHODES AVENUE 0

HEATH ROVERS 2

DIVISION I

Source : Herts & Essex Observer

Source : Herts & Essex Observer

HATFIELD HEATH 1 LITTLE HALLINGBURY 2

PREMIER DIVISION

The heavy going proved a handicap to both sides in the local derby.

Source : Herts & Essex Observer

ELSENHAM 5 HARTAM ROVERS 1

DIVISION I CHALLENGE CUP

Elsenham's 5-1 win over Hartam Rovers in the Division I Challenge Cup quarter finals was a personal triumph for centre-forward Blackwell, who scored four goals.

Source : Herts & Essex Observer

RHODES AVENUE 4

BISHOP'S STORTFORD SWIFTS RESERVES 1

DIVISION I

After a season or two in the doldrums, Rhodes Avenue staged a welcome revival.

Source : Herts & Essex Observer

SAWBRIDGEWORTH 3 DEBDEN 0

PREMIER DIVISION CUP SEMI-FINAL

At the April Management Committee meeting, the Chairman spoke of High Laver Sports and said this season they have won the League's Premier Division and this was the third year running they had won it and wondered if the League could present them with a special trophy for their achievement.

It was decided to present High Laver Sports with a special trophy.

Source : Herts & Essex Observer

BISHOP'S STORTFORD SWIFTS RESERVES 2

HEATH ROVERS 2

DIVISION I

It was a red-letter day for Heath Rovers at Cricketfield Lane, goals by Derek Maynard enabling them to pull back a 2-0 deficit and become Division I champions. There was a double celebration, too, for Ron Hampton, who became the fifth Rovers player to notch 50 first team appearance. Heath Rovers reached the Premier Division after only three years in the League and the fourth of their existence.

PREMIER DIVISION CHALLENGE CUP FINAL

SAWBRIDGEWORTH 1 P0TTER STREET 1

(Abandoned during Extra-Time)

During the first period of extra-time in the final of the 1961/62 Premier Division Cup between Sawbridgeworth and Potter Street at Rhodes Avenue, the light became so bad that the referee was forced to divest himself of his black jacket because it was causing confusion against the Sawbridgeworth team's strip. For some minutes he was running around in a singlet and shorts until a suitable shirt could be found. The game was eventually abandoned, and the match replayed.

There was no score in the first half. The scoring was opened eight minutes after the restart, Wright heading in Wood's cross. Reverting to defensive tactics, Potter Street looked likely to hang on to their slender lead until Stafford, coming up with the forwards, made the opening for Revell to equalise.

Source : Herts & Essex Observer

SAWBRIDGEWORTH

Source : Herts & Essex Observer

BIRCHANGER

DIVISION II CHALLENGE CUP FINAL

BIRCHANGER 3 HIGH LAVER RESERVES 2

Birchanger carried off the Division II Cup at Rhodes Avenue beating High Laver Reserves 3-2. While they fully deserved their win there were times when the defence adopted desperate measures, which were not always justified, to break up High Laver's attacks

Gradually getting into their stride, Birchanger forged ahead in the 26th minute, P Brown netting with a sharp drive that W French allowed to slip through his hands. This success was short-lived as four minutes later J Hawkins equalised with a terrific drive that gave A E Banks no chance.

Ten minutes after the restart G Sampford restored Birchanger's lead with a magnificent header and gave them the confidence they had been lacking.

The result was put virtually beyond doubt after 77 minutes when G Sampford got his second goal.

Laver's A Winright broke through on one or two occasions, but his low centres deceived everyone, including his own forwards. It was not until the last minute that High Laver reduced the deficit, A Porter scoring from Hawkins' centre.

Source : Herts & Essex Observer

DIVISION I CHALLENGE CUP FINAL

ELSENHAM 2

HATFIELD BROAD OAK 1

As was anticipated, in view of the strength of both teams, the final at Rhodes Avenue was very closely contested with the result in doubt right up until the final whistle.

The scoring was opened 10 minutes before the interval, Rawlinson crossing for R Blackwell to head a neat goal in an Elsenham break away.

The scores were levelled in the 55th minute, however, a move down the middle enabling B Field to run through and beat Blackwell with a deflected shot.

After Elsenham had survived further pressure on their goal, Cook, at the other end, dealt with one or two long range shots before the Broad Oak defence was split wide open by a movement on the Elsenham left-wing in the 80th minute and Jones steered the ball just inside the post for the decisive goal.

PREMIER DIVISION CHALLENGE CUP FINAL REPLAY

POTTER STREET 2 SAWBRIDGEWORTH 1

Losing finalists in the two previous seasons, Potter Street found it third time lucky at Rhodes Avenue. Although they were on top for most of the match the Street did not get the decisive goal until 10 minutes from time.

Potter Street had the incentive of an early lead, Freestone making the opening in the third minute for Wright to leave Warwick well beaten.

Sawbridgeworth's equaliser in the 33rd minute came from the penalty spot, Revell being the successful marksman after Kirby was fouled by the goalkeeper.

Defences dominated the game until the 80th minute when a free kick on the edge of the Sawbridgeworth penalty area taken by Snell was punched out by Warwick to Freeman, who netted from close range through a crowd of players.

TAKELEY FOOTBALL CLUB IS DISBANDED

Takeley Football Club is to be disbanded. This was the decision made after a long discussion at the club's annual meeting.

The main reasons are financial and lack of support generally. The accounts presented by Mr M J Shuttlewood, Treasurer, showed a debit of £5.

The Chairman, Mr B Robinson, and the Treasurer, were appointed trustees.

Takeley Football Club has had a continuous existence of over 30 years and since the Second World War has once held the championship of the Bishop's Stortford and Stansted and District League and twice runners-up.

The decline in the club's fortunes began a few years ago when the ground was changed from the centre of the village to a rather inaccessible spot in Hatfield Forest.

At the meeting, the President, Mr A L Frost, referred to the great loss sustained by the club in the death of Mr H Rusher who for many years had helped in every possible way. Mr Rusher acted as linesman, groundsman, team secretary and in fact in any capacity he could be of service.

SHIELD TO MARK TREBLE

Source : Herts & Essex Observer

As a memento of winning the Premier Division for the third consecutive season, High Laver were presented with a special commemorative shield at the League's annual Presentation evening in 1962.

Mr V R Knight, Vice-Chairman of the Delphian League, said that frequently league officials were referees, as he was himself. Footballers sometimes saw a bad referee, but referees sometimes saw bad footballers, which was a point should not be forgotten by the players.

STORTFORD LEAGUE MAKE-UP

At the League's Annual General Meeting it was proposed that to save travelling long distances Division II would be split into North and South zones. Mr Kime, Vice-President, asked if clubs paid a differential rate with coaches on long and short journeys. The Little Hallingbury club confirmed that they did on longer journeys.

Mr Kime proposed that the committee's recommendations for the Divisions be adopted. This was seconded by Little Hallingbury and carried.

However, the 1962/63 normal season was abandoned due to the very bad weather conditions.

1962/63 SEASON		
League Competition	**Winners**	**Runners up**
Premier Division	Bishop's Stortford Swifts	Potter Street
Division I	Elsenham	Little Hallingbury
Division II	No Competition (Abandoned)	
League Cup		
Premier Division	Hatfield Heath	Bishop's Stortford Swifts
Division I	Elsenham	Manuden
Division II	No Competition (Abandoned)	

Source : Herts & Essex Observer

BISHOP'S STORTFORD SWIFTS 2 HATFIELD HEATH 3

PREMIER DIVISION

With his head between the ball and a team-mate's knee, this was an uncomfortable moment for Roy Nicholls, the Hatfield Heath centre-half.

**GREAT HALLINGBURY 3
MATCHING UNITED 4**

DIVISION 2 SOUTH

Although they dominated the game for long periods, Great Hallingbury's hundred percent record went by the board when they were beaten on their own ground by Matching United. The game was marred by a number of unfortunate incidents, culminating with a United player being sent off and Capewell, of Great Hallingbury, being carried off four minutes before time.

Source : Herts & Essex Observer

At the start of the season Sawbridgeworth had intended to change their colours to Black Shirts with white trimmings which the League had taken exception to.

At the October Management Committee meeting the Chairman said he had spoken to Sawbridgeworth's Honorary Secretary, Mr G Stafford, about the colours and Mr Stafford said they were seeing a taylor in Sawbridgeworth to see if anything could be done about the shirts and if his answer was no, Sawbridgeworth were going to buy a new set of shirts. Sawbridgeworth had had a fortnight in which to alter them and until that time was up the League could not do anything and he asked the matter to be left to him, this was agreed.

At the following meeting in November, League Secretary, Mr Baker, explained the telephone conversation he had with the Chairman, Mr Bruty. Mr Bruty had visited Sawbridgeworth and said the shirts had had a white band inserted on the front of the shirts and had had a conversation with a referee who was satisfied with them, but, Mr Bruty said that if further complaints were received we would have to go into the matter then.

.

Source : Herts & Essex Observer

HATFIELD BROAD OAK 1 HATFIELD HEATH 2

PREMIER DIVISION CUP

Hatfield Broad Oak's chance of progressing in the Cup received a severe jolt when they were forced to kick off a man short. It was not until the 35th minute that Clarke put in an appearance and by then the Heath were in front. For the remainder of the game the home team staged a spirited revival but were unable to get on level terms.

The winter of 1962-63 was the coldest for 200 years in Britain. It began abruptly just before Christmas in 1962. The weeks before had been changeable and stormy, but then on 22 December a high-pressure system moved to the north-east of the British Isles, dragging bitterly cold winds across the country. This situation was to last much of the winter.

As can be seen from the photos taken at Rhodes Avenue, the home of Bishop's Stortford Football Club, terrible conditions led to sporting events all over the country were severely disrupted including the Bishop's Stortford, Stanstead and District League.

Source : Herts & Essex Observer

Source : Herts & Essex Observer

In February 1963, the League recognised the impossibility of making up the fixture leeway caused by the freeze-up and abandoned the outstanding programme.

The Premier Division and Division I were divided into groups of six teams, the winners of each group playing off for the divisional championships.

The League cups continued, and in fact would be the only programmes for Division II teams. Promotion and relegation were suspended.

Correspondence was received in March from the Herford League regarding the Inter-League match. After discussion it was proposed by Mr Harrision that owing to the weather conditions and the congestion of fixtures, we withdraw from the Inter-League competition for this season. Withdrawal from the competition was agreed.

The committee also decided that owing to the very adverse weather and the season's very congested fixture list and the subsidiary competition all clubs be allowed to play not more than two senior players in any games for the remainder of the season. A senior player is one who has played 6 or more games in a senior division.

BOY 'KEEPER DIES IN CUP TIE

In April 1963, with his parents, younger brother and sister watching from the touchline, 16 years-old Michael Dover, the Albury goalkeeper, was fatally injured just before half-time in a match against Elsenham.

As he went out to gather the ball Michael was in collision with one of his own team, fell to the ground and did not recover. He was taken to the Herts & Essex General Hospital, Bishop's Stortford, and found to have passed away.

The first reaction of the team was not to play again that season, but Mr Horace Dover, a former player, and the current club Secretary, told them, 'Don't give up playing, carry on and win. My son would have wanted it that way.'

Source:

Barbara Hudgell

Michael Dover was still attending Hadham Hall School where he was also a top performer at basketball, athletics, gymnastics and tennis. He hoped to take up accountancy when he left but would have welcomed a career in football and gave every promise of achieving that ambition. One of the best young goalkeepers in the district, he had already attracted the attention of senior clubs, and Arsenal's Chief Scout intended to come and watch him play.

Michael's ability had twice impressed a Bishop's Stortford representative and it had been hoped he would join the club for the following season.

At Hadham Hall School plans were made to buy a special cup in his memory. Captain A W Mack, the Physical Education master said, 'We shall inscribe it The Michael Dover Cup and it would be for every year.'

Albury Church was filled to capacity for the funeral of Michael Dover. The pathway to the church was lined with nearly a hundred wreaths, many of them from football clubs against whom Michael had played.

As the coffin was carried into the church a guard of honour was formed by players from Albury and Elsenham, who met in the young goalkeeper's last match. Among those that were present were representatives of the Albury club, of the Bishop's Stortford, Stansted and District League, and most of the teams that play in it. They were joined by many local residents including Prince Frederick of Prussia and Princess Bridget, fellow pupils and members of the staff at Hadham Hall School.

In his address the Rector of Little Hadham, the Reverend Peter Bide, who officiated, praised Michael's habit of always doing his best in whatever field he chose to exert himself.

DEATH OF FOOTBALL ENTHUSIAST, MR A L RUSHFORTH

One of 58 year-old Mr A L Rushforth's main interests was football. At the time of his death he was Vice-President of the Newport Football Club and Vice-Chairman of the League. For some years he was Chairman of Newport.

In his younger days, Mr Rushforth played for Walden Town. His hometown was Saffron Walden until he moved to Newport in 1949.

Mr Rushforth left a wife and three children.

At the May Management Committee, the Chairman opened the meeting by a few moments silence for Mr Dover and Mr Rushforth.

Mr Thorne reported on the inquest of Mr Dover. A letter to Mr Bruty from Mrs Rushforth was read to the committee.

DIVISION I CHALLENGE CUP FINAL

ELSENHAM 3 MANUDEN 1

In one of the best League Cup Finals seen at Rhodes Avenue for many years, Elsenham took the Division I trophy by beating Manuden 3-1. Two players stood out in a match that provided the large crowd with plenty of action and thrills – Adrian Jones of Elsenham and Peter Stooks, the losers' goalkeeper.

Hat trick specialist Jones got another and Stooks was in great form bringing off a number of magnificent saves.

Jones opened the scoring after 15 minutes with a great shot, which Stooks could only palm into the top corner of the net.

After 25 minutes good approach work by Jaggard and Rawlinson made the opening for Jones' second goal, and 10 minutes later he completed his hat trick with an effort which would have graced any match. A pass was sent through to him at waist high and, with his back to the goal, Jones swivelled to hook the ball past Stooks.

Five minutes after the change of ends Manuden reduced the leeway through the persistence of Trigg, which had been apparent in the first period. Neatly robbing Suckling and goalkeeper Suckling, he virtually walked the ball into the net.

PREMIER DIVISION CUP FINAL

HATFIELD HEATH 4 BISHOP'S STORTFORD SWIFTS 2

On the defensive for two-thirds of the game, Hatfield Heath shocked the Swifts by twice breaking away to score in the closing minutes at Rhodes Avenue.

Swifts went straight into the attack and when Mick Thurley opened their account in the 14th minute it looked like the signal for a runaway victory.

Part of the attraction of football, however, is its uncertainty and a few seconds before the interval the underdogs got on level terms through Roy Howard, who just beat Mollison to a centre from the left.

There was another shock in store for Swifts in the 47th minute, Peter Nicholls putting them in arrears with a fine solo effort in which he evaded three determined tackles before cutting in and shooting past Mollison.

From that point it was all Swifts, and the equaliser just had to come, the scorer being Les Stock, who calmly chipped the ball past Turner instead of blazing at the net.

Putting everything in attack, Swifts were caught on the hop when a breakaway on the right saw Roy Howard beat Hunt in a race for possession and net from a narrow angle.

It was Heath's reward for sticking grimly to their task could easily have resigned themselves to defeat, and two minutes later they clinched the issue, Peter Nicholls scoring with a close-range shot.

PREMIER DIVISION SUBSIDIARY COMPETITION

BISHOP'S STORTFORD SWIFTS 5 POTTER STREET 1

Potter Street were hammered into defeat by a much superior side in the final of the League Subsidiary Competition at Rhodes Avenue. All soccer skills came from the Swifts, who dominated the play and made Potter Street look a very uncultured team.

Potter Street had the edge for 15 minutes at the start of the game when Swifts were without Fred Maskell.

During this spell Street scored their only goal, netted in the seventh minute by centre-forward Bernard Walters from a cross by inside- left Crossan.

Potter Street's dominance came to an end in the 15th minute when Maskell, a last-minute replacement for Stock, completed Swifts team.

From the moment Maskell stepped on to the pitch – he started with a raid on the right-wing – Swifts gave their opponents the run-around.

In the 26th minute they got a deserved equaliser, Haskell lofting the ball into the penalty area for Mick Thurley to head home.

Five minutes before the interval centre-forward Ray Hammond netted to give Swifts the lead – from a Maskell pass.

In the second half Swifts cruised home easy winners, additional goals coming from Mick Thurley, Ray Hammond and Fred Maskell.

Source : Herts & Essex Observer

ELSENHAM

Last season was Elsenham's best ever in spite of the difficulties caused by the freeze-up. Beaten only five times in 34 matches, they achieved a notable hat trick by winning the

Division I League and Challenge Cup competition, together with the Saffron Walden District knock-out cup.

The team scored a total of 151 goals with 51 against, the ace marksman being Adrian Jones, who netted 62 to break the club record for the second successive time.

SURPRISE PRESENTATION AT FOOTBALL DINNER

Source : Herts & Essex Observer

League Officers and their guests at the Annual Dinner and Dance.

Mr Charles French, Secretary of Sheering Football Club and Mr Howard Pyle, Treasurer of Hatfield Heath Football Club, were awarded long service certificates of the Essex Football Association.

The surprise presentation of the certificates was made at the Annual Dinner and Dance of the League by the President Mr George Wilson.

Mr French, a committee member of the Sheering club from 1919 to 1939 and from 1947, was also Secretary of the West Essex Border Charity Cup and was formerly a referee for 21 years.

Mr Pyle was a committee member of the League from 1947 to 1959, President of the Junior Inter-League Cup since 1955, President of the West Essex Border Charity Cup from 1952 and Treasurer of Hatfield Heath Football Club for 18 years.

Proposing the toast to the ladies and guests, Mr W Bruty, League Chairman, welcomed guests who included representatives of the Harlow, Thurrock Thames-side and Hertford Leagues and from the Bishop's Stortford and Harlow clubs.

There were special tributes to Bishop's Stortford FC. Referring to the club's Amateur Cup run, 'To be in the last eight out of 202 clubs is a dam fine performance,' said Mr Bruty.

Replying to the toast, Mr H W White, President of the Thurrock Thames-side Combination, congratulated Bishop's Stortford Swifts – 'an up and coming club for several years' – for winning the Premier Division.

DEATH OF MR 'BOB' BAKER ANNOUNCED

Secretary of the League since full-scale activities were resumed in 1946, following the wartime activities, Mr Bob Baker, was suddenly taken ill at his home and sadly passed away.

Aged just 47, Mr Baker was a native of Rye Park, but had lived in Bishop's Stortford for the past 24 years. In his younger days he played football for Nazeing and later became a referee.

During the last war he served with the 8th Army signals at Alamein and throughout the victorious desert campaign later going with the 'Desert Rats' to Italy where he was awarded the British Empire Medal.

LEAGUE REJECT HIGHER FEES FOR REFEREES

A move to increase the match fee for referees to 15 shillings a game in the League, to bring them into line with other leagues, was defeated at the League's Annual General Meeting.

Club representatives were told that other local leagues had increased the fees to 15 shillings which in some ways enticed referees away from the League – paid 12/6d a game.

Mr Lionel Thorne, the Referees' Secretary, opposed the amendment to the rules. He said that referees did the job for the love of the sport and money was not of prime importance. By not increasing the fees he did not think that it would lead to an even more acute shortage of referees.

By a very narrow vote the amendment to the rule was lost. Mr R Harrison, the Fixture Secretary, termed the past season as 'one of the most difficult' as far as fixtures were concerned.

At the beginning of the season 408 games were arranged. At the start of the bad weather 211 had been played. In early February, the position was the same, so the League programme had to be scrapped in favour of an emergency competition.

A special meeting was called to re-arrange the Officers of the League following the death of Mr Baker.

The Chairman opened the meeting with a few moments silence in memory of the late Honorary Secretary Mr R E Baker B.E.M.

The Chairman threw the meeting open for suggestions for Honorary Secretary after informing the meeting of his views on the matter. After a lengthy discussion it was decided unanimously that Mr Harrison resign his Vice-Chairmanship in order to fill the vacancy of Honorary Secretary. Mr Harrison agreed and thanked the meeting for their confidence placed in him. He also agreed to carry on as Fixtures Secretary on view of the difficulty in being able to fill this office. Mr Harrison then stated that in order to carry out these two offices it was essential that he had an assistant. Mr George Reed was elected Honorary Assistant-Secretary in addition to his present office of Honorary Treasurer.

Mr Thorne was elected to fill the vacancy of Vice-Chairman caused by the resignation of Mr Harrison. Mr Thorne was also to continue in his present position of Honorary Referees Secretary. Both Mr Reed and Mr Thorne agreed to take their new additional offices and both suitably thanked the meeting.

Mr Reed then stated that he received a letter from Debden Football Club with regard to a fund being raised in appreciation of the long service given to the League by Mr Baker. The Management Committee were also of this opinion and it was decided to open such a fund and on the proposition of Mr Camp and seconded by Mr G Banks and carried the fund to be called the Mr R E Baker Memorial Fund, and all clubs advised of its existence thus giving them the opportunity subscribe if they so desired. The Honorary Secretary advised them, as necessary.

The Chairman then suggested that owing to the fact that we had several Hertfordshire clubs in membership of the League we should affiliate to the Hertfordshire Football Association in addition to the Essex County Football Association. This was carried.

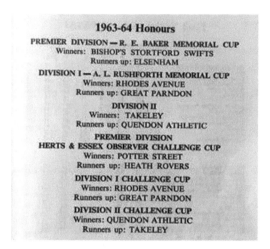

Takeley's first team reappeared for the 1963/64 season and were promoted at the end of the season as Division II champions. The club lost only one of their 22 games and scoring 178 goals.

At the September Management Committee the Honorary Treasurer announced that the R E Baker Memorial Fund stood at £14 14s 0d.

Mr Thorne proposed that the League donate to both the Hertfordshire and Essex Football Associations' Benevolent Funds. The Chairman proposed we donate £2 2s 0d and this was carried.

After the Annual General Meeting Blue Star, Brent Pelham, Epping Youth and Great Hallingbury withdrew before the season started

In September 1963 Jim Hartley made his 100th first team appearance for Heath Rovers and became the first of the club's players to achieve that distinction.

Source : Herts & Essex Observer

SHEERING 3 BISHOP'S STORTFORD SWIFTS 9

PREMIER DIVISION

Stortford Swifts had little difficulty in preserving their unbeaten League record.

Source : Herts & Essex Observer

BISHOP'S STORTFORD SWIFTS

BISHOP'S STORTFORD SWIFTS RESERVES 0

RHODES AVENUE 5

DIVISION I

Their performance in the top-of-the-table clash at Cricketfield Lane stamped Rhodes Avenue, who had a 100 percent record, as worthy leaders of Division I. In midfield there was little to choose between the two teams, but Swifts Reserves could not match the power of Ron Bonney and John McCarthy in Avenue's attack.

The Rhodes Avenue team were runaway winners of the Division I championship and completed the double by taking the Division I Challenge Cup.

RHODES AVENUE 5 HARTAM ROVERS 0

DIVISION I

BISHOP'S STORTFORD SWIFTS 4 DEBDEN 2

PREMIER DIVISION

Already assured of the Premier Division championship, the Swifts still had an important target in their final game – to preserve their unbeaten run.

Showing considerably improved form, they achieved their ambition, repeating the previous season's impressive performance.

Starting off in fine style, Swifts looked as though they would get a hatful of goals, but it was Debden who opened the scoring. Allowed plenty of room by Barltrop, the left-winger crossed for Diggons to crash the ball into the net.

Responding in a lively manner to the set-back, the home team went close to equalising on several occasions, the Debden goalkeeper coming into the picture with some good saves.

Eventually Les Stock pulled the ball back from the bye-line for the diving Mick Thurley to level the scores with his 50th goal of the season.

Keeping control of the game after the break, Swifts went further ahead when Mick Thurley ran on to a through pass and netted. After Les Stock had headed the fourth goal, the home team relaxed somewhat, but without losing the initiative. Stock and Mick Thurley both forced the goalkeeper to make good saves.

When Debden reduced the arrears, it was from the penalty spot. Diggons making no mistake after Smith had unnecessarily handled the ball.

DIVISION II CHALLENGE CUP FINAL

QUENDON ATHLETIC 2 TAKELEY 1

Runaway winners of League Division II, Takeley were confidently expected to complete the double in the Cup Final at Rhodes Avenue, but Quendon Athletic upset the form book by winning 2-1.

Both goals had narrow escapes before Quendon opened the scoring in the 42nd minute, Waites snapping up Eldred's back-pass and scoring with a simple shot that went in off Day's legs.

The second half was only three minutes old when Grandsen increased Athletic's lead following a corner on the right.

DIVISION I CHALLENGE CUP FINAL

RHODES AVENUE 3 GREAT PARNDON I

Source : Herts & Essex Observer

RHODES AVENUE

Jubilant Rhodes Avenue players chair their skipper, Brian King, after completing the Division I double. The club remained unbeaten in the League winning 20 0f 22 matches scoring 111 goals.

There was no real excitement until the 15th minute, when D Bonney was brought down in the penalty area, but from the spot R Bonney blazed his shot high over the bar.

In the second half, having been forced back on the defensive, Avenue were somewhat fortunate to find themselves in front after 62 minutes. Porter, who had a very quiet first half, ran on to King's through pass and his shot from a narrow angle passed under Knight's body and headed it inside the post.

A minute later Knight dropped the ball when harassed by McCarthy, who slipped it to Porter and banged in the return pass from close range.

Avenue's lead was quickly reduced, a Haywood corner being headed into the goalmouth by Elliott out of Bruty's reach, Springham's attempted clearance cannoning off Pegg into the net.

Minutes from time McCarthy netted his second goal putting the result beyond doubt.

The Herts and Essex Observer had gifted a trophy to the League and it was named The Herts and Essex Observer Cup for the winners of the Premier Division Challenge Cup Final.

At this time, the League decided to purchase new cups for the League Championships. It was agreed to purchase three in all, at a cost of £40. It was proposed by D Camp and seconded by D Wright that the Division I Cup should be engraved 'A L Rushforth Memorial Cup' subject to permission of Mrs Rushforth. Permission was given by Mrs Rushforth.

PREMIER DIVISION CHALLENGE CUP FINAL

THE HERTS & ESSEX OBSERVER CUP

POTTER STREET 3 HEATH ROVERS 0

It was a new Premier Division Cup, known as The Herts & Essex Observer Cup, for which Potter Street and Heath Rovers played at Rhodes Avenue at the end of the 1963/64 season.

Once again, the under-dogs came out on top. Having been successful in both League matches, Heath Rovers were clear favourites to beat Potter Street but were defeated in no uncertain manner.

It was a 30-second goal which started the Rovers' slide, Richard Hoad dropping a corner, the fifth kick of the game, on to the foot of Mick Greenhouse, who banged the ball into the net.

Four minutes after the interval, Gordon Freeman increased Potter Street's lead, having hit the bar a minute earlier.

He rushed in to scramble the ball over the line when a fine header by Lou Greenhouse rebounded from the post.

The issue was put beyond doubt a quarter of an hour from the end, McKenzie mistiming Mick Greenhouse's low drive from 25 yards.

Two minutes from time David Wood, schemer-in-chief of the Potter Street attacks, pushed a long pass between two defenders, Gordon Freeman bringing the ball under control. and slipping it through from close range.

Source : Herts & Essex Observer

Source : Dave Wood

POTTER STREET

HERT'S JUNIOR CUP FINAL

BISHOP'S STORTFORD SWIFTS 1 CROXLEY CASUALS 2

Bishop's Stortford Swifts were hoping to become the only junior side to have the chance to win the Hert's Junior Cup since 1927 when Sawbridgeworth had won the title.

In the final, Swifts had to play Croxley Casuals from the Watford & District League at Clarence Park, St Albans. The game was originally to be played on Good Friday but was postponed after an inspection found the pitch to be waterlogged and re-arranged to be played on April 9th.

In the re-arranged game, played in windy conditions on a now bone-dry pitch, the Casuals took the lead in the first half, but Stock managed to equalise for Swifts just before half-time. After 58 minutes Croxley were reduced to ten men and from that moment were hardly in the match, except that Swifts were simply unable to put the ball in the net. The game went into extra-time with Swifts constantly on the attack and Croxley defending stubbornly. In the 108th minute, however, Croxley managed to scrape a winning goal against all the odds.

A CELEBRATION DINNER FOR FOOTBALL CHAMPIONS

SUCCESS AFTER YEAR IN WILDERNESS

Takeley Football Club champions of Division II of the League, and runners-up in the Division II Challenge Cup, held a celebration dinner and dance at the Silver Jubilee Hall. Some 115 players, supporters and friends attended.

President Mr A L Frost, presided, and said the club had no money, no team and no ground. Now they had an excellent ground, a good team, and a substantial bank balance.

This success, he said was due to the hard work of the officers, committee, and members – and to the wholehearted support of all sections of the community.

Next season, he continued, the club would be in Division I of the League, and it hoped to run a second team in Division II.

League Chairman, Mr W A Bruty, proposing the toast to the club, said, how glad they were to have Takeley, a team with a long tradition, back in the League once more.

He was struck, he went on, by the number of young people at the dinner, and he was sure they would do more-good by joining a football club than becoming Mods or Rockers.

Mr Bruty then presented the championship cup to Mr G Perry, captain, and medals to members of the team.

Responding to the toast, Mr R Bradley, Secretary, said the team had won 21 out of 22 League matches, scored 178 goals and had only 27 scored against them, and gained 42 out of 44 possible points.

Proposing the toast to the League, Mr B Robinson, Takeley F C Chairman, said that with the coming growth of population in the area they would have an ever increasing role to play.

They would probably have to organise intermediate football, but there was no doubt the officers of the League would be quite capable of doing so.

Mr Frost then presented an inscribed barometer to Mr Jack Shuttlewood, who served the club for many years as player, captain and Treasurer.

Replying, Mr Shuttlewood said he had enjoyed his long stay with the club and regretted his leaving the village had made it impossible for him to continue to take part in the club's activities.

The toast to the visitors was proposed by Mr D Phillips and responded to by Mr G Reed, League Treasurer.

SPECIAL SHIELD PRESENTED TO THE SWIFTS

Source : Herts & Essex Observer

At the League's Annual Dinner, held at Long's Ballroom, when presentations were given to the successful clubs, cups were also given to the runners-up for the first time.

Bishop's Stortford Swifts were awarded the new Premier Division Championship Cup named the R E Baker Memorial Cup, in memory of the League's late secretary, Mr R E Baker.

Rhodes Avenue were awarded the new Division I Championship Cup named the A L Rushforth Memorial Cup, in memory of the League's late Vice-Chairman.

An additional surprise was in store for Bishop's Stortford Swifts when the League also awarded the club a special shield in honour of its outstanding achievements, Premier Division champions, runners-up in the Premier Division Challenge Cup and the losing Finalists in the Hert's Junior Cup.

Chairman of the League, Mr W A 'Bill' Bruty, proposed a toast to the guests saying that the Cup Finals had been held at Rhodes Avenue, home of Bishop's Stortford FC and, but for them, the League might well have been forced to ask for a little more money from the clubs. Mr Arthur Dimond, Chairman of the Harlow Referees society made a response to the toast.

61 GAMES WERE CANCELLED LAST SEASON

A total of 61 games, or 12.5%, of the matches of the League were cancelled last season. This was 2% higher than the previous season.

Altogether 130 games had to be rearranged by the Secretary and Fixtures Secretary, Mr Roy Harrison. But, on the whole, clubs in the League co-operated 'wonderfully' with fixtures, said Mr Harrison at the League's Annual General Meeting.

The League began the season without two long-serving officials. Four days after the previous Annual Meeting the Secretary Mr 'Bob' Baker, passed away. Earlier Mr A L Rushforth, the Vice-Chairman, also passed away. Two Challenge Cups were dedicated to the memory of the two officials.

Finals of all cups last season were described as 'a great financial success.' The Premier Division Cup, in which the new Herts & Essex Observer trophy was competed for had an income of £48 12s 6d. The Division I final brought in the same and the Division II final just 5s 8d less.

Mr G Reed, Treasurer, reported that the League finished the year with a balance in hand of £64 – £12 up on the previous season.

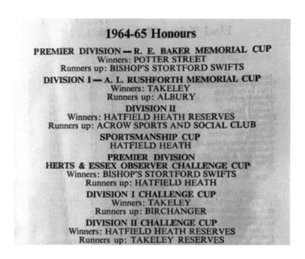

1964-65 Honours

PREMIER DIVISION — R. E. BAKER MEMORIAL CUP
Winners: POTTER STREET
Runners up: BISHOP'S STORTFORD SWIFTS

DIVISION I — A. L. RUSHFORTH MEMORIAL CUP
Winners: TAKELEY
Runners up: ALBURY

DIVISION II
Winners: HATFIELD HEATH RESERVES
Runners up: ACROW SPORTS AND SOCIAL CLUB

SPORTSMANSHIP CUP
HATFIELD HEATH

PREMIER DIVISION
HERTS & ESSEX OBSERVER CHALLENGE CUP
Winners: BISHOP'S STORTFORD SWIFTS
Runners up: HATFIELD HEATH

DIVISION I CHALLENGE CUP
Winners: TAKELEY
Runners up: BIRCHANGER

DIVISION II CHALLENGE CUP
Winners: HATFIELD HEATH RESERVES
Runners up: TAKELEY RESERVES

Little Hallingbury withdrew after the Annual General Meeting and before the season started.

Following the 11th anniversary of Bishop's Stortford Swifts and after just over a decade of playing at Cricketfield Lane the club had to move on.

The Cricketfield Lane ground was due for development for a new school to be built. There had been an unwritten agreement between the Swifts and the Hert's County Education Department, in particular, Northgate End, and they now needed larger premises. While this was a shock to the club at that time, the situation was viewed with mixed feelings. On the one hand they would be losing a pitch with a slope they knew intimately, on the other it was seen as an opportunity to escape the primitive facilities, provided the club could find a better situation.

The Chairman of Bishop's Stortford Swifts, Derek Smith, had an idea of writing to one of the trustees of the ground at Silver Leys, Geoffrey Sparrow, who owned the Sparrows shop in North Street, Bishop's Stortford.

Smith asked if Bishop's Stortford Swifts FC could be considered for a pitch at Silver Leys. 'It was, Mr Sparrow who championed their cause.'

Silver Leys had two football pitches, used by Rhodes Avenue (Premier Division) and Hartam Rovers (Division I). There were also some other buildings that previously formed part of an Italian Prisoner of War Camp at the end of World War II.

Silver Leys was an area of land to the North-West edge of Bishop's Stortford, part of an estate once owned by Tresham Gilbey (a former President of the League), son of Sir Walter Gilbey who had succeeded to the title of Baronet Gilbey of Elsenham Hall, Essex. After Tresham Gilbey's death in 1947, there was difficulty in selling of the estate. Eventually, that part of the land known as Silver Leys was gifted by the estate for the benefit of the town and administered by Trustees.

Almost as famously at this time, Silver Leys was also used to play Polo. Boyd Gibbons was a builder originally from London, who had made his fortune building Council and private estates in the area immediately after the war. He also owned a gravel pit sited on what was, at the time, part of the approach to the then sleepy Stansted Airport. Gibbons was a keen horseman and indulged himself by organising Polo matches that involved teams containing celebrities.

Bishop's Stortford Rugby Club also played at Silver Leys, but both football and rugby were severely affected when horses tore the pitches to shreds. Even in the course of a polo game, during the pause for the next chukka, spectators could be asked to 'heel' the turf to give the horses the benefit of a better surface to give the small hard wooden ball a chance to roll smoothly. There were some in Stortford who did not take to Gibbons, but the town was much taken with the opportunity to see celebrities and sometimes, royalty. These polo events were, therefore, well attended and many welcomed the opportunity to witness a spectacle new to the area.

Swift's Chairman, Derek Smith, was hopeful that his request for a pitch at Silver Leys would be granted. Pending a decision, the club used one of the new pitches at Grange Paddocks, provided by the local Council. While Swifts did have the opportunity to use Grange Paddocks, the playing surface, unfortunately, saw many stones on it. Also, the club had to provide their own nets before the commencement of any games and had no changing facilities. These pitches were sited on land further north of the Causeway and running parallel to the Causeway, with an opening near the Fox public house. The move was only temporary and gave the club the opportunity to carry on playing in the town. The Swifts eventually moved to Silver Leys in December 1964.

While it may not have been realised at the time, the enforced move away from Cricketfield Lane turned out to be a blessing in disguise. The Cricketfield Lane little ground was a school-sized pitch that before each game needed to be remarked and larger goal posts erected. Indeed, it could be argued that had the club not been forced to source its new home at Silver Leys it might not have survived and prospered.

Peter Hunt, one of Swift's founder members, remembers that the hut at Silver Leys was shared for the latter half of the first season with another club, Rhodes Avenue, who played on the adjacent pitch. Swifts were only able to play at Silver Leys when Hartam Rovers, who had previously shared the facilities with Rhodes Avenue until the end of November, had to depart and in fact disbanded at the end of that season. Rhodes Avenue also departed and disbanded at the end of that season.

The Council football pitches at Grange Paddocks were used for the first time in 1964 by Heath Rovers (including Reserves), Millars Sports and temporarily by Bishop's Stortford Swifts (including Reserves).

BISHOP'S STORTFORD SWIFTS 4

HATFIELD HEATH 2

PREMIER DIVISION

This was one which did not get through when Bishop's Stortford Swifts opened their Premier Division programme with a win over Hatfield Heath by 4-2.

Source : Herts & Essex Observer

TAKELEY 6 BIRCHANGER 0

DIVISION I

Birchanger's goalkeeper was caught on the wrong foot when Ken Yates (white shirt) slipped in Takeley's second goal.

Source : Herts & Essex Observer

Source : Herts & Essex Observer

HEATH ROVERS 1 BISHOP'S STORTFORD SWIFTS 3

PREMIER DIVISION CHALLENGE CUP

A misunderstanding between Roberts and Smith soon after the restart gave Fields the opportunity to equalise from close range. However, Bishop's Stortford Swifts went on to win 3-1.

The League planned to re-engrave the Sportsmanship Cup but the cup was too thin. The League agreed to sell the cup and purchase a new one.

The League also agreed that a badge should be awarded to any player who had played three games for the League Representative team.

BISHOP'S STORTFORD SWIFTS 1 HEATH ROVERS 0

PREMIER DIVISION

The Heath Rovers goalkeeper was unable to do anything about Terry Applin's shot which decided the match at Silver Leys.

Source : Herts & Essex Observer

Source : Herts & Essex Observer

ELSENHAM 3 HATFIELD HEATH 0

PREMIER DIVISION

Elsenham come close but were unable to score here but ran out 3-0 winners.

DIVISION II CHALLENGE CUP FINAL

HATFIELD HEATH RESERVES 5 TAKELEY RESERVES 1

The game started at a cracking pace which was maintained throughout the first half, but clearly it couldn't last and the second period was tame by comparison.

Within two minutes of the start a defensive lapse gave Bayford the opportunity to open the scoring, but five minutes Packer equalised after getting possession near the half-way line.

A long and hopeful lob, by Clark put the Heath in front and before the break they scored again though Dave Brown.

The scoring was completed early in the second half. A goalkeeping error left Brown through for his second goal which he scored with a rasping shot. Minutes later Hermitage netted after a scramble in the goalmouth.

DIVISION I CHALLENGE CUP FINAL

TAKELEY 3 BIRCHANGER 1

Already assured of the Division I championship, Takeley rounded off the double by winning the divisional Cup Final in front of a large crowd at Rhodes Avenue.

The scoring was opened by Carter in the 15th minute, but it was not long before Chapman restored the balance after dispossessing Lawson.

It was Robinson's mistake which enabled Carter to restore his team's lead. Taking a wild swing at a ball down the middle, the Birchanger player only half connected, sat down with a thud, and left Carter with a clear run through.

Only a dramatic save by Lawson, who divided to push Cornell's drive over the bar, prevented an equaliser, but Birchanger's hopes finally faded five minutes from time when Carter rammed the ball home from close range.

PREMIER DIVISION CHALLENGE CUP FINAL

BISHOP'S STORTFORD SWIFTS 2 HATFIELD HEATH 1

Source : Herts & Essex Observer

A goal by Swifts in each half at Rhodes Avenue ended the Heath's dream of a double, their reserves having won the Division II trophy the previous week.

Although they conceded the first goal, Swifts came back strongly and should have won by a wider margin, Terry Applin alone missing three good chances.

The credit for Heath's goal belonged mainly to Johnny Collins. His cross from the wing had goalkeeper Barry Roberts and two players from each side leaping for possession, the ball skidding off Mick Maley's head into his own net.

Just before the interval Swifts equalised with the best goal of the match. When Peter Hunt dropped the ball into the goalmouth Turner was rather slow off the mark and Joe Ventre nipped in to nod the ball over him for a glorious goal.

The decisive goal came early in the second half following a scramble in the Heath goalmouth. Applin flicked a pass to Brock Thurley, whose drive from close range gave Turner no chance.

SOCCER CREAM IS IN THE LOCAL LEAGUES

'When playing football it is better to have played and lost than not to have played at all,' said the League Chairman, Mr W Bruty, at the League's Annual Dinner when proposing the toast to the ladies and guests.

He added that naturally one congratulated the winners of a competition, but at the same time always felt sorry for the losers.

Mr Bruty went on to praise the work of the officers he had working with him and said they were a 'great team.' Anything he asked them to do for him they did without complaint. 'They work extremely hard and I am grateful for their services,' he said.

Club Secretaries were also praised by Mr Bruty, who said that without them the clubs would be in a bad way. 'The only way to have a good club is to have a good Secretary,' he added.

On a night of praise, Mr Bruty congratulated Mr G H Wilson, President of the League, on completing 15 years' service with the Hertfordshire Football Association.

He also paid tribute to Mr Ivan Tuthill, Secretary of the Chelmsford and Mid-Essex Combination who was not only a county FA representative but who had a lot to do with the Chelmsford prison team.

Mr Bruty commented : 'Recently I met an ex-prisoner who could not speak highly enough of the work that Mr Tuthill had done for the prisoners, and he said he thought he was doing a wonderful job.'

Replying to the toast, Mr Len Menhinick, Secretary of Chelmsford City Football Club, said that the 'lads' who played football in the League were extremely lucky. 'You have a great League and great officers,' he said.

Congratulating Mr Bruty on the completion of 16 years as Chairman, Mr Menhinick said :

'Bill is a bloke in a million, and quite frankly I don't know how he has done what he has.'

He added : 'You will all be pleased to know that he has been awarded a gold medal award for long service to the Essex Football Association.'

Mr Menhinick concluded by saying that soccer played in the League and in junior football was the cream. 'The glamour is with the professionals, but here in local soccer is the cream,' he added.

A long-service award was made to Mr George Wilson by the Hertfordshire Football Association, in recognition of 15 years membership. Mr Wilson was also President and Chairman of Bishop's Stortford FC as well as President of the League.

The first winners of the Sportsmanship Cup were Hatfield Heath with High Laver second and Bishop's Stortford Swifts Reserves third.

Hatfield Heath Annual Awards evening

MORE TEAMS IN THE STORTFORD LEAGUE

It was decided at the League's Annual General Meeting that during the coming season, there would be 13 teams in each division of the League.

Mr W Bruty, the Chairman giving details of the coming changes, said the new entries would include some clubs who wished to re-join the League and had been recommended by the Management Committee.

Details of a new scheme to encourage each club to provide a linesman for the League were outlined by Mr L Thorne.

He told the meeting, which was attended by a delegate from every club except Quendon, that at a meeting of the Referees' Association recently, the question of the clubs' sportsmanship was discussed, and then it was decided that they would like to encourage the clubs to have a regular linesman.

'This will benefit the clubs as well as the referees,' Mr Thorne said, 'and we felt it might help if we gave a trophy each year to the best club linesman.'

Mr Bruty earlier reported that at a meeting of the Hertfordshire Football Association, a long service award for 15 years' service to Hertfordshire Football was awarded to the League's President, Mr George Wilson.'

'I think this is a great honour, and we are all extremely proud of his great record,' commented Mr Bruty.

Presenting the Treasurer's report, Mr G Reed said the general account had cash at the bank of £31 19s 1d, and the social account £29 5s 6d.

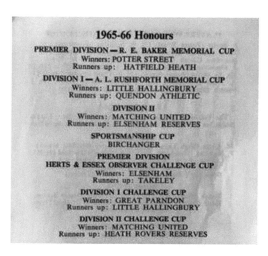

1965-66 Honours

PREMIER DIVISION — R. E. BAKER MEMORIAL CUP
Winners: POTTER STREET
Runners up: HATFIELD HEATH

DIVISION I — A. L. RUSHFORTH MEMORIAL CUP
Winners: LITTLE HALLINGBURY
Runners up: QUENDON ATHLETIC

DIVISION II
Winners: MATCHING UNITED
Runners up: ELSENHAM RESERVES

SPORTSMANSHIP CUP
BIRCHANGER

PREMIER DIVISION
HERTS & ESSEX OBSERVER CHALLENGE CUP
Winners: ELSENHAM
Runners up: TAKELEY

DIVISION I CHALLENGE CUP
Winners: GREAT PARNDON
Runners up: LITTLE HALLINGBURY

DIVISION II CHALLENGE CUP
Winners: MATCHING UNITED
Runners up: HEATH ROVERS RESERVES

Heath's prison 'nap'

H.M. Prison, Chelmsford ... 1
Hatfield Heath 5

ON the strength of being awarded the Stortford, Stansted and District League's Sportsmanship Cup last season, the Heath were invited to visit the prison on Saturday, and emerged comfortable winners of a friendly.

On a bumpy pitch and in the face of a strong wind, both teams took some time to master the conditions. Heath opened the scoring when Hermitage rounded a defender and sent in an angled shot which gave the goalkeeper no chance.

Straight from the restart the prison equalised through their inside-left, who took full advantage of a muddled defence.

The visitors took command in the second period, Hobday restoring their lead by heading through from a corner. Hermitage and Brown put them further in front, before Bayford completed the scoring from the penalty spot.

I understand that this game was organised by Bill Bruty and there was an estimated crowd of 500.

Source : Herts & Essex Observer

The October Management Committee meeting opened with members standing in silence to the memory of the late L G Lewis. A letter of condolence was sent to Mrs Lewis.

Source : Herts & Essex Observer

HATFIELD HEATH

PREMIER LEAGUE RUNNERS-UP

DIVISION I CHALLENGE CUP FINAL

GREAT PARNDON I LITTLE HALLINGBURY 0

In front of a large crowd, Little Hallingbury lost the chance to complete a notable double when they were beaten by an 89th minute goal.

The all-important goal came after an otherwise uninspiring game, but it was one to be remembered.

A long clearance out of defence sparked off a chase for the ball between inside-right Wilson and a Hallingbury defender. Wilson won, and his cross from near the by-line eluded goalkeeper Bruty, but not the head of inside-left John Quinn who was steaming up in support. His superb header was way above the standard of football being played.

DIVISION II CHALLENGE CUP FINAL

MATCHING UNITED 2 HEATH ROVERS RESERVES 0

The scoring was opened after 25 minutes, J Brown moving on to a through ball and putting Matching on the victory trail.

The second half only served to emphasise the superiority of Matching, who went further in front on the hour. A neat constructive movement found R Judd with only Coxall to beat, and he left the goalkeeper stranded with a clever lob.

MATCHING UNITED

PREMIER DIVISION CHALLENGE CUP FINAL

ELSENHAM 2 TAKELEY 0

In the picture above no one seems to be quite sure where the ball is as Takeley tried to break through. Things looked black for Takeley when left-winger Maurice Shuttlewood was carried off (right) in the 40th minute.

A crowd of 1,200 saw Elsenham take their second trophy of the season by winning the Premier Division Challenge Cup by beating Takeley 2-0. The game was full of fight, thrilling saves and hairsbreadth escape at both ends, with not a little skilful football thrown in for good measure.

The scoring opened after 10 minutes when Takeley goalkeeper Pat Lawson, probably dazzled by the sinking sun, missed a corner from the right. The ball fell at the feet of Jones, who scored easily.

In the second half Elsenham occasionally broke away on the wings and it was from such a move that they got their clincher. When Mick Ellis crossed the ball, Jaggard running in, hit a half volley high into the net for a glorious goal.

The cup and medals were presented by Mr G H Wilson, the League President.

ALWAYS TRY AND GIVE THE JUNIOR CLUBS A HELPING HAND

Source : Herts & Essex Observer

Relationships between senior amateur clubs and junior amateur clubs in the district always had been good, and the senior clubs should assist the junior clubs in every possible way, Mr Alex Masie, manager of Hertford FC. Mr Massie, a former Scottish International, was speaking at the Annual Dinner of the League.

He said that senior amateur clubs could not do without the juniors, and likewise the juniors could not manage without the assistance from the seniors.

Replying to the toast of the ladies and guests, Mr Massie went on to pay tribute to Bishop's Stortford Football Club on the winning the Athenian League Division I.

Proposing the toast of the ladies and guests, Mr W Bruty, Chairman of the League, also paid tribute to Bishop's Stortford for the support they had given to the League.

They had always allowed the League to use their ground for the League's Cup Finals and had always helped in every way possible, he told the 250 people present.

The League was never refused at Stansted either, he added and there was another club always willing to give support.

The trophy presented to Mr Fred Bruty, of Hatfield Heath, as the first ever Linesman of the Year.

At the start of the League's Annual General Meeting on 6th July 1966, Vice-Chairman, Mr Lionel Thorne, apologised for the absence of the Chairman, Mr W A Bruty, who had been representing the Essex FA at a reception given by the Harlow Corporation for the Uruguayan football team who were playing the 1966 World Cup. Of course, Uruguay played against England in the opening game of the World Cup at Wembley on 11th July. At the same meeting, a letter was read to the members informing them that Mr Lionel Thorne had resigned as Referees Secretary.

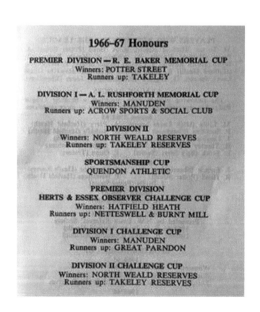

1966–67 Honours

PREMIER DIVISION — R. E. BAKER MEMORIAL CUP
Winners: POTTER STREET
Runners up: TAKELEY

DIVISION I — A. L. RUSHFORTH MEMORIAL CUP
Winners: MANUDEN
Runners up: ACROW SPORTS & SOCIAL CLUB

DIVISION II
Winners: NORTH WEALD RESERVES
Runners up: TAKELEY RESERVES

SPORTSMANSHIP CUP
QUENDON ATHLETIC

PREMIER DIVISION
HERTS & ESSEX OBSERVER CHALLENGE CUP
Winners: HATFIELD HEATH
Runners up: NETTESWELL & BURNT MILL

DIVISION I CHALLENGE CUP
Winners: MANUDEN
Runners up: GREAT PARNDON

DIVISION II CHALLENGE CUP
Winners: NORTH WEALD RESERVES
Runners up: TAKELEY RESERVES

Source : Herts & Essex Observer

HEATH ROVERS 3 LITTLE HALLINGBURY 1

PREMIER DIVISION

Source : Herts & Essex Observer

SAFFRON WALDEN YOUTH CENTRE 10

ELSENHAM RESERVES 1

DIVISION I

It looks like a rugby tackle on Manuden's Brian King, but in fact the Hatfield Broad Oak player on the ground was making a desperate effort to take advantage of a scoring chance.

Source : Herts & Essex Observer

Source : Herts & Essex Observer

MANUDEN 6 HATFIELD BROAD OAK 0

DIVISION I

Hatfield Broad Oak got the ball in the net once during the game at Manuden, but unfortunately it was their own! Laurence Cook headed the wrong way.

Source : Herts & Essex Observer

BISHOP'S STORTFORD SWIFTS RESERVES 4 SAFFRON WALDEN YOUTH CENTRE 0

DIVISION I

The Walden Youth Centre goalkeeper got his hand to Dick Sweetman's penalty but could not prevent the ball from entering the net.

In March 1967, the League received a letter from the Honorary Treasurer of Bishop's Stortford Football Club inviting the Honorary Secretary to contribute an article based along the lines of the League for publication in their Club Handbook for 1967/68. The Honorary Secretary readily agreed but asked that any club who had a knowledge of the Stansted and District League and the Bishop's Stortford and District Junior League from 1922 until their amalgamation in 1936 to let him know.

Source : Herts & Essex Observer

MANUDEN 4 ACROW SPORTS 3

DIVISION I CHALLENGE CUP

A thriller was expected when 100% Manuden clashed with their closest challengers for the Division 1 title in the League cup semi-final, and the spectators were not disappointed. With 20 minutes to go Acrow Sports were leading 3-0 and it looked as though the home side could say goodbye to their unique record, but then Manuden made a switch which worked wonders. John Maley moved from left-back to inside-left and completely transformed the game with a hat-trick. Together with a goal from Peter Selves, Manuden took the lead with just three minutes to go when John Maley completed his hat-trick.

The Debden goalkeeper clearing his lines under pressure.

TAKELEY 5 DEBDEN 0

PREMIER DIVISION

Source : Herts & Essex Observer

DIVISION II CHALLENGE CUP FINAL

NORTH WEALD RESERVES 3 TAKELEY RESERVES 1

After 15 minutes Shelsher initiated the move which led to the vital first goal. The ball bounced awkwardly in the Takeley goal area, and although Peacock left his line, and there were two other defenders close by, Williams was allowed to nip in and score.

Following a partially cleared corner in the 25th minute, North Weald increased their lead, Monk taking advantage of yet another mix-up in the Takeley defence.

Seven minutes later Takeley got right back in the game when Baines scored the goal of the match. Whitter came through and made a pass which Baines took in his stride and netted a low drive from 20 yards.

The issue was decided after 65 minutes, good work by Williams and Shelsher making the opening from which Ferguson scored.

Source : John Maley

MANUDEN

DIVISION I LEAGUE AND CUP WINNERS

DIVISION I CHALLENGE CUP FINAL

MANUDEN 3 GREAT PARNDON 2

After 22 minutes Groom was fouled in the area, and ex-Bishop's Stortford player, Ray Garret, smashed home the spot-kick. Six minutes after that, Green belted home a sizzling shot after Hunt parried a fierce from live-wire winger Terry Shoebridge.

Great Parndon hit back in the second half and they got the first on the hour when winger Pitt flew up his flank, just kept the ball in play on the touchline, rounded full-back Maley and centred for Alan Mead to head home.

Two minutes later Pitt ran on to a free-kick and drove the ball past Clarke to keep Parndon's more than alive.

After Shoebridge – undoubtedly the best forward on view – had gone close following a good run, Manuden drafted John Maley into attack, and he netted the winner after 70 minutes with a hard shot from close in.

PREMIER DIVISION CHALLENGE CUP FINAL

HATFIELD HEATH 3 NETTESWELL AND BURNT MILL 1

(AFTER EXTRA-TIME)

In a game governed more by stamina than by footballing ability, Hatfield Heath were taken to extra-time by a brave Burnt Mill side before being rightfully claimed the Premier Division Challenge Cup for the third time in the past decade at Rhodes Avenue.

Heath took the lead after 35 minutes at a time when a goal was desperately needed a lift the match out of the depths to which it had sunk.

Although crowded out by at least three defenders, lanky inside-left Elms collected the ball inside the area and netted via the post.

Denis Elms scores Heath's first goal despite the attention of two Burnt Mill defenders.0

Source : Herts & Essex Observer

Turner made a bad mistake which led to Mill equalising seven minutes from time. Teenager Ling collected the ball from right- winger Underwood and shot hard towards the far corner. Turner appeared to have the ball covered but dropped at the last minute into his net.

In extra-time centre-forward Brown robbed Bardwell near the by-line and shot over his head into the far corner of the net.

Five minutes before the end, Hobday completed a grand solo run to put the issue beyond doubt.

Source : Herts & Essex Observer

HATFIELD HEATH

Champagne flowed in the dressing room after Heath's victory.

JUNIORS SAY 'THANKS' TO BIG BROTHER

Without valuable assistance from Bishop's Stortford Football Club, the local League would almost certainly be in the 'red' said Mr W A Bruty, Chairman of the League, at the Annual Dinner.

Mr Arthur Dimond, Football League referee and Chairman of the Harlow & District League, said he was glad to see such strong ties existing between the two Leagues.

After the speeches, a gold watch was presented to Mr Lionel Thorne, for 13 years the League's Referees' Secretary and also Appointments Secretary of the North-West Essex Referees' Society, for loyal service to the League.

To mark the achievement of winning the Premier Division for three years in succession, Potter Street were awarded a plaque in recognition of their success.

Mr George Lindsell, the North-West Essex Referees' Society's Vice-Chairman, commented that club linesmen were a great asset to the League, and he thanked them all for the work they had done.

Some of the officials who attended the League's 1967 Annual Dinner and trophy presentations.

CHALLENGE CUP SEMI-FINALS TO BE PLAYED ON NEUTRAL GROUNDS

At the League's Annual General Meeting, Debden FC proposed that all cup semi-finals be played on neutral grounds instead of the first drawn club's home ground. After a lengthy discussion and a good number of clubs willing to place their grounds at the disposal of the League for these the proposal was carried.

The Chairman gave a brief talk on forming a Selection Committee as a separate body from the Officers and Management Committee to select future representative teams for the Inter-League matches etc. After some discussion, Mr Charlie French, Chairman of Sheering FC, volunteered to undertake this task together with Mr W J Gilbert, Honorary Secretary of Saffron Walden Town FC and Mr K Buttress, Honorary Secretary of Elsenham FC.

It was reported that just prior to the end of the season the League had 885 players registered of which 735 had played.

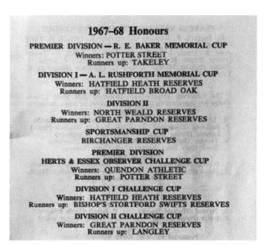

1967–68 Honours

PREMIER DIVISION — R. E. BAKER MEMORIAL CUP
Winners: POTTER STREET
Runners up: TAKELEY

DIVISION I — A. L. RUSHFORTH MEMORIAL CUP
Winners: HATFIELD HEATH RESERVES
Runners up: HATFIELD BROAD OAK

DIVISION II
Winners: NORTH WEALD RESERVES
Runners up: GREAT PARNDON RESERVES

SPORTSMANSHIP CUP
BIRCHANGER RESERVES

PREMIER DIVISION
HERTS & ESSEX OBSERVER CHALLENGE CUP
Winners: QUENDON ATHLETIC
Runners up: POTTER STREET

DIVISION I CHALLENGE CUP
Winners: HATFIELD HEATH RESERVES
Runners up: BISHOP'S STORTFORD SWIFTS RESERVES

DIVISION II CHALLENGE CUP
Winners: GREAT PARNDON RESERVES
Runners up: LANGLEY

HEATH ROVERS SEARCHING FOR THEIR OWN GROUND

One of the most affluent of junior football clubs and seeking a ground of their own – that's Heath Rovers, founded in 1958 with the growth of the Parsonage Estate.

Club Manager, John Dickinson said : 'We have several hundred pounds in the bank for this purpose, and we might be able to get a grant. We feel that somewhere locally there must be a landowner with a bit of land lying dormant which he would be willing to lease or even sell us.'

How does a club reach a state of affluence? Mr Dickinson said he thought it was entirely due to the organisational ability of the club's fund raising expert – the committee man whose sole job is to raise funds.

On the playing side Heath Rovers have lost the services of the club's top goal-poacher of last season Brian Simmonds, who hit 44 goals. He has joined Bishop's Stortford Football Club.

The club is running three Saturday teams: in the BSSDL, Premier Division and Division I, and in the Premier Division of the Hertford and District League. And this season, to ensure that all the 40-plus players on their books have a game if they wish, they have entered a Sunday morning side in the Harlow League.

The club holds its final trial for the coming season on Saturday afternoon. And like any progressive club, is always on the look-out for new players. I was proud to be one of those players.

HARDLY A BALL WAS KICKED

It was D – for dismal – day for sport. In the homes of League and club Secretaries the telephones rang to convey the gloomy message – 'our game is off.' Quickly it became apparent that sport had taken its worst knock from the weather since the long hold-up during the winter of 1962/63.

Roy Harrison, Honorary Secretary, wrote an article about the History of the Bishop's Stortford, Stansted and District League in the Bishop's Stortford Football Club's Official

1967/68 Handbook. In the article he mentioned the Minutes of the League which exist from the middle 1930's.

Source : Herts & Essex Observer

ACROW SPORTS 1 MANUDEN 6

PREMIER DIVISION

Source : Herts & Essex Observer

HEATH ROVERS 1 QUENDON ATHLETIC 1

PREMIER DIVISION

Heath Rovers gave a very much off-key display and were lucky to share the points. It was not until the last ten minutes, after Athletic had taken the lead, that the home side woke up to get the equaliser with time fast running out.

MANUDEN 2 SAFFRON WALDEN RESERVES 1

PREMIER DIVISION

Track suited Bill Clark, the Manuden goalkeeper, came well prepared for the artic conditions. Goals by the Maley brothers, John and Mick, gave Manuden a 2-0 half-time lead. Saffron Walden Reserves pulling one back after the break. Looking on, referee Bill Bruty.

BISHOP'S STORTFORD SWIFTS RESERVES 3

ALBURY 1

PREMIER DIVISION

Closely covered by skipper John Sewell (number 4), Richard Blayney, Swifts goalkeeper, clears a high ball during the 3-1 victory against Albury at Silver Leys.

YOUNG MAN WHO LOVED SOCCER DIES DURING MATCH

A young Bishop's Stortford sportsman who lived for football died playing the game he loved. David Robinson was buried still wearing the football kit in which he died.

David, 6 feet 4 inches, playing for Birchanger Reserves, collapsed on the field soon after the start of the match with Langley at Birchanger.

Attempts to revive him with the kiss of life mouth to mouth resuscitation failed.

His death was a blow to local football, In particular it was a great shock to Stortford Colts Football Club, the team which he helped to build-up from scratch and which he became Manager and Treasurer.

Source : Harlow Citizen

STORTFORD COLTS

Just before his death, in readiness for the Colts' Cup Final, David had bought two bottles of champagne and booked a room at the Bishop's Stortford Working Men's Club for a win or lose celebration.

The events surrounding his death were described by the Secretary of Birchanger Football Club, Mr George Banks, who was acting as a linesman during the game.

'The ball had gone out for a goal kick and I was going up the field to watch it being taken when someone called my name. David was lying on the flat out in the goalmouth. I went across and helped to pick him up. He was groaning.'

'His collapse had no connection with the match as no-one was near him when it happened. In fact, no-one saw him go down. He was carried to the local Working Men's Club. About 15 minutes later, someone came to tell me that it was far more serious than we thought. I walked in. I tried to massage him and give him the kiss of life.'

'When a doctor arrived, he tried to revive him, but without success.'

The game was abandoned.

Mr Banks commented later : 'He lived for football, not the national stuff, but the local games. We are going to miss him. He was a tower of strength to the club. We are thinking of doing something to keep him in mind.'

David lived with his parents in Benhooks Avenue, Bishop's Stortford.

Five years previously, he had joined Birchanger Football Club and later joined the committee and trained the younger players.

In the 1963/64 season, he helped form Stortford Colts Football Club, who played in the Harlow & District Sunday League, Premier Division. During their first two seasons David commanded a regular centre-half position.

Around that time, he had presented the club with a cup for a sportsman of the year award.

BISHOP'S STORTFORD SWIFTS RESERVES 2

HATFIELD BROAD OAK 2

DIVISION I CHALLENGE CUP

Source : Herts & Essex Observer

DIVISION II CHALLENGE CUP FINAL

LANGLEY 1 GREAT PARNDON RESERVES 1

(AFTER EXTRA-TIME)

In some respects, Langley were fortunate to have a second bite at the Division II Cup cherry. With the scores level at 1-1 Parndon were awarded a second half penalty for a foul which Mead shot over the bar.

With veteran former Stansted player Brian Kemp pushing forward a stream of astute passes, Langley had slightly the better of the first half, but could only manage one goal.

This came after 17 minutes when Stone chased a long ball down the middle and kicked it almost out of Harvey's hands into the net.

Having seen Wilson make a brilliant save from Mead, Parndon drew level on the hour, the Langley defence failing to cut out a cross from the right which left-winger Chalk netted.

DIVISION I CHALLENGE CUP FINAL

HATFIELD HEATH RESERVES 5

BISHOP'S STORTFORD SWIFTS RESERVES 2

Source : Herts & Essex Observer

Source : Herts & Essex Observer

Four penalties were awarded during the Division II Cup Final at Rhodes Avenue. Heath made full use of theirs, but on both occasions, they had a spot kick Swifts failed.

It was against the run of play that the Heath went in front after a quarter of an hour, a quick break caught Swifts' defence badly positioned and Des Brown scored with Blayney well off his line.

Always quicker on the break, Heath gave the opposition another shock when Thomas put then two up and they were within inches of a third soon afterwards. Thomas beat Blayney to the ball on the penalty area but saw his shot bounce off the top the bar.

By switching King and Hunt, Swifts showed up better at the start of the second half, their recovery sparked off in the 55th minute when Tim Hopkins netted with a shot from just inside the penalty area.

Appropriately Fred Maskell levelled the scores with a magnificent goal. His free kick from way outside the box was blocked, but the ball came back to him and he left Mascall groping for a sizzling low drive.

For a time, the Heath had to defend desperately with Mascall handling the greasy ball confidently. Swifts first big chance came when they were awarded a penalty for a foul, but Maskell shot wide.

Heath regained the lead through Bellamy, who hit a beauty from 30 yards and a minute later went further ahead. With Blayney beaten John Sewell prevented a certain goal with a running catch of which any cricketer would have been proud. Blayney beat out Des Brown's spot kick, but with Swifts' defence standing like statues, Thomas followed up to net.

Swifts hopes were momentarily revived when they were awarded their second spot kick, only for Mascall to tip John Challis's shot over the bar.

Shortly after the Heath goalkeeper had made a brilliant save from Maskell, the penalty saga came to an end with Des Brown driving the ball past Blayney after his namesake was brought down.

DIVISION I CHALLENGE CUP FINAL

HATFIELD HEATH RESERVES 3

BISHOP'S STORTFORD SWIFTS RESERVES 0

A crowd of around 300 saw Hatfield Heath Reserves clinch the Division I title and complete the double when they repeated their Cup Final success by beating Swifts Reserves. Once again, the spectators were treated to a wonderful display of goalkeeping by Mascall, who broke the hearts of the Swifts' forwards.

The first half was goalless but in the second half Heath, prompted by Bellamy and Des Brown controlled the midfield play, going in front when Stracey's corner went into the Swifts' net off John Challis's head. Peter Hermitage got their second when Blayney could only parry a shot to his feet and clinched the issue with a third near the end.

Source : Herts & Essex Observer

HATFIELD HEATH RESERVES

MEMORIAL FUND IS CREATED

The memory of David Robinson who collapsed and died while playing for Birchanger is to be perpetuated by a memorial fund opened by the club in connection with Stortford Colts the team of which he was Secretary.

A match between the two clubs was held at Rhodes Avenue with gate receipts together with other income from the match, devoted to the fund, which was used to purchase a memorial trophy.

'This, the clubs felt, would help to remember David, who lived for local football, and died while playing,' commented Mr George Banks, the Birchanger Secretary.

PREMIER DIVISION CHALLENGE CUP FINAL

QUENDON ATHLETIC 3 POTTER STREET 1

It was a triumphant return to Rhodes Avenue, where in the past he played many a fine game for Bishop's Stortford, for Quendon Athletic skipper Brian Wilson. His injury-hit team, fourth from bottom of the table, sprang a major surprise by beating Potter Street, champions of the Premier Division for the fourth successive season, in the divisional Cup Final.

For the large crowd of supporters there was an early taste of what was to come. After five minutes John Grandsen, who proved a real handful for veteran full-back Ron Hoad, pushed through a pass of slide rule precision for Dave Bonney to crash the ball into the Street net.

There was a distinct suspicion of offside about the champions' equaliser, scored by Dave Turner from Pete Smith's pass.

It was as the result of a dreadful mix-up in the Street penalty area that Quendon regained the lead. With three or four players lying in a heap and Bruce Gibson out of his goal, Waites coolly lobbed the ball into the net from around 25 yards.

Street's hopes of pulling the game out of the fire virtually disappeared when stylish wing half Jim Lambie handled just inside the box. Waites sent his spot kick wide, but the referee ordered a re-take on the grounds that Gibson had moved too soon, and this time Brain Wilson made no mistake. Strong protests by the Street were waived aside.

DIVISION II CHALLENGE CUP FINAL REPLAY

GREAT PARNDON RESERVES BEAT LANGLEY

NORTH WEALD RESERVES

HELP OF STORTFORD CLUB IS VALUED BY LEAGUE

The assistance and interest of Bishop's Stortford Football Club was valued, said Mr W Bruty, Chairman of the League, at their Annual Dinner and Dance.

Without the assistance of the club, which had told them the ground was available whenever they wanted it, the League would be financially in a much poorer state.

Mr Bruty, who was proposing the toast to the ladies and guests, said the League were also indebted to Stansted FC for their assistance. He thanked his officers who had 'a hell of a job in the season. And some clubs do not make it easier.'

Responding, Mr B R Baker, a well-known League Referee, and a representative of the Football Association, praised the energy and enthusiasm that went into junior football. It was right and proper that the Football Association should be represented at the dinner. He said it was good to see a local senior club interested in the League and working with it.

Hatfield Heath boys celebrating at the League Dinner – Roy Nicholls (Manager), Norman Mascall, Geoff Pegg, Alan Hermitage, David Brown, John Collins and Peter Nicholls.

HATFIELD HEATH RESERVES MADE HISTORY

In the course of his annual report at Hatfield Heath Football Club's annual meeting, the Secretary, Mr A G Perry, said that last season the reserves made club history by completing the Division I League and cup double.

LEAGUE FALLS INTO LINE – SUBSTITUTES

It was decided at the League's Annual General Meeting that in common with most other leagues and competitions, the League would allow the use of substitutes in season 1968/69.

The David Robinson Memorial Trophy, for the player who died at Birchanger during the season, was shown to the meeting by Mr George Banks, who organised the cup fund.

He thanked everyone for raising £75 so far and said that the trophy would be played for annually between the Harlow League and the Bishop's Stortford, Stansted and District League.

Mr Bruty explained that the money raised from the annual match would go towards any person or body who they felt needed it.

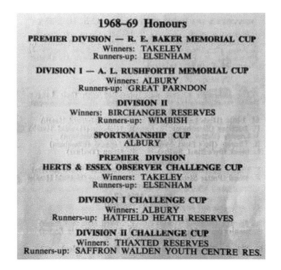

1968–69 Honours

PREMIER DIVISION — R. E. BAKER MEMORIAL CUP
Winners: TAKELEY
Runners-up: ELSENHAM

DIVISION I — A. L. RUSHFORTH MEMORIAL CUP
Winners: ALBURY
Runners-up: GREAT PARNDON

DIVISION II
Winners: BIRCHANGER RESERVES
Runners-up: WIMBISH

SPORTSMANSHIP CUP
ALBURY

PREMIER DIVISION
HERTS & ESSEX OBSERVER CHALLENGE CUP
Winners: TAKELEY
Runners-up: ELSENHAM

DIVISION I CHALLENGE CUP
Winners: ALBURY
Runners-up: HATFIELD HEATH RESERVES

DIVISION II CHALLENGE CUP
Winners: THAXTED RESERVES
Runners-up: SAFFRON WALDEN YOUTH CENTRE RES.

ACROW SPORTS 2 ELSENHAM 9

PREMIER DIVISION CHALLENGE CUP

HATFIELD HEATH 2 SAFFRON WALDEN YOUTH CENTRE 2

PREMIER DIVISION

Centre-forward Alf Jenkins (quartered shirt) who scored both of the Heath's goals is seen narrowly losing a race for possession and getting the better of a heading duel.

The League Division II game between Thaxted Reserves and Sheering Reserves was abandoned 15 minutes from time after fighting had broken out in both areas. When the referee, Mr Perry of Bishop's Stortford, called the players off Thaxted were leading 2-1. This had been the third time Thaxted had been involved in violent scenes on the field.

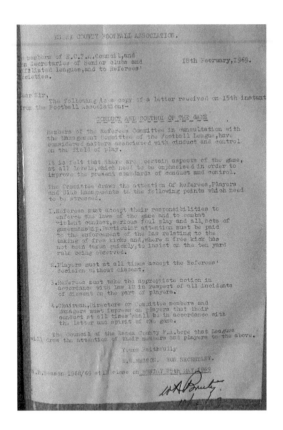

Letter received from the Essex County Football Association regarding 'Conduct and Control of the Game' – a subject close to Bill Bruty's heart.

DIVISION II CHALLENGE CUP FINAL

THAXTED RESERVES 1

SAFFRON WALDEN YOUTH CENTRE RESERVES 0

The decisive goal in the 71st minute when Hart's crisp drive rebounded of the post and Elliott, following up closely pushed the ball home.

ALBURY

Source : Herts & Essex Observer

DIVISION I CHALLENGE CUP FINAL

ALBURY 5 HATFIELD HEATH RESERVES 0

Source : Herts & Essex Observer

Norman Mascall, the Heath's goalkeeper, making one of a number of fine saves.

The ace in the Albury pack was left-winger Mick Petchey, who broke his leg in a pre-season friendly for Bishop's Stortford Reserves and had only played a couple of games since.

Hat trick Mick Petchey started the Albury goal rush with a pile driver on the volley in the 35th minute which Norman Mascall in the Heath goal could hardly have seen.

The second Petchey goal came after 53 minutes, four minutes after skipper Brian Chipperfield had scored number two for Albury. Petchey unleashed a cannonball carbon copy of his first goal to put the issue beyond doubt.

The fourth goal came after a defence-splitting through ball from Trevor Novell left Petchey with only the goalkeeper to beat. Five minutes later, in the 70th minute, Rob Newman completed the rout when he flicked the ball home.

HERTS JUNIOR CUP FINAL

MILL END SPORTS 2 HEATH ROVERS 1

The result of the Herts Junior Cup Final at St Albans, which was a disappointment for the team from Bishop's Stortford, hinged very largely on a second half incident. Trailing 2-1, Heath Rovers were denied what they felt was an obvious penalty which, had it been awarded, might well have put a completely different complexion on the game.

John Redfern, Rovers centre-half headed their goal just before half-time.

PREMIER DIVISION CHALLENGE CUP FINAL

TAKELEY 5 ELSENHAM 0

Too hurried in their use of the ball, Takeley had a let-off when Graham Jaggard hooked the ball against the bar but they settled down to take the lead after 25 minutes. Elsenham's defence was at sixes and sevens when Shuttlewood was left with only Ayres to beat.

Any hopes Elsenham may have had of pulling the game round virtually disappeared 10 minutes after the restart. Ayres called for the ball which he failed to collect and Shuttlewood rammed it into the net.

Takeley increased their lead when Trower headed through Shuttlewood's pass to finish off a move he had started on the left flank Two minutes later Ayres was at fault when Shuttlewood completed his hat trick, but to their credit Elsenham fought back strongly, forcing Wise to make a number of good saves.

Ayres also made a fine save when Shuttlewood hit one on the turn, but the goal-hungry Takeley leader struck again near the end, netting at the second attempt with a shot that went in off the post.

GOOD SPORTSMEN OF ALBURY ROUND OFF THE SEASON'S SUCCESSES

Albury, who had already completed the Division I League and cup double sealed their success when they were presented with Sportsmen Trophy at the League's Annual Dinner.

'Albury have shown that they can combine match-winning football with clean play,' said Mr Bill Bruty, League Chairman, when he announced the decision. 'It is an example that all clubs could follow.'

Earlier, tribute had been paid to Mr Bruty by his Vice-Chairman, Mr Lionel Thorne. 'No organisation can run without proper leadership and Mr Bruty provides this lead.' Said Mr

Thorne. Each season he makes it his ambition to visit every club in the League and also those clubs in the area he represents on the Essex Association.'

'Bill also visits the referees' associations and gets to know both sides of the question when he deals with some of you naughty players,' Mr Thorne continued, 'This helps enormously when we are ready to blow our tops and Bill calms us down by saying, we are here to foster football not to kill it.' Mr Thorne concluded by mentioning that his Chairman seemed to spend all his time and energies on football. 'How he manages to do a job of work as well I just do not know.' He commented.

Source : Herts & Essex Observer

Mr George Wilson, League President, presenting the Division I championship trophy to Brian Chipperfield, Albury.

After the tribute, the League made a presentation to its auditor, Mr C Searle of a pen and pencil set.

'He has serves us well for the past 12 years,' said Mr Bruty, 'and he keeps a tight hold on our treasurer, George Reed. Indeed he will not let George spend a penny unless he really has to – not that George tries very much.'

It was Mr Bruty who had proposed the toast to the guests and he mentioned the difficulties of the season.

'There was such a congestion of matches to be played at the end of the season that I did not think we would get through,' he commented. 'But we did, and it was mainly due to the hard-working, and under-thanked, club secretaries. Without them we could not have a League and without the work they put in this League would not be as good as it is.'

He concluded by mentioning that the evening, apart from being a chance to make the presentations to the clubs was a 'thank you' to the ladies for allowing their husbands to play football every Saturday.

RECORD NUMBER OF CLUBS IN LOCAL LEAGUE

Next season the League would have a record number of teams, 48 in all, and to cater for all applications the League would be divided into four divisions.

Several delegates at the Annual General Meeting made the point that the new Premier Division looked overloaded.

It was one of the teams in the top division who had the most cup commitments, said one delegate. They consequently had the most difficulty in completing their League programme.

To compensate for the comparatively few League games in Division II and Division III, a new League Challenge Cup will be competed for next season between all 22 clubs of those two divisions.

The new cup would be in addition to the separate League cups, for each division. Mr George Wilson was presenting the trophy.

Mr G Reed, the Treasurer told the meeting that the receipts from the three League Cup Finals last season were the highest in the 10 years he had been in office,

He added : 'The revenue from these finals are in fact our main source of income,' And he thanked the Bishop's Stortford club for making their ground available for the matches to be played.

The money raised from the Premier Division final was £113 13s 6d; from the Division I final was £85 5s 6d and from the Division II final £42 5s 6d.

Mr Reed reported a balance in the bank of nearly £220, and also announced that referee's fees would be increased from 15s to £1 and linesman's fees from 10s to 15s from the coming season.

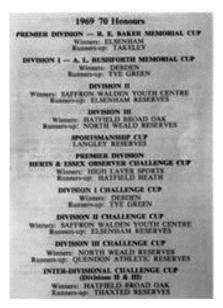

The 1969/70 season saw the League expanded to include Division III League and Challenge Cup competitions as well as the Inter-Divisional Cup contested by clubs in Divisions II and III. This brought the number of teams in the League to 47. The season also saw the League's first female secretary, Mrs D Trott from Hatfield Broad Oak.

It was decided to run a Challenge Cup Competition for teams in Divisions II and III for the season 1969/70 to bolster their fixture lists. The President Mr George Wilson said he would be pleased to donate a cup for the competition.

TAKELEY 0 ALBURY 6

PREMIER DIVISION CHALLENGE CUP

The Premier Division Cup holders, Takeley, made an inglorious exit at the first hurdle of the competition, being beaten by the very efficient Albury side, who scored six goals without reply.

Source : Herts & Essex Observer

Chris Newman (number 8) scoring Albury's fifth goal.

Source : Herts & Essex Observer

During pressure by Takeley, Richard Brown headed clear

from close to the line.

Source : Herts & Essex Observer

BISHOP'S STORTFORD SWIFTS RESERVES 1

TAKELEY RESERVES 0

DIVISION I

Roy Wacey, of Swifts Reserves and Michael Phillips of Takeley tussle for possession in the match at Silver Leys which Swifts Reserves won 1-0.

SUGAR PERRY AND JIM LAMBIE RECEIVE LEAGUE PLAQUES

In 1969, Sugar Perry of Hatfield Heath and Jim Lambie of Potter Street who were regular members of the League team during the sixties received League Plaques for representing the League on ten or more occasions.

Jim Lambie later became a referee. Before coming south to Harlow, he played for Queen's Park in the Scottish League and appeared at Hampden Park on two occasions. Jim was also a committee member for the League's representative side for several years.

John King began his career in 1966 when he signed for Bishop's Stortford Swifts. They described him as 'a welcome addition to the reserve defence, tall, lanky with his distinctive coloured hair and the ability to make good tackles.' In season 1970/71, he made a number of appearances for Bishop's Stortford Reserves. In 1976 John joined S.J.F.C. and played for the League representative side. John then played and managed Sheering Football Club.

The Seventies

46 clubs provided teams for the League during the seventies and there was an average of 48 teams per year playing in the League.

There were 5,204 League games played and 25,178 League goals scored.

Harlow based Great Parndon became the first team from the League to win the Essex Junior Cup when they beat Mersey Island 2-1 in 1972. Takeley became the second club to win the competition in 1975 by beating Stanway Rovers 1-0 in 1975. Both these finals were played at the home of Grays Athletic FC.

Albury, Takeley and Great Parndon dominated the Premier Division in the seventies. Albury won the championship 4 times, Takeley 3 times and Great Parndon 2 times. The same clubs won the Premier Division Cup on 7 occasions between them and were also runners-up also on 7 occasions.

During the seventies and eighties many of these club's players represented the League in competition and friendly matches:-

Albury - P English, C Newman, R Newman, T Novell, M Petchey,

K Devlin, T Collins, G Cornell

Takeley – J Smith, R Yeoman, M Skingle, C Baines, J Cogan,

S Baines, M Seymour, T Clarey, M Ryan

Great Parndon - C Humphries, D Thomas, P Smith, E Hawliczek,

I Smith, A Trott, M Young, D Fullen, J Johnson, F McGinley

Source : Herts & Essex Observer

TAKELEY 1 HATFIELD HEATH 3

PREMIER DIVISION

Takeley goalkeeper George Clayden clears the ball before the Heath's striker can reach it

Source : Herts & Essex Observer

Source : Herts & Essex Observer

HATFIELD BROAD OAK 11 QUENDON ATHLETIC RESERVES 2

INTER-DIVISIONAL CUP

The only game to survive the arctic conditions that week. Hatfield Broad Oak went on another of their goal sprees. Malcolm Skingle was unlucky but figured among the goal-scorers.

ELSENHAM 5

HATFIELD HEATH 1

PREMIER DIVISION

Elsenham stepped up their bid for the Premier Division title with a convincing 5-1 win in this top-of-the-table battle with striker Bradbury netting four times.

Heath centre-half Bob Jerrard resists a challenge by Adrian Jones.

(Below) – Hermitage running in to net Heath's first half goal following a well-taken free kick.

Source : Herts & Essex Observer

Source : Herts & Essex Observer

Source : Herts & Essex Observer

It should have been a goal but Johnson gets a hand to a shot from Tony Hobday.

MANUDEN 1 HATFIELD HEATH 2

PREMIER DIVISION CUP

Hatfield Heath reached the final of the Premier Division Cup with a fine win over Manuden 2-1, at Elsenham.

(Above) – It should have been a goal but somehow Johnson, the Manuden goalkeeper, got a hand to the shot from Tony Hobday, to push the ball past for a corner. On Hobday's left is Peter Hermitage.

DIVISION I CHALLENGE CUP FINAL

DEBDEN 1 TYE GREEN 1 (AFTER EXTRA-TIME)

Source : Herts & Essex Observer

'It is mine' says goalkeeper Chris Matthews, who played a major role in keeping the margin of Elsenham's defeat to a single goal.

DIVISION II CHALLENGE CUP FINAL

SAFFRON WALDEN YOUTH CENTRE 1 ELSENHAM RESERVES 0

The only goal, scored eight minutes from time, settled the match. It was the only real excitement in a mediocre display from both teams.

A shot by Saunders ended up in the net only to be disallowed by the referee. It was Richard Thompson fastening on to a Saunders' rebound and then driving the ball home that gave the Youth Centre the deciding goal.

Source : Muma Caz Pupa Malcy

SAFFRON WALDEN YOUTH CENTRE

PREMIER DIVISION CHALLENGE CUP FINAL

HIGH LAVER 2 HATFIELD HEATH 1

After dominating the first 40 minutes the Heath ran out of steam and High Laver, who rarely looked anything more than 'also-rans' in the first half, powered home to take the cup by 2 goals to 1.

After ten minutes, intercepting a back-pass, Peter Hermitage got Hatfield Heath's goal despite a brave attempt by goalkeeper Shield to keep the ball out.

Before half-time Laver's left-winger Ken Hawkins took the ball to the by-line but his far post cross deceived the defence and Dave Hawkins, on the opposite flank, bundled the ball into the net.

After 67 minutes a low hard cross from Powell beat Turner and Dave Hawkins on the spot to volley home.

At the end it was Ayling, of High Laver, who received the trophy from Mr A L Frost, a Vice-President of the League.

HATFIELD BROAD OAK

Hatfield Broad Oak were the first winners of the Inter-Divisional Cup and were also Division III League winners.

A record was created by two Division III teams during the season which has not beaten by teams in either Division III or any higher Division. Hatfield Broad Oak scored a record 130 goals while Langley Reserves conceded a record 156 goals.

INTER-DIVISIONAL CHALLENGE CUP FINAL

HATFIELD BROAD OAK 5 THAXTED RESERVES 0

The first goal was the best of the match. Broad Oak's 16 year-old winger, Malcolm Skingle, who gave full-back Coughlan a roasting throughout, crossed from the line and Lee crashed the ball high into the net from the edge of the box.

Thaxted had hardly recovered when Skingle and Everett worked their way into the area and Lee prodded the ball home again via a post and Bunting's back.

The Thaxted goal survived a rain of shots in which Lee should have doubled his score at least before Payne notched the third, shooting home from the edge of the box following a right-wing corner.

Winger Everett snapped up two late opportunities for Broad Oak.

DIVISION I CHALLENGE CUP FINAL REPLAY

DEBDEN 2 TYE GREEN 1

Debden took 207 minutes to settle the Division I Cup Final and complete the Division double.

The opening moves were nearly all Tye Green, but it was Debden who scored first, against the run of play, with the game only ten minutes old. Jimmy Watson sent a free-kick low into the area for Colin Diggons to hit the ball into the net.

Debden held out until the 36th minute. Two headers, one from Parker and the other from Jones, had already caused some anxious moments for Moule, but with Garaty turning to hit a shot on the volley from close in the goalkeeper was left with no chance.

Just when extra-time looked a distinct possibility Adams took his chance to clinch the game.

High Laver Reserves would not be appearing in the League Division III Cup Final. Laver got through to the final against North Weald Reserves by defeating Quendon Reserves and Harlow Metal, but after subsequent long and involved protests about ineligible players, the League threw Laver out of the final and ordered Quendon and Harlow Metal to play in the semi-final.

DIVISION III CHALLENGE CUP FINAL

NORTH WEALD RESERVES 3

QUENDON ATHLETIC RESERVES 1

Warwick put Quendon into the lead after a quarter of an hour, when a long ball found him able to chip past Meachin.

But within seven minutes North Weald were back on level terms. Burling missed a chance in front of goal when the ball bounced awkwardly for him, but the resulting goal-kick was picked up by Monk, who punted the ball back into the area for Burling to knock it home.

The crunch came in the 75th minute when a probing cross from Jessop found Burling in the centre to head home his and Weald's second goal.

Source : Graham Ingold

ELSENHAM

ACCLAIM AND A GOLD WATCH FOR MR BILL BRUTY

Source : Herts & Essex Observer

Mr Bill Bruty receives acclaim, applause and a gold watch at the League's Annual Dinner.

Mr Bruty had just finished his 21st year as an officer of the League and his 20th year as Chairman.

Acclaim came from Mr Len Menhinick of the Essex County Football Association : 'Bill works hard for football all over the place. Indeed he spends all his spare time on junior soccer in the area,' he said.

And from the League's senior Vice-President, Mr A L Frost : 'Bill is as straight as a gun barrel. Whether people have complaints about the running of the League, or if they think it runs smoothly, we all know he is fair.'

'The strongest and the weakest clubs receive equal consideration from him, and from over 50 clubs in the League there are very, very few complaints that ever go to the County Association.'

'To my mind, the success of this League is due almost entirely to the work of Bill Bruty. Yet, although a lot of work is involved here, he does so much for soccer outside the League as well.'

Applause came from the 200 members and guests. The gold watch was presented to Mr Bruty on behalf of the League by the President, Mr George Wilson, and the object of the praise and congratulations replied : 'It's all a great surprise and all I can say is, Thank You.'

Earlier Mr Bruty, proposing the toast to the guests, had remarked on the League's first season with four divisions as 'very successful,' and added there were 1,004 registered players and that 1,152 result cards had been dealt with during the season.

He also said 'thank you' to Mr Gerry Rowlins, Secretary of Netteswell and Burnt Mill and member of the League Management Committee, who was emigrating to Australia.

Replying to the toast, Mr Menhinick said that the League continued to go from 'strength to strength and had just completed a very successful season.'

TAKELEY CELEBRATE A FINE SEASON

One of the district's best known players in the not too distant past, Mr Ken Yeats, had something to say about the changing face of football when proposing the toast to 'The Club' at Takeley Football Club's dinner.

He advised players not to concern themselves with technicalities, but to remember that the main purpose of the game was enjoyment which depended largely on good sportsmanship.

Mr Yeats congratulated a very successful season with the first team having won the Bardfield Cup and finished as runners-up in the Stortford League Premier Division. In addition the reserves achieved a very respectable position in Division I.

The support the club had enjoyed, Mr Yeats went on, proved the wisdom of moving the pitch from the forest to the centre of the village. Much had been done to improve the facilities on the ground, including drainage and the building of a new pavilion.

Responding, the President, Mr A L Frost, referred to the first team's storming finish in winning their last 17 League matches to get within two points of the champions, Elsenham.

The club's present leading position in local football was a tribute to the energy and enthusiasm of the officers and members, Mr Frost commented.

INELIGIBLE PLAYERS NEW RULE CHANGE

At the League's annual meeting the Treasurer, Mr G Reed reported a loss of £115, leaving a balance of £189 in the account.

Particular attention was drawn to the fact that in the previous season three League Cup Finals had raised £249, whereas last season's six finals had made only £204.

To try to meet allegations of teams fielding ineligible players, clubs would have the right to demand signatures of opposing players immediately after a match.

These can then be forwarded to the Registration Secretary for comparison if necessary.

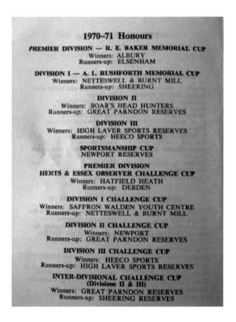

1970–71 Honours

PREMIER DIVISION — R. E. BAKER MEMORIAL CUP
Winners: ALBURY
Runners-up: ELSENHAM

DIVISION I — A. L. RUSHFORTH MEMORIAL CUP
Winners: NETTESWELL & BURNT MILL
Runners-up: SHEERING

DIVISION II
Winners: BOAR'S HEAD HUNTERS
Runners-up: GREAT PARNDON RESERVES

DIVISION III
Winners: HIGH LAVER SPORTS RESERVES
Runners-up: HEECO SPORTS

SPORTSMANSHIP CUP
NEWPORT RESERVES

PREMIER DIVISION
HERTS & ESSEX OBSERVER CHALLENGE CUP
Winners: HATFIELD HEATH
Runners-up: DEBDEN

DIVISION I CHALLENGE CUP
Winners: SAFFRON WALDEN YOUTH CENTRE
Runners-up: NETTESWELL & BURNT MILL

DIVISION II CHALLENGE CUP
Winners: NEWPORT
Runners-up: GREAT PARNDON RESERVES

DIVISION III CHALLENGE CUP
Winners: HEECO SPORTS
Runners-up: HIGH LAVER SPORTS RESERVES

INTER-DIVISIONAL CHALLENGE CUP
(Divisions II & III)
Winners: GREAT PARNDON RESERVES
Runners-up: SHEERING RESERVES

HEATH ROVERS COMPLAIN TO THE COUNCIL ABOUT THE PITCHES AT GRANGE PADDOCKS

In September 1970 Heath Rovers launched a strong attack on the playing conditions and facilities at Grange Paddocks – administered by Bishop's Stortford Urban Council.

The club complained :-

1)   That the pitches had not been rolled, cut or marked properly for the opening for the opening of the season.

2)   That the Council have turned round the pitches this season, which has reduced the number from a possible five to three.

3)   That the Council has at the same time, increased the number of teams allowed to use the pitches. This, say Heath Rovers will leave them in a 'deplorable state' at the end of the season.

4)   That the toilet facilities are 'non-existent' and the changing accommodation 'completely inadequate.'

The Rovers warn – in a letter to the Herts and Essex Observer – 'The football teams of Bishop's Stortford cannot look to the future with much confidence while things remain as they are at Grange Paddocks.'

Mr Ron Cox, the Council's Surveyor, admitted that the changing facilities were giving cause for concern.

GRANGE PADDOCKS PITCHES GET 'DANGEROUS LABEL'

Later in the month, a warning came that that the condition of the pitches at Grange Paddocks are so dangerous that 'a broken leg could easily result.'

The latest criticism comes from Boars Head Hunters, new boys in the League.

Manager Derek Burden, expressing fears about the safety of the ground, said : 'The goalmouths were re-turfed only two weeks before the start of the season. The ground there is already completely dead, with divots being kicked up whenever there is a miskick.'

'It will be terrible when it gets wet, we will be sticking in it.'

This, said Derek, was when the risk of players being seriously injured would be greatest.

He added : 'To have done the job properly, the goalmouths should have been re-turfed at the end of the season, not a couple of weeks ago.'

Derek also backed criticism of the lack of running water and changing facilities. 'You don't need to open the changing room doors. You can get through the holes in the walls,' he said.

The Council were getting 'between £6 and £10' a week from the pitches. They should provide water and a tea room for the money.

Source : Herts & Essex Observer

Newly promoted Debden had every reason to be satisfied with their debut in the Premier Division by holding champions Elsenham to a 1-1 draw. Having taken the lead in the second half, they threw away a golden opportunity of consolidating their position by missing a penalty (above). It was not until late in the game that Elsenham equalised, their scorer pictured below.

Source : Herts & Essex Observer

ELSENHAM 1 DEBDEN 1

PREMIER DIVISION

Source : Herts & Essex Observer

HATFIELD HEATH 1 ALBURY 3

PREMIER DIVISION

Robert Newman's spot kick after less than a minute had Mel Turner, the Hatfield Heath goalkeeper, going the wrong way.

Source : Herts & Essex Observer

HEATH ROVERS 0 ALBURY 4

PREMIER DIVISION CUP

From the expressions on their places, Rovers defenders clearly anticipated trouble as Robert Newman, Albury's goal ace, gets on the move.

Source : Herts & Essex Observer

HATFIELD BROAD OAK 1 GRANGE PARK 1

DIVISION II

The goal scored by Everitt was insufficient to prevent a home defeat. They paid the penalty for missing a number of scoring chances in each half. Note the goalkeeper wearing glasses.

Source : Herts & Essex Observer

HEECO SPORTS 6 DEBDEN RESERVES 2

DIVISION III

Typical of the conditions which most matches were played that week were those at Grange Paddocks, Bishop's Stortford, where Debden Reserves goalkeeper, Charlie Clarke, is seen taking an involuntary mud bath.

HUT PLAN

In February, Heath Rovers application for a changing hut to be erected at Grange Paddocks was recommended – subject to planning approval – by the Bishop's Stortford Urban Council.

At a meeting, a member of the Surveyor's Department reported on a plan submitted by the football club and suggested that the hut be built nearer to the proposed Rye Street car park.

SAFFRON WALDEN RESERVES 2 HATFIELD HEATH 0

PREMIER LEAGUE

More like ballet than soccer as Saffron Walden Reserves mount an attack on the Hatfield Heath goal.

Robin Nettle and Alan Ball were the scorers for Walden Reserves.

Source : Herts & Essex Observer

DIVISION III CHALLENGE CUP FINAL

HEECO SPORTS 1 HIGH LAVER RES 0

INTER-DIVISIONAL CUP FINAL

GREAT PARNDON RESERVES 5 SHEERING RESERVES 0

Sheering were beaten out of sight by a side who were superior in almost every department.

Parndon got on to the victory trail after 15 minutes when Hawliczek left Ashton groping for a glorious drive from outside the penalty area.

Five minutes before the break, the Sheering defence was caught wide open and although Gunn slipped as the goalkeeper came out to challenge he was able to get up and stroke the ball into the net.

Any hope Sheering may have had of pulling the game round virtually disappeared within five minutes of the restart when Bray increased their arrears from a Chalk cross.

Knighton collected Chalk's pass in midfield and streaked past the Sheering defence to make it 4-0 with a fine goal,

The scoring was completed in the closing minutes by Kilbours when the Sheering defence was again caught wide open.

DIVISION II CHALLENGE CUP FINAL

NEWPORT 3 GREAT PARNDON RESERVES 0

Newport upset the applecart with a clear-cut victory and their goalkeeper 'Diggy' Didcot, who must have broken the hearts of the Parndon players with a near faultless performance.

The Newport defence had to work hard to keep their goal in-tact. But as so often happens it was the team less in the picture as an attacking force who broke the deadlock. A sudden sharp thrust caught the Parndon defence on the hop and Westwood whipped the ball into the net.

After 37 minutes play Newport had their supporters yelling with delight as they went two up when Ingram put the finishing touch to a slick move with a close range shot.

Parndon's hopes finally faded 16 minutes from time when they conceded a penalty and goalkeeper Traveller was beaten by Butcher's spot kick which he should have saved, the ball appearing to pass through the goalkeeper's legs.

DIVISION I CHALLENGE CUP FINAL

NETTESWELL AND BURNT MILL 0 SAFFRON WALDEN YOUTH 1

Only a handful of spectators watched a game which seldom rose above mediocre, neither side ever getting to grips with the problems presented by the hard ground and a lively ball.

The decisive goal came almost immediately after the restart, Bounders hooking the ball over Tripp's head.

PREMIER DIVISION CHALLENGE CUP FINAL

HATFIELD HEATH 3 DEBDEN 2 (AFTER EXTRA-TIME)

Hatfield Heath made another successful visit to the George Wilson Stadium winning the League's Premier Division Cup.

And the Heath did it the hard way. They conceded a penalty, twice fell into arrears and lost Hobday through injury early in the game before snatching the verdict in extra-time.

The penalty came early in the game – a harsh award for what appeared to be accidental hands – and from the spot Watson had long-serving goalkeeper Mel Turner going the wrong way.

At the time Heath were down to 10 men, Hobday having gone off to receive attention on the touchline. He returned after a few minutes, but soon had to go off for good and was replaced by Bruty.

The scores were levelled by S Reville, who forced the ball over the line from close range. But right on the interval Lindsell edged Debden in front again with a superb header from a corner.

The balance was restored by Stone's crisp drive into the top corner of the net.

The Heath had the edge in the additional period during which the decisive goal was knocked in by Elliott following a corner.

President, Mr George Wilson, presents the Premier Division Cup to **HATFIELD HEATH** captain Billy Dean.

Source : Herts & Essex Observer

APPLAUSE FOR LEAGUE CHAIRMAN

Source : Herts & Essex Observer

Albury skipper Peter English collected the Premier Division Cup from League President Mr George Wilson.

Source : Herts & Essex Observer

Proving that you do not always have to win to get among the silverware, Newport Reserves skipper, John Rushforth, receives the cup for the most sporting team in all divisions.

Over 300 people at Rhodes Avenue at the League's Annual presentation applauded when it was announced Mr Bill Bruty was celebrating his 21st as Chairman of the League.

In proposing the toast to the ladies and guests, Mr Bruty paid tribute to the men who had helped the League.

He thanked the League President, Mr George Wilson, and said he did not know what the League would have done without his support.

Mr Bruty spoke of the close association they had with Bishop's Stortford Football Club, who always allowed them to use the facilities at Rhodes Avenue and Stansted Football Club, who were always ready to help.

The principal guest, Mr Maurice Jeffers, Assistant-Secretary of the Essex FA, said that the large attendance reflected the healthy state which the League was in.

SUDDEN DEATH OF MR 'WALLY' DAY

Mr Walter John 'Wally' Day well known over the past 35 years died suddenly in Bishop's Stortford. He was 53.

Wally Day, a native of Bush End, had lived in Hatfield Heath for 40 years.

He was married and left a widow.

Wally Day had been Registration Secretary of the League since 1966. League Chairman Bill Bruty referred to Mr Day as a 'great gentleman,' and League Secretary, Mr Roy Harrison, called his death, 'a great loss.'

Wally Day was also Chairman of the West Essex Border Charity Cup.

He was Vice-Chairman of the Hatfield Heath Football Club, and for 16 years had been the club's Secretary. He first played for the Heath in 1935.

For 22 years he had organised the flower and vegetable show at the annual Heath football and cricket club fete.

Mr Arthur Perry, the Heath's football club Secretary, said : 'Wally did his work with efficiency and dedication. Local football and the Heath will be the poorer.'

LEAGUE INCREASES SUBSCIPTIONS

At the 50th Anniversary Annual General Meeting on 8th July the deaths were announced of the League's Honorary Registration Secretary Mr W.J. Day and Vice-President Mr A C Harris, both of whom had died suddenly in the days before the meeting.

Members of the League paid tribute to Mr Day's work and a two-minute silence was observed.

At the meeting it was proposed that the vacancy caused by the death of Mr A C Harris be filled by Mr L H J Thorne, this was carried unanimously.

It was then proposed by Mr G Reed and seconded by Mr G H Wilson that Mr W A Bruty and Mr L H J Thorne be made Life-Presidents in gratitude for all the work both these gentlemen had done for the League over so many years. This was carried unanimously.

The League decided to increase their subscriptions in all four divisions by £1 at the meeting. The subscriptions were now Premier Division (£2.50), Division I (£2.25), Division II and III (£2).

Among the changes in rules was one that no club would be able to play three players in any division who had played six or more games in a higher division. This tightened the control as three players from the higher division could play in a lower division before, it was reported.

Another rule alteration was that all sides must enter cup competitions instead of having the right to withdraw.

Any club playing 'ringers' may have points forfeited and awarded to the opposing side (this is to be at the discretion of the League Management Committee).

Any clubs who suspect 'ringers' can demand all the signatures of the opposing side after the game in question. This will then be checked against the registration list.

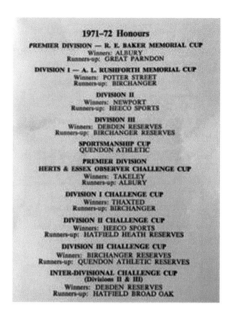

SCORED TWO THEN BROKE LEG

Hatfield Broad Oak Football Club received another severe blow when their captain Roy Field broke his leg.

Roy's injury is a particularly bad setback as he is an outstanding clubman and an excellent captain. As he is 36 a question mark must hang over his future. He has been playing football for 20 years mainly with Broad Oak as well as four years with Heath Rovers.

One of the many occasions on which Birchanger Reserves striker Bill Wright caused panic in the Quendon Athletic Reserves defence.

Source : Herts & Essex Observer

DIVISION III CHALLENGE CUP FINAL

BIRCHANGER RESERVES 10 QUENDON ATHLETIC RESERVES 0

Not so much a football match as a slaughter. Quendon were never in with a chance in the Division III Cup Final at the George Wilson Stadium and it quickly became only the question of the margin of Birchanger's victory.

Playing against the wind in the first half, Birchanger went into the dressing room at half-time with a 2-0 lead.

Afterwards they completely dominated the game and Athletic having little but courage to offer.

Hat tricks were notched by Wright and Abbott, with Maley, Gray, Buttle and Ball also getting one each.

Mr Lionel Thorne, a Vice-President of the League, presented the cup to Gray, the Birchanger skipper following their 10-0 win.

INTER-DIVISIONAL CHALLENGE CUP FINAL

DEBDEN RESERVES 2 HATFIELD BROAD OAK 1

Fox, the most dangerous Debden forward, gave his side the lead after nine minutes when his shot was deflected past Cook in the Broad Oak goal.

With the wind advantage, Broad Oak put on the pressure and Chris Baker equalised in the twenty-nineth minute. He pounced on hesitancy in the defence to slide the ball into the net.

With ten minutes left, Pledger ran on to a good through pass and crossed for Adams to turn the ball into the net and give Debden the trophy.

DIVISION II CHALLENGE CUP FINAL

HEECO SPORTS 3 HATFIELD HEATH RESERVES 0

Heeco had the incentive of a goal within two minutes of the start, Tim Novell heading through from a melee which developed in the Heath goalmouth.

More constructive in midfield, Heeco continued to dominate the game in the second half, going further ahead when Brandon left Flack groping for a well taken shot.

The final nail in the coffin was hammered home in the last minute, Foreman's shot going off the goalkeeper.

DIVISION I CHALLENGE CUP FINAL

THAXTED 1 BIRCHANGER 0

In a dull first half Thaxted were clearly the better side and should have gone ahead.

The second period opened with both sides showing far more dash and spirit.

The second period opened with both sides showing far more dash and spirit. After an early Birchanger burst Thaxted broke away, a move between Greenwood and Luckey giving the latter a sight of the target from twenty yards and his fine shot completely beat Stagg.

Source : Herts & Essex Observer

PREMIER DIVISION CHALLENGE CUP FINAL

TAKELEY 4 ALBURY 3

'Mugger' Smith opened the scoring for Takeley when he smashed home a free kick from the edge of the box but it was not long before Saunders equalised with a splendidly taken goal.

Before and after the goal the woodwork was hit at each end and there were similarly narrow escapes before a neat move down the Albury right ended with Saunders putting them in front seven minutes before the interval.

In the second half both sides had strong appeals turned down and Albury had a goal disallowed for offside before the scores were levelled. Peter Trower raced through the stretched Albury defence to hammer his shot past Chipperfield.

Takeley went ahead when Ivor Parrish took full advantage of a muddle in the Albury defence which was again at fault ten minutes from time when Smith netted easily.

But Albury were not finished and a minute later Peter English rammed home a free kick and up to the final whistle the Takeley defence had to absorb considerable pressure.

Source : Herts & Essex Observer

Takeley skipper Mick Ryan has no bigger fan than his son Patrick, pictured on dad's shoulders proudly displaying the cup.

ESSEX JUNIOR CUP FINAL

GREAT PARNDON 2 MERSEA ISLAND 1

Great Parndon became the first team from the League to win the competition.

GUEST OF HONOUR PLAYED FOOTBALL 50 YEARS AGO

Guest of honour at the Annual Dinner of Takeley Football Club was Mr Arthur Piper, who was a prominent figure in local football 50 years ago. Mr Piper played for Takeley and later for Bishop's Stortford, excelling equally at football and cricket.

Mr Piper proposed the toast to Takeley Football Club. He recalled the early history of the club and particularly its revival after World War I, followed by very successful years in the now defunct Dunmow and District League.

Mr Piper spoke of the hard work of the Chairman, Bert Robinson; Secretary, Ron Bradle; and Treasurer, Harold Munns, and said that their long years of service showed that a happy atmosphere existed between the officers and the members.

President A L Frost in reply, welcomed Mr & Mrs Piper, and also Mr G Banks, Press and Match Secretary of the League.

Mr Frost spoke of the fine performance of the club in defeating Albury in the Final of the League Challenge Cup and said the team owed much to the inspiring leadership of their captain, Mick Ryan.

He thanked the ladies and the caterers for providing tea for players and spectators at home games.

The President concluded by suggesting the club should look to the future by organising and coaching the many teenage boys in the village, as the older players could not be expected to go on for ever.

Sportsman of the Year trophy was awarded to 'Mugger Smith,' who scored 53 goals during the season. The presentation was made by Ron Bradley.

Mick Ryan then expressed his appreciation of the support he had received from players and officers, and particularly of the hard work of team manager Jim Scraggs.

LEAGUE CELEBRATED ITS GOLDEN JUBILEE

Quendon Athletic may not have put their village on the map in the way that Great Parndon did but they earned it a great deal of goodwill.

At the 50th anniversary dinner of the League, Quendon Athletic received the coveted Sportsman's Cup, the trophy which the League awards to the most sporting side in its divisions.

But they had to share the large amount of goodwill generated by the dinner – which was attended by 270 people – with three of the League's hardest working officers, the President, George Wilson, Secretary Roy Harrison, and Treasurer George Reed, who all received presentations from the League Chairman, Bill Bruty, in recognition of their services.

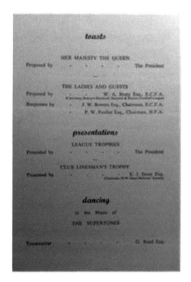

Among the presentations at the League Dinner was one by the Chairman, Mr Bill Bruty to the President, Mr George Wilson.

BOOST FOR CLUB FINANCES

At the League's Annual General Meeting, Mr A E Dimond, Chairman of the Harlow League, at the invitation of Mr W.A. Bruty, spoke regarding the 50th Anniversary of the League, and the friendship which had existed between the Harlow & District League and the Bishop's Stortford, Stansted & District League for the last 20 years. He then presented the League, through Mr Bruty, with a pennant from the Harlow & District League to mark the occasion.

The introduction of the requirement for each team to buy 25 tickets for the Cup Finals has put the League on a much sounder financial footing.

The Treasurer, Mr George Reed, reported that the League had a balance £151.78 at the bank compared to £30.69 at the end of the previous season.

The sale of tickets brought in £235 but the cost of trophies was just under £200.

The Secretary, Mr Roy Harrison, also referred to the new scheme in his report. 'One thing that is here to stay if the League is to continue to function is that teams must purchase tickets for the finals by the first of January each year.'

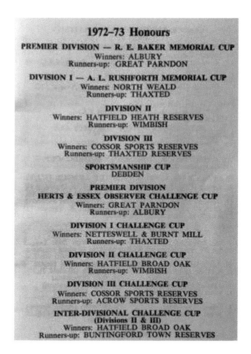

1972–73 Honours

PREMIER DIVISION — R. E. BAKER MEMORIAL CUP
Winners: ALBURY
Runners-up: GREAT PARNDON

DIVISION I — A. L. RUSHFORTH MEMORIAL CUP
Winners: NORTH WEALD
Runners-up: THAXTED

DIVISION II
Winners: HATFIELD HEATH RESERVES
Runners-up: WIMBISH

DIVISION III
Winners: COSSOR SPORTS RESERVES
Runners-up: THAXTED RESERVES

SPORTSMANSHIP CUP
DEBDEN

PREMIER DIVISION
HERTS & ESSEX OBSERVER CHALLENGE CUP
Winners: GREAT PARNDON
Runners-up: ALBURY

DIVISION I CHALLENGE CUP
Winners: NETTESWELL & BURNT MILL
Runners-up: THAXTED

DIVISION II CHALLENGE CUP
Winners: HATFIELD BROAD OAK
Runners-up: WIMBISH

DIVISION III CHALLENGE CUP
Winners: COSSOR SPORTS RESERVES
Runners-up: ACROW SPORTS RESERVES

INTER-DIVISIONAL CHALLENGE CUP
(Divisions II & III)
Winners: HATFIELD BROAD OAK
Runners-up: BUNTINGFORD TOWN RESERVES

At the November Management Committee meeting Mr Bruty said that Mrs Day had asked us to accept a cup in memory of her late husband 'Wally.' The cup is to be known as the W J Day Memorial Cup 1971. The cup is to be competed for annually by the Champions and Challenge Cup holders of the Premier Division. Should these two clubs be one and the same, then the Champions and the losing finalists of the Challenge Cup will compete.

In January Manuden were allowed to withdraw from the League.

In 1973, Brian Bayford, who was Secretary of Bishop's Stortford FC and member of Hertfordshire Football Association at that time, was elected as a Vice-President of the League.

Source : Herts & Essex Observer

ALBURY 6 HIGH LAVER 2

PREMIER DIVISION Robert Newman scoring his second goal in Albury's win.

DIVISION III CHALLENGE CUP FINAL

ACROW SPORTS RESERVES 3 COSSOR SPORTS RESERVES 5

The battle of the works clubs ended with Cossor Sports Reserves comfortable winners.

From the start Cossor looked more dangerous up front and it seemed only a matter of time before they went in front. The goal came from Armstrong in the 15th minute, but almost immediately Gdabeo missed a good chance of putting Acrow on level terms.

There was an element of luck about the Harlow team's second goal, Turner's shot being deflected sufficiently to leave goalkeeper Rix without a chance.

Both sides missed scoring chances in the second half before Acrow got back in the game, Page's corner-kick being punched into the top of his own net by Brettle. But it was not long before Cossor's two goal lead was restored by Longman, whose shot deceived Rix and crept inside the post. Five minutes later Longman struck again following a good run down the wing by Dodman.

Acrow's hopes were revived when Bunting got their second goal, but back came Cossor for Carter to score and it was not until the last minute that Bunting netted Acrow's third.

DIVISION II CHALLENGE CUP FINAL

HATFIELD BROAD OAK 4 WIMBISH 2

Broad Oak's victory was a personal triumph for striker John Williams, who walked off with a hat trick under his belt.

It was somewhat against the run of play and with a slice of luck that Broad Oak opened their account after 30 minutes, keeper Butcher allowing William's header from a corner to slip through his hands. Just afterwards, the same player missed a good chance by shooting wide when he was left with only the keeper to beat.

Broad Oak increased their lead through Ted Field, who fastened on to a weak goal kick and cut into the box to net from a narrow angle.

Wimbish fell further behind as the result of wrongly anticipating an offside decision, which would have been justified, and Williams went through to score easily. Williams completed his hat trick before the opposition staged their late revival which brought them goals by Crouch and Bacon, not to mention other anxious moments for the Broad Oak defence.

Source : Roy Bacon

WIMBISH

INTER-DIVISIONAL CHALLENGE CUP FINAL

HATFIELD BROAD OAK 3 BUNTINGFORD TOWN RESERVES 1

Having previously won the Division II Cup, Broad Oak completed a notable League double by winning the Inter-Divisional Cup.

And once again their hero was striker Jerry Williams who repeated the hat-trick he notched in the earlier match.

Fords struck first through Stobart, but by half-time Williams had levelled the scores.

Afterwards, Broad Oak, who had made a number of changes from the winning line-up four days previously, took charge of the game. Within five minutes of the restart Williams gave them the lead with a brilliant goal and he went on to put the issue beyond doubt by climbing high to head in an accurate cross.

DIVISION I CHALLENGE CUP FINAL

NETTESWELL AND BURNT MILL 3 THAXTED 2

(AFTER EXTRA-TIME)

Holders of the Division I Cup, Thaxted, looked all set to retain the trophy when they established a 2-0 lead during the first 45 minutes. But the Mill staged a fine second half recovery and went on to snatch the decisive goal near the end of extra-time.

Not only did the Mill come from behind to achieve success, but in the 85th minute they had goalkeeper Whiston taken to hospital suffering from concussion after making a brave save at the feet of a Thaxted forward. It was not until the start of the extra-time that the Mill brought on a substitute.

The treacherous pitch, which had been thoroughly soaked earlier in the day made it almost impossible to play constructive football, a number of promising movements by both teams being spoilt by the ball sticking in the mud.

Thaxted went into the lead after 15 minutes through Saych, who hammered home a penalty for hands and for a time the cup holders did most of the attacking. In the 42nd minute they went further ahead when Wright worked his way into the box and left Whiston well beaten with affine shot high into the net.

In the second half the Mill's persistence paid off on the hour when Payne ran on to a long ball over the top of the Thaxted defence and steered his shot just under the bar. Five minutes later Parker levelled the scores and although Thaxted came back strongly in the closing stages, they were unable to retrieve their lost advantage.

With extra-time rapidly running out and a replay looking a distinct possibility Eiffert made a night of glory for the Mill.

Source : Herts & Essex Observer

NETTESWELL & BURNT MILL

PREMIER DIVISION CHALLENGE CUP FINAL

ALBURY 2 GREAT PARNDON 3

For the second successive season the League's Premier Division double eluded Albury.

Parndon got the vital early goal after only five minutes play. Johnstone heading through a cross from the right and for a time they dominated the exchanges. But they also had their anxious moments, notably when Robert Newman had Young scrambling to get his shot away and then when they survived a hectic goalmouth melee following a corner.

Parndon were more direct in their approach however and went two up after half an hour. Thomas outpaced the Albury defence and crossed for Johnstone to knock in his second goal.

Albury's revival began six minutes later when they won a free kick on the edge of the penalty area and Robert Newman's shot found its way through the defensive wall.

It was almost immediately afterwards that Parndon lost Myers when he fell heavily and was taken to hospital with a suspected broken wrist and up to the interval their defence was under pressure.

The equaliser came in the 48th minute, Chris Newman's spot kick, awarded for hands, going in off the post and this was the signal for increased pressure on the Parndon defence. The goal had a narrow escape when Smith's shot on the turn bounced off the bar and Robert Newman went close with a crisp drive when the ball came out from a corner.

With extra-time looming Parndon broke away and snatched the verdict with a brilliant goal, Smith latching on to the ball and beating two defenders in a confined space before leaving Chipperfield groping for his shot. Albury tried desperately hard to save the game. Prime was close to doing so with a drive which passed inches over the bar.

Mr John Barry, a League Vice-President, presenting the Premier Division Cup to the **GREAT PARNDON** captain.

Source : Herts & Essex Observer

CHAMPIONSHIP HAT-TRICK

Source : Herts & Essex Observer

Garry Godfrey (Cossor Sports), Phillip Brookwell (Hatfield Heath Reserves), Mervyn Jessop (North Weald) and Peter English (Albury).

Albury player Peter Newman was presented with a trophy at the League's Annual Dinner to mark the club winning the Premier Division championship three years in succession.

The chief guest was Mr Len Menhinick, a member of the Essex FA and a former Secretary of Chelmsford Football Club.

He congratulated the officers on the efficient way the club was run and paid tribute to club secretaries.

'I congratulate Secretaries of clubs, especially those of clubs at the bottom of the League. It is easy to run a club if you are at the top but not so easy if you are down at the bottom,' he said.

SPORTSMANSHIP TROPHIES INTRODUCED

At the League's Annual General Meeting on 9th July, It was proposed that Mr Brian Bayford, who was a member of the Herts FA, and also Honorary Secretary of Bishop's Stortford FC be elected as a Vice-President. This was carried unanimously. Mr Bayford, who was at the meeting, thanked the League, and said he would be pleased to accept.

It was announced that a Sportsmanship Cup would be presented to the overall winning team and plaque for the Divisional winners.

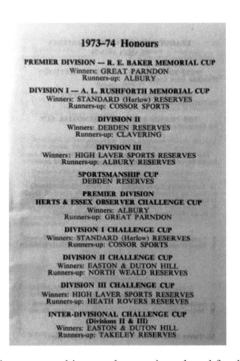

1973-74 Honours

PREMIER DIVISION — R. E. BAKER MEMORIAL CUP
Winners: GREAT PARNDON
Runners-up: ALBURY

DIVISION I — A. L. RUSHFORTH MEMORIAL CUP
Winners: STANDARD (Harlow) RESERVES
Runners-up: COSSOR SPORTS

DIVISION II
Winners: DEBDEN RESERVES
Runners-up: CLAVERING

DIVISION III
Winners: HIGH LAVER SPORTS RESERVES
Runners-up: ALBURY RESERVES

SPORTSMANSHIP CUP
DEBDEN RESERVES

PREMIER DIVISION
HERTS & ESSEX OBSERVER CHALLENGE CUP
Winners: ALBURY
Runners-up: GREAT PARNDON

DIVISION I CHALLENGE CUP
Winners: STANDARD (Harlow) RESERVES
Runners-up: COSSOR SPORTS

DIVISION II CHALLENGE CUP
Winners: EASTON & DUTON HILL
Runners-up: NORTH WEALD RESERVES

DIVISION III CHALLENGE CUP
Winners: HIGH LAVER SPORTS RESERVES
Runners-up: HEATH ROVERS RESERVES

INTER-DIVISIONAL CHALLENGE CUP
(Divisions II & III)
Winners: EASTON & DUTON HILL
Runners-up: TAKELEY RESERVES

The individual divisional sportsmanship awards were introduced for the 1973/74 season.

FARNHAM REVIVAL

After a lapse of 20 years Farnham FC is being revived and will compete in League Division III. In addition it is hoped to arrange friendlies for most Sunday mornings.

As a prelude to the re-entry into competitive football, Farnham played 27 friendlies last season winning 11 of them.

The Chairman/Manager Mr W Nott has high hopes of a successful season. Most of the players competing for positions in the League team are young and inexperienced, but he thinks he has the nucleus of a good side once the youngsters gain experience.

■ Stortford League side Tye Green 1973-74. Back row left to right: Nipper Vinton (manager), Allan Tye, Johnny Ship, Phil Jones, Ray Moles, Derek Budd, Ray Hayter, Micky Day. Front row: Barry Etherington, Norbert Creed, Graham Cole, Arthur Strivens, Gordon Costello. ★ (683)

Source : Harlow Citizen

TYE GREEN

ACROW SPORTS RESERVES 2

NEWPORT RESERVES I

DIVISION III CHALLENGE CUP

Acrow Reserves completed a memorable day for the club by reaching the Division III Cup Semi-Final after being a goal down after the interval.

Source : Herts & Essex Observer

292

LETTER FROM BISHOP'S STORTFORD, STANSTED & DISTRICT FOOTBALL LEAGUE

BILL BRUTY

Congratulations from the Bishop's Stortford, Stansted & District League and sincere thanks - I don't know what we would have done without B.S.F.C. My first visit to their ground was in 1931 when I attended a League Cup Final and from that day to this the B.S.F.C have let my League play all its Cup Finals on its ground.

We have some 1,200 players registered with our League and they all know how close our association is with the B.S.F.C.

What can we wish the Club in their Centenary Year?

A good ground (they have got that).

A good committee to run the club (they have got that)

A good Playing Squad (Under Ted - not much better in the League).

So let us all wish that the F.A. Amateur Cup, in its last year, will come to rest in the Club's Board Room.

Thi is my 50th Year in Football (24 years as Chairman of our Local League) and I say a personal 'Thank you Gentlemen of the B.S.F.C for the help you have given Junior Football in the District.'

DIVISION III CHALLENGE CUP FINAL

HIGH LAVER RESERVES 3 HEATH ROVERS RESERVES 0

INTER-DIVISIONAL CHALLENGE CUP FINAL

EASTON AND DUTON HILL 4 TAKELEY RESERVES 1

After taking an early lead Easton went on to a deserved victory in the Inter-Divisional Cup Final at Rhodes Avenue.

From the kick off Easton made the running and their reward soon came when Paul Perry headed home after seven minutes.

Takeley began to settle and trouble the Easton defence but they could not take full control of the midfield and once again it was Easton who broke through in the 31st minute to score. Bill Wright put the cross through to Paul Perry, whose powerful shot was touched by the goalkeeper before falling into the net.

After the interval Takeley searched desperately for a goal but they lacked the finish and Easton were the ones who increased their lead. A pass from Bill Deack in the 56th minute was picked up by 16-year-old Terry Hollingsworth, who beat a defender and the goalkeeper before slotting the ball in from 12 yards.

But Takeley were still not beaten and in the 73rd minute they finally got their reward. Substitute George Lilley tackled past the defence and goalkeeper and cracked the ball into the net.

Easton clinched their victory four minutes later after a free kick, awarded for a foul just outside the penalty box. The kick was taken by Terry Brewer and Paul Perry was there to head on to Bill Deack who scored from close range.

DIVISION I CHALLENGE CUP FINAL

COSSOR SPORTS 2 STANDARD (HARLOW) RESERVES 3

Cup tie fever raged in the cold and the rain at the George Wilson Stadium. But the three or four hundred fans were nearly all from Harlow and had come to yell encouragement to their sides.

The wintry conditions may well have something to do with the cracking pace both sides set and kept up amazingly well. Cossor, whose supporters seemed dominant at first, looked a good bet in the early stages when they went into a 2-0 lead, through Longhurst. His second was a converted penalty.

But Standard were only waiting for their second wind, and Fullen and Dear had put them on equal terms before the interval.

In the second half Hillier's goal gave Standard the lead and never looked like losing after this.

DIVISION II CHALLENGE CUP FINAL

EASTON AND DUTON HILL 2 NORTH WEALD RESERVES 1

(AFTER EXTRA-TIME)

Easton completed their cup double by winning the Division II cup at the George Wilson Stadium.

All the goals were scored in extra-time after the first 90 minutes were played with neither team finding the net.

During the first period of extra-time Easton eventually scored. Paul Perry pushed the ball home from close range after the goalkeeper had fallen.

But North Weald were not beaten and scored the equaliser in the second period. A penalty was given for hands and Drane made no mistake from the spot.

The winning goal came five minutes before the final whistle. From a dead ball situation, Brewer crossed to Wright, whose powerful shot went into the corner of the net.

PREMIER DIVISION CHALLENGE CUP FINAL

ALBURY 3 GREAT PARNDON 2

Two well-matched sides provided top-class entertainment when Albury earned the Herts & Essex Observer Cup by the odd goal in five. Even Stortford host officials shared the excitement as the village supporters roared home their men,

In this Premier Division final tie, as in those of the League's other divisions, the lads seemed to pull out reserves of speed and energy to bustle throughout the 90 minutes. Play was a little rough at times but referee Mr C Pooley had a firm grip on the situation after booking a player from each side.

Alan Cherry, the Parndon goalkeeper, was unlucky to get hurt, but carried on gamely to serve the Harlow side well. And indeed it was Parndon who opened the scoring, through striker John Johnson after 15 minutes. Soon afterwards the Parndon attack had the chance of another easy one but threw this away to their final undoing.

Albury's Chris Newman put them on level terms just before the interval. But the best was still to come, and the floodlit second half was to prove packed with action, in which both sides could have pushed the score along by more careful marksmanship.

As it was, Benny Smith was the first to make no mistake, putting Albury ahead again in the 55th minute. But Parndon struck back again two minutes later when Ivor Smith put them on level terms.

The minutes ticked by as the supporters clamoured for the decider. came, to a frenzy of village enthusiasm, when Keith Devlin ripped in Albury's third goal three minutes from time. Parndon tried all they knew to snatch another, but it was too late.

Albury skipper, Peter English, held aloft with the trophy.

Source : Herts & Essex Observer

BROAD OAK'S TOP PLAYERS

Hatfield Broad Oak's Sports Association Annual Dinner and Dance was another big social success with an attendance of 170, which Mr Reg Simons described as a great encouragement to the committee.

He referred also to the football club's decision to reinstate the reserve team after a period of five years and said they had done well to finish in third position in their division.

MR FOOTBALL GETS A TELLY

For 50 years' devoted service to local football, Mr Bill Bruty was presented with a colour television at the Annual Dinner of the League.

As well as the television set, which was given by the clubs in the League and many other footballing friends, Mr Bruty was presented with a cheque and the Management Committee of the League pledged to buy his television licence for the rest of his life.

Making the presentation. Mr John Barry spoke of the tremendous work done by Mr Bruty who was quite overcome with emotion, thanked everyone and said that the presentation had come as a complete surprise.

Source : Harlow Citizen

Guest speaker at the dinner Mr Arthur Barrett, from the Essex FA, congratulated the League on its good record and thanked it for all its work with junior football. He also mentioned Mr Bruty's loyal service to football in the county.

Mr Bruty presented Mr George Wilson, President of Bishop's Stortford Football Club, a silver salver from the League in recognition of the club's centenary year and their success in the Amateur Cup.

At the League's annual General Meeting Mr Bruty thanked all present, for the wonderful gift of a colour television set, which was presented to him at the League's Annual Dinner.

The Hatfield Heath/Broad Oak area of the county seemed to have been particularly expert at breeding loyal men in the field of football. At the Hatfield Heath end-of-season dinner, George Brown was presented with a long-service from the Essex FA for his 37 years association with the club. George started as a player in 1937, played regularly for the next 15 years and in 1953 was made a committee member.

Source : David Brown

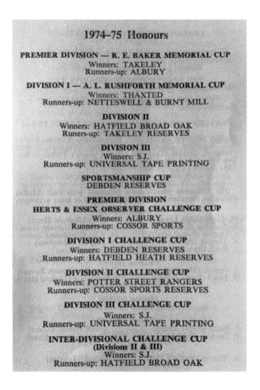

1974–75 Honours

PREMIER DIVISION — R. E. BAKER MEMORIAL CUP
Winners: TAKELEY
Runners-up: ALBURY

DIVISION I — A. L. RUSHFORTH MEMORIAL CUP
Winners: THAXTED
Runners-up: NETTESWELL & BURNT MILL

DIVISION II
Winners: HATFIELD BROAD OAK
Runers-up: TAKELEY RESERVES

DIVISION III
Winners: S.J.
Runners-up: UNIVERSAL TAPE PRINTING

SPORTSMANSHIP CUP
DEBDEN RESERVES

PREMIER DIVISION
HERTS & ESSEX OBSERVER CHALLENGE CUP
Winners: ALBURY
Runners-up: COSSOR SPORTS

DIVISION I CHALLENGE CUP
Winners: DEBDEN RESERVES
Runners-up: HATFIELD HEATH RESERVES

DIVISION II CHALLENGE CUP
Winners: POTTER STREET RANGERS
Runners-up: COSSOR SPORTS RESERVES

DIVISION III CHALLENGE CUP
Winners: S.J.
Runners-up: UNIVERSAL TAPE PRINTING

INTER-DIVISIONAL CHALLENGE CUP
(Divisions II & III)
Winners: S.J.
Runners-up: HATFIELD BROAD OAK

Ray Johnstone recently told me that Great Parndon left the League in 1974 to play in the now defunct South Essex League until 1976.

One of the reasons for leaving the League was to get a higher standard of competition and Arthur Dimond said that he could get the club into the Essex Senior League if they could get a private ground. The club's Chairman, Fred Rolleston, looked at buying some suitable sites but ultimately decided against it.

Another reason was that the Essex Junior Cup, which Great Parndon had won three times , rules restricted the number of players from previously winning clubs from entering it (only eight players). The club therefore entered the Essex Intermediate Cup, playing the second teams of clubs like Leytonstone, Ilford and Dagenham.

In 1974, the Jack Cottrill Memorial Cup for the 'Secretary of the Year' was introduced.

S.J.F.C. joined the League in 1974 and in their first two phenomenal seasons achieved two trebles and scored no fewer than 216 League goals. It was success all the way for the club who also enjoyed similar triumphs in the Harlow & District Sunday League. SJFC did not lose a cup game in the League until 7th May 1977 when they were beaten by Thaxted in the Division I Challenge Cup Final.

In October Wimbish were allowed to withdraw from the League and as the club had not completed 75% of their fixtures their record was expunged.

SHEERING 2

GREAT PARNDON RESERVES 2

DIVISION I

Source : Herts & Essex Observer

HATFIELD BROAD OAK

RESERVES 6

ACROW SPORTS RESERVES 2

DIVISION III

Action from a game that was played despite a downpour. Broad Oak took the opportunity to hammer Acrow Sports Reserves and move into second place in the table.

Source : Herts & Essex Observer

'SCANDALOUS' CONDITIONS AT THE PADDOCKS

The lack of proper facilities for the large number of footballers using the nine pitches at Grange Paddocks at the time of the year was described as 'scandalous.'

For the players – many of them boys aged 10 to 11 – there was not adequate changing accommodation, no toilets and no showers or other washing facilities.

The criticism came from Councillor V H Shoebridge at Bishop's Stortford Town Council.

The nearest public lavatory was three-quarters of a mile away, and for those who use Grange Paddocks one-and-a half mile round trip.

'Another thing which sticks out is the lack of water,' he said. 'About three weeks ago I was asked by a team manager to go into the swimming pool and get a bucket of water for the first aid kit but was refused.'

'There are no washing facilities for muddy hands or boots. We are denying children and the adults who use Grange Paddocks while other areas have fantastic facilities.'

'If you want to return courtesy to a team you just have nothing to offer them. They get off their coach and have to change, leaving their clothes laid out on ground sheets.'

Councillor Mrs V Sparrow said that temporary accommodation had been approved pending the establishment of more permanent facilities when the money was available.

The town Mayor, Councillor Vic Wallis, said : 'Members of this Council are fully aware that in the dying days of the former Council it was agreed there would be changing facilities complete with showers and toilets.'

'This was passed over to East Herts and £5,000 provided.'

The sum was 'totally inadequate' said Councillor Roy Strong. He went on : 'this is why there is temporary accommodation costing £500. Something like £10,000 would be needed if Bishop's Stortford Urban Council's suggestion were to be carried out.'

Councillor Mrs V Sparrow said that £4,000 was still earmarked for changing facilities at Grange Paddocks.

'This is a matter of real urgency,' said Councillor Wallis. 'I know our members on East Herts Council will press for this matter, It needs top priority.'

The town Council was to write to East Herts stressing the urgency of the situation. Councillor T Sharrock said : We could send it in the words of a prayer.'

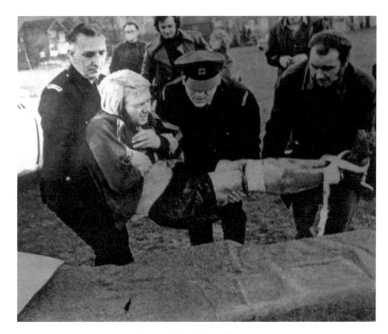

Source : Herts & Essex Observer

ACROW SPORTS 0 NORTH WEALD 3

PREMIER DIVISION

There is no more sombre sight in football than a player being stretchered off. Richard Thompson of Acrow Sports was taken to hospital with a suspected broken ankle from the game against North Weald. An x-ray revealed nothing more than extensive bruising. The game was switched to Thaxted as Acrow Sports ground was unfit.

At the Management Committee meeting in March Mr Harrison reported that at the request of the Chairman, he attended a little function at the home of Mrs J Cottrill, for the purposes of accepting on behalf of the League, a silver cup in memory of her husband Mr Jack Cottrill which was presented by Mr P J Rogers, Industrial Relations Manager on behalf of Standard Telecommunication Laboratories Limited. It was thought that by the Management Committee, that it might be presented annually to the best Club Secretary of the League, if a suitable system could be found.

At the following meeting, Mr Harrison reported that he had written to both Mr P J Rogers of ITT and Mrs Cottrill informing them that the 'Jack Cottrill Memorial Cup' would be presented each year to the best Club Secretary of the League, provided a suitable scheme could be arranged to determine same.

'POTTING SHED' CHANGING ROOMS

There will be no improvement to the changing facilities on Grange Paddocks playing fields, Bishop's Stortford, and the hire price of the ground and a 'ramshackle hut' to change in is to go up from £1.10 to £3.00 per game – a staggering increase of nearly 200%.

The price increase for all council playing fields was recommended by a recent Leisure Service Committee meeting.

The same department of the East Herts District Council's decision to shelve the improvement scheme for the changing facilities has angered local users of the playing fields.

The price increase has still to be agreed by full council. It would then go ahead subject to approval by the Price Commission, but football clubs in the area are to send a deputation of objectors to the meeting to present a petition.

Source : Harlow Gazette

Some feel that East Herts Council should not 'shelve arbitrarily' something that was started by the old Bishop's Stortford UDC before re-organisation.

Youngsters in the area face an equally large increase – two youth sides who use pitches there face a jump from 55p to £1.50 per game.

Director for Leisure Services, Mr Brian Slade recently wrote to Stortford Town Council and told them that although £4,000 had been provided in the estimates for changing accommodation, it was unlikely that any improvements would be made while the current economic climate continues.

The situation at the moment :

The 'huts' provided have no lighting.

There are no toilet facilities.

There is no running water so players – both men and boys – go home covered in mud.

The windows of the huts have been broken and are now boarded up meaning they are pitch dark inside.

There are no longer benches or hooks to hang clothes.

The divisions in the huts have been broken down,

PREMIER DIVISION CHALLENGE CUP FINAL

ALBURY 4 COSSOR SPORTS 0

Albury never looked back once they had nosed ahead midway through the first half.

The other three goals came at peak psychological moments and destroyed a plucky young Cossor side.

Ben Smith netted from close range a minute before the interval to give Albury a comfortable 2-0 lead and then Chris Newman bounced into the picture with goals in the 50th and 51st minutes.

Source : Herts & Essex Observer

DIVISION I CHALLENGE CUP FINAL

DEBDEN RESERVES 3 HATFIELD HEATH RESERVES 1

DIVISION II CHALLENGE CUP FINAL

POTTER STREET RESERVES 2 COSSOR RESERVES 1

S.J.F.C. proved they had stamina playing two Challenge Cup Finals in a week and emerging unbeaten.

The planned Division III Challenge Cup Final between S.J.F.C. and Universal Tapes was postponed as the Rhodes Avenue pitch was waterlogged. This was good news for S.J.'s Pat Brazzier who was to have served a one match suspension.

DIVISION III CHALLENGE CUP FINAL

S.J.F.C. 3 UNIVERSAL TAPES 3 (AFTER EXTRA-TIME)

In the Division III Challenge Cup, S.J. had to pull back from a 3-1 deficit to draw 3-3.

After 20 minutes a good ball from P Barker put T Saunders away on the left. He crossed deep and R Saunders headed back across the goal for R Baton to nip in and score a good headed goal.

Pat Brazzier wiped out the one-goal deficit after 10 minutes, with a well-placed header, but Saffron Walden-based Universal Tapes, the underdogs pressed on at the and led 2-1 at the interval.

S Millership and R Saunders were quick on the break for Tapes and T Saunders took a nice one-two with R Saunders round two defenders and slotted home a great second goal for Tapes.

In the second half S.J. pushed hard but C Reed made two great diving saves, Then came a quick break by J Wren down the left. His cross was perfectly headed on and T Saunders outpaced the S.J. defence to hit the ball home to give Tapes a 3-1 lead.

After this S.J. piled on the pressure. Man-of-the-match Colin Ealey pulled one back, running the length of the pitch before hitting an unstoppable shot into the roof of the net. Although losing Jimmy Windley through injury, S.J. kept up the pressure and snatched the equaliser when A Coote handled in the area and Mick Barry converted the penalty.

In extra-time Brazzier came close to breaking the deadlock when he hit the bar, but Tapes held on to force a replay.

INTER-DIVISIONAL CHALLENGE CUP FINAL

S.J.F.C. 4 HATFIELD BROAD OAK 2

A first half hat-trick by Graham Baker gave S.J. a 3-0 interval lead and a 4-2 win against Division II Champions, Hatfield Broad Oak, in the Inter-Divisional Challenge Cup Final.

A Mick Barry, Chris Brace, Glenn Thurley move ended with Thurley rounding goalkeeper George Clayden before scoring the fourth soon after the interval.

Broad Oak never gave up trying and hit back when goalkeeper Newton made a rare mistake and the other coming from Ivor Parrish.

DIVISION III CHALLENGE CUP FINAL REPLAY

S.J.F.C. 2 UNIVERSAL TAPES 1

S.J.F.C. wound up a marvellous first season in the League by winning the Division III Challenge Cup replay. They beat Universal Tapes 2-1. Tapes were leading 1-0 with only minutes to play when Pat Brazzier headed in a Glenn Thurley corner.

Just before the final whistle Brazzier scored the winner with a 25-yard direct free kick.

In their first season in the League S.J. also won the Division III title and Inter-Divisional Challenge Cup.

ESSEX JUNIOR CUP FINAL

TAKELEY 1 STANWAY ROVERS 0

A 43rd minute goal from Malcolm Skingle was sufficient to bring the Essex Junior Cup to Takeley for the first time.

It was not until the morning of the match that it was decided that the game could be played but some belated spring sunshine made conditions comparatively pleasant for the players

Takeley kept the side that had done so well in the previous two games with Mike Phillips at full-back and Dave Thurgood on the substitutes bench.

The Colchester side had the most impressive record having won five trophies in the previous season and were lying second in the Premier Division of the Colchester and Essex League being four points behind the leaders with five games in hand.

However, in the competition, Stanway had the more convincing record having clear cut in every round, whereas Takeley were forced to extra-time in three games.

Takeley started in convincing fashion and it soon became apparent that Skingle was to be the main threat to Stanway's defence.

In the first 20 minutes, Stanway survived four menacing attacks. Skingle put Clive Baines through and Newstead saved on the line. Peter Baker had a header tipped over the bar and both Peter Trower and Baines again brought the goalkeeper into action.

The Takeley back-four showed great skill in turning defence into attack and began a movement involving Baines and Trower.

Skingle cut in and drove a swerving-shot inches into the near post giving Takeley the lead.

Source : Tim Clarey

TAKELEY

PREMIER DIVISION AND ESSEX JUNIOR CUP WINNERS

NEW COUNCIL FEES THREATEN LEAGUE CLUBS

Protests from soccer clubs facing extinction because of increased fees for pitches were to be put before a special meeting of the community services committee of East Herts Council.

A Council spokesman said there had been a 'substantial' number of protests from clubs using the pitches, and these would be considered.

Clubs and organisations, in addition to letters to the Council, have lobbied a number of local Councillors.

The pictures concerned are those at Grange Paddocks and an official of the North-West Essex Sunday League said that three tentative resignations from that League had been received, as a result of the increases.

The Bishop's Stortford, Stansted and District League joined forces with the McMullen's Hertford and District League in adding their protests.

The increases were approved by a meeting of the full Council. The charge of £1.10 per pitch for seniors was increased to £3.00 and from 55p to £1.50 for juniors under 16.

A Council spokesman said there was nothing to stop any organisation writing to the Council and asking for a reduction in their fees.

One League official said the clubs believed that, taking into account referee's fees, it would mean putting up their match fees for the players to 50p per match and this was ridiculous, particularly in view of a lack of changing accommodation and other facilities at Grange Paddocks.

But the Council spokesman said the clubs had had the facilities 'cheaply' in the past. Divided among 22 players using the pitch, the increase was not very much.

It had to be pointed out, said the spokesman, that the Council was merely following a national trend and a Government directive that fees for leisure and amenity services must be more 'realistic.'

SPECIAL AWARD FOR TAKELEY

A memento was presented to Mr 'Pip' Willett – who had left the district for his services to the League at the Annual Dinner and Dance.

Another was awarded to Takeley in recognition of their feat in winning the Essex Junior Cup.

Chairman Mr Bill Bruty said that apart from Great Parndon in 1972, the last time the cup was won by a team in the area was before the turn of the century in 1896/97, when Saffron Walden triumphed.

Proposing the toast to the ladies and guests, Mr Bruty congratulated the team who had won trophies during the season and praised the hard working club Secretaries and League Officers for their efforts in a difficult year.

Mr Frank Holloway, secretary of the Hertfordshire FA responded.

SOCCER WILL COST THE CLUBS MORE

At the League's Annual General Meeting Mr Bruty introduced Mr Brian Curtis who had recently been elected as a member of the Hertfordshire FA.

Later Mr Bruty paid tribute to the officers who, through varying reasons had retired from the League. He made special mention of Mr R C Harrison, the new Vice-Chairman, for his work as Honorary Secretary over the last twelve years and asked that his sincere thanks and appreciation be recorded.

Roger Brinsford succeeded Roy Harrison, and Roger told me that he only arrived in Bishop's Stortford in the late sixties but was fortunate enough to meet Roy as they both worked for the ANZ Bank.

Roger told me that the those who served on the League's Management Committee were wonderful characters who gave so much to local football.

The balance sheet was submitted by the Treasurer, Mr G Reed, showed that income, including the balance of £141.01 from the previous season was £912.63. After meeting expenses there was an increased credit balance of £176.89.

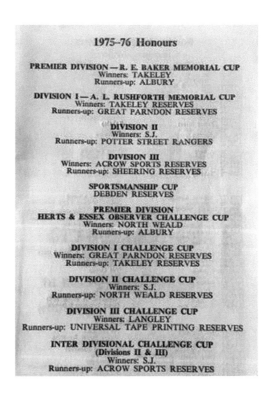

1975–76 Honours

PREMIER DIVISION — R. E. BAKER MEMORIAL CUP
Winners: TAKELEY
Runners-up: ALBURY

DIVISION I — A. L. RUSHFORTH MEMORIAL CUP
Winners: TAKELEY RESERVES
Runners-up: GREAT PARNDON RESERVES

DIVISION II
Winners: S.J.
Runners-up: POTTER STREET RANGERS

DIVISION III
Winners: ACROW SPORTS RESERVES
Runners-up: SHEERING RESERVES

SPORTSMANSHIP CUP
DEBDEN RESERVES

PREMIER DIVISION
HERTS & ESSEX OBSERVER CHALLENGE CUP
Winners: NORTH WEALD
Runners-up: ALBURY

DIVISION I CHALLENGE CUP
Winners: GREAT PARNDON RESERVES
Runners-up: TAKELEY RESERVES

DIVISION II CHALLENGE CUP
Winners: S.J.
Runners-up: NORTH WEALD RESERVES

DIVISION III CHALLENGE CUP
Winners: LANGLEY
Runners-up: UNIVERSAL TAPE PRINTING RESERVES

INTER DIVISIONAL CHALLENGE CUP
(Divisions II & III)
Winners: S.J.
Runners-up: ACROW SPORTS RESERVES

PLAYERS PLAN PROTEST STRIP

More than 150 footballers planned to change in the open in a protest demo.

The streak was the idea of Graham Melvin and Peter Carr of Tower Rovers and Transmeridian respectively, 'This is not a sporting gesture but a serious attempt to improve changing facilities at Grange Paddocks football grounds,' said Mr Melvin.

The footballers formed a line along the Paddocks and change from their everyday clothes into football kit in full view of the public.

Mr Carr said : 'The Paddocks have three changing huts for nine pitches which can involve as many as 200 people. The conditions are chaotic. The huts are just like shells with no lighting or heating and holes in the ceilings and floors, and players have had their gear stolen as well.'

'The fees for pitches trebled in the close season to £3, and there have been no improvements by the Council, even though they put aside £4,000 in the last financial year for improving sporting facilities.'

Mr Richard Lock, East Hertfordshire District Council's sports officer said : 'The sum of £4,000 was put aside, because of the year's estimates for facilities and to extend the use of the Paddocks changing rooms, because of their present inadequacy.'

'And in this year's estimates we decided to put aside £20,000 to give the players adequate changing rooms, showers, storage, lighting and heating, as £4,000 did not seem a large enough sum.'

However, the demo, due mainly to the weather did not quite go to plan.

Essex County referee Mr Geoff Biggs who has been refereeing at Grange Paddocks wrote to the Minister of Sport, Mr Denis Howell, complaining about the changing conditions.

Mr Biggs said : 'These bureaucratic councillors of ours really get on my nerves. As a referee I thought if the council is not going to do anything I would write to Mr Howell. He has played football and been a referee in the past and he might be sympathetic.'

'The playing surface over there is ok but the changing room accommodation is terrible.'

Source : Herts & Essex Observer

In January 1976, news of a proposed twenty per cent increase in pitch charges at Grange Paddocks, Bishop's Stortford, was greeted with alarm and dismay by officials of the football leagues and clubs concerned. There were warnings that several clubs might not be able to carry on playing at Grange Paddocks.

The increases were proposed by the East Herts Council's community group's committee to help meet the rising cost of operating amenities in 1976.

Many local football clubs in their comments had once again moaned about the lack of facilities at the Paddocks.

Charges went up substantially in 1975 and the proposals would have raised them from £3 to £3.60.

Secretary of Rye Rovers, one of the League's sides, Peter Sellars, commented, 'In view of the changing facilities there, this increase, is a bit of a farce.'

'I thought the £3 fee was extortionate anyway' he added, 'much more than I had to pay in my hometown of Sheffield.'

'We were a new club coming into the League and the finances are very tight.'

'Obviously, we will pay the increase because we have to, but it will be very hard to find.'

'Our match fees are 50p at the moment, which does not sound very much until you consider that some of our players are still at school and this has to come out of their pocket money. I can't yet say if we will have to put the fees up, this is something we'll have to talk over as a club.'

A spokesman for East Herts Council, Mr Richard Lock, sports officer, said, 'There just isn't the money available to improve the facilities at the Paddocks at the moment.'

'I think the whole Council is aware of the desperate plight of Grange Paddocks as far as changing rooms are concerned, but while we are in this period of economic restraint, any money is difficult to find.'

'We have got to save £122,000 – or increase income – in order to achieve nil growth, which is the instruction from the government that there should be no increased expenditure when there are increased commitments.'

At the February Management Committee meeting, Mr Brinsford reported that the inaugural meeting of the East Herts Sports Advisory Council was due to be held on 11th February.

LINESMAN RAN OFF WITH BALL

A bitter attack on the behaviour of a Great Parndon Reserves linesman was made by Hatfield Heath Secretary Sugar Perry after an incident in the 88th minute of the top-of-the-table clash.

'Our winner was disputed and when referee Ernie Fairhurst allowed the goal the Parndon linesman came on the pitch, picked up the ball and ran off to the dressing room with it.'

'Two Parndon players pulled off their shirts and suggested the game be abandoned but our skipper insisted that he retrieve the ball and finish the 90 minutes. Heath completed a 3-2 victory to stay second, one point ahead of Parndon. Mr Fairhurst said : 'I have reported the matter to the Essex Football Association and have no further comment.'

Source : Harlow Gazette

MR LIONEL THORNE – SERVANT OF LOCAL SOCCER

Mr Lionel Thorne of Nelson Road, Bishop's Stortford, was an officer in the League for 18 years.

He was formerly Honorary Referees' Appointments Secretary in North-West Essex, but when that was put in the hands of the leagues in 1953, Thorne became the first Honorary Referees' Secretary.

It was a post that he held for 13 years with the League and between 1963 and 1971 he was also Vice-Chairman of the League, When he retired from that post he was made a Life Vice-President and continued to take a great interest in all levels of local football.

DIVISION III CHALLENGE CUP FINAL

LANGLEY AND UNIVERSAL TAPE PRINTING RESERVES DREW

(AFTER EXTRA-TIME)

DIVISION I CHALLENGE CUP FINAL

GREAT PARNDON RESERVES 3 TAKELEY RESERVES 2

Source : Harlow Gazette

GREAT PARNDON RESERVES

DIVISION II CHALLENGE CUP FINAL

S.J.F.C. 2 NORTH WEALD 2 (AFTER EXTRA-TIME)

Fine attacking football by both teams produced one of the best League Cup Finals seen at the George Wilson Stadium for a long time.

North Weald went into the lead after 30 minutes through a blunder in the S.J. defence. S.J. drew level after 50 minutes. Vealey pushed the ball to Thurley, whose pass split the North Weald defence and Baker was on hand to slot it home.

After 57 minutes S.J. took the lead with a magnificent goal scored by Baker who was 25 yards out on the left, and he hit the ball on the volley to give the goalkeeper no chance.

Two minutes from time North Weald equalised. A long ball went to the winger, over the S.J. defence and he ran on to lob the ball past the advancing goalkeeper, Newton.

INTER-DIVISIONAL CHALLENGE CUP FINAL

S.J.F.C. 7 ACROW SPORTS 1

S.J.F.C. won the Inter-Divisional Challenge Cup for the second year running with a power-packed performance.

Peter Vealey put S.J. ahead after the Acrow goalkeeper could only parry a Graham Baker header and Chris Bird volleyed home a Colin Ealey corner, but Acrow Sports Reserves got back into the game with a goal that came from a mix-up in the S.J. defence.

In the second half S.J. turned the screw and goals followed. Baker rounded a defender and rammed home number three, and then headed in after a fine run by Ealey. An own goal added to Acrow's troubles.

Colin Dance and Baker made another goal for Bird and S.J. finished with a dream goal, the ball not being touched by an Acrow player from a goal-kick until Vealey slammed the ball home from an acute angle.

PREMIER DIVISION CHALLENGE CUP FINAL

ALBURY 3 NORTH WEALD 4

The game had started predictably enough with Albury going ahead when Petchey crossed from the left and Chris Newman slammed the ball home.

Within a minute the whole pattern of the game changed. Weald equalised through Dave King, who went on to complete a hat-trick. Weald, went in front after 14 minute and then got a third in the 33rd minute when sheer persistence by Phil Adam, who forced his way past four tackles in the penalty area, led to Alan Pottell netting with an overhead kick after the goalkeeper could only parry the shot by Adams.

Albury pulled back two goals, both by their outstanding player, Robert Newman in the 48th and 59th minutes. Then, just as suddenly as when they first scored, Weald snatched the lead again in the 73rd minute.

It was the biggest cup upset for years on the League's competitions, but it did not become reality until a sensational last minute when Chris Newman netted at the fourth attempt in a scramble in front of goal only to have the effort disallowed by the referee, who had blown for time.

Albury protested 'vehemently' and part of the crowd of nearly 500 spilled on to the pitch but the referee asserted that the ball had not crossed the line for what would have been Albury's equaliser until after the final whistle.

Source : Herts & Essex Observer

Source : Harlow Gazette

NORTH WEALD

DIVISION III CHALLENGE CUP FINAL REPLAY

LANGLEY 2 UNIVERSAL TAPE PRINTING RESERVES 1

HERTS JUNIOR CUP FINAL

ALBURY 1 WHITWELL 1 (AFTER EXTRA-TIME)

The teams observed a minutes silence in memory of a Whitwell player killed in Italy.

Whitwell led 1-0 at half-time and the equaliser came from Albury with their first real move, the ball being played man to man out to Chris Newman, whose cross created chaos in a crowded goalmouth and Robert Newman drove the ball home.

The teams played out extra-time and the replay would take place at Rhodes Avenue.

Source : Herts & Essex Observer

CHRIS AND ROBERT NEWMAN - ALBURY

HERTS JUNIOR CUP FINAL REPLAY

ALBURY 1 WHITWELL O

Albury, who became the only club from the League to win the Herts Junior Cup, did more, much more, than win the Herts Junior Cup before a 600 crowd at the George Wilson Stadium. They proved that the standards of the League were higher every season with Albury following in the paths of Takeley and Great Parndon.

A super second half team performance saw Albury lift the Herts Junior Cup at the George Wilson Stadium.

After 25 minutes of the second half, Chris Newman worked space for himself on the right before sending through a ball which split the Whitwell defence. Trevor Novell latched on to the pass and side-footed the ball past the advancing goalkeeper for the only goal of the game.

Source : Harlow Gazette

ALBURY – HERTS JUNIOR CUP WINNERS

DIVISION II CHALLENGE CUP FINAL REPLAY

S.J.F.C. 2 NORTH WEALD 2 (AFTER EXTRA-TIME)

The Division II Cup Final was still not resolved after a replay.

Good defensive play prevented either side from scoring, until North Weald took the lead when their left-winger crossed the ball and a forward slotted it home from close in.

S.J. equalised soon after when Vealey headed home a Baker cross past a defender on the line.

A mix up in the S.J. defence led to North Weald taking the lead again.

In the second half S.J. put on the pressure but could not break down North Weald's defence and S.J. forwards wasted a couple of good chances. North Weald had the ball in the net, but it was disallowed for hands.

The S.J. equaliser, 15 minutes from the end, was scored by Brazzier, with Vealey and Brazzier inter-passing before he slammed it home.

In extra-time S.J. came close on several occasions, but North Weald nearly stole it towards the end when they hit the post with the S.J. defence wide open.

Source : Roger Brinsford

S.J.F.C.

DIVISION II CHALLENGE CUP FINAL SECOND REPLAY

S.J.F.C. 4 NORTH WEALD 0

S.J.F.C. completed a unique second clean sweep hat-trick with an emphatic win over North Weald Reserves in the Division II Challenge Cup. In doing so, they also competed in a game rare to the League – a second replay in a Cup Final. Herts FA Official and League Chairman Bill Bruty said after the game, 'This is the first time since I became involved in the League that a Cup Final has gone to three matches.' However, this was, in fact, the third time that a Cup Final had gone to a second replay.

The first occasion that a team won a League Cup Final after two replays was in season 1949/50 when Green Tye eventually defeated Takeley Reserves 3-1 in the Division II Cup Final. The second occasion was at the start of the 1954/55 season when the 1953/54 season Division II League Cup Final went to a second replay with Birchanger beating Rhodes Avenue 1-0.

What surprised a number of people at Stansted was how, after two close previous encounters, one team could suddenly produce four goals without reply.

SJ secretary Jeff Dallimore thought he had the explanation, 'In the previous games, there was always only one goal in it. Someone would score and then the other side would undoubtedly equalise. Neither team ever built up a confidence-boosting lead. Before this match, the lads knew that to get a two-goal lead would probably be enough.'

Two goals from Glenn Thurley in the first half and a further two goals from Colin Ealey wrapped it up.

FIVE TROPHIES ON THE TABLE

Takeley Football Club celebrated a record season with a dinner and dance.

There was certainly plenty of reason to rejoice with the top table adorned with five trophies – Premier League and Division I Championships, Saffron Walden Cup first and reserve sections and the West Essex Border Charity Cup.

Chairman Mr Mick Ellis welcomed the guests and thanked officials, players and helpers for their part in making the season such a great success.

In reply, Mr Bill Bruty, an Essex County representative, said that although the club had had an outstanding record last season, it had been through hard times and was now reaping the award for the old stalwarts who had stood by it in times of trouble.

IT'S BEEN A GREAT, GREAT SEASON

Source : Herts & Essex Observer

The good, though not perfect, record of players in the League came in for praise at the League's Annual presentation.

The League's disciplinary record was touched on by Mr Len Menhinick, Chairman of the Chelmsford Sunday League and Essex county area representative.

He congratulated the League on another successful season, he said that in 1,000 league and cup matches the League had only 9 players sent off – an average of one every 111 games.

He praised the officers of the League, pointing out that President, Mr George Wilson, had held office since 1957 and listing his other offices and achievements.

Mr Wilson presented the League trophies and the Club Linesman's Trophy was given to Dick Mumford (Waggoners) by Mr Eric Swan, Vice-President of the North-West Essex Referees' Society.

Albury and Takeley once more stole the limelight with the lion's share of success. Takeley, the Premier Division champions again won the West Essex Border Charity Cup and reached the fourth round of the Essex Intermediate Cup. Dick Yeoman had represented the county in the Southern Counties Amateur Championship

And Albury of course brought the Herts Junior Cup home as well as finishing as runners-up in the Premier League and the Premier Cup Final.

Albury were presented with a special plaque from the League to mark their Herts Junior Cup success.

Mr Bill Bruty said that in 550 matches in the League that season only eight players had been sent off. 'It's a good record – and it's not a good recording that it's eight too many. Next year let us see if we can bring the eight down to none.'

He thanked all Secretaries and clubs participating in the League helping to make it a success. That season the League had gone from strength to strength with Albury completing the third of three victories in four years in county cups by winning the Herts Junior Cup.

'If you doubt, we've had a good season, then tell me another League that can lift three county trophies in four years. I do not think you will not find that anywhere in England.'

He also mentioned the successes of Takeley, who won the Premier Division for the second year, reached the fourth round of the Essex Intermediate Cup and won the Saffron Walden Cup, the Saffron Walden Reserve Cup, the Division I championship and the West Essex Border Cup.

But he emphasised that Albury and Takeley were not the only teams the only teams in the Stortford League and congratulated all the winning clubs, especially S.J.F.C., who completed a unique second treble in two seasons.

Mr Bruty summed up the League's performances, 'We've had a great, great season.'

Tim Clarey (Takeley) receiving the Premier Division Championship Trophy

Dickie Amott (Takeley Reserves) receiving the Division I trophy

Division III Championship
Acrow Sports

Premier Division Sportsmanship
Award - Acrow Sports Manager
Mike Hathaway

Jim O'Connor (Grange Park)
picks up the Division II
Sportsmanship Trophy

Division III Sportsmanship Award
Eastons & Duton Hill

George Wood (North Weald) winner
of the Secretary of the Year Award

Peter Newman, Secretary of Albury,
the club winning the Herts Jun Cup

Chris Newman (Albury) and Dick Yeoman (Takeley) receive plaques in recognition of representing the League team on ten occasions.

Mr E Swan, Vice-President of the North-West Essex Referees Society presents the Club Linesman's Trophy to Dick Mumford of Waggoners.

Fred Newman

A great sporting character, Mr Fred Newman, who retired as Chairman of **ALBURY** Football Club, received warm tributes and gifts in recognition of his great service to the club over 41 years, at the club's Annual Dinner.

The club's gift was an inscribed silver tray and the players presented him with an inscribed wall mirror.

A man who loved football all of his life and put everything into the game. Fred Newman – known in his younger days as Juddy – started with the club in 1927 and, excluding the war years had been going since then. He made many friends in football all over the area – and also a few enemies in the sporting sense of the word.

His retirement as Chairman did not mean he would be missing from the football scene. He hoped to start a junior side and train the young lads his way.

'If you can talk to youngsters and knock it into them when they are young you can get a good side' he said. 'I'd like to get a school of twenty lads, play a few friendly games then enter a junior league.'

'Sport keeps lads of the street and stops a lot of vandalism and petty crime. We have no trouble with our youngsters in Albury and I think it is mostly because they are keen footballers.'

Fred came from an old footballing family. His father who died in 1975 at the age of 94 was a keen footballer in his day and was club treasurer for about 12 years. His sons carried on the tradition – Peter, Christopher, Robert and Trevor – and his grandson, Paul Woolard, in the reserves.

Fred played for Albury for twenty-six seasons. When he hung up his boots, he became groundsman/first aid/teaboy until 1975 when his son Peter – who became Secretary/Manager of the club – took his place.

'I played my first game for the club on Boxing Day, 1927, in the snow. We beat Hadham Villa 1-0 and I was lucky enough to score the goal.'

He played in every position – including goalkeeper on odd occasions when someone was injured.

'I still hold the record for the club of 38 goals from the outside -right position,' he said. 'I believe in wing men. Wing men are the success of many clubs and it brings entertainment to the game.'

He was very proud of Albury's record, 'In the last eight years they have not failed to win a major honour of some description, and this year crowned it by winning the coveted Herts Junior Cup. – competing 400 clubs throughout the county.'

'I hope that in the coming season they will be more successful than ever before. They are the finest set of set of men I have been with – a great bunch of lads. I can't speak too highly of them. I don't think they've got an enemy in the world.'

Fred had been Chairman of the club for eight years when he handed over to the new Chairman, Mr P Church.

INCREASED PROFITS

At the League's Annual General Meeting Mr Bruty paid tribute Mr Lionel Thorne who had sadly passed away during the season Mr Bruty spoke of the work that he had done for the League and for the Referees in particular.

The Honorary Treasurer reported that the balance of the League's bank account was £357.40. Treasurer, Mr G Reed, made special reference to the increased donations and higher profit from the Cup Finals and Annual Dinner.

983 players registered, 29 transfers and 42 registrations cancelled.

There had been 10 dismissals and 90 cautions in the season.

There had been 67 referees (handbook).

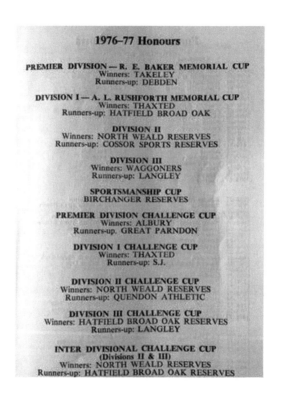

1976–77 Honours

PREMIER DIVISION — R. E. BAKER MEMORIAL CUP
Winners: TAKELEY
Runners-up: DEBDEN

DIVISION I — A. L. RUSHFORTH MEMORIAL CUP
Winners: THAXTED
Runners-up: HATFIELD BROAD OAK

DIVISION II
Winners: NORTH WEALD RESERVES
Runners-up: COSSOR SPORTS RESERVES

DIVISION III
Winners: WAGGONERS
Runners-up: LANGLEY

SPORTSMANSHIP CUP
BIRCHANGER RESERVES

PREMIER DIVISION CHALLENGE CUP
Winners: ALBURY
Runners-up. GREAT PARNDON

DIVISION I CHALLENGE CUP
Winners: THAXTED
Runners-up: S.J.

DIVISION II CHALLENGE CUP
Winners: NORTH WEALD RESERVES
Runners-up: QUENDON ATHLETIC

DIVISION III CHALLENGE CUP
Winners: HATFIELD BROAD OAK RESERVES
Runners-up: LANGLEY

INTER DIVISIONAL CHALLENGE CUP
(Divisions II & III)
Winners: NORTH WEALD RESERVES
Runners-up: HATFIELD BROAD OAK RESERVES

END OF £382,000 DISPUTE IN SIGHT –

WILL MEAN MORE FACILITIES AT GRANGE PADDOCKS

Two years of dispute over which Council, East Herts or Bishop's Stortford, was entitled to the capital sum of £382,000, was to be resolved in a settlement, which would provide Bishop's Stortford with much-needed facilities.

It was proposed that the town Council would withdraw all claim to the capital sum provided the District Council undertook to provide changing rooms and other facilities at Grange Paddocks at a cost of not less than £40,000 so that the project could be carried out in 1977/78.

The Secretaries of the two major local leagues, Mr Brian Curtis and Mr Roger Brinsford welcomed the news that Grange Paddocks was likely to have a £40,000 facelift.

Mr Curtis said : 'I am pleased to learn that there is, at least, some progress on the provision pf proper changing rooms at Grange Paddocks.'

'These facilities have been urgently required for many years, not only by players in the North-West Essex Sunday League but by many youth teams using Grange Paddocks. Proper covered changing rooms are essential for the youth of the town.'

'I would like to acknowledge the help given by Councillors who have campaigned on our behalf. However, I am sceptical about the developments as proposals have come and gone in the past, and I prefer to reserve my gratitude until the scheme is finally completed.'

Mr Brinsford commented : 'I welcome the news, and what a Christmas present for the footballers who use Grange Paddocks week after week.'

'I do hope that when the plans are being drawn up the authorities will consult the various leagues for their suggestions and ideas. When an amount of money such as this is being spent, it would be a pity if there were say shortcomings in the final product through lack of consultation with the bodies who have the necessary experience of what is required.'

ON-OR-OFF FEE ANGERS CLUBS

A clause in the agreement for the hire of soccer pitches at Grange Paddocks from East Herts District Council was worrying clubs.

It seemed that if a club's game was called off or was postponed, then the club would have to forfeit the fee for the hire of the pitch.

Commented Mr Roger Brinsford, Secretary of the Bishop's Stortford, Stansted and District League : 'While the League only have five teams playing at Grange Paddocks we are obviously concerned that the clubs have to pay for the pitches when matches are called off by referees. It is even more disturbing that that the Council are still charging when they themselves postpone the games.'

'It is difficult enough for clubs to survive with the high rental charged, and I am surprised that the Council are choosing this way to penalise the clubs further.'

Speaking for the Council, information officer Mr Sid Newman said : 'We have received several complaints about the clause, and the matter will shortly be the subject of a special report, after which changes are sure to be made.'

GREAT PARNDON 6 NETTESWELL & BURNT MILL 2

PREMIER DIVISION

Man-of-the-match Ivor Smith scored a hat-trick and steered Great Parndon to victory in a match that at one point became so physical a riot seemed imminent. Parndon ran out winners 6-2.

Source : Herts & Essex Observer

GREAT PARNDON

Source : Herts & Essex Observer

NETTESWELL & BURNT MILL

TAKELEY 2 DEBDEN 1 – PREMIER DIVISION

Source : Herts & Essex Observer

TAKELEY

Source : Herts & Essex Observer

DEBDEN

Tony Neeves joined Debden at the start of the season as player/manager.

Neeves was Manager of Saffron Walden until last season.

THAXTED 1 ELSENHAM 0

DIVISION I

Source : Herts & Essex Observer

THAXTED

Source : Harlow Gazette

ELSENHAM

DIVISION II CHALLENGE CUP FINAL

NORTH WEALD RESERVES 4 QUENDON ATHLETIC 1

North Weald Reserves made up for the previous year's defeat after three matches against S.J.F.C. by convincingly beating Quendon Athletic by four goals to one. And they did it at the first attempt with Cooper hitting a fine second half hat-trick and a further goal coming from Alexander. Quendon's goal came from Grandsen.

Source : Harlow Citizen

NORTH WEALD RESERVES

Source : Herts & Essex Observer

QUENDON ATHLETIC

DIVISION III CHALLENGE CUP FINAL

LANGLEY 2 HATFIELD BROAD OAK RESERVES 2

(AFTER EXTRA-TIME)

Watched by a crowd of 300, Langley went ahead after 15 minutes through Gerry Mardell but Broad Oak fought back and on the half-hour Andrew Trott set the game alight with an equaliser.

On the stroke of the halfway break in extra-time, John Cutmore forced his way through from the halfway line and turning the impossible into a great goal with a run past a wall of defenders and a neat shot into an empty net.

Langley carried on piecing together their painstaking moves and were rewarded for some fine football – played despite atrocious conditions – with an equaliser from George Reynolds seven minutes from time.

Source : Herts & Essex Observer

LANGLEY

Source : Herts & Essex Observer

HATFIELD BROAD OAK RESERVES

INTER-DIVISIONAL CHALLENGE CUP FINAL

NORTH WEALD RESERVES 4 HATFIELD BROAD OAK RESERVES 1

Hot favourites North Weald came one step nearer winning the treble when they added the Inter-Divisional Cup to the impressive list of successes this season.

This match had many similar to their victories last week, The score was identical, in Weald's favour, with one of their players, Stewart Alexander, scoring a hat-trick.

Weald combatted the slippery conditions to ensure victory with two goals in the second half that killed Broad Oak's slender chances of a revival.

With the ball skidding along the rain-soaked pitch, Weald were quick to assert their dominance.

For the first 20 minutes it was one-way traffic and it came as no surprise that Weald took the lead after several close chances, Alexander's shot skimmed along the ground and went in through the legs of Boswell in the Broad Oak goal.

Goal number two came a few minutes later from Brian Maille, who made hard work of an open goal when his shot went in off the post.

Surprisingly, Broad Oak managed to notch a goal right on half-time when Trott saw his shot parried on to the post by Weald goalkeeper Green and trickle over the line.

Thoughts of a revival were quickly dashed five minutes after the interval when Alexander showed his cool head in tight situations by elegantly slotting home his shot.

Weald's obvious thirst for action provided Alexander with numerous chances to complete his hat-trick before he finally scored with a deflection.

Source : Harlow Citizen

NORTH WEALD RESERVES

DIVISION 1 CHALLENGE CUP FINAL (AFTER EXTRA-TIME)

THAXTED 3 S.J.F.C. 1

Source : Harlow Citizen

THAXTED

S.J. did most of the pressing in the first half but only scored one goal and that had a strong element of luck; a Glen Thurley free-kick beat a wall of defenders and an unsighted keeper in the 25th minute and S.J. were in front deservedly.

Ten minutes from time Thaxted got the equaliser they deserved when Kevin Eldred centred and George Luckey headed home.

There was no further score until the stroke of half-time of extra-time, even though Thaxted, by now, were threatening, to run amok.

Thaxted's goal had a similar element of luck about it as S.J.'s, and again came from a free-kick. Reg Sage fired in the kick, the keeper could not hold it and Malcolm Rivers pushed the ball home from close range.

Five minutes from time Eldred returned an earlier Luckey compliment and turned in his compatriot's cross for number three.

Source : Herts & Essex Observer

S.J.F.C.

DIVISION III CHALLENGE CUP FINAL REPLAY

LANGLEY 0 HATFIELD BROAD OAK RESERVES 1

After 210 minutes of tension-filled football, Hatfield Broad Oak Reserves snatched victory from unlucky Langley with a solitary goal. It came just after the interval when, even at that stage, extra-time seemed a distinct possibility.

13 minutes into the second half Kevin Gunn slipped his constant shadow, in the form of Langley defender Pegrum, to leave himself free in the area and slot the ball home from close range.

PREMIER DIVISION CHALLENGE CUP FINAL

ALBURY 3 GREAT PARNDON 2

"BEST WE'VE SEEN YET" SAYS BRUTY

Albury 3, Great Parndon 2
Stortford League Premier Div Cup Final

STORTFORD League chairman Bill Bruty said after this thrilling Stortford League Premier Division cup final on Saturday: "That was the best game that has been seen at Stortford all season."

It certainly had all the ingredients that go to make a great cup tie. Two well-matched teams who finished third and fourth in the league table played an end-to-end game which first saw one side take the initiative, then the other.

Albury started quickly but missed a couple of good chances which could have put them on an early road to victory. Having weathered the storm, Parndon came back and took the lead after 20 minutes when Albury keeper Rust collided with a defender and missed a cross from the left completely, leaving Billy Webb to slot the ball home.

There was no further score before the interval but 10 minutes into the second half Great Parndon went two up. Good work by Graeme Burden down the right flank ended with a cross for Dave Piercey to head home and Parndon were well on top.

But they made the mistake of trying to sit on their lead and Albury fought back with devastating results. Mick Petchey reduced the arrears with a goal that always looked on the cards and Parndon were put under ever-increasing pressure.

On a break, they felt they could have been awarded a penalty after Burden was unceremoniously bundled to the floor but it was not given and the Albury attacking paid in the end. Robert Newman equalised with 18 minutes left and brother Chris hit the winner just seven minutes from time to complete their great comeback.

Source : Harlow Citizen

SPONSOR FOR LEAGUE

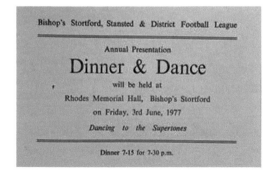

Bishop's Stortford, Stansted & District Football League

Annual Presentation

Dinner & Dance

will be held at

Rhodes Memorial Hall, Bishop's Stortford

on Friday, 3rd June, 1977

Dancing to the Supertones

Dinner 7-15 for 7-30 p.m.

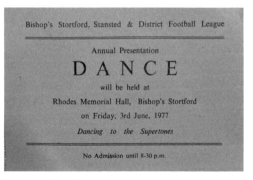

Bishop's Stortford, Stansted & District Football League

Annual Presentation

D A N C E

will be held at

Rhodes Memorial Hall, Bishop's Stortford

on Friday, 3rd June, 1977

Dancing to the Supertones

No Admission until 8-30 p.m.

The League was almost certain to be sponsored for the following season.

News of the deal was announced at the League's Annual Dinner and Dance.

Chairman, Mr Bill Bruty made the announcement, saying that Don Burlingham Associates had made an offer for the next three years. The Management Committee had been delighted to accept.

League Secretary Mr Roger Brinsford said afterwards that there were still one or two things to be ironed out but the whole package should be sorted by the Annual General Meeting.

Mr Brinsford added : 'We are obviously delighted. We came near to sponsorship three seasons ago and were disappointed when it fell through and have been on the look-out for a suitable sponsor ever since.'

The sponsorship agreement would need the ratification of the Annual General Meeting to go ahead, but this looks only a formality.

Other highlights of the event were the special presentation made to Vice-Chairman, Mr Roy Harrison and Treasurer, Mr George Reed, on completing 21 and 20 years respectively as officers of the League. Both were presented with clocks by League President, Mr George Wilson.

Both recipients also received long-service certificates, along with Fixtures Secretary, Mr George Banks from the Vice-Chairman of the Essex County FA, Mr Doug Stuart.

The toast of the ladies and guests, who swelled the company to 280, was proposed by Mr Bruty, who welcomed representatives of the Harlow, North-West Essex Sunday and McMullen Hertford and District Leagues. The response was given by Mr Jack Hooper, of the Essex FA.

Mr R C Harrison

Mr G Banks

Mr G Reed

Source : Herts & Essex Observer

SPONSOR CASH TO TAME BAD BOYS

The League may use some of its new sponsorship money to stamp out bad behaviour on the field.

The League was to be sponsored by Don Burlingham Associates Ltd., of Bishop's Stortford. Mr Bill Bruty revealed that the sponsorship amounted to £250 per year for the following three years.

Mr Bruty, who recalled that previous negotiations for sponsorship by Greene King had broken down a few years previously, said that the spadework for the new agreement had been done by League Secretary, Mr Roger Brinsford.

The sponsorship would help the clubs and the first of a number of suggestions for use of the money was making the League directories free instead of £2.50 per head.

The main suggestion Mr Bruty put before the meeting – to be considered by the Management Committee – was that there should be a sportsmanship pool run on similar lines to the Rothman's Isthmian League. The sum of £20 would be allotted to each division and each team would be given eight points. A sending-off would cost a club two points and a caution, one point.

Earlier, Mr Bruty had warned offenders that misbehaviour on the field would not be tolerated. 'Last season we had 20 players sent off and ten the year before. I can assure you that the League Management Committee will not hesitate to use the new rule on misconduct.'

The rule he referred to empower the Management Committee to refuse, cancel or suspend the registration of any player found guilty of undesirable conduct and to disqualify the player from participation in any or all games in the League. It is an FA rule and compulsory for the League.'

The meeting voted in favour of sponsorship and left the Management Committee to work out details of the various schemes.

The Treasurer reported that the balance of the League's bank account was £451.45.

950 players registered, 41 transfers and 49 registrations cancelled.

There were 20 dismissals and 102 cautions as of 24th May 1977.

There were 61 referees (handbook).

SERVICE MEANS WORK!

Most people think of the football season lasting from August to May but for Roger Brinsford the season continues throughout the year.

He is Secretary of the Bishop's Stortford, Stansted and District League and retiring Referees' Secretary of the North-West Essex Sunday League. He is also Secretary of the David Robinson Memorial Trophy (the annual match) between the Harlow and Bishop's Stortford Leagues) and a non-executive officer of the Essex FA.

These positions entail a year-round programme of work. The reason for his retirement as Referees' Secretary of the North-West Essex League after four years is that he felt that he could not do justice to the job alongside his many other commitments.

'It was a carefully considered decision. I decided that with both leagues developing fast I could not give sufficient time to both positions; it would not have fair to the leagues in question.'

His involvement with local soccer started eight years ago when he moved to the area from his native Worcestershire. He played for Transmeridian, his firm's side in the London Banks League and also had half a season with Hatfield Heath before having his first taste of officialdom.

He has been Referees' Secretary of the North-West Essex League since September 1972 and has had four very successful seasons in that position. In the 1974/75 season the Bishop's Stortford, Stansted and District League approached him with the offer of being Press and Match Secretary, an offer he found too good to refuse.

With so many responsibilities resting on the shoulders of one man, that man must have the right approach to the tasks.

'My approach is to present a face as professional as possible to the League but at the same time retaining a sympathetic ear. A large part of my job in that respect is public relations work, and there is not one secretary of any club in the Stortford League that I am not on first name terms with. If you know people you are dealing with it makes your job much easier. It also makes for better understanding and co-operation with the clubs.'

Although he has not been involved with local soccer as long as some people in the area, Brinsford has the sort of position that demands a great deal of knowledge of the area's football.

He has to be aware of changes and conflicts and has to form opinions to control new situations. One thing that does disturb him is the increasing degree of bad conduct on the field, especially from young players.

Discipline is important for the survival and the sight of players mimicking the worst elements of the professional game and paying the penalty with disciplinary action worries Brinsford.

'It saddens me to see players who regard football as their recreation from a week's work spoil it by bad behaviour.'

Looking at the brighter side, one recent piece of good news to the local soccer scene was the introduction of sponsorship of the North-West Essex League who are going to be sponsored by a local firm of financiers and now have the task of deciding how to spend the money.

'I welcome the thought of sponsorship but there must be a constant flow of sponsors to make it work. The money must also be used wisely and for the good of the game.'

Looking critically at the Bishop's Stortford, Stansted and District League, Brinsford maintains that there is only one real problem, not enough players are becoming involved in the running of their clubs.

Regarding the structure of the League, he is quite happy with its development. Although not at saturation point, it has a workable number of clubs and the right number of divisions, he feels.

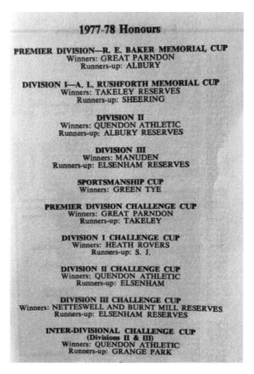

W.J. (WALLY) DAY MEMORIAL CUP

Winners : ALBURY **Runners-Up** : TAKELEY

In 1977 - Don Burlingham Associates (Commercial) Ltd became the sponsor of the League for three seasons.

The number of substitutions allowed during matches in the League were increased to two by each side for the 1977/78 season.

It was reported that Keith Miller, a referee registered with the League for eleven seasons, had been promoted to the Football League's Linesmen's list. A letter of congratulation was sent to Mr Miller.

W.J. (WALLY) DAY MEMORIAL CUP FINAL

ALBURY 3 TAKELEY 1

It was intended that the match should be staged on the opening day of each succeeding season and the following year's competitors would be the Division I Champions and Cup winners. By maintaining a four year cycle, it would give teams from the lower divisions an opportunity of competing for an additional trophy.

Takeley started off well, but after six minutes gave away a simple goal. A bouncing ball in the box caught the defence in two minds. Seymour came out and a ricochet off a defender left Barry Trott with an open goal.

After the break Ivor Parrish levelled the score pushing home a cross from Peter Trower.

Then Albury went further ahead when Stobart rammed home a cross from Trott and ten minutes from time the same player scored again with a hard rising drive to make Albury worthy winners.

Albury got the better of this tussle with Takeley for possession.

Source : Harlow Citizen

Source : Harlow Citizen

ALBURY

CHARITY GAME PULLS IN THE FANS

Over 200 people turned up at Stansted's Hargrave Park to see a team composed of members of the Management Committees of the League and the North-West Essex Sunday League play a side from the North-West Essex Referees' Society.

The Management Committees won 5-3 after being a goal in arrears after only two minutes when the Stortford League Secretary, Roger Brinsford, converted a penalty awarded by referee Don Burlingham for handball.

Source : Roger Brinsford

Source : Roger Brinsford

The match raised over £12 for soccer charities – the benevolent funds of the Essex Referees' Association, the Hertfordshire Football Association and the Essex County Football Association. Rayment's gave a cup for the match and was presented by Mr Bob Parker, licensee of the Three Tuns, Bishop's Stortford. Goal scorers were Brinsford, David Cush and Norman Brown for the referees and Ray Field (3), Ray Fach and John Glumsden for the Management Committee.

Source : Herts & Essex Observer

GREEN TYE

Paul Jolley proved a handful for Manuden's defence when he scored a hat-trick in Green Tye's sweeping 5-0 win in the Inter-Divisional Cup.

Source : Herts & Essex Observer

HATFIELD BROAD OAK

HATFIELD HEATH

The nearest of neighbours and the keenest of rivals. On this occasion the Heath ran out 3-1 winners in the Premier League.

MANUDEN

Source : Herts & Essex Observer

THAXTED

DIVISION III CHALLENGE CUP FINAL

NETTESWELL & BURNT MILL RESERVES 4

ELSENHAM RESERVES 2 (AFTER EXTRA-TIME)

Elsenham battled their way back into the final with two superbly taken goals. They forced the game to extra-time but Netteswell, who were always in command, put paid to their little revival with two goals in the first period.

Elsenham had to wait until well into the second half before a defensive error let Robert Adcock in to crash home the ball with only the keeper to beat. The move started with a fine through ball from Elsenham striker Lovelock which Netteswell's Paddy Monk couldn't quite reach, and Adcock was clear to level the scores.

Netteswell started the game at a rip-roaring pace and took the lead after only seven minutes. Paddy Monk floated in a high kick for Roy Stephenson to soar above the Elsenham defence and head powerfully past the motionless keeper.

Elsenham seemed to be well out of the running when they gave away a penalty shortly after. And Pierre Eiffert made absolutely sure of Netteswell's second as he casually slotted the ball to keeper Porter's right.

Elsenham pulled one back just before the break when a high through ball left Mick Lovelock clear to rattle a first time shot which gave keeper Irish no chance.

Elsenham's second took the game to extra-time where they hoped to continue their revival. But their high hopes were dashed when Eiffert got his second direct from a corner. The ball sailed across the face of the goal and to everyone's surprise hit the angle and bounced in.

Elsenham fought on for the equaliser but it was Netteswell who added to their tally with a fine effort from Danny Sweeney after a good attacking run. He shook off two defenders before hammering the ball past Porter to give his side the game and the cup by a comfortable two goal margin.

Source : Harlow Citizen

NETTESWELL & BURNT MILL RESERVES

DIVISION II CHALLENGE CUP FINAL

ELSENHAM 2 QUENDON ATHLETIC 3

Within 15 seconds of the start of the second half, Quendon were seemingly dead and buried.

A Mick Lovelock goal had just put Elsenham 2-0 in the lead and they seemed as if they were about to capitalise on their first half ascendancy.

However, Quendon's Paul Brown had other ideas and his brace of goals put his side on the victory trail.

In between, Paul Warwick had grabbed a 59th minute equaliser after veteran Brian Wilson's chip forward had been deflected on to Warwick's head by an Elsenham defender.

DIVISION I CHALLENGE CUP FINAL

HEATH ROVERS 2 S.J.F.C. 1

Heath Rovers used old-fashioned methods to carry off the Division I Cup.

The final came to life ten minutes into the second half when Rovers took the lead. Pirie chased a long ball from Godwin and challenged Kitchener and keeper Mynott. When the ball broke free Pirie was brought down by Kitchener and from the penalty spot Metson sent the keeper the wrong way. Five minutes later Rovers went further ahead when Aldis ran on to a ball from Wheeler and hit the back of the net.

With five minutes left, keeper Francis made his only mistake of the match. He appeared to have a Baker shot covered, but it slipped from his grasp into the net.

But Rovers had the final say with the last kick of the match. Skipper Dave Nicholas was tackled just inside the penalty area. Lying on his back he spotted the keeper coming off his line and hit the ball into the far corner of the net.

HEATH ROVERS

S.J.F.C.

Source : Herts & Essex Observer

PREMIER DIVISION CHALLENGE CUP FINAL

TAKELEY 1 GREAT PARNDON 2

Source : Harlow Citizen

TAKELEY

Source : Harlow Citizen

GREAT PARNDON

Takeley scored in the 34th minute with an out-of-character soft goal. Peter Trower sent a hopeful 20 yard shot towards the goal and was surprised when Mascall fumbled the ball and let it slip into his net.

Parndon scored five minutes after the interval when Johnson headed home from close range from an Ian Smith cross.

Then came the penalty and the turning point in the game. From the spot-kick Elms shot hard but Mascall saved the day.

That single save gave Parndon new life and minutes later they took the lead when Johnson scored from close range.

INTER-DIVISIONAL CHALLENGE CUP FINAL

QUENDON ATHLETIC 3 GRANGE PARK 1

BOB CALLS A HALT AFTER 533 GAMES

After 533 games for Heath Rovers, 42 year-old Bob Whitelock decided to hang up his boots. He was presented with an inscribed tray to mark his record number of appearances for the club.

Bob first played for Rovers in 1961 and since then had been both a regular and outstanding player. He also received the Player of the Year award.

The club's Chairman, he said that he had stayed with Rovers because there always been a good atmosphere in the club.

He added that a number of young players had been introduced to the first team and they had started to bring success to the club.

Before joining Rovers, Bob spent a couple of years with Spurs youth team and played for Bishop's Stortford at one time, making a few appearances in the first team.

Source : Herts & Essex Observer

AWARDS FOR HEATH ROVERS OLD TIMERS

THE Barn Theatre Company's Old Tyme Music Hall production was upstaged by five of Heath Rovers' old timers on Saturday night.

The five, pictured above with ex-clubman Derek Wright (far right) have chalked up nearly 2000 appearances for the Bishop's Stortford-based club.

Pride of place went to Bob Whitelock

who reached 500 games before calling it a day at the end of the season. Bob also took the player of the year award and stays with the club as chairman.

More than 130 people turned up for the music hall at Bishop's Stortford Boys High school where awards also went to Martin Pirie and Hugh Davidson (Saturday and Sunday leading goalscorers),

Valerie Paul – who won the secretary's cup for cleaning three sets of kit every week – and a whole host of players with 100 and 200 appearances.

● Pictured (left to right) are: Ron Hampton (400 games), Ernie Paul (300), Brian Doyle (300), Jim Hartley (300), Bob Whitelock (500) and Derek Wright, who presented the awards. (792)

Source : Harlow Gazette

NEW ESSEX FA AREA REPRESENTATIVE

For the first time in more than 20 years, local football would vote for their choice of Essex FA Area Representative.

'Uncle' Bill Bruty had been returned unopposed since he was elected to the post in 1955 and had done a wonderful job for local football.

However, his decision to accept a life membership of the Essex Football Association left a gap and two men were proposed for the area four vacancy.

They were Arthur Dimond, President and Chairman of the Harlow & District League, and Roger Brinsford, General Secretary of the Bishop's Stortford, Stansted and District League.

Arthur was the popular and unanimous choice of the Harlow League's Management Committee after 25 years' service from the League's inception.

League Secretary Ken Blackburn said the committee was agreed there could only be one person capable of taking over the reins and his selection would be fine recognition of his services.

Arthur refereed the first Harlow League Cup Final on the Green Man Field and since his retirement from the Football League Referee's list had devoted even more time to Essex football.

Roger was given his chance because the Stortford League is affiliated to the Essex FA as well as the Hertfordshire FA.

He was Press and Match Secretary for the League in the 1974/75 season before taking over as General Secretary in 1975 and was also active on the local referees' list.

DEATH OF ROY HARRISON ANNOUNCED

Source : Herts and Essex Observer

Vice-President Roy Harrison who had served as a League officer in a several positions for many years passed away in April 1978 at the age of 71.

He had lived in the area for the greater part of his life, first in Hatfield Heath and later in Grange Road and Hillside Avenue, Bishop's Stortford.

He worked at the Australian and New Zealand Bank in the city until his retirement at the age of 63 but was best known locally for his 22 year association with the League. He had been an official from 1956 until the time of his death and was presented with a clock in recognition his long service.

From 1956 until 1959 he was Press and Match Secretary; from 1959 until 1970, Fixtures Secretary; from 1963 to 1975 he was Secretary of the League and from 1975 to date was Vice-Chairman.

Mr Harrison also received the Essex County Football Association Meritorious Service award.

A referee from 1949 to 1958, he held the Referee's Association Meritorious Service Award, presented to him a few years ago when he was Treasurer of the North-West Essex Referee's Society.

FOR LIFE

Source : Harlow Observer

The grand old man of local football, Mr Bill Bruty, accepted a nomination to become a life member of the Essex Football Association. He would be elected at the annual meeting.

Under the county's rules there can only be a maximum of six life-members who have completed 21 years' service to the Council.

League Secretary, Roger Brinsford said : 'The honour accorded to Bill is not easily earned and speaks volumes for the service he has given this area since becoming group representative in 1955.'

TAKELEY FC WITHDRAW FROM THE LEAGUE

Takeley's teams withdrew from the Bishop's Stortford, Stansted and District League at the end of the 1977/78 season to compete in higher level football in the Essex Olympian League. The club have since progressed to the Essex Senior League.

PRAISE FOR THE GRAND OLD MAN OF SOCCER

Source : Herts & Essex Observer

Trophy Winners at the Annual Dance

At the 1978 League's Annual Presentation newly elected Essex County FA life member, Mr Bill Bruty, standing in for League President George Wilson, who, due to a very bad cold, was missing his first League dinner in 21 years as President, spoke of his love for local soccer and its characters. More than 300 people heard Mr Bruty speak of fond memories and old friends.

He also had high marks for the League's disciplinary record , 'There were 1,350 bookings in Essex last season, 79 from the Stortford League' it is good to see the figure down on the year before and I hope that next year's will be even lower,' he said. There were also 14 players sent off.

Mr Arthur Dimond, Chairman of the Harlow & District League, and the Essex Senior League, thanked Mr Bruty for his unstinting service to local soccer.

'Many local footballers have a great deal to thank this man for,' he said. 'Now the Essex County FA have honoured him with perhaps the ultimate accolade, and they could not have chosen a finer man.'

Brian Grimshaw (Acrow Sports) stamped his name on the Linesman of the Year award for the second year running and fourth time in all.

'FIVE DIVISIONS' MOVE REVEALED

At the League's Annual General Meeting, Mr Bruty paid tribute to the late Mr Roy Harrison, who had passed away in May, and outlined the service which he had given to the League over many years. The meeting stood in his memory.

To help ease the fixture caused by bad weather, the splitting of the League into five divisions had been considered, Secretary Roger Brinsford said in his report to the League's annual meeting.

'The Management Committee did discuss the possibility but with the withdrawal of High Laver and the two Takeley teams, it was felt that we should continue for another season at least with the present set-up.'

1,036 players registered, 37 transfers and 45 registrations cancelled.

There had been 14 dismissals and 79 cautions as of 2nd April 1978.

There were 65 referees (handbook).

The Treasurer reported that the balance of the League's bank account was £910.54.

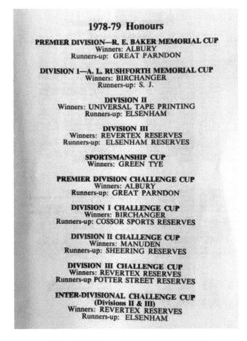

1978-79 Honours

PREMIER DIVISION—R. E. BAKER MEMORIAL CUP
Winners: ALBURY
Runners-up: GREAT PARNDON

DIVISION 1—A. L. RUSHFORTH MEMORIAL CUP
Winners: BIRCHANGER
Runners-up: S. J.

DIVISION II
Winners: UNIVERSAL TAPE PRINTING
Runners-up: ELSENHAM

DIVISION III
Winners: REVERTEX RESERVES
Runners-up: ELSENHAM RESERVES

SPORTSMANSHIP CUP
Winners: GREEN TYE

PREMIER DIVISION CHALLENGE CUP
Winners: ALBURY
Runners-up: GREAT PARNDON

DIVISION I CHALLENGE CUP
Winners: BIRCHANGER
Runners-up: COSSOR SPORTS RESERVES

DIVISION II CHALLENGE CUP
Winners: MANUDEN
Runners-up: SHEERING RESERVES

DIVISION III CHALLENGE CUP
Winners: REVERTEX RESERVES
Runners-up POTTER STREET RESERVES

INTER-DIVISIONAL CHALLENGE CUP
(Divisions II & III)
Winners: REVERTEX RESERVES
Runners-up: ELSENHAM

W.J. (WALLY) DAY MEMORIAL CUP

Winners : SHEERING Runners Up : HEATH ROVERS

Sponsored by Don Burlingham Associates (Commercial) Ltd

W.J. (WALLY) DAY MEMORIAL CUP FINAL

SHEERING 4 HEATH ROVERS 0

Peter Vealey scored the first goal after a constructive move, and Doug Wiltshire soon added a second. Two further goals were added in the second half by Chris Hellmers and Russell Adams.

HATFIELD HEATH

Prior to their resounding 5-1 win over local rivals Hatfield Broad Oak.

CLAVERING

DIVISION II CHALLENGE CUP FINAL

MANUDEN 3 SHEERING RESERVES 1

MANUDEN

Manuden outclassed Sheering Reserves to clinch a well-deserved Division II League and Cup double.

After half an hour Manuden had done everything but score. The first signs of frustration up front were showing when Isherwood hooked a great shot beyond Murphy in the Sheering goal. With their tails well up Manuden had the Sheering defence in a muddle, and it came as no surprise when Isherwood hit his second a minute before half-time.

After 57 minutes a long ball was pumped into the Sheering box, and in the confusion a defender handled. Referee Dyer had no hesitation in pointing to the spot, and up came Isherwood to place the ball into the right hand corner of the net. In the dying minutes Sheering scored a consolation goal when a shot slipped underneath keeper Slater's body.

Source : Herts & Essex Observer

SHEERING RESERVES

DIVISION III CHALLENGE CUP FINAL

REVERTEX RESERVES 3 POTTER STREET RESERVES 0

Tony Irish opened the scoring for Revertex Reserves after 20 minutes. Keith Barnard added a second but the final goal did not come until six minutes to go.

Roy Stephenson robbed a defender, left two men for dead in a 20 yard sprint and then placed the ball perfectly into the far corner of the net.

Source : Harlow Observer

REVERTEX RESERVES

INTER-DIVISIONAL CHALLENGE CUP FINAL

ELSENHAM 2 REVERTEX RESERVES 3

Source : Herts & Essex Observer

ELSENHAM

Playing one of his last games for Revertex before moving from the area, striker Roy Stephenson thrilled a Rhodes Avenue crowd with a stunning hat-trick.

Stephenson opened the scoring after 33 minutes when he was put through by Tony Irish to leave Porter with no chance.

The second half opened in spectacular style. In the 53rd minute, Stephenson ran fully 50 yards, leaving two defenders in his wake, to bury the ball in the back of the net.

Two minutes later, he completed his hat-trick when he beat the offside trap after another long run.

In the 72nd minute Elsenham pulled a goal back. A shot hit keeper Day's legs and Russell Banks was on hand to drive home the rebound.

Following a corner two minutes later, Laurence Devon headed home and Revertex had to withstand constant pressure from a revitalised Elsenham right up to the final whistle.

DIVISION I CHALLENGE CUP FINAL

BIRCHANGER 2 COSSOR SPORTS RESERVES 0

Source : Herts & Essex Observer

BIRCHANGER

Source : Herts & Essex Observer

COSSOR SPORTS RESERVES

Two goals within a minute gave Birchanger their first Bishop's Stortford, Stansted and District League trophy for 17 years at the George Wilson Stadium before a crowd of 350.

The first goal saw Graham Baker head home a cross by Neil Fullalove and a minute later Tony Dellow sped away to lob a bouncing through ball over the keeper's head for number two.

OLYMPIAN FUTURE FOR ALBURY?

Albury are not letting their hopes of following arch rivals Takeley into the Essex Olympian League soccer dim reality.

Rumour has been rife in the last few days that the club intend making the jump out of the Bishop's Stortford, Stansted and District League pretty soon. But Secretary and first team Manager Peter Newman said in clipped tones : 'Let's get the facilities right first.'

Albury currently chasing a League and cup double in the Premier Division, are engaged in dressing room improvements costing an estimated £800.'

Mr Newman said: 'Olympian League or any other league, the first thing we must do is get our facilities dead right. At the moment, we are having shower units installed for each dressing room in our building, which has been enlarged.'

'To start with, you have to think about which comes first, the chicken or the egg. You either have good facilities with no players or a good side with no facilities. When we are getting our ground in good order, we must also think about our players of the future – the two must come good at the same time.'

'We don't want just one good side we must also have a good reserve side and must get more support. We don't get as much as much local support as Takeley, for instance, good as we are, and we are planning a sponsored walk or some other sponsored event.'

'It would be better for us to work hard at making one fund-raising event a success than a whole series of ventures that might provide nothing.'

PREMIER DIVISION CHALLENGE CUP FINAL

ALBURY 2 GREAT PARNDON 0

Albury opened the scoring one minute into the second half when Trott headed home a cross by Peter English from the right with the keeper and two defenders all half-committed.

The goal upset Parndon's rhythm, and they had hardly got over the shock when Trott forced his way down the left in the 66th minute to cross for Chris Newman to head a picture goal.

Source : Harlow Citizen

ALBURY

A PAT AND A SLAP !

Congratulations and warning went hand in hand at the Annual Dinner and Dance and presentation of the League.

They both came from Bill Bruty, Chairman of the League and a life member of Essex FA. He praised clubs for another successful season but added a tough note on discipline after a warm word for the club secretaries on whose most responsibilities fell.

'I hope that next year's record is better than this.' He told 230 officials and guests. 'This year we had 19 sendings off and 84 cautioned. That is not good enough, so please impress on your team that sportsmanship cost nothing, but it means such a lot.'

Len Menhinick, the Chairman of the Chelmsford and District Sunday League and also a member of the Essex FA, also had a kind word for club secretaries. 'It is very easy to run a club when everything is going well but it is difficult to run a club when things are going not so well.'

Likewise he had a word or two to say about discipline. 'Sportsmanship is the most important thing in football,' he said.

He backed Mr Bruty's appeal for better behaviour on the field but added that the Stortford League had a better disciplinary record than any club in Essex. 'I don't know about Hertfordshire, but I wouldn't think it rates pretty high.'

He congratulated the League on a successful, if traumatic season with more matches postponed than ever before, 'You have a great bunch of officers,' he said.

Source : Roger Brinsford

Roger Brinsford was presented with a pair of roller skates to mark his energetic League secretaryship again during the year.

Sugar Perry, Hatfield Heath, who took the Secretary of the Year award.

Source : Harlow Observer

Source : Roger Brinsford

Bill Bruty presents the Premier Division championship trophy to Albury skipper Peter English.

Richard Marriott with the Linesman's Trophy

Source : Harlow Observer

A surprised Mike Steed receives an engraved plate for his three years as Referees' Secretary.

Source : Roger Brinsford

Some of the winners with their trophies at the Annual Dinner and Dance.

LEAGUE SUBS ROCKET

Clubs will have to pay much more to belong to the League next season with subscriptions rising from between £3-£3.50 to £20-£26, depending on their Division.

But the new levy will include the cost of club directories and tickets for the Cup Finals – each of which were charged separately.

The referees fee was also increase from £2 to £2.50.

Warning of the rises, approved at the League's annual meeting, was given in the report of League Secretary, Roger Brinsford.

Some of the sponsorship, by Don Burlingham Associates (Commercial) Ltd., was used to help defray the cost such items as printing and stationery, he said.

'It was unfortunate that when the agreement was concluded, the Management Committee endeavoured to pass all the monetary benefits possible on to the clubs. As a result, we did not increase subscriptions in line with the escalating costs 'to provide us in running the League and we were eventually forced to levy £5 from each team before the season ended.'

Mr Brinsford said that to avoid a similar situation arising, 'substantially' increased fees were being sought for next season 'to provide us with a platform, not only to monitor inflation, but also to make future increases on a much smaller and, if necessary, more regular basis.'

He said disciplinary figures were running at the level of two seasons ago, having shown a slight increase over the previous season, and the Management Committee had written to five clubs regarding their disciplinary records.

The Treasurer reported that the League's bank balance was £128.83.

997 players registered, 31 transfers and 23 registrations cancelled.

There were 4,448 league games played and 20,165 league goals scored.

There had been 19 dismissals and 84 cautions as of 1st May 1979.

There were 69 referees (handbook).

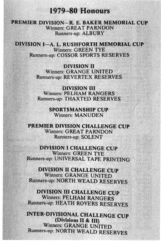

1979–80 Honours

PREMIER DIVISION—R. E. BAKER MEMORIAL CUP
Winners: GREAT PARNDON
Runners-up: ALBURY

DIVISION I—A. L. RUSHFORTH MEMORIAL CUP
Winners: GREEN TYE
Runners-up: COSSOR SPORTS RESERVES

DIVISION II
Winners: GRANGE UNITED
Runners-up: REVERTEX RESERVES

DIVISION III
Winners: PELHAM RANGERS
Runners-up: THAXTED RESERVES

SPORTSMANSHIP CUP
Winners: MANUDEN

PREMIER DIVISION CHALLENGE CUP
Winners: GREAT PARNDON
Runners-up: SOLENT

DIVISION I CHALLENGE CUP
Winners: GREEN TYE
Runners-up: UNIVERSAL TAPE PRINTING

DIVISION II CHALLENGE CUP
Winners: GRANGE UNITED
Runners-up: NORTH WEALD RESERVES

DIVISION III CHALLENGE CUP
Winners: PELHAM RANGERS
Runners-up: HEATH ROVERS RESERVES

INTER-DIVISIONAL CHALLENGE CUP
(Divisions II & III)
Winners: GRANGE UNITED
Runners-up: NORTH WEALD RESERVES

W.J. (WALLY) DAY MEMORIAL CUP

Winners : MANUDEN **Runners-Up** : UNIVERSAL TAPE PRINTING

Sponsored by Don Burlingham Associates (Commercial) Ltd

Phillip Newman was a one club man, joining Sheering Football Club. Phillip also played for the League representative side on a number of occasions. He was also a member of the League Management Committee from 2004 to 2016.

The Eighties

48 clubs provided teams for the League during the eighties and there was an average of 44 teams per year playing in the League.

There were 4,448 League games played and 20,165 League goals scored.

During the decade Great Parndon and Hatfield Broad Oak each won the Premier Division on four occasions. In the other two years N.A.L.G.O. won the title.

Great Parndon also won the Premier Division Challenge Cup four times while Hatfield Broad Oak were successful on three occasions.

The number of teams competing in the League fell from 49 to 38 during the decade and although several reserve teams joined the League in fact 17 reserve teams had been withdrawn by their parent clubs. Between 1986 and 1989 the League lost 232 players.

Long serving clubs Debden and Jim O'Connor's Grange Park withdrew from the League in the decade.

On 1st April 1980, the League's Representative team won the West Essex Inter-League Cup Competition for the third time at the Epping Town FC ground beating the Romford & District League by 2 goals to 1.

W.J. (WALLY) DAY MEMORIAL CUP FINAL

MANUDEN 2 UNIVERSAL TAPE PRINTING 1

Manuden, Division II Challenge Cup winners last season, beat League winners Universal Tapes 2-1. First Half goals from Oakley and Budd won a match that was as close and well contested as the final score suggests.

Source : Herts & Essex Observer

MANUDEN   **UNIVERSAL TAPE PRINTING**

PITCH FEES INCREASE

Clubs from the two major local football leagues were to hold an urgent meeting to discuss East Herts Council's proposed 100% increase in pitch fees at Grange Paddocks.

Representatives from the two leagues were to discuss the announcement that the Council was considering increasing the charges from £4.16 to £8.25.

Although delighted with the news that the changing rooms would soon be ready, the leagues were surprised all clubs would be charged for the use of showers. That, they claimed, was a complete reversal of earlier policy.

'The Council has changed its mind. The clubs do not mind paying £5.55 for decent facilities but many do not want to use the showers,' said North-West Essex League fixtures Secretary Bill Fegan.

When plans were originally announced for the new changing rooms, the Council charges would naturally go up but showers would be paid for as and when used. This suited the clubs, many of whose players lived within walking distance of the Paddocks.

Clubs were notified that due to increased VAT, pitch charges at the beginning of the new season would be £5.55 less a 20% discount for the present lack of changing facilities.

But the Council's Community Services Committee met to consider officers' proposals that the pitch fee should be £8.25 including showers with effect from October 6th. Officers made the stipulation that until the facilities were complete, clubs would just be charged £5.55 less the 20% discount.

Officers in a report to the committee, said : 'The cost of providing showers is a substantial part of the total cost of the provision of changing facilities.'

They also said there is no method of ensuring the teams using changing rooms in East Herts, who have not hired showers, do not in fact use them 'and its apparent that there is some abuse of this.'

The two major local leagues decided that clubs should have the chance of airing their views on paying £2.70 per home match for showers – which many will not use.

ALGERIANS TRAIN WITH HEATH ROVERS

Heath Rovers became the first local junior team to give trials to a group of foreign players. Four Algerians were due to train with Rovers at Grange Paddocks and play in trial matches for the Club's three Saturday's teams.

The players, who worked for Algerian Airways and were on three-year apprenticeships at Stansted Airport, all signed on for the Club.

But Secretary, Hugh Davidson, said : We have not guaranteed them football. We will have to see what they are like. They all speak English, so that shouldn't provide any problems and all have played football before.'

ROGER THE REFEREE COMES INTO FOCUS

ROGER Brinsford, best known locally as a football administrator — he is secretary of Bishop's Stortford, Stansted and District Football League — on Saturday found himself in the spotlight as a referee.

At the North-West Essex Referees' Society annual presentation buffet disco at the Barn Theatre, Dunmow, a surprised Roger was presented by the FA divisional officer, Arthur Dimond, with the society's meritorious service award — the first time that this annual award has gone to a referee not an officer or committee member of the society.

Vice-chairman Michael Steed, announcing the award, said that Roger's work and attitudes typified the best example of "rank and file" membership of any sports society — ever ready for years to play his part in routine working of the referees society.

The opportunity had arisen this year to spotlight Roger's contribution to the society because he single-handed organised a social event which raised nearly £250 for the society's golden jubilee fund.

The other main local referees award of the year — the Frank Bidwell Trophy to the most promising new referee, went to 17-year-old Howard Shoebridge, of Northolt, Bishop's Stortford.

The donor, personally making the award, said Howard, who had been refereeing for two years, had developed his enthusiasm for refereeing when as a schoolboy he was club linesman to Stansted FC reserve team and after a year as a youth league referee, he was now successfully officiating in two local adult leagues as well as being the youngest linesman on the Essex and Herts Border Combination. His age and enthusiasm gave him much promise for the future.

Eighty referees and guests attended the evening, including the president of the Essex Referees' Association, Mr T. Gee, Essex FA life vice-president, Mr Bill Bruty, and representatives of local leagues, Mr G. Banks (Bishop's Stortford and District League) and Mr D. Metson (North-West Essex Sunday League).

ROGER BRINSFORD

Source : Herts & Essex Observer

Source : Herts & Essex Observer

GREAT PARNDON   DEBDEN

Source : Harlow Gazette

SHEERING   THAXTED

357

ALBURY　　　　　　　　**GREAT PARNDON**

DIVISION II CHALLENGE CUP FINAL

GRANGE UNITED 2 NORTH WEALD RESERVES 1

On a bone hard pitch both teams found it hard to control the ball. Both sides used the long high ball to good effect. In the 13th minute Weald went ahead when a free-kick from the right was touched on to Mark Ginn, who cleverly lobbed the ball over goalkeeper Gurden from close range.

The goal was scored against the run of play as Grange had forced three corners in succession only a couple of minutes earlier.

Grange kept trying and came close when one of their front runners broke with the Weald defence waiting for an offside whistle that never came. But keeper Green made an important save.

Grange applied pressure immediately after the break and a great 20-yarder was parried by the keeper. In the 52nd minute Grange got a deserved equaliser from a Mark Nicholas lob.

They began to get on top and went ahead in the 58th minute, when Mick Collins beat the offside trap and ran on to dribble the ball past the keeper and slot home.

Weald made a great effort to get back on terms and had a good shot scrambled away, but this proved to be their best chance and it was Grange who collected the cup.

GRANGE UNITED　　　　　　**NORTH WEALD RESERVES**

DIVISION III CHALLENGE CUP FINAL

PELHAM RANGERS 4 HEATH ROVERS RESERVES 3

Pelham began to attack from the kick-off and after seven minutes had a good effort saved by Miller.

It was Heath Rovers, however, who went ahead slightly against the run of play when a high bouncing ball beat the Pelham defence who had pushed up to the half-way line. Mezhoud ran through and cleverly beat the advancing goalkeeper with a ground shot.

Pelham continued to push forward and were twice caught out by balls lobbed over the defence. Only good goalkeeping by Surtees kept them from going further behind at this stage.

Heath Rovers scored a second goal after half-an-hour when Claydon hit a high shot from the left corner of the of the penalty box which found the top corner of the net. Pelham reduced the arrears within a minute when Hagger headed in from a corner on the left.

They then had a good long shot pushed over the bar by the keeper before drawing level in the 35th minute when Hawkes slotted home a good goal from another corner from the left.

Six minutes later another corner caused chaos in the Heath Rovers area and Hagger was again on hand to put Rangers ahead.

The second half was dominated by Pelham Rangers and goal number four came after 55 minutes when indecision in the Heath Rovers defence allowed Cook to score off the keeper's body. In a rare second half raid by Rovers they were awarded an 82nd minute penalty which James converted to give them hope, but Rangers held out for another eight minutes of high excitement.

Source : Herts & Essex Observer

PELHAM RANGERS   **HEATH ROVERS RESERVES**

ELSENHAM   **HEATH ROVERS**

DIVISION I CHALLENGE CUP FINAL

GREEN TYE 4 UNIVERSAL TAPES 0

A hat-trick from danger man Teddy Prior set Green Tye on the way to victory.

His fine individual performance capped a display of strong running and incisive passing from the whole team.

Green Tye took an early grip on the game on the game with two first half goals, both of which stemmed from mistakes at the centre of a Universal Tape defence which was badly missing the settling influence of regular central defender Paul Goodyear.

After 12 minutes, Green Tye skipper Dave Gosling lofted a free-kick into Universal Tapes penalty area from deep inside his own half and Tape's keeper Alan Tite, seemed to hesitate as the ball bounced on the hard ground before travelling in a slow arc over his despairing backward dive. Five minutes later Green Tye struck again after Dave Porter's ill-advised pass across his own goal was intercepted sharply by Teddy Prior who ran on and despatched the ball low to the keeper's right.

These two early blows seemed to kill off the challenge from the Universal team, who were always struggling to control the skilful prompting of Ronnie Page in midfield, and the opportunism of Teddy Prior up front. Tite made up for his previous error early in the second half, coming out to save a point-blank shot after Prior had been sent clear by Page.

But there was no stopping the two Green Tye players, and in the 67th minute Page's finely judged cross from the left dipped over the Universal defence and was thumped high into the net by Prior after he had raced in from the right. Universal almost got one back after Tony Boyce and Tony White combined skilfully in the 73rd minute, but Boyce's final shot lacked conviction. Three minutes later, Prior's sharpness told again when he completed his hat-trick with a fine first time volley at the near post following a cross from Dave Wright.

The Tape's team ran bravely throughout the 90 minutes, and Manager Mike Hathaway was well pleased with their 'tremendous effort,' but it was Green Tye Manager Dick Mumford who was celebrating after his team's 'excellent performance.'

GREEN TYE   **UNIVERSAL TAPES**

PREMIER DIVISION CHALLENGE CUP FINAL

GREAT PARNDON 1 SOLENT 0

An early goal settled a furious League leader's clash. Parndon settled first but it was Solent who were the first with a quick break after a long clearance. A desperate clearance by a defender saved the day and another Solent shot from 20 yards was off target.

The decider came in the 13th minute when Parndon were awarded a free-kick on the left of the box and a perfectly judged kick was headed home by Ivor Smith.

Parndon got into their stride with another shot from the right wing which was pushed over the bar for a corner which in turn led to a goalmouth scramble and a disallowed goal.

Solent began to get back into the match but good work from the midfield was squandered by their forwards' lack of urgency. They created few chances except for isolated shots which the Parndon keeper took easily.

Parndon may well have made it two when seconds before half-time a bad defensive error let in a forward who shot against the post.

The second half saw both defences on top and neither side had many chances. Parndon again looked the more dangerous with a header just wide from a free-kick and shot which hit the post in the last two minutes.

GREAT PARNDON   **SOLENT**

ESSEX JUNIOR CUP FINAL

GREAT PARNDON 4 RIO ATHLETIC 1

A hat-trick from Bob Johnstone set Parndon on their way to victory in the Essex Junior Cup Final at Witham.

Rio took an early grip and after 21 minutes, winger Dave McCarthy got free on the right, and his quick low cross was touched into the net by Michael Callison.

GREAT PARNDON

The strong running of Jeff Hilton helped to stem the tide of Rio's midfield, and Frank McGinlay, back after a three-week absence, out jumped taller opponents to win several crucial high balls.

In the 26th minute Parndon hit back. A corner from Johnny Johnson was headed powerfully against the inside of the post by Bob Johnstone, and the ball was helped over the line by a hapless defender.

Parndon began to wrest the initiative from their Dagenham opponents, and the wily Johnny Johnson began to control matters in midfield.

In the 50th minute, Parndon took a deserved lead when a corner on the left was flicked on at the near post by full-back Freddie Phillips, and Bob Johnstone was at hand to head it high into the net.

Parndon made the game safe in the 85th minute, Hilton took a free-kick just outside the Rio penalty area and when his gentle chip was returned to him via a Rio defender, he clipped the ball back and this time Bob Johnstone headed it down for brother Ray Johnstone to crash into the net.

Parndon's final goal came a minute before the end, and it typified their fine team performance, Stuart Smith raced back 40 yards to dispossess a Rio player, and after Ivor Smith had picked the ball up and played a one-two with Johnson, he crossed it from wide on the right to the far post and Bob Johnstone raced in to complete his hat-trick.

NEW RAP FOR THE BAD BOYS

The bad boys of soccer got a rap from George Banks Vice-Chairman of the League at the Annual Dinner and Dance.

He told the assembled members and guests – which included Harlow League Vice-Chairman and Treasurer Peter Pengelly – that the League had a bad record for last season on the misconduct side.

'The record of 24 dismissals and 146 cautions is bad for a league of this size. In fact it is terrible,' he said.

Mr Banks said the League's Management Committee had spent many hours discussing the problem and warned would-be offenders. 'You have got to learn to play football with your feet and not with your mouth.'

He proposed a toast to the ladies and guests, including in his welcome, Arthur Dimond, Essex FA Group VI Representative and retiring Chairman of the Harlow and District League, Brian Curtis, Secretary of the Coaching Committee of the Herts Football Association and Chairman of the North-West Essex Sunday League and Jim Gill (Vice-Chairman) and Vic Wallice (Secretary) representing Bishop's Stortford Football Club.

The response was given by Ken Daish, Secretary of the Referees' Committee of the Hertfordshire Football Association, who also referred to the lack of discipline that marred a good season for the League.

Mr Daish said, 'it was a way of showing off and said that some players tried to turn it into more than a game of football by dissent, which was the major cause of cautions.'

He reminded players and officials that referees had to start somewhere, just like players, and all the referees who got to the top had humble beginnings on the field. 'Rule one must be that the referee is always right.'

Mr Daish congratulated the League on winning the West Essex Inter-League competition and Great Parndon on completing the quadruple by taking the Essex Junior Cup, the Premier Division Championship and Cup and the West Essex Border Charity Cup.

Chairman Bill Bruty, who presided in the absence through illness of President George Wilson and Mrs Wilson, presented a plaque to Great Parndon Secretary Brian Vernon to mark the club's feat in winning the Essex Junior Cup for the second time.

Mr Bruty paid tribute to the work of all his officers in turn, in particular Secretary Roger Brinsford, who was the toastmaster, and presented the trophies.

Richard Marriott (Albury) was presented with the Linesman of the Year award for the second consecutive year. He is seen receiving his award from Bernard Ellis, Chairman of the North-West Essex Referees Society.

League Chairman Bill Bruty (centre) presents the Premier Division championship trophy to Great Parndon Manager, Phil Smith, and Captain Ray Johnstone.

Brian Vernon, Great Parndon Secretary, receives the plaque to mark his club's winning of the Essex Junior Cup.

Pelham Rangers (Division III) and Manuden (Division II) each received their Sportsmanship awards.

Secretary of the Year Barry Mutimer (Cossor Sports).

Source : All photos - Herts & Essex Observer

At the 1980 Annual General Meeting, the Chairman, Mr Bruty, spoke of forming another cup competition for the Division Three clubs instead of the usual cup competition, It was to form a League Cup basis using two divisions of four clubs, the winners of each to play each other in the final. This would give the clubs more games.

1,075 players registered, 36 transfers and 26 registrations cancelled.

There had been 24 dismissals and 146 cautions.

There were 56 referees (handbook).

W.J. (WALLY) DAY MEMORIAL CUP

Winners : THAXTED RESERVES Runners-Up : PELHAM RANGERS

Sponsored by Don Burlingham Associates (Commercial) Ltd

W.J. (WALLY) DAY MEMORIAL CUP FINAL

THAXTED RESERVES 2 PELHAM RANGERS 1

(AFTER EXTRA-TIME)

Source : Herts & Essex Observer

GREEN TYE

365

PARNDON STALWART DIES AGED 73

Harry Burton, a stalwart of the Great Parndon team throughout the 1930's died at the age of 73.

He was well-known to many people in Great Parndon where he lived.

Both his sons played for Parndon, and Harry kept up his interest in the club until the end.

Source : Herts & Essex Observer

Source : Harlow Gazette

ALBURY

Source : Harlow Gazette

SHEERING

On 7th April 1981 at a League Management Committee meeting the Honorary Treasurer, George Reed, requested that his name be disassociated with minutes regarding the League

Presentation Function despite the otherwise unanimous approval of the contents of the minutes by the remainder of the League Management Committee.

The Honorary Treasurer had expressed strong criticism at every meeting since September over the distribution of tickets at the Annual Dinner in previous years and, the way in which the Chairman and Honorary General Secretary had handled the matter. Up to an hour at each one of those meetings had been lost through his repeated reference to this and other items, involving the Honorary General Secretary, such as the running of the League Challenge Cup Finals. He had not received the backing of the League Management Committee over these charges and because of the lack of reasonable time, items on the agenda or due for fuller discussion had to be held over when they should have received immediate attention in the normal course. Following this meeting the Chairman received the resignation of one of the League Management Committee members.

At the following meeting, the Honorary Treasurer spoke at length regarding his feelings, as did many of the committee. After considerable discussion it was proposed that the minute should stand in its entirety. This motion was carried by 10 votes to 1! The Chairman then asked the Honorary Treasurer for his resignation which he considered was a fair reflection of the lack of confidence expressed by the meeting. The Honorary Treasurer refused to resign adding he would consider his position during the next couple of weeks.

The minutes were than signed as a true record after appreciation had been expressed for the work that Mr A.G. Perry had done for the League over many years. Mr Perry had resigned from the Committee as he was dissatisfied over the conduct of the Honorary Treasurer.

Source : Saffron Walden Reporter

ACROW SPORTS

Harlow referee made the big time after being appointed a Football League official. John Moules began his career in the Bishop's Stortford, Stansted and District League in 1968.

Source : Harlow Gazette

MATCH-DAY SPONSORSHIP AND MATCH BALL

The League was delighted that they were able to find sponsors for all Cup Finals. This was the first occasion that it had ventured into this particular field and it proved highly successful.

The first sponsor was the Herts & Essex Observer Group.

DIVISION I CHALLENGE CUP FINAL

POTTER STREET RANGERS 2 POTTER STREET 0

Potter Street held its own local derby at Rhodes Avenue in the Division I Challenge Cup Final.

Source : Herts & Essex Observer

POTTER STREET RANGERS   POTTER STREET

DIVISION II CHALLENGE CUP FINAL

N.A.L.G.O. 1 LANGLEY 0

N.A.L.G.O. put the pressure on Langley throughout the game, but good defending and a measure of bad luck for N.A.L.G.O. kept Langley in the game.

N.A.L.G.O. were well marshalled by their skipper Peter Haywood and despite good work by Mays, Smith, Gregory, and Thorpe, the goals just would not go in.

The winner did not come until the last minute when winger Tony Smith scored from a set piece 35 yards out.

PREMIER DIVISION CHALLENGE CUP FINAL

SOLENT 2 GREAT PARNDON 1

Five minutes from half-time, Great Parndon came within a whisker of scoring on three separate occasions.

Their failure to press home this attack probably lost them the game, allowing Solent's crisp attacking football to claim their first victory over in six games, and the Premier Division Cup.

Man of the match was Jeff Hilton in the Solent midfield, whose impressive footwork and tireless running launched attacks against his old club.

With only four minutes gone a push in the back on a Solent forward gave away a penalty and Hilton confidently scored from the spot.

Parndon, accepting their defensive role far too readily, battled against Solent's crisp attacking moves, which constantly threatened the Parndon goal.

Tony Liddle and Ken O'Connell's sharp and passing holes in Parndon's right wing, while Lawrence William's running threatened their left.

A 20 yard drive from Tony Liddle which skimmed the bar was followed by a free-kick. Tony Liddle stepped over the ball leaving it for Ken O'Connell to thump into the far corner, putting Solent two up after 20 minutes.

Graham Col's midfield work eased the pressure on Parndon but it was not until the last five minutes that a defensive error allowed him space on the left-wing. His cross skidded across the treacherous surface water in Solent's defenceless goalmouth only to miss Ray Johnstone's outstretched foot by inches.

Minutes later a Solent defender headed off the line, followed by a Frank McGinlay shot that went just over.

It took Parndon a further 14 minutes in the second half before Ivor Smith turned neatly in the box to slam the ball home from short range and claw back for Parndon.

Neither side however looked like scoring as the second half developed in to a midfield struggle of attrition where Jeff Hilton and Danny Fullen were the stars.

In the closing minutes Parndon pushed for an equaliser, laying siege to Solent's packed defence. A corner fell to John Johnson but the ball was scrambled away.

Solent had to survive a further four minutes of injury time before taking the cup, well-earned by their superior attacking play by and midfield passing.

INTER-DIVISIONAL CHALLENGE CUP FINAL

N.A.L.G.O. 1 NEWPORT 0

N.A.L.G.O. clinched the treble having dismissed Newport .

It was the fourth meeting between the two teams and for the fourth time, Newport didn't look like scoring against a very strong N.A.L.G.O. defence.

Solid work by Dave Forrest and a great game by Steve Burgess laid the foundation for the win, But the goal did not come until the second half when a nervous Newport goalkeeper let in a 45 yard Gary King effort which bounced over his head.

Special mention must go to N.A.L.G.O. goalkeeper Ian Vernon who has kept 15 clean sheets this season with some fine saves – including one in each cup final.

DIVISION III CHALLENGE CUP FINAL

ACROW SPORTS 1 UNIVERSAL TAPE PRINTING RESERVES 2

This game held at Catons Lane Saffron Walden FC was the first occasion that the League brought a final to the Northern extremity of the League.

In the local derby final, during which three players were booked, UTP Reserves ran out winners 2-1.

Source : Saffron Walden Reporter

UNIVERSAL TAPE PRINTING RESERVES

ESSEX JUNIOR CUP FINAL

SOLENT 3 TATE & LYLE 1

After going a goal down Solent put on a brave performance to defeat Tate & Lyle.

Solent began well at a hard pace and hit the bar after 10 minutes. Tate & Lyle broke away though and took the lead two minutes before the break.

Solent broke out in the second half and put on a fine display of attacking football and within five minutes of the restart they equalised. A good run by Williams led to O'Connell firing home from close range.

Five minutes later Solent took the lead when Liddle ran on to a through ball by Gates to shoot home from 12 yards and with Solent constantly pressurising the Tate & Lyle defence it was no surprise when Boyle headed home the goal which made sure of the trophy.

SWIFTS TURN THE CLOCK BACK

Twenty-five years after their first League match, Bishop's Stortford Swifts celebrated with a veterans match against Takeley at Silver Leys.

Source : Herts & Essex Observer

BISHOP'S STORTFORD SWIFTS   **TAKELEY**

With a minimum age of 35, the teams turned the clock back to give a rare display of Old Swifts' characteristic close passing game, which contrasted well with Takeley's more direct but often effective long ball game.

Neither team was self-conscious about their age and, determined to enjoy themselves, created a number of diversions. One Swifts player started the first half on crutches while at half-time the Takeley first-aid lorry complete with white clad attendants and stretchers joined the scene.

Neither were needed as the veterans gave a fine display of attacking football with a bag of five goals.

Eddie Miller scored two for the Swifts and John Gregory added a third. Takeley scorers were Mick Ellis and Mick Ryan with a penalty.

Mr Roger Brinsford, who refereed the game had little to do on such a sporting occasion which had none of the evils of dissent, swearing and the intentional foul characteristic of the modern game!

THE GLORY WINNERS

After finally winding up the 59th and possibly longest season, the League celebrated with their annual award presentation and buffet dance.

Mr Bill Bruty, the League's Chairman explained that that he had been with the League since 1930/31 and this, he felt, had been the hardest season. He thanked the players, club officials and members of the Management Committee who had all worked so hard.

Mr Bruty welcomed the guests who included Rex Blackman from the Harlow and District League, Graham Ward from the Hertford and District League, Bill Fegan from the North-West Essex Sunday League and Alex James, Chairman of Harlow Council. Mr James ended the presentations by thanking Mr Bruty. 'Over the years, the name of Bill Bruty has stayed with the League. I hope he will receive the benefit of his work for many years.'

TICKET ROW COMES TO A HEAD

Roger Brinsford's worst year since taking office came to a head with a clash with Treasurer George Reed at the League's Annual General Meeting.

The clash was over the discretion used by Mr Brinsford and Chairman, Mr Bill Bruty, in allocating complimentary tickets for the 1980 Annual Dinner.

Both brought the row into the open at the meeting, but Vice-President, John Barry, presiding, cooled the tempo. 'This can do no good to the League if we let it get out of hand,' he said.

He continued, Management Committee members did a lot of valuable work and this would not be very enjoyable if there was bickering.

No further reference was made to the clash and the meeting accepted Mr Brinsford's report in which he said : 'To say this season has been a bitter disappointment is a gross understatement. Both on and off the field, it has been the worst year since I took office and in the opinion of many, the worst in their memory as well.'

'The League was late finishing, the senior representative side did not get a game and the disciplinary figures continued to rise.'

Mr Brinsford said he and the Management Committee were concerned at the attitude of players and clubs towards their opponents, the game in general and the League in particular.

'Over the years the League and its clubs, has been noted for the friendliness and hospitality while at the same time remaining competitive. This season all the goodwill built up over many seasons appears to have disappeared.'

Mr Reed thanked Mr Don Burlingham for his sponsorship and reported that Mr Brian Skingle of Brian Skingle Sports had kindly agreed to sponsor the League for the coming three seasons. After the formal presentation of a cheque for £400, a further £100 would be in vouchers for sportsmanship awards. The Honorary General Secretary then informed the members that approval would now be sought from the Essex FA to change the name of the

League to the 'Brian Skingle Sports, Bishop's Stortford, Stansted & District League' for the term of the sponsorship.

The meeting agreed to a proposal that all players will wear numbered shirts the season after next. Mr Brinsford said this was to bring the League into line with both the Herts and Essex Football Associations' thinking, and this was strongly supported by referees, especially when they had to administer cautions.

1,075 players registered, 25 transfers and 42 registrations cancelled.

There had been 26 dismissals and 145 cautions as of 19th May 1981.

There were 56 referees (handbook).

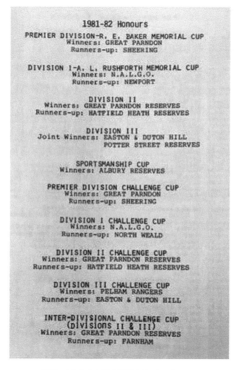

1981-82 Honours

PREMIER DIVISION-R. E. BAKER MEMORIAL CUP
Winners: GREAT PARNDON
Runners-up: SHEERING

DIVISION I-A. L. RUSHFORTH MEMORIAL CUP
Winners: N.A.L.G.O.
Runners-up: NEWPORT

DIVISION II
Winners: GREAT PARNDON RESERVES
Runners-up: HATFIELD HEATH RESERVES

DIVISION III
Joint Winners: EASTON & DUTON HILL
POTTER STREET RESERVES

SPORTSMANSHIP CUP
Winners: ALBURY RESERVES

PREMIER DIVISION CHALLENGE CUP
Winners: GREAT PARNDON
Runners-up: SHEERING

DIVISION I CHALLENGE CUP
Winners: N.A.L.G.O.
Runners-up: NORTH WEALD

DIVISION II CHALLENGE CUP
Winners: GREAT PARNDON RESERVES
Runners-up: HATFIELD HEATH RESERVES

DIVISION III CHALLENGE CUP
Winners: PELHAM RANGERS
Runners-up: EASTON & DUTON HILL

INTER-DIVISIONAL CHALLENGE CUP
(DIVISIONS II & III)
Winners: GREAT PARNDON RESERVES
Runners-up: FARNHAM

W.J. (WALLY) DAY MEMORIAL CUP

SOLENT / GREAT PARNDON shared the trophy

Sponsored by Brian Skingle Sports

W.J. (WALLY) DAY MEMORIAL CUP FINAL

SOLENT 1 GREAT PARNDON 1

After carving up the honours in last season's Premier League, champions Great Parndon and cup holders Solent clashed again in the season's traditional opener, the Wally Day Memorial Cup.

But a further 90 minutes as the blistering heat of Rectory Field still not divide the teams.

Playing a virtually unchanged side from that which beat Parndon in the final of last season's cup, Solent struck from the start with a shock goal. Two minutes into the game Jeff Hilton saw a gap in the Parndon defence and shot from 25 yards. The ball curved away from the keeper and lodged in the far corner of the net, leaving Brian Morton motionless.

Solent went from strength to strength as their speedy winger Lawrence Williams launched endless attacks down the left wing demonstrating a control and tenacity that taxed every inch of the Parndon defence marshalled by their captain, Ray Johnstone.

Douggie Sheppard and Ken O'Connell's hard work in midfield allowed no let up in the Solent attack but it was not until Williams went on his own that a second goal looked imminent, he fought his way past three defenders only to shoot wide.

Parndon rarely strayed into the Solent penalty box, dominated by the sturdy figure of central defender, Don Watters and the neat footwork of right-back Colin Gates.

After the break it was Parndon's turn. Their earlier policy of letting the ball do the work began to pay off as the Solent players tired in the heat.

Parndon substitutes Colin Hawkins and Bill Bailey came on, giving more sting to the attack and after 20 minutes the scores were level. Bob Johnstone received a flick from Colin Hawkins and he slammed the ball home from close range.

Solent, whose midfield machine refused to let up counter attacked with neat first time passing but this time Ray Johnstone had his way in the Parndon defence. In fact Parndon could have clinched it when with 15 minutes to go Bob Johnstone hit the bar with a header.

The game was marred in the closing minutes when Solent's Billy Herriot kicked out at Graham Cole in an off the ball incident, leaving the Parndon spectators demanding a sending off, but both players were booked. A penalty claim by Solent was rejected soon after and the game threatened to boil over before coming to a timely close, leaving the two giants of the League to share the trophy.

Source : Herts & Essex Observer

SOLENT

GREAT PARNDON

S.J.F.C.

GREEN TYE

DEATHS OF BILL BRUTY AND GEORGE WILSON ANNOUNCED

In late 1981 the deaths were announced of the Vice-President and Chairman, Bill Bruty and President of the League, George Wilson, both served the League for many years. Following the death of Mr Bruty, the League introduced The W A (Bill) Bruty Memorial Trophy.

A LIFEETIME OF SERVICE TO SPORT AND VILLAGE ENDS

BILL BRUTY DIES AT 72

Village coalman, Parish Councillor and life-long sportsman William Alfred 'Bill' Bruty passed away two weeks after celebrating his 72nd birthday.

Mr Bruty was a widower. There was no family, and he was survived by a sister and nephew. Her died on the day of his sister-in-law's funeral.

The Bruty family moved to Hatfield Heath in the late 1880s. Bill's father and Uncle Fred, moved from London and established their coal merchant's business.

Mr Bruty was educated at the old village school and worked on a poultry farm until the coal business acquired its first lorry when he joined the firm as its driver. He continued the business until he retired.

During the second world war he served as a Sergeant in the Home Guard.

Throughout his life, Bill Bruty served the community in many ways, including being a Parish Councillor for many years. He was Vice-Chairman of Hatfield Broad Oak Parish Council when he retired.

But it was as a sportsman he was best known. Although his main interest was football, he played cricket for the village for many years and was at one time captain and Secretary of the village cricket club, He was also a keen darts player.

He was one of the pioneers of the Hatfield Heath show and fete, which was one of the villages highlights in the post-war years where he was the auctioneer. He also founded many trophies and medals.

Affectionately known as 'Uncle Bill,' Bill Bruty had been one of the best-known and most popular of local football administrators. He first played for Hatfield Heath in 1924 when he was 14. He played at right-half and his brother Dick Bruty was right-back. He had a number of games for the club that season and he won a runners-up medal in the old Rodings and District League. He was the club Secretary from just before the first world war until 1950. He was made a Life-President in 1950. Previous to his election as Chairman, he had served as Vice-Chairman for two years.

In September 1955, he succeeded Mr A Frost of Takeley, as the Essex Football Association representative for the area, a position he held until 1978 when he was made a life member. County FA committees he served on included the Executive Council, disciplinary, junior competitions, sanctions and the referees' committee. He was also a referee assessor and was a member of the benevolent fund committee.

Mr Bruty had also been Honorary Treasurer of the West Essex Border Charity Cup competition and Vice-Chairman of the West Essex Inter-League competition.

At an Annual Presentation, a few years earlier Mr Arthur Dimond, Chairman of the Harlow & District League, and the Essex Senior League, had thanked Mr Bruty for his unstinting service to local soccer. 'Many local footballers have a great deal to thank this man for,' he said. 'Now the Essex County FA have honoured him with perhaps the ultimate accolade, and they could not have chosen a finer man.'

Tributes were paid to Bill Bruty when more than 200 people turned out for his funeral at Hatfield Heath Reformed Church.

Mr Arthur Dimond, a close friend, spoke movingly about the high regard in which Bill was held throughout football.

He was both 'a lion and a lamb,' expecting high standards, but ever ready to help where needed. In addition to family mourners and representatives of the Parish Council, of which he had been a member for so long, leading football figures from all over the area turned out in force to pay last respects to a much-loved man who was such an inspiration to young and old.

A sea of wreaths and flowers was sent from far and wide, including a replica football pitch with players sent by the officers and committee of the Bishop's Stortford, Stansted and District Football League.

Representatives from his Hatfield Heath home club included the President Mr Howard Pyle and club Secretary, Sugar Perry, a long-standing friend and neighbour.

'Bill was a marvellous man. He did as much not only for the game, but for thousands of people who enjoy football. We shall miss him.'

Hymns at the funeral service including 'Mine eyes have seen the coming of the glory of the Lord' which was Bill's favourite.

Reverend John Hannah, a newcomer to the village, said that judging by the congregation, Bill was not only greatly loved in his own village, but by the football world way beyond.

MR SOCCER – LEGEND IN HIS LIFETIME

'Mr Soccer,' George Wilson was a legend in his own lifetime and not surprisingly he was made a life President of Bishop's Stortford Football Club in recognition of his service over many, many years.

He started humbly in local circles before the last war, but by the end he had won every honour there was to bestow in Bishop's Stortford.

He was born in Derbyshire and came to Bishop's Stortford in 1928 when he acquired the wholesale tobacconists in Bridge Street where he worked a full week until well into his eighties. Along with the office of President of Bishop's Stortford Football Club and President of the Bishop's Stortford, Stansted and District League, Mr Wilson had also been President of the North-West Essex Referee's Society, President of the North-West Essex Sunday League and a Life Vice-President of the Hertfordshire Football Association from whom he had a long service medal.

His immense contribution was marked when Bishop's Stortford Football Club's Rhodes Avenue ground was named after him.

In earlier years he was one of the first Royal Navy radio operators, serving in the first world war.

He was a member of the St Michael's Lodge of Freemasons,

He left a wife, son and daughter.

Essentially a proud man, he nevertheless mingled with Mr Public every day of his life and even at Rhodes Avenue his raincoat-covered figure, stooping but with a jaw that spelt determination, was to be found on the terraces. He was affectionately known as 'The resident President' but he was no figurehead. He helped cut the pitch, paint the dressing rooms and install railings at the club until he was well into his eighties.

Only in his last few months, when he still made every effort to keep in touch despite the mounting years, was he to be found in the VIP lounge.

He hated hangers-on and did not mince his words. But he possessed the charm of sincerity and, though he would be the last to admit it, he liked to be liked.

To all he gave his judgement and guidance, and he will be remembered by all who met him as Mr Soccer, a man who became a legend in the town he adopted.

Vice-Chairman Mr L.G. Banks paid tribute to Bill Bruty and George Wilson. It was agreed that the positions of Chairman and President would remain until the next Annual General Meeting as a mark of respect. Mr Banks would assume the duties of Chairman until that time.

During the eighties, some clubs had to be warned about the conduct of not only their players but also their supporters and this eventually led to expulsion from the League for some clubs.

In 1981, following a request from the Management Committee, Solent had to provide written assurance regarding the conduct of their supporters so that they were able to continue in the League.

Source : Herts & Essex Observer

NEWPORT

378

Source : Herts & Essex Observer

GREAT PARNDON

Most teams reckon their League unbeaten records in matches but Great Parndon calculate theirs in seasons.

Parndon have been unbeaten in the League since September 1979. The last team to have beaten them was Thaxted.

Source : Herts & Essex Observer

HATFIELD HEATH

DIVISION III CHALLENGE CUP FINAL

PELHAM RANGERS 1 EASTONS & DUTON HILL 0

Pelham Rangers pulled off a shock 1-0 win over Eastons & Duton Hill.

Rangers went in front after 34 minutes when Robert Wagstaff charged down the right-wing and cut inside a defender to slot the ball home between the keeper and the far post.

EASTONS & DUTON HILL

NAMED WINNERS OF DIVISION III CHALLENGE CUP

DIVISION II CHALLENGE CUP FINAL

HATFIELD HEATH RESERVES 0 GREAT PARNDON RESERVES 2

Substitute Bill Bailey's goal a few minutes from time gave Great Parndon Reserves a two-goal lead in the Division II Cup Final. A goal in the first half by Terry Haydon had given the Parndon team the lead in the 29th minute.

GREAT PARNDON RESERVES

DIVISION II CHALLENGE CUP WINNERS

HATFIELD HEATH RESERVES

DIVISION II CHALLENGE CUP RUNNERS-UP

DIVISION I CHALLENGE CUP

N.A.L.G.O. 2 NORTH WEALD 1 (AFTER EXTRA-TIME)

N.A.L.G.O.'s Kevin Gregory hit the bar from the spot after a Weald defender handled a Ray Mays shot, the first time he has missed in over two years.

N.A.L.G.O. opened the scoring after 25 minutes after the interval when Howard Davis snapped up a half chance, but North Weald bounced back four minutes later to equalise.

Substitute Russell Pugh lifted N.A.L.G.O. as the game went into extra-time and Ray Mays grabbed the winner with a scorching shot.

N.A.L.G.O.

Source : Harlow Gazette

NORTH WEALD

Source : Harlow Gazette

Essex Area FA representative Arthur Dimond presents the Essex Junior Trophy Area Winners Pennant to N.A.L.G.O. manager Peter Sweet and skipper Pete Haywood.

In season 1981/82 N.A.L.G.O. won the Division I League Championship and Challenge Cup double and were also Essex Junior Trophy winners.

INTER-DIVISIONAL CHALLENGE CUP FINAL

FARNHAM 0 GREAT PARNDON RESERVES 4

A combination of good work from defenders Warwick and Luckey and edgy finishing restricted Parndon to one goal before the break.

Bailey got it, cutting in from the wing to send a fine shot past keeper Long.

Richard Head scored the crucial second goal in the 65th minute, and Bailey added another soon after.

Bailey completed his hat-trick in the last minute of the game, beating three players on the way.

GREAT PARNDON

SHEERING

PREMIER DIVISION CHALLENGE CUP FINAL

GREAT PARNDON 2 SHEERING 0

Great Parndon ruined Sheering's first visit to Rhodes Avenue for over 25 years winning 2-0. Great Parndon had contested this particular final in seven of the last nine seasons.

Parndon took the lead after 25 minutes after Sheering needlessly conceded a corner and Johnson swung the ball in from the right for Ray Johnstone to head home.

Substitute Graham Smith collected the ball midway in the Sheering half and weaved his way past defenders before scoring with a tremendous curling shot into the top corner.

ESSEX JUNIOR TROPHY FINAL

N.A.L.G.O. 2 UNICORN 1

Unicorn, from Hornchurch, went ahead in the second half after N.A.L.G.O. had missed all their early chances.

Kevin Ball and Peter Haywood kept things tight in the N.A.L.G.O. defence as Brian Thackeray and John MacLennan took over the midfield and it was winger Ray Mays who finally won the trophy with two classy goals.

REFS HONOUR TOMMY AT 50TH ANNIVERSARY

Referees from the North-West Essex Society chose the occasion of their 50th anniversary dinner to honour founder-member Tommy Gee.

To mark his 50 years of service society members elected him as their first life Vice-President – a gesture that came as a complete surprise to Tommy.

Source : Harlow Gazette

Committee member Mike Steed praised his wonderful record since he began refereeing in 1927. During that time he had been elected a life member of the Essex Referees Association and had received the Referees' Association Service Meritorious Service Award.

Tommy received a silver salver from Bernie Ellis. Mrs Gee received a large bouquet of flowers.

The Frank Bidwell award to the most promising young referee was collected by Jim O'Connor on behalf of Russell Adams.

Jim O'Connor received the North-West Essex Society's Meritorious Service Award from Charlie Brown, Chairman of the Essex Referees' Association.

Arthur Diamond, the Essex Football Association's representative, presented Bill Bruty a long service award from the Essex Football Association.

ROGER BRINSFORD RESIGNS AS GENERAL SECRETARY

At the final meeting of the League Management Committee on 7th May 1982, Mr Banks advised the meeting that he had received the resignation of the Honorary General Secretary to take effect from the Annual General Meeting. Mr Brinsford was to become the Honorary Secretary of Bishop's Stortford Football Club subject to ratification at their Annual General Meeting. He was thanked for his services to the League.

HATFIELD HEATH'S ANNUAL DINNER AND DANCE

Highlight of the Hatfield Heath Football Club's Annual Dinner and Dance was the inaugural presentation of the George Brown Clubman Trophy to Secretary 'Sugar' Perry for his contribution to the running of the club.

The dinner celebrated a successful season during which the Heath's Reserve team won the Saffron Walden Reserves Cup and runners-up in both the League Division II and Division II Challenge Cups.

Other presentations made were – Walter Day Sportsman Trophy, Alan Day; First team Player of the Year, John Clarke and Reserve team Player of the Year, Ian Batram.

Guest speaker at the dinner was Football League referee John Moules.

LEAGUE RECEIVES NEW TROPHY IN MEMORY OF UNCLE BILL

Celebrations at the Bishop's Stortford and Stansted and District League's 60th Anniversary Presentation Dinner were tinged with sadness.

For the memories of two highly popular and respected figures in the football world – Bill Bruty and George Wilson – were uppermost in people's thoughts.

In his speech of welcome to the guests, League Chairman-elect, George Banks, paid tribute to the two men who both died in 1981.

And the response by guest of honour, Arthur Dimond, the Essex FA Area Officer, also recalled 'Uncle' Bill and George with affection.

A highlight of the dinner was the presentation of the W.A. (Bill) Bruty Memorial Cup. The splendid trophy, donated by Bishop's Stortford FC Chairman Eddie Bentley, was accepted on behalf of the League by President-elect John Barry.

Special plaques were awarded to Great Parndon marking their third consecutive League title and N.A.L.G.O., who won the Essex Saturday Junior Trophy.

There was also a special presentation to Roger Brinsford, the League Secretary who was due to take over as Secretary of Bishop's Stortford FC.

Source : Roger Brinsford

EDDIE BENTLEY/JOHN BARRY   **FRED NEWMAN – ALBURY RES**

Source : Roger Brinsford

Club representatives who picked up trophies at the League's Annual Dinner and Dance.

TRIBUTES PAID TO BILL BRUTY AND GEORGE WILSON

The League's Annual General Meeting opened with a short silence in memory of Mr W A Bruty and Mr G H Wilson.

The retiring Secretary Roger Brinsford also paid tribute to George Wilson and Bill Bruty, former President and Chairman respectively of the League, who both died in 1981.

Mr L G Banks, Vice-Chairman, proposed that Mr J E Barry be elected President for the coming season. This proposition was carried unanimously. Mr Barry made a suitable reply of thanks.

The Vice-Chairman also proposed that Mr R L Brinsford and Mr G Reed be elected as Vice-Presidents. This was carried unanimously.

The Honorary General Secretary confirmed that the League intended to withdraw from the West Essex Inter-League competition but matches would be arranged during the coming season. He said that the Selection Committee had put in a lot of unrewarding work, with the team taking the field on only one occasion.

Mr Banks paid tribute to the contribution Roger Brinsford had made to the League during his eight years-service for which he was warmly thanked.

'Roger has done a really marvellous job' said Mr Barry, 'we shall certainly miss him.'

Mr Brinsford replied saying how much he had enjoyed being with the League and the friendships that he had built up.

Mr Barry also praised the work of George Reed, who was making his 24th Treasurer's report.

Both Roger Brinsford and George Reed were made League Vice-Presidents.

Mr D J Wingrove was elected as Honorary General Secretary.

970 players registered, 23 transfers and 26 registrations cancelled.

There had been 20 dismissals and 97 cautions up to 5th May 1982.

There were 58 referees (handbook).

```
          1982-83  Honours
PREMIER DIVISION-R. E. BAKER MEMORIAL CUP
        Winners: GREAT PARNDON
        Runners-up: ALBURY

DIVISION I-A. L. RUSHFORTH MEMORIAL CUP
      Winners: HATFIELD BROAD OAK
    Runners-up: GREAT PARNDON RESERVES

             DIVISION II
          Winners: CLAVERING
        Runners-up: GRANGE PARK

             DIVISION III
       Winners: BIRCHANGER RESERVES
   Runners-up: BUNTINGFORD TOWN RESERVES

          SPORTSMANSHIP CUP
       Winners: HEATH ROVERS 'A'

W. A. (BILL) BRUTY MEMORIAL CUP
       Winners: PITNEY BOWES
       Runners-up: ALBURY

  PREMIER DIVISION CHALLENGE CUP
      Winners: GREAT PARNDON
     Runners-up: HATFIELD HEATH

     DIVISION I CHALLENGE CUP
   Winners: GREAT PARNDON RESERVES
     Runners-up: GRANGE UNITED

     DIVISION II CHALLENGE CUP
   Winners: EASTONS & DUTON HILL
     Runners-up: GRANGE PARK

    DIVISION III CHALLENGE CUP
    Winners: ELSENHAM RESERVES
    Runners-up: ALBURY RESERVES

 INTER-DIVISIONAL CHALLENGE CUP
      (Divisions II & III)
  Winners: POTTER STREET RESERVES
       Runners-up: MANUDEN
```

W.J. (WALLY) DAY MEMORIAL CUP

Winners : N.A.L.G.O. Runners-up : NEWPORT

Sponsored by Brian Skingle Sports

W.J. (WALLY) DAY MEMORIAL CUP FINAL

N.A.L.G.O. 3 NEWPORT 2

N.A.L.G.O. added another trophy with a narrow victory over old rivals Newport.

After twenty minutes the lead came when a through ball beat the offside trap and after Smith had skilfully lobbed over Newport keeper Richard Cracknell, Howard Davis steamed in to flick home a header at the near post.

In the 27th minute Ray Mays made it 2-0 when a corner from the left was headed down for him to fire home from close range .

Newport fought to haul themselves back into the game and thanks to a mistake in the N.A.L.G.O. defence were rewarded for their efforts when Ian Mack slotted home.

With a minute to go to half-time Newport were awarded a penalty when a N.A.L.G.O. defender was penalised for pushing at the near post. Newport skipper and manager, Bruce Ingham, made no mistake with the spot kick to send the sides in at the break at 2-2.

With extra-time approaching N.A.L.G.O. clinched the trophy when a move involving Davis and Kevin Gregory was finished by Mays to secure a 3-2 win.

Source : Harlow Gazette

N.A.L.G.O.

THREE YEARS UNBEATEN IN THE LEAGUE

In September 1982, Great Parndon's 2-1 win at Hatfield Heath meant that they, had gone three years without defeat in the League.

Their last League defeat had been on 2nd September 1979, going down 2-1 to Thaxted.

PARNDON BEATEN

Great Parndon suffered their first League defeat for over three years when they lost 2-1 to Pitney Bowes.

Great Parndon Secretary Brian Vernon said : 'It had to happen sometime and it might help the team as they treated every game like a cup tie, not wanting to get beaten.'

FUTURE OF PELHAM RANGERS DISCUSSED

At an emergency League Management Committee meeting on 7th November 1982 the case of legality of some players of Pelham Rangers FC who had appeared in the Division III Challenge Cup Final on 17th April 1982 was discussed.

The League had requested the Hertfordshire Football Association to investigate the case.

The Hertfordshire Football Association, for who their representative, Mr Brian Curtis, had done an exceptional job in this case, used a photograph which appeared in the local press to uncover substantial evidence which led to the club being charged and found guilty of misconduct.

Investigations showed that six of the Pelham Cup Final team had started the season with the now defunct Harrow FC in the Waltham and District League and had been suspended by the Herts Football Association after a match was abandoned because of violence on the field.

The six, Mark Salter, Peter Riddle, Gary Norf, Andy Norf, Philip Holtby and Christopher Holtby, all from Ware, signed for Pelham Rangers using false names and addresses and played a total of 41 games for the club between them.

The decision of the Herts FA was:

1)   That Pelham Rangers FC were fined £50.00

2)   That the Division III Challenge Cup be returned to the League and that the Club pay for the obliteration of their name

3)   Each of the 6 players that were suspended at that time be fined £20.00, which the Club must guarantee payment and had to be paid by 31st December 1982.

After lengthy discussion, each of the following decisions were made by the Management Committee:

1)   The registration of the 6 players named be immediately cancelled and that they be banned from registering with any club in the League for a minimum of 5 years.

2)   Two officials of the Club playing registrations be cancelled immediately and both be banned from playing or taking any future official duty within the League for a minimum of 5 years.

3)   A special General Meeting be called with the Management Committee's recommendation that Pelham Rangers FC be expelled from the League.

4)   The Club be fined a total of £30.00 for fielding 6 ineligible players in the Division III Challenge Cup Final.

5)   The Club be fined a total of £60.00 for fielding 3 ineligible players in each of the first 4 League games of the season and the points be awarded to their opponents.

6) That Eastons & Duton Hill be awarded the Division III Challenge Cup for season 1981/82 and the records amended accordingly.

PELHAM RANGERS EXPELLED FROM THE LEAGUE

On 22nd November 1982 at a special general meeting of the League Pelham Rangers FC were expelled from the League.

The chairman of the League, Mr L G Banks, outlined the background which led to the League requesting the Hertfordshire Football Association to investigate the legality of some of the Pelham Rangers FC's players who had appeared in the Division III Cup Final on 17th April 1982, in which they defeated Eastons & Duton Hill.

In addition to the punishments already imposed on Pelham Rangers by the Herts FA and the League Management Committee this Special General Meeting was called to ballot on the motion 'The Management Committee recommend that Pelham Rangers FC be expelled from the League.'

Mr Banks clarified that should they be expelled and the Management Committee would consider any future application by the club to re-join the League. He said : 'There is nothing to stop the club applying for League membership next season using different officials and the League ban should not stop Rangers playing in the North-West Essex Sunday League.'

Fifty ballot papers were distributed with six clubs having two delegates in attendance and ten clubs with one delegate in attendance. The remaining eight votes were from the five officers and three Vice-Presidents in attendance.

The ballot resulted in a majority of 49 votes to 1 vote in favour of the motion that Pelham FC be expelled from the League.

It was agreed by the meeting that the fine for non-attendance of the club at the meeting should be waived and it was further agreed that £94-00 outstanding in fines must be paid by 31st December 1982 or it would be reported to the Herts FA.

The League Chairman then presented the Division III Challenge Cup for season 1981/82, which had been returned by Pelham Rangers FC, to Eastons & Duton Hill.

The Pelham Rangers Secretary, Tony Boyton, said : 'I did not know anyone had been banned when we played in the Cup Final. There's not a lot we can do – its pay up or pack up.'

He added : 'I have no grumbles. I bent the rules and the players acknowledge they have. I can understand them wanting to play.'

DEATH OF MR C J SEARLE ANNOUNCED

It was announced that Mr C J Searle, who had been the League's Honorary Auditor, passed away in early 1983.

HATFIELD BROAD OAK

ELSENHAM RESERVES

DIVISION III CHALLENGE CUP FINAL

ELSENHAM RESERVES 4 ALBURY RESERVES 3

In an all-out attacking Cup Final Elsenham pipped Albury, with the result not decided until the 85th minute, at Rhodes Avenue.

Ironically, it was a defensive error by Elsenham which enabled Albury to take a fourth minute lead when, in the middle of a goal mouth melee, one of their defenders put the ball past his own goalkeeper.

Elsenham had to wait until the 30th minute for their equalise and once again it was served up by the opposing defence. Nigel Taylor latched onto a poor back-pass, rounded the keeper and scored from an acute angle.

The second half was only three minutes old when Elsenham took the lead. Another defensive lapse in the Albury area saw Burgess fail to clear and Bar nipped in to score.

Shortly afterwards a fluke long shot from K Wheatley sailed into the net with the Elsenham keeper Service at fault.

Elsenham's lead was restored on the hour when Albury keeper Pomfrett missed a Robin Nettle corner and then proceeded to pull down Cracknell as he shaped up to shoot. Nettle lifted the spot kick high into the net to make it 3-2.

Albury pressed hard for another equaliser, but it seemed as if the match was slipping away from them. But then in the 82nd minute substitute Hollylee tried a speculative shot from 30 yards, Service failed to pick the shot out of the floodlights and it went in.

Elsenham replied almost immediately when Nettle floated a free kick into the area and Cracknell guided a header past Pomfrett.

In 1983 an award was made to Mr J Boucher who was retiring after ten years' service (Revertex and Netteswell and Burnt Mill) on the League Management Committee.

DIVISION II CHALLENGE CUP FINAL

EASTONS & DUTON HILL 5 GRANGE PARK 0

After 20 minutes Morris applied the final touch to put Eastons in front and in the 31st minute Walker bundled the ball over the line to make it 2-0. Morris made it 3-0 5 minutes after the break and Grange Park fell further behind in the 70th minute when Simmons clipped the ball home off the inside of the post. Eastons completed their tally 11 minutes from time when Day drilled home a penalty.

Source : Harlow Gazette

EASTONS & DUTON HILL

GRANGE PARK

DIVISION I CHALLENGE CUP FINAL

GREAT PARNDON RESERVES 1 GRANGE UNITED 1

(AFTER EXTRA-TIME)

Grange United belied their lowly League position to hold Great Parndon Reserves to a draw for the second time during the season. A goal apiece, in quick succession by Peter Godden of Grange United and Grant Matthews was the result after 120 minutes.

GRANGE UNITED

Source : Harlow Gazette

GREAT PARNDON RESERVES

INTER-DIVISIONAL CUP FINAL

POTTER STREET RESERVES 3 MANUDEN 0

Potter Street Reserves Cup Final triumph owes nothing to their penalty-taking ability – they missed two spot kicks.

Clive Wollard missed his hat-trick when he drove a low kick against the keeper's right hand post and minutes later David Llewellyn fired over the bar.

Manuden's initial flurry had soon died and Wollard put the Harlow side ahead after 10 minutes when he broke through the middle following a move with Trevor Keeble and Llewellyn. Two minutes later he missed his penalty, awarded when Manuden skipper Kevin Stone brought down Martin Horn.

Manuden came close but then Horn broke through only to be sent sprawling as Paul Stapleton and John Dowling converged on him. Llewellyn put the penalty over the bar.

Potter Street showed their superiority but only had a 1-0 lead at half-time.

Manuden improved after the interval, with Dave Roach bustling into the area.

Potter Street finally scored again after 84 minutes when Llewellyn went down the left wing, pushing the ball inside for Horn to slot home at the near post. A minute later, Wollard robbed Downing on the right, cut back from the by-line and hammered in a low shot, ensuring Potter Street Reserves of their first cup.

POTTER STREET RESERVES   **MANUDEN**

PREMIER DIVISION CHALLENGE CUP FINAL

GREAT PARNDON 4 HATFIELD HEATH 0

A hat-trick in the first 28 minutes by Stewart Smith ended this Cup Final as a contest at Rhodes Avenue. Veteran winger Johnny Johnson headed home a cross in the 56th minute to make it 4-0.

HATFIELD HEATH

THE FIRST W. A. (BILL) BRUTY MEMORIAL CUP FINAL

PITNEY BOWES 2 ALBURY 0

Refereed by the 'younger' Bill Bruty, nephew of Bill Bruty.

When 'Uncle Bill,' as he was affectionately known, died in September 1981 the League decided that they should provide a suitable testimonial in memory of a man who is sadly missed and who was a sterling servant to local football.

Source : Harlow Gazette

PITNEY BOWES

Source : Harlow Gazette

ALBURY

Pitney Bowes became the first winners of the new W A (Bill) Bruty Memorial Cup at Rhodes Avenue.

There was no score in the first half but in the 57th minute Pitney Bowes' Stapleton knocked a long ball and Lakin squeezed his shot between the advancing keeper and the near post to open the scoring. Five minutes before the end Bowes increased their lead.

Referee 'young' Bill Bruty, nephew of 'Uncle Bill,' after whom the cup was named, played a great advantage, allowing Tom Tilley to continue even though he was held back.

And from the edge of the box Tilley clipped the ball across for full-back Martin Coaley to run in on the blindside of the Albury defence and slot home.

After the game Eddie Bentley, President and Chairman of Bishop's Stortford FC, presented the gleaming new cup to its first winners. Eddie donated the solid silver trophy for the competition, which was started this season.

DIVISION I CHALLENGE CUP FINAL REPLAY

GREAT PARNDON RESERVES 2 GRANGE UNITED 0

ESSEX JUNIOR CUP FINAL

GREAT PARNDON 3 BOREHAM 1

Great Parndon fought back from a goal deficit to win the Essex Junior Cup at Witham, delighting their many supporters who made the trip.

The League Premier Division side became only the second team to have won the cup three times.

The match was closer than the score line suggests and Great Parndon Secretary, Brian Vernon, said : 'Boreham were a good young side and stretched us in the first half. When they went ahead they looked good enough to win.'

Their goal came early in the second half, but Parndon fought back and Bon Johnstone volleyed home the equaliser from Brian Becker's long free-kick after 70 minutes.

Boreham bounced back and Brian Morton pulled off a brilliant save that earned a standing ovation from the crowd and swung the game.

An inspired Stuart Smith finished a solo run that started deep in the Boreham half by putting Parndon ahead and they then knew the hat-trick was on.

John Johnson made it a certainty with the third goal, finishing off a move with Graham Cole and Ray Johnstone.

Great Parndon had proved their worth, but Brian Vernon was quick to praise their supporters, saying : 'We might not have done it without them,'

Source : Harlow Gazette

GREAT PARNDON FC

Great Parndon FC celebrated another highly successful season with a presentation evening. The club carried off five trophies during the season including the Essex Junior Cup, the Premier Division title, Premier Division Challenge Cup, Division I Challenge Cup and Division I Runners-Up Cup.

The Player of the Year Trophy was shared by Stewart Smith and Colin Hawkins. Players Player was Fred Phillips and Clubman of the Year Paul Howells. Reserve Player of the Year was Steve Henry and Reserve Players Player, and Clubman of the Year was Mark Riddle.

A GREAT LEAGUE – BUT THAT TITLE!

League Chairman George Banks gave a warm welcome to the guests of the League at its Annual Dinner.

He thanked League sponsor Brian Skingle and all the officials who had worked tirelessly for the League, then praised their most successful club, Great Parndon, winners of the Premier League title and cup and the Essex Junior Cup. Brian Curtis, representing the Herts Football Association, gave a witty reply, but found giving the League its full title a bit of a mouthful, so he hung a Skingle Sports placard round his neck!

President John Barry presented the trophies.

Source :

Herts & Essex Observer

Source : Herts & Essex Observer

'BAD BOYS' FIGURE AT AN ALL-TIME HIGH

Elsenham will have a team in the League next season after all. Their first team pulled out to join the Halstead League, but an application for their reserves was welcomed at the League's Annual General Meeting.

Secretary Dave Wingrove reported a successful year, though there was a sour note with the number of cautions and dismissals, which reached an all-time high. 'It's not enough for us to say that it is the same everywhere, an improvement must be made if we are all to continue to enjoy the game at this level,' he said.

President John Barry said he hoped to see a significant decrease in the numbers of offenders next season.

904 registered players, 14 transfers and 21 registrations cancelled.

There had been 27 dismissals and 165 cautions up to 28th April 1983.

There had been 52 referees (handbook).

Hatfield Heath's Dinner and Dance marked the end of an era for the club.

'Sugar Perry,' Secretary of the club for 17 years and only the third Secretary since the war, announced that the was stepping down.

Mr Perry who was one of the League's longest-serving Secretaries, was presented with a certificate of long service by the Essex County Football Association representative, Arthur Dimond.

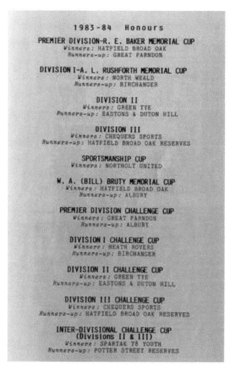

1983-84 Honours

PREMIER DIVISION-R. E. BAKER MEMORIAL CUP
Winners: HATFIELD BROAD OAK
Runners-up: GREAT PARNDON

DIVISION I-A. L. RUSHFORTH MEMORIAL CUP
Winners: NORTH WEALD
Runners-up: BIRCHANGER

DIVISION II
Winners: GREEN TYE
Runners-up: EASTONS & DUTON HILL

DIVISION III
Winners: CHEQUERS SPORTS
Runners-up: HATFIELD BROAD OAK RESERVES

SPORTSMANSHIP CUP
Winners: NORTHOLT UNITED

W. A. (BILL) BRUTY MEMORIAL CUP
Winners: HATFIELD BROAD OAK
Runners-up: ALBURY

PREMIER DIVISION CHALLENGE CUP
Winners: GREAT PARNDON
Runners-up: ALBURY

DIVISION I CHALLENGE CUP
Winners: HEATH ROVERS
Runners-up: BIRCHANGER

DIVISION II CHALLENGE CUP
Winners: GREEN TYE
Runners-up: EASTONS & DUTON HILL

DIVISION III CHALLENGE CUP
Winners: CHEQUERS SPORTS
Runners-up: HATFIELD BROAD OAK RESERVES

INTER-DIVISIONAL CHALLENGE CUP
(Divisions II & III)
Winners: SPARTAK 78 YOUTH
Runners-up: POTTER STREET RESERVES

W.J. (WALLY) DAY MEMORIAL CUP

Winners : CLAVERING Runners-Up : EASTONS AND DUTON HILL

Sponsored by Brian Skingle Sports

Buntingford Town Reserves were excluded from the League in 1983 due to their continued unsporting conduct.

The League Management Committee reported that they had received a letter from Sheering FC requesting that they be allowed to wear the name of their sponsor, the 'Juicy Duck' on the front of their shirts. As they had enclosed a letter granting them permission from the Essex FA, the Management Committee had no objection.

W.J. (WALLY) DAY MEMORIAL CUP FINAL

CLAVERING 5 EASTONS & DUTON HILL 3

Because Division I was reduced to 9 teams, it was of concern that there would be a relatively low number of games for the clubs. At a League Management Committee meeting on 4th

October 1983 Mr Jim O'Connor, being a representative for Division 1 of the Management Committee, had enquired of clubs in the division if they were happy with this and the majority were in favour of extra competition matches. After a lengthy discussion, it was agreed to leave the Challenge Cup as a knockout competition but to allow the division to play for the Wally Day Memorial Cup on a two-group basis, with the winners of each group playing off in the Final. There would be no mementoes for the players or officials and the proceeds would go to charity as in the past. The final would be played in September.

The Chairman and Honorary Treasurer reported on the success of a meeting with the League's Sponsor in October 1983. Mr Skingle was pleased with the results of the first 3 years of sponsorship and agreed to a further 2 years of sponsorship, at an increase of 10%, with an option on the third year, which would be season 1986/87, at a further increase of 10%. The Management Committee agreed that this was a fine agreement and everything possible should be done to promote the name of the League's Sponsor as a show of gratitude for his interest in the League.

Source : Herts & Essex Observer

ALBURY V HATFIELD BROAD OAK

FAREWELL TO REFEREE

After 19 years Bernard Ellis retired from refereeing in December 1983. Before taking up the whistle he played soccer for Stansted, in the Herts County League and Bishop's Stortford in their Spartan League days.

Source : Harlow Gazette

HATFIELD BROAD OAK

PREMIER LEAGUE AND W.A. (BILL) BRUTY MEMORIAL CUP WINNERS

DIVISION III CHALLENGE CUP FINAL

CHEQUERS SPORTS 2 HATFIELD BROAD OAK RESERVES 0

Chequers became the first League Cup winners of the season. The table leaders, in their first season in the League, scored a goal in each half without reply against Hatfield Broad Oak.

Source : Herts & Essex Observer

CHEQUERS SPORTS **HATFIELD BROAD OAK RES**

DIVISION I CHALLENGE CUP FINAL

BIRCHANGER 3 HEATH ROVERS 4

A goal-splattered second half saw Heath Rovers upset the form book to win the cup at Rhodes Avenue.

The first-class facilities at the George Wilson Stadium didn't engender that kind of play from the teams in the first half but the match came alive after the break.

Birchanger will rue their missed chances and Heath Rovers snapping up opportunities as they dominated the first half but trailed 1-0 at the break.

Early Birchanger pressure saw Graham Baker shoot over after Ralph Clark's pass, then Peter Vealey shot wide of the mark after he had been fed by Neil Fullalove,

Heath Rovers keeper and captain Simon Godwin kept his side in the game with a good save from Chris Ball's long range header.

Birchanger's Bob Grant saw his effort headed off the line and then, against the run of play, Heath Rovers went ahead with a dream of a goal.

A disputed free-kick was awarded on the edge of the Birchanger area, John Beeston ran over the ball and Eddie Aldis hit a curling free-kick that beat the five-man wall.

Divisional runners-up Birchanger thought they had drawn level four minutes after the restart but Steve Harvey's 'goal' was disallowed for offside.

Then, with a quick attack, Heath Rovers went 2-0 up as Birchanger pushed forward and David Morland latched onto a clearance from defence and shot home past the advancing Mick Dellow.

In the 62nd minute it was 2-1 with Birchanger's Mick Fullalove heading home following a corner.

Now the game was really alive and Birchanger pushed forward looking for an equaliser. Dellow had to pull off a fine save to keep his side from going further behind as he stopped substitute Howard Shoebridge from scoring.

But Ralph Clark made it 2-2 as he beat the offside trap and with only keeper Godwin to beat shot home.

Then Heath Rovers scored a minute later through a right wing cross-shot from Aldis that went in off a post.

Still the action wasn't over, Birchanger pushed everyone forward again, a long ball caught them out and Brendan Heath flicked the ball on to Shoebridge who, seeing the keeper off his line, shot.

Dellow got his hand to the ball but could only turn and watch it arc into the net.

With three minutes to go Clark made it 4-3 with a header but Birchanger ran out of time.

Birchanger were without their normal first choice keeper, Duncan Wright. He was getting married and therefore missed his team's defeat.

Source : Herts & Essex Observer

HEATH ROVERS   **BIRCHANGER**

DIVISION II CHALLENGE CUP FINAL

EASTONS & DUTON HILL 1 GREEN TYE 2

For 60 minutes at least, Eastons & Duton Hill looked like retaining the Division II Cup.

Twice Green Tye had goals disallowed and Eastons keeper Chris Milczarek was unbeatable the rest of the time. Green Tye kept up the pressure even though they trailed 1-0 and after 60 minutes Paul McComb – who netted one of the two disallowed goals – equalised.

Ten minutes from time Peter Smith headed the winner and Green Tye lifted the trophy for the first time.

Eastons had gone ahead after 55 minutes when Colin Day chested down a cross by Andy Matthews and drove the ball home.

Source : Herts & Essex Observer

GREEN TYE   **EASTONS & DUTON HILL**

PREMIER DIVISION CHALLENGE CUP FINAL

ALBURY 0 GREAT PARNDON 1

Small wonder that this Premier Division Cup Final attracted some 250 spectators – the biggest attendance so far this season for a League final. The teams were meeting in the final for the fifth time in the last decade and Great Parndon snatched the winner 15 minutes from time to take a further step towards yet another League and cup double. Scoring chances were few and far between but Glenn Thurley nearly broke the deadlock – and turned the game Albury's way – when he went on a splendid solo run which ended with a shot just over the bar. Ten minutes later the Harlow side snatched the only goal of the game when Bob Johnstone gave Albury goalkeeper Dave Reed no chance with a fine 25 yard drive. It was Parndon's third successive Premier Division Cup Final win.

Source : Harlow Gazette

ALBURY

PREMIER LEAGUE CHALLENGE CUP AND W.A. (BILL BRUTY) MEMORIAL CUP RUNNERS-UP

Source . Harlow Gazette

GREAT PARNDON

PREMIER LEAGUE RUNNERS-UP AND PREMIER LEAGUE CHALLENGE CUP WINNERS

INTER-DIVISIONAL CHALLENGE CUP FINAL

POTTER STREET RESERVES 1 SPARTAK 78 YOUTH 2

Source : Harlow Gazette

POTTER STREET RESERVES

INTER-DIVISIONAL CUP RUNNERS-UP

ESSEX JUNIOR CUP FINAL

HATFIELD BROAD OAK 1

CARIBBEAN INTERNATIONAL RESERVES 2

Hatfield Broad Oak are counting themselves unlucky after losing an incident packed Essex Junior Cup Final at Witham.

They had a goal disallowed late in the game and Trevor Search played for 80 painful minutes with three broken bones in his face after being elbowed in an aerial duel.

Caribbean, from the Ilford and District League, went ahead five minutes after the break, then scored again 10 minutes later but Search pulled one back 10 minutes from time.

Hatfield Broad Oak, the fourth League finalist in five years sent a disputed penalty over the bar five minutes from time.

W.A. (BILL) BRUTY MEMORIAL CUP FINAL

ALBURY 1 HATFIELD BROAD OAK 4 (AFTER EXTRA-TIME)

Albury, contesting the final for the second successive season, looked the highly competent side they are, though there were no goals before the interval, seemed set to end their five years without a trophy win.

Indeed, only a couple of fine saves by Broad Oak keeper Bob Brane prevented Albury from taking a deserved lead.

He dived bravely at the feet of Mark Saggers when the Albury striker was through and then made the save of the game when tipping over a drive from Ken Ridgeley.

Broad Oak came more into the picture in the last 15 minutes of the first half and Albury keeper David Reed did well to thwart Steve Dean. Albury still held the upper hand but Broad Oak were ominously finding their touch.

The second half was only three minutes old when Dean cut down the bye-line and dropped a cross on to the head of Kevin Field to nod home from inside the six-yard area.

Broad Oak looked again full of goals and Albury wilted, but suddenly Albury equalised.

Brane's clearance from the edge of his penalty area was gathered in the centre circle by Ray Prior, who lobbed a 45-yard ball over the keeper's head and into the back of the net. It was quick thinking and perfect execution. Broad Oak had the better of the remaining time in the 90 minutes, though Prior almost stole the game for Albury with a left-foot shot in the last seconds that Brane did well to tip over the top.

Broad Oak substitute Steve Holdgate was booked for a hard challenge within a minute of coming on but, after the referee had threatened to abandon before the start of extra-time because of a spectator worse for drink, the game got under way and his side quickly established their supremacy.

Kevin Gunn made it 2-1 within five minutes and Chris Serdet virtually made the game safe with another goal five minutes later. Then Serdet burst through on a 40-yard run taken over by Dean, who finished clinically. The second period of extra-time was a formality.

Source : Harlow Gazette

HATFIELD BROAD OAK   ALBURY

In May, letters on behalf of the League were sent to Keith Miller by the Honorary General Secretary and the Honorary Referees Secretary congratulating him on his appointment to the Football League Referees list. Keith Miller replied thanking the League for their good wishes, regretting that dear old Bill Bruty was not around to see it.

At the League Annual General Meeting the Chairman, Mr L G Banks, conveyed his disappointment that three games in the Premier Division were un-played at the end of the season and explained the measures he hoped to take in his capacity as Honorary Fixtures Secretary to prevent a reoccurrence of the problems experienced in arranging the final outstanding matches. He also commented on the increase in dismissals and cautions and assured everyone that the Management Committee would look closely at the persistent offenders next season. It was agreed that a plaque should be awarded to Hatfield Broad Oak at the Annual Dinner in recognition of reaching the Essex Junior Cup Final. It was also agreed to award Great Parndon a plaque at the Annual Dinner in recognition of winning the Premier Division Challenge Cup for three consecutive seasons. CCDC

976 players registered, 26 transfers and 55 registrations cancelled.

There had been 24 dismissals and 102 cautions up to and including 28th April 1984.

There had been 53 referees (handbook).

A LEGEND OF BROAD OAK

Source : Herts & Essex Observer

As the curtain finally came down on the soccer season, Roy Jones of the Herts & Essex Observer, talked to one of the living legends of Hatfield Broad Oak.

Roy Field was born 48 years ago in the same house he occupies today in Park Terrace, Dunmow Road.

He has been with Hatfield Broad Oak Football Club ever since he was 15 – apart from a five-year spell with Heath Rovers. Of his term with Rovers, he says; 'I had a point to make and when I made it, I came back.'

He certainly did. As a player, he was a bustling centre-forward in the Nat Lofthouse mould and he celebrated his return with 70 goals in 1967/68. It was a club record that has never been beaten.

A broken leg put paid to his playing career 11 years ago. He remembers it was a cup match at Hatfield Heath and, typically for a servant of Broad Oak, also remembers that his club won the match.

He led Broad Oak to the League Division I championship last season and added the Saffron Walden Reserve Cup to the honours the club collected.

But it was the past season that his management career really blossomed. He took the club to unprecedented success, the team winning League Premier Division championship. The W A (Bill) Bruty Memorial Cup and the Saffron Walden Cup. More significantly, perhaps, Broad Oak reached the final of the Essex Junior Cup.

They lost the match but Roy Field was not too bothered. 'It would have been great to win the county cup, but my prime ambition was the League championship' he said. 'I have always wanted Broad Oak to win the title, and the Essex Junior Cup Final was a bonus.'

His recipe for success was simple. 'I used to play it hard but fair,' he said. 'We have some good players in the village and they have attracted others to help make us a winning outfit. But the main thing was for the team to try – and they did just that.'

Field sees next season as a different season. 'It would be good to have a go at the League again but every game is going to be like a Cup Final – everyone will want to beat us after this season.'

He was unworried. 'Personally. I like a challenge. I am a fighter and I like to win and the team is the same. We'll be trying hard.'

Was he happy with all the success the club had won. 'I am never happy,' he said, 'but we did have a good season.'

With a squad of 14, his side played 40 matches, winning 32 and drawing 2. Significantly for a former goal scorer, his side hit 153 goals against 48.

It was a proud record for a proud man leading a proud club. Whatever happens next season, or in seasons after that. Roy Field remains a living legend in the villages.

SERVICE IS REWARDED

The backroom boys were among the award-winners at the League's annual dinner-dance .

There were three awards for 15-years long and valued service to Essex soccer, presented by county Chairman Dave Pond.

One recipient was Terry Ball, Treasurer of Birchanger since 1958, a member of the League's Management Committee since 1960 and its Registration Secretary since 1975.

The other two awards went to Hugh Savill (Secretary of Langley since 1969) and John Grandsen (Secretary of Quendon since 1967).

Source : Herts & Essex Observer

Dave Pond presenting awards to Hugh Savill and Terry Ball

League Chairman George Banks presenting Dave Barrick (Potter Street) with the Secretary of the Year award and Geoff Goff, Treasurer of the North-West Essex Referees Society presenting Peter Grey (Birchanger) with the Club Linesman of the Year award.

League President John Barry presenting Hatfield Broad Oak Manager Roy Field and Trevor Search with the trophy for the League Premier Division championship.

SPONSOR VALUE

The £400 from Brian Skingle Sports for sponsorship of the League brought warm words from League President, John Barry.

At the League's Annual General Meeting he appealed for member clubs to support the firm.

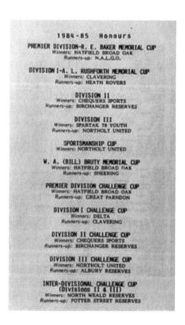

1984-85 Honours

PREMIER DIVISION-R. E. BAKER MEMORIAL CUP
Winners: HATFIELD BROAD OAK
Runners-up: N.A.L.G.O.

DIVISION I-A. L. RUSHFORTH MEMORIAL CUP
Winners: CLAVERING
Runners-up: HEATH ROVERS

DIVISION II
Winners: CHEQUERS SPORTS
Runners-up: BIRCHANGER RESERVES

DIVISION III
Winners: SPARTAK 78 YOUTH
Runners-up: NORTHOLT UNITED

SPORTSMANSHIP CUP
Winners: NORTHOLT UNITED

W. A. (BILL) BRUTY MEMORIAL CUP
Winners: HATFIELD BROAD OAK
Runners-up: SHEERING

PREMIER DIVISION CHALLENGE CUP
Winners: HATFIELD BROAD OAK
Runners-up: GREAT PARNDON

DIVISION I CHALLENGE CUP
Winners: DELTA
Runners-up: CLAVERING

DIVISION II CHALLENGE CUP
Winners: CHEQUERS SPORTS
Runners-up: BIRCHANGER RESERVES

DIVISION III CHALLENGE CUP
Winners: NORTHOLT UNITED
Runners-up: ALBURY RESERVES

INTER-DIVISIONAL CHALLENGE CUP
(Divisions II & III)
Winners: NORTH WEALD RESERVES
Runners-up: POTTER STREET RESERVES

W.J. (WALLY) DAY MEMORIAL CUP

Winners : BIRCHANGER Runners-Up : NORTH WEALD

Sponsored by Brian Skingle Sports

RAY GETS SKINGLE LEAGUE JOB

A quest for honours by the League takes on a fresh dimension with the appointment of a new Manager for the representative side.

Great Parndon's Player-Manager, Ray Johnstone, has been given the job by the League Management Committee.

He was the only playing member of the former five-man selection committee and he aims to 'get a successful blend of uniformity and continuity.'

He feels his long career with Great Parndon has given him good judgement and he is solely responsible for selection, although helped in other duties by Sheering's Charlie French and Potter Street's Mick Phillips.

Ray's first test comes with the Dave Robinson Memorial Trophy match against the Harlow and District League and he has high hopes of winning the Herts Inter-League Competition.

He has been instrumental in much of Parndon's success and says : 'I like to win.'

That should be warning enough for any opposition…..

W.J. (WALLY) DAY MEMORIAL CUP FINAL

BIRCHANGER 3 NORTH WEALD 3 (AFTER EXTRA-TIME)

BIRCHANGER WON 7-6 AFTER PENALTIES

Birchanger's adept penalty-taking and a fine save by their keeper, Len Clayden, gave them the Wally Day Memorial Cup after an extra-time shoot out against North Weald.

Honours were even at 2-2 after 90 minutes at the George Wilson Stadium and both sides scored once more in extra-time.

Even penalties looked like they may not split the teams. After five penalties each, it was 4-4, Birchanger's Peter Vealey missing before North Weald's Martin Warner hit the right-hand post.

Penalty scorers up to then had been Dave Dodd, Steve Roberts, Sean Horrigan and Tim Jones for North Weald, Neil Fullalove, Mick Fullalove, Graham Baker and Chris Ball for Birchanger.

From then on the cup would go to the first side to stay one ahead and Dave Dodd and Neil Fullalove kept it even, as did Steve Roberts and Mick Fullalove.

But then North Weald's Horrigan fired too close to Clayden, who smothered the ball, and Birchanger's Peter Vealey drove his kick high into the back of the net, before racing jubilantly back to his team-mates.

It was a gripping finale to an exciting final, contested in two pools by the League champions and cup winners of each division, for the cup that commemorates the former League Registration Secretary and Hatfield Heath Secretary.

North Weald, last season's League Division I winners, went ahead after three minutes, Alan Pottle racing on to a through-ball to fire home.

Birchanger had an effort disallowed before Chris Ball, Ralph Clark and Graham Baker combined in a diagonal move that split North Weald's defence, leaving Baker to score after 21 minutes.

A minute later Birchanger went ahead, this time Colin Dance finding Clark with a long ball and the centre-forward cutting in from the left before shooting in off the near post.

North Weald's equaliser came after 72minutes, substitute Keith Wix heading home Steve Roberts' corner.

Goals again came within a minute of each other in extra-time, Clayden appearing to hold Martin Werner's low header but the ball bobbing over the line, then Graham Baker levelling for Birchanger after a goalmouth scramble.

JUVENTUS LEAVE THE LEAGUE

Juventus resigned from the League on the 3rd of October 1984 and as the club had not completed 75% of their fixtures their record was expunged.

DEATH OF MR LES FROST ANNOUNCED

In October 1984, the death of Mr Les Frost, a Vice-President of the League was announced. As well as being a Vice-President of the League, Mr Frost had been associated with Takeley FC for over 50 years and had been headmaster at Takeley Primary School.

Mr Frost's football career started in 1919 with a junior club. A year later he played for March FC, competing with semi-professional clubs in the Peterborough and Cambs League. What looked like a promising career came to a sudden temporary stop when he dislocated his knee in a playing accident in 1923. He was forced to rest for two seasons, and when eventually he took the field again, he had to reconcile himself to the fact that senior football was too great a strain on his knee.

The 1931/32 season found him as centre-forward and team mate of Peter Smith with Chelmsford Rangers. The next season his name was associated with Takeley for the first time. Together with Mr A Collison he got Takeley on the football map again, and on the field did his share as centre-forward and captain.

When he finally decided to hang up his boots, in 1948, he was 47 years old.

During the war he tried to keep the club going, organising matches with troops stationed in the district and in 1946 when the club restarted, he was elected Chairman.

Tim Clarey said that he was a lovely man and a great ambassador for local junior football.

Following the Herts Inter-League Cup Semi-Final at the George Wilson Stadium on 30th January 1985, it was agreed that the Honorary General Secretary should write to the opponents, the Mid-Herts League, requesting they go halfway towards the cost of staging the match as there was a loss of £50.85. This was carried unanimously by the clubs.

The Chairman then made the following statement.

'On Wednesday, 30th January 1985, the League Representative side played in this competition at the George Wilson Stadium, this was after your Secretary had one game cancelled and had to work hard to get this game staged. Some Officers and Committee men were at the game manning the gates etc, the only people that were missing were members of the League to support them.'

'The outcome of the game was that we not only lost the match by the one goal scored but also when expenses had been met, we lost £50.00.'

'I have noticed that this follows the pattern of our Finals which we have on the ground, only certain clubs support the League every year. It appears that now your Treasurer and the late Chairman secured sponsorship a lot of clubs are under the illusion that this solves all the League's financial troubles, they could not be further from the truth. If we do not get more support at the Finals, which are the life blood of the League, then fees will have to be raised, for every year the cost of running the League grows, you only have to study the balance sheet to see this.'

'If, on the other hand, the support is not forthcoming because of lack of faith in the Officers of the League then it is your duty to express this at the next Annual General Meeting.'

The Honorary General Secretary supported this statement adding that unless there was an improvement in attitude by some of the member clubs, then he would not be standing for re-election next season.

The Chairman commented 'At the Annual General Meeting of the League, the Management Committee put forward a proposal that a Representative team should be entered into the Herts Inter-League Competition.'

DIVISION III CHALLENGE CUP FINAL

ALBURY RESERVES 2 NORTHOLT UNITED 5

An Alaster Mollinson hat-trick inspired Northolt United to a convincing victory in this Division III League Cup Final at Rhodes Avenue.

Source : Harlow Gazette

DELTA

DIVISION I CHALLENGE CUP FINAL

DELTA 2 CLAVERING 2 (AFTER EXTRA-TIME)

Delta were in their first season in the League having spent 24 years in the Harlow & District League

Clavering came to Rhodes Avenue for the first time in 30 years, the last occasion being in season 1951/52 when they defeated Manuden for this particular trophy.

Delta's exciting striker Richie Taylor opened the scoring in the sixth minute. Collecting a fine through ball he beat Clavering defender Steve Miller to shoot home from five yards inside the area.

The outcome looked settled 13 minutes into the second half as Giles struck a crisp right foot drive inside the far post, giving Nick Phillips no chance.

Victory celebrations turned sour for Delta as the ball flashed across their box and the left leg of Fox made firm contact to steer Clavering back into the game.

And four minutes later they drew level, mainly with the help of a disastrous goalkeeping error by Gristwood.

Hagger picked up a loose ball midway inside Delta's half and cut diagonally past three defenders to the corner flag. Then, he hooked back a swirling cross which Gristwood, yards off his line, let drop over him into an open goal.

Source : Herts & Essex Observer

CLAVERING

Source : Harlow Gazette

CHEQUERS SPORTS

DIVISION II CHALLENGE CUP FINAL

CHEQUERS SPORTS 3 BIRCHANGER RESERVES 0

Real drama surrounded Chequers' cup success at Rhodes Avenue as the Harlow side had to draft striker Eric Kelly into goal when concussion to regular keeper forced him to leave the field four minutes from half-time.

Goals from Terry Edgell, direct from a corner, Henry Barnes and Edgell again saw Chequers take the cup.

BIRCHANGER RESERVES

PREMIER DIVISION CHALLENGE CUP FINAL

HATFIELD BROAD OAK 3 GREAT PARNDON 2

A goal in the first 30 seconds gave Hatfield Broad Oak a winning start.

Great Parndon never really recovered after Steve Dean slipped a loose ball under goalkeeper Paul Smith.

And 20 minutes later Broad Oak went further ahead when a move down the left ended with Kevin Field rounding two defenders to fire home.

Great Parndon then launched their first serious attack and Bob Johnstone's crisp half-volley struck the bar following a corner.

He soon made up for his disappointment by breaking clear of the defence and, although he stumbled, Johnstone scrambled the ball home.

Broad Oak continued to press forward and after the break and were rewarded in the 65th minute when Dean scored his second, latching on to a long ball, which he drove in low and hard past Smith.

Parndon reduced the deficit in the last minute when Graham Pringle went on a jinking run, forcing a way through to shoot into the corner of the net.

HATFIELD BROAD OAK   GREAT PARNDON

INTER-DIVISIONAL CHALLENGE CUP FINAL

NORTH WEALD RESERVES 2 POTTER STREET RESERVES 1

North Weald keeper Mark Jones made the type of save at Rhodes Avenue that wins Cup Finals.

In their first attack of the game Weald's Sid Wix broke into the area and converted confidently to make it 1-0. Wix was dominant on the left and supplied Weald's second goal, cutting in from the bye-line he crossed for Andrew Owen to head powerfully into the corner.

Potter Street reduced the arrears to 1-2 through a Colin Hill drive from 10 yards.

So North Weald took the cup deservedly for the second time in their history adding to their 1977 success.

Source : Harlow Gazette

NORTH WEALD   **POTTER STREET RESERVES**

W.A. (BILL) BRUTY MEMORIAL CUP FINAL

HATFIELD BROAD OAK 2 SHEERING 1

Holders Hatfield Broad Oak came from behind to retain the W.A. (Bill) Bruty Memorial Cup, so adding a second honour to the League Premier Division Challenge Cup.

They had to wait until the 76th minute for their winner, a close range header by Trevor Search following Kevin Gunn's corner, to reward their steam roller like assaults on the Sheering goal.

Sheering, the first Division I club to reach the final, often had their backs to the wall, but could not believe their luck, when after 12 minutes Wayne Cracknell's cross was spooned past his own keeper by Broad Oak skipper Doug Felton.

A Neil Cutmore cross was met at the near post by Gunn, but his flicked header flashed across the goalmouth, before being hacked to safety.

The long-expected goal arrived four minutes later when Kevin Field latched on to a Cutmore throw-in before unleashing a thunderbolt shot from the edge of the area which flew in off Robert Quinn's hands.

Steve Dean was the most unfortunate, after twice seeing his goal-bound efforts blocked on the line, but Search's header keeps the trophy in Hatfield Broad Oak for another year.

DIVISION I CHALLENGE CUP FINAL REPLAY

DELTA 3 CLAVERING 1 (AFTER EXTRA-TIME)

BROAD OAK SAY 'WELL DONE, LADS'

Hatfield Broad Oak congratulated themselves at their Annual Dinner on a vintage season that brought them as much success as the previous year.

The club won the League Premier Division League and Cup, the Saffron Walden Cup, the W.A. (Bill) Bruty Memorial Cup and the West Essex Border Charity Cup.

A NIGHT OF CELEBRATION –

BUT LEAGUE'S TROUBLES NOT FORGOTTEN

The troubles that have tarnished local football were put aside at the League's Annual Dinner.

League Chairman George Banks' speech cordially welcomed the 180 guests, but to the trouble-makers he said : 'Take your boots and play elsewhere,'

And in reply, principal guest Hertfordshire Football Association Chairman Bill Daulby stressed that individual trouble-makers must be penalised, as banning a club will not stop its players joining another team.

Those were the only stern words during an evening of celebration, when the club's elder statesmen, such as Sheering's Charlie French, joined in the fun with footballers young enough to be his grand-children.

League Treasurer George Reed, who organised the evening, was toastmaster and League President John Barry presented the awards.

Source : Harlow Gazette

Club representatives with their trophies at the League Annual Dinner and Dance.

Source : Herts & Essex Observer

Sportsmanship award winners : Dick Street (Sheering Reserves), John Godwin (Heath Rovers), Bob Gerrard (Hatfield Heath) and Neil Whitbread (Northolt United).

Source : Herts & Essex Observer

N.A.L.G.O. Manager Peter Sweet and Roy Field whose Hatfield Broad Oak side pipped N.A.L.G.O. for the Premier Division championship.

Smiles from Clavering's Division I champions.

Always smiling, always popular, Charlie French shows off Sheering Reserves sportsmanship award.

The President, Mr J E Barry, then asked the Meeting to stand for a short silence in memory of the late Mr A L Frost, a League Vice-President who had passed away.

JUVENTUS GET THUMBS DOWN

Juventus were refused permission to re-enter at the League's Annual General Meeting.

The club had pulled out of League at the beginning of the season when they lost their Secretary, but the League's Management Committee had accepted their application to re-join at a meeting in May.

But club delegates voted against Juventus, some worried that they might pull out again, others worried that the present side might contain members of the Juventus team excluded from the Rayments North-West Essex League at the end of the 1984/84 season.

The League made it clear that they intend to get tough with offenders on the pitch as sendings-off and bookings are at an all-time high.

League Chairman George Banks spoke for everyone when he said : 'Football was a game for recreation and not an excuse for fighting.'

It was not just misconduct that was an issue. With three matches not played last season, the Chairman called for more co-operation from the clubs in rearranging postponed fixtures.

In an attempt to ease this problem, the League amended a rule extending the time limit for notifying the League of a postponement, from seven to ten days.

Great Parndon's Brian Vernon felt strongly about the matter and said : 'I believe that clubs should not be allowed to call a game off, especially those who run first team and reserve teams.'

He added : 'I am not criticising the League, but sides should not be able to call them off because Joe Bloggs wants to get married and several of the players want to go along. My club had to play eleven games in a month at the end of last season because of matches called off.'

There were 14 rule amendments, notably a increase in the fine, from £2 to £5, for an indiscipline on the field.

All fines for both players and clubs were increased, to keep intact the League's image of good sportsmanship.

1,007 players registered, 29 transfers and 30 cancelled registrations.

There had been 50 dismissals and 173 cautions as of 28th May 1985.

There had been 55 referees (handbook).

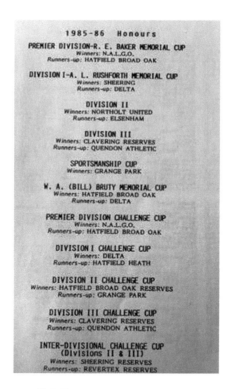

W.J. (WALLY) DAY MEMORIAL CUP

Winners : NORTHOLT UNITED Runners-Up : SPARTAK 78 YOUTH

Sponsored by Brian Skingle Sports

The competition returns to the original cycle of playing the League Champions against the Cup Winners of each division in rotation.

W.J. (WALLY) DAY MEMORIAL CUP FINAL

NORTHOLT UNITED 2 SPARTAK 78 YOUTH 0

Bishop's Stortford Swifts 'A' withdrew from the League as of 15th March 1986 due to a lack of players. As the club had not completed 75% of their fixtures their record was expunged.

DIVISION III CHALLENGE CUP FINAL

CLAVERING RESERVES 2 QUENDON ATHLETIC 1

Clavering Player-Manager John Webb was the hero of his side's triumph as the reserves lifted a League trophy for the first time.

His side trailed 1-0 at half-time and they received another setback early in the second half when right-winger Steve Shelsher went off with an ankle injury.

John Goddard came on at right-back and Webb moved up front. But Quendon still did not yield to pressure until five minutes from the end of normal time when Keith Harste crossed from the left and the ball bounced invitingly for Webb to squeeze in at the far post.

The two top teams in Division III – both with a good chance of championship honours – looked set for a replay until five minutes from the end of extra-time when the Quendon goalkeeper could only parry away a shot by John Wagstaff and Webb hammered the ball home.

Quendon had gone ahead in the first ten minutes when an optimistic back-pass by Wagstaff was intercepted by Paul Warwick, who scored.

The game was largely won in midfield where John Butcher proving that junior soccer was not all kick and rush.

Source : Herts & Essex Observer

CLAVERING RESERVES   **QUENDON ATHLETIC**

DIVISION II CHALLENGE CUP FINAL

GRANGE PARK 1 HATFIELD BROAD OAK RESERVES 2

Hatfield Broad Oak improved on their last appearance – in the 1984 Division III Cup Final, where they lost to Chequers Sports – by winning the Division II Cup with two second half goals.

The victory was secured on the merit of their second half performance after a competitive Grange Park marginally held the edge in the first half, though they failed to create many clear-cut chances.

With Broad Oak's star player, Dave Miles, beginning to control the midfield, Broad Oak took the lead midway through the second half.

Striker Jim Francis was put in the clear and he rammed the ball home, a 20 yard drive which he dipped just under the bar.

Broad Oak's advantage was further extended in the second minute. Substitute Steve Orwin directed the ball accurately past the wall into the net from a free-kick just outside the penalty area.

In a last determined effort by Grange to save their cup hopes, they pulled a goal back three minutes from time.

Striker Roy Wheeler was put down the right by Lenny Fisher and he cut inside to shot low into the corner – but it was just too late.

Source : Herts & Essex Observer

HATFIELD BROAD OAK RESERVES   GRANGE PARK

INTER-DIVISIONAL CHALLENGE CUP FINAL

SHEERING RESERVES 2 REVERTEX RESERVES 2

(AFTER EXTRA-TIME)

.

Source : Anne Murphy

SHEERING RESERVES

PREMIER DIVISION CHALLENGE CUP FINAL

HATFIELD BROAD OAK 1 N.A.L.G.O. 0

N.A.L.G.O. won the Herts & Essex Observer Cup for the first time in dramatic fashion at Rhodes Avenue.

With the match heading for extra-time substitute Jammy Stapleton, who had only been on the field five minutes, scored with only his second touch two minutes from time to end Hatfield Broad Oak's two-year reign as the League's Premier Division Cup holders.

N.A.L.G.O.'s winner was no more than they deserved because once they had contained Broad Oak's early exuberance, they began to exert their influence on the game.

N.A.L.G.O.'s power from the midfield just gave them the edge up until the interval and they were unlucky not to score from a series of chances they created during the first half.

The League's leaders' first attempt almost gave them the lead when Barry Paffett drove a free-kick just over the bar from 20 yards with Broad Oak goalkeeper Stuart Fuller stranded,

Kevin Gregory also came close but N.A.L.G.O.'s best chance fell to Simon Green. An incisive run by Tony Smith set up the chance for Green, who hit his shot just wide of the post.

If N.A.L.G.O. had been unlucky not to score in the first half, they must have been cursing themselves for missing a penalty in the 50th minute. Broad Oak's Kevin Gunn handled but Gregory placed the ball high and wide of the left upright.

The penalty shocked Broad Oak into action and within minutes they came close to scoring themselves. Their endeavour, which they showed throughout the match, was rewarded with a free-kick but Kevin Field hit the rebound from his original shot over the bar.

Green again almost scored for N.A.L.G.O. but then Stapleton came on for John Clark and he scored what proved to be the winner.

With time running out, Broad Oak pressed for an equaliser but Field's shot just went wide of the post and N.A.L.G.O. were at last home and dry.

Source : Herts & Essex Observer

| N.A.L.G.O. | HATFIELD BROAD OAK |

FIXTURE CHAOS HITS TOP TEAMS

The League has extended its season for the second time in six weeks to accommodate teams still suffering from a fixture crisis.

The season was originally scheduled to finish in April but the new May17 deadline, which will give teams an extra three weeks to complete their League and cup programme, comes after last month's decision by the League Management Committee to extend their see son until May 10.

Delta, who have not been beaten for 23 games, are enjoying their most successful season ever but reaching three Cup Finals now means they are facing the mammoth task of playing 14 games in 20 days.

Delta lined up against Hatfield Heath in the Division I Cup Final on Tuesday, while on Saturday they play Hatfield Broad Oak in the W.A. (Bill) Bruty Memorial Cup Final at Rhodes Avenue.

Their season should be brought to a climax when they meet Progress Rovers in the Essex Junior Trophy Final at Aveley on April 30th, but this will still leave them with more than half their League games still to play.

Delta's Secretary, Colin Wright, said he did not know how they would fit all the games in and there was a strong possibility they would not complete the League programme.

He added that Delta might only play enough matches to secure the required number of points to win promotion.

Playing so many matches in such a short time could see their promotion challenge falter with many of the first team members unable to play in midweek.

Mr Wright said : 'Our success is costing us dear and it may well mean that we could miss out on promotion, which was our main aim for the season.'

'If we cannot win enough points to win promotion, we will be writing to the League shortly saying that if a vacancy arose in the Premier Division next season, we hope we will be considered to take that place.'

W.A. (BILL) BRUTY MEMORIAL CUP FINAL

DELTA 1 HATFIELD BROAD OAK 4

Hatfield Broad Oak completed a hat-trick of victories in exhilarating style in the W.A. (Bill) Bruty Memorial Cup.

The reigning Premier Division champions were head and shoulders above the team of the moment, Delta, who suffered their first defeat in 24 games.

In the first half Broad Oak established what proved to be an impregnable advantage by running up a two-goal in the first 15 minutes.

Kevin Gunn, whose speed and skill caused Delta innumerable problems until he was substituted, steered home a cross from Perry Chandler in the fourth minute and 11 minutes later, Gunn ran on to a long ball to lob the ball into the net past the advancing goalkeeper from 18 yards.

Delta responded by throwing players forward in a series of inventive moves but Broad Oak, who always defended in numbers, were difficult to break down with sweeper Doug Felton in majestic form.

In the second half Delta came close to reducing the deficit through Scott Harrison but their cup hopes ended when Broad Oak scored the third in the 51st minute.

Kevin Field's goal was a killer blow but there was no way back when Doug Felton hit a 30-yard rocket into the top corner in the 68th minute for Broad Oak's fourth.

Martin Neagus pulled a consolation goal back for Delta in the 71st minute but by than the Division I side were dead and buried.

Source : Herts & Essex Observer

SHEERING

DIVISION I CHALLENGE CUP FINAL

DELTA BEAT HATFIELD HEATH

INTER-DIVISIONAL CHALLENGE CUP FINAL REPLAY

SHEERING RESERVES BEAT REVERTEX RESERVES

COUNCIL TO BE EXCLUDED NEXT SEASON

Despite being given assurances by both the Chairman and Secretary of the Council FC that fines had been paid, the club played Sheering on 5th May 1986 when in fact the fines had not been paid and they were under a sine-die suspension.

The General Secretary, Mr Wingrove, confirmed that he had written to Council FC on 24th April warning them of the serious consequences if they played any games whilst they were under suspension.

The match, which Sheering won 5-0, had consequently caused the League a lot of embarrassment and it was agreed to report the matter to the Essex County Football Association, along with all the players registered with the club.

The Treasurer, Mr Reed, also reported that the club had outstanding fines of £15 dating back to February 1986 and the club's Annual Dinner ticket fees of £30 also remain unpaid.

It was agreed to fine the club a further £5 and £2 respectively and also report to the Essex County Football Association that they were now owing the League the sum of £52.

In view of these problems, along with the disgraceful disciplinary record of the club over the past two seasons, it was agreed that attitude was totally unacceptable, and the club should no longer be associated with the League.

It was further agreed that the points from their remaining three matches be awarded to their opponents and it be recommended to the Annual General Meeting that they should not be re-elected to the League for the next season.

Council were excluded from the League in 1986 due to their continued misconduct and the points for their last three matches were awarded to their opponents.

It was agreed to award Hatfield Broad Oak a special plaque at the Annual Dinner in recognition of their winning the W.A. (Bill) Bruty Memorial Cup for three consecutive seasons.

LONG SERVICE RECOGNIZED

Years of loyal service were acknowledged when Hatfield Heath Football Club president Howard Pyle was presented with an engraved rose-bowl at the club's annual dinner and dance.

He is also retiring as the club's treasurer after 40 years. His wife was presented with a basket of flowers.

It was one of two awards given for over 30 years' service to the club. Bob Jerrard was presented with a special award for having played for Hatfield Heath for 30 years.

PRAISE TO THE HIGHEST

Praise was heaped upon the League at its Annual Presentation evening by guest of honour Arthur Dimond.

Mr Dimond, the Essex County Football Association area representative paid a special tribute to Essex Junior Trophy winners Delta.

He said : 'I saw them four times in the competition and was very proud, their conduct was superb.'

Mr Dimond also described the work of League Chairman and Fixture Secretary as 'fantastic' and praised Secretary Dave Wingrove for his efforts.

And a special Essex Football Association long-service award was made to Dave Barrick, who has been Secretary of Potter Street FC since 1968 but was also involved with the League before this date.

The guests had been welcomed in the absence of unwell Mr Banks by League President, John Barry.

As well as Mr Dimond, they included Vice-Presidents, Brian Bayford, Jack Nichols and Howard Pyle, the League's longest-serving Vice-President.

Also present were Brian Curtis and Dick Mumford of the Rayment's North-West Essex Sunday League, and Ernie Fairhurst of the Harlow and District Referees' Society.

A special award was made by Mr Barry to Referees' Secretary, John Mayhew, who in three years, has had only two matches not covered by an officially appointed referee.

Source : All photos Herts & Essex Observer

Sheering's Chris Hellmers (left) received the Linesman's trophy on behalf of Russell Adams. Northolt United's John Brown (centre) receives the Secretary of the year award from League President John Barry. Referees Secretary, John Mayhew (right) received a special award for his work.

LEAGUE KICKS OUT COUNCIL

Council have been thrown out of the League. At the Annual General Meeting, clubs voted overwhelmingly for their ejection for their conduct last season.

Chairman, George Banks said : 'Several clubs had made complaints about Council and also the club told us they had paid some money owing to the Committee when it had not.'

In a reference to Council, League Secretary, Dave Wingrove, said : Unfortunately, it is still the few clubs which make the records look bad and the Management Committee has again had to recommend to the Annual Meeting that a club finds itself in another League next season.'

1,009 players registered, 21 transfers and 12 registrations were cancelled.

There had been 178 cautions and 38 dismissals as at, 13th May 1986.

There were 53 referees (Handbook).

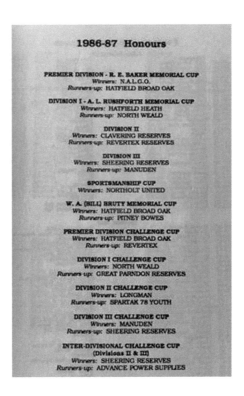

W.J. (WALLY) DAY MEMORIAL CUP

Winners : N.A.L.G.O. Runners-Up : HATFIELD BROAD OAK

Sponsored by Brian Skingle Sports

W.J. (WALLY) DAY MEMORIAL CUP FINAL

N.A.L.G.O. 4 HATFIELD BROAD OAK 1

Hatfield Broad Oak must be wondering what they have to do to beat League Premier Division champions and cup holders N.A.L.G.O.

After finishing runners-up to them in both those competitions, Broad Oak dominated for long periods in the W.J. (Wally Day) Memorial Cup but were again second best.

Within four minutes Broad Oak were ahead as Steve Dean drew the goalkeeper before playing the ball wide to Kevin Field, whose shot was all but kept out by a defender.

Most of the play was in N.A.L.G.O.'s half, but they equalised after 35 minutes when Broad Oak goalkeeper and skipper Stuart Fuller dropped Gary King's free-kick and Kevin Gregory fired home.

Seven minutes later N.A.L.G.O. went ahead when Gregory curled a free-kick round a defensive wall and past the unsighted goalkeeper.

N.A.L.G.O. effectively won in the 66th minute when Fuller could only parry Ray Mays shot and Gary Day tucked away the loose ball.

The final goal came in the 90th minute when Lee Law outstripped the defence from the halfway line.

Source : Herts & Essex Observer

HATFIELD BROAD OAK **N.A.L.G.O.**

SPONSORSHIP DEAL AGREED

In January 1987, the Honorary General Secretary and Mr Brian Skingle discussed the future sponsorship for the next 3 years. Mr Banks outlined the agreement that was reached on Mr Skingle's proposals which were generally favourable to the Management Committee.

Mr Skingle also agreed to allow the League to obtain their trophies from another source if it were a better proposition than he could offer.

Before taking a vote on the recommendation for Brian Skingle Sports Ltd to continue sponsorship with the League for the next 3 seasons, it was agreed the Honorary General Secretary should write to Mr Skingle requesting assurances regarding the forthcoming season before the next Management Committee meeting.

Following the discussions regarding sponsorship the Honorary Treasurer received a communication from Brian Skingle which gave the Management Committee enough assurances to recommend that the League take up a further agreement of sponsorship as offered by Brian Skingle Sports Ltd when the current agreement expired at the end of the season.

At the Management Committee meeting in May 1987, Mr Wingrove explained that he would not be seeking re-election as Honorary General Secretary for the 1987/88 season. Various ideas were proposed to Mr Wingrove in the hope that he would continue as Honorary General Secretary, but the demands of continuing in this position were not practicable for him under the present organisation.

The Chairman proposed Mr Wingrove reconsider his resignation in the light of suggestions made and reply to the Management Committee meeting.

At the next meeting in May 1987 Mr Wingrove said that he had decided to continue as Honorary General Secretary but also expressed his disappointment that having covered the position of Honorary Assistant-Secretary over the past 5 years with no extra expense, the League could not agree to any compensation associated with carrying out this job.

A lot of Cup Finals were postponed due to the weather (see League committee meetings notes).

DIVISION I CHALLENGE CUP FINAL

GREAT PARNDON RESERVES 1 NORTH WEALD 2

(AFTER EXTRA-TIME)

Two goals from Tim Williams clinched the first leg of a possible trophy treble for North Weald.

His match-winning effort came two minutes into extra-time at Rhodes Avenue.

But the result of the first League Cup Final to survive this season was a personal tragedy for Parndon's Karl Shuttlewood.

He had put his team in front with a spectacular goal, which deserved to be a cup clincher.

Both sides combatted the blustery the blustery conditions well to produce an entertaining match in front of a disappointingly small crowd.

Parndon threatened first, after just two minutes, when promising youngster Ian Henderson's free-kick was flicked on by Warren Perkins to Lee Rawlins, who jinked inside a challenge but then saw his shot blocked by Weald keeper Mark Jones's legs at close range,

At the other end, Williams turned the ball into the net after the whistle had sounded for offside. Weald went close again after 27 minutes when Sean Horrigan's swerving free-kick from 30 yards out on the left hit the bar with Parndon keeper Mark Loxton beaten.

Five minutes later Parndon thought that they had broken the deadlock. Kelvin Quinn carried the ball forward before finding Neil Whitbread who swivelled and hit a tremendous shot from outside the box pas t back-peddling keeper Jones.

Referee Denis Williams gave the goal but then ruled it out for offside after spotting linesman Peter Draycott's flag.

Weald survived again in the 37th minute when Lenny Geddes intercepted Horrigan's back-pass, but Jones came out to half-block and Andrew Owen ran back to complete the clearance.

Parndon continued to push forward at the start of the second half. Whitbread's curling free-kick from near the left-hand corner flag landed on the roof of the net; and Jones had to turn round a far-post header by Rawlins from Bradley Booth's corner.

But, with 20 minutes left, Shuttlewood broke the deadlock in amazing fashion. There seemed no danger when he collected a loose ball fully 40 yerds out – but in a flash he hammered a brilliant shot into the far corner.

Perkins tested keeper Jones with another long-distance shot as Weald wobbled momentarily, but the village side fought back and Edwards was thwarted by Loxton before Williams equalised in the 76th minute.

Phil Needham's free-kick from the left was palmed upwards by Loxton, leaving Williams to score with a glancing header.

Parndon, who were forced to re-shuffle after losing Henderson with a painful shoulder injury, almost regained the lead five minutes later. Quinn put Whitbread through on the left with

Weald appealing in vain for offside, but Jones blocked the blocked the first effort and recovered well to hold the follow-up shot.

North Weald stunned Parndon by taking the lead for the first time early in extra-time. Williams fired in a shot from well outside the box and keeper Loxton looked aghast when the ball flashed just inside a post. Weald's greater experience gave them a critical advantage as Parndon's youngster's tried to pull the game round in the extra period.

Horrigan, with a free-kick, and David Smith-Galer with a chip both went close to increasing the North Weald lead as the teams kept up the entertainment to the final whistle.

Source : Harlow Gazette

NORTH WEALD   **GREAT PARNDON RESERVES**

PREMIER DIVISION CHALLENGE CUP FINAL

HATFIELD BROAD OAK 4 REVERTEX 1

Hatfield Broad Oak enjoyed a 'Field Day' as they regained the Premier Division cup in sensational fashion.

Ted Field opened the scoring and Kevin Field struck twice as the village side marched in victory.

And the old adage 'what a difference a goal makes' was surely coined after a game like this one.

For 70 minutes the teams slugged it out without creating many chances. But once the deadlock was broken, goals rained in from all angles – five in seven minutes as the final took on a completely different look.

The tidal wave of scoring began when Bruce Search sent Ted Field through on the right. Revertex keeper Paul Austin has rushed out of his area to act as an emergency sweeper several times in the game, but he couldn't rescue his side with a fly-hacked clearance on this occasion – Field got there first and was able to fire into an unguarded net.

Broad Oak increased their advantage a minute later when Steve Dean reached the bye-line on the right and crossed for Kevin Field to score with a flying near-post header.

Revertex threw themselves a lifeline within four minutes when Mick Hawkins rolled a short pass across the edge of the penalty area for Mick Gallagher to fire a fine shot into the far corner.

But straight from the restart Broad Oak regained their two goal advantage. Dean ran at the heart of the Revertex defence and drove a right foot shot past Austin's left hand to make it three goals to one.

Spectators were still trying to catch their breath when Broad Oak added a fourth a minute later. Dean again attacked the Revertex rear-guard down the right and his cross looped over Austin, leaving Kevin Field to head the ball down and over the line.

Remarkably, Broad Oak could have scored twice more in the next five minutes as well.

Ted Field's cross caused more panic in the ruffled Revertex defence, but Kevin Field was denied a hat-trick by Colin Stagman's desperate challenge and as Dean moved in – a foul on Austin saved the Harlow side.

Then Kevin Field set up Garry Field but, from a great position, he shot wide.

Revertex were understandably shell-shocked, but they pushed men forward to the end and sub Chris Quinn saw a shot held by Broad Oak keeper Stuart Fuller.

The damage had been done, though with Broad Oak setting up their winning position in remarkable fashion.

The goal flood made everyone forget the earlier lack of incident. As Jimmy Greaves would say, 'football's a funny old game.'

Source : Harlow Gazette

HATFIELD BROAD OAK   **REVERTEX**

W.A. (BILL) BRUTY MEMORIAL CUP FINAL

HATFIELD BROAD OAK BEAT PITNEY BOWES

DIVISION III CHALLENGE CUP FINAL

MANUDEN 2 SHEERING RESERVES 1 (AFTER EXTRA-TIME)

A David Roach goal in the first minute of extra-time earned Manuden the Stortford League Division III cup at Rhodes Avenue.

Roach stabbed home a corner amid a moment of panic and confusion in the Sheering box – one of the few times when the Sheering defence, marshalled vocally by John King, looked vulnerable.

The late crack in the usually tight Sheering back line proved costly, however, as they failed to pull out a late equaliser – only Geoff Romaine going close with a shot which was deflected over.

But, on balance, Manuden deserved the win. In a game of few clear-cut chances, their forwards always looked the more likely to provide the finish.

And the victory also rewarded some stiff battling in the middle and a fine calming influence in defence.

The first half was a quiet affair with only two real chances in the opening half-hour.

First Brendan Heath fired a fierce shot from 25 yards which Sheering goalkeeper Gavin Hammond gathered at the second attempt.

Then Ian Druce burst through for Sheering but Manuden keeper Mick Buckler narrowed the angle well, forcing Druce to go wide and shoot into the side-netting.

But what the early part of the half had lacked in excitement, the final five minutes before the break more than made up for with two goals in as many minutes.

Manuden took the lead after 41 minutes when Heath strode onto a through ball, taking his time before slotting a controlled shot past Hammond.

A defensive disaster ended with keeper Buckler letting the ball slip past him and Sheering's Paul Munn winning a chase with Micky Murphy for the honour of slamming the loose ball over the line from about six inches.

Honours even, both sides gritted their teeth for the second half, but neither could break the deadlock which instead of loosening as the players tired, it became more stifled.

So it was quite a shock in the end that, when side's started their extra-time bout, Manuden sprung so swiftly into the lead – Roach doing the honours by converting a corner from five yards.

The goal tipped the momentum Manuden's way and Paul Bruton, who deserved a goal for his efforts up front, almost added a third but his effort, minutes after the winning goal, was deflected wide for a corner.

Source : Cliff Fox

MANUDEN DIVISION III RUNNERS-UP AND DIVISION III CHALLENGE CUP WINNERS

DIVISION II CHALLENGE CUP FINAL

LONGMAN BEAT SPARTAK 78 YOUTH

GRANGE PARK   QUENDON ATHLETIC

A Larry Jolley goal seven minutes from the end of the Saffron Walden Reserve Cup Final gave Jim O'Connor's Grange Park special reasons to celebrate. The effort clinched a 1-0 win over Quendon Athletic and secured their first trophy in their 20-year history.

SHEERING

INTER-DIVISIONAL CHALLENGE CUP FINAL

ADVANCE POWER SUPPLIES 1 SHEERING RESERVES 2

Sheering Reserves swept away the disappointment of losing their divisional Cup Final – three days earlier by toppling Advance Power Supplies to take the Inter-Divisional Cup.

In their second final appearance at Rhodes Avenue, Sheering changed their kit and changed their luck – clinching victory thanks to a late goal by John McHugh.

The final looked set to go to extra-time before McHugh capped a battling Sheering performance by capitalising on a fine turn and pass by Ian Druce to score the 82nd minute winner. But that wasn't McHugh's only contribution to Sheering's victory – he also set up their first goal after 68 minutes when Hagan netted an equaliser to Dave Lambert's opening second half goal for Advance.

Following an even if uninspiring first half – intriguing most of all for the nifty control of tricky Advance striker Tony Mansfield and midfielder Nick Hunt – the second half exploded into action after two minutes.

Advance's Paul Downey bundled the ball into the Sheering area, bringing it down past a pack of bemused defenders before letting it lose to Lambert who made no mistake, firing home a shot with only keeper Gavin Hammond to beat. But 11 minutes later McHugh, who had spent an unrewarding first half chasing through balls into the Advance box, suddenly helped swing the game back in Sheering's direction.

His sweet cross fell just right for Hagan who connected perfectly, sending a concise effort past Advance's keeper Mark Stevens.

Minutes later Sheering almost took the lead when Hagan picked up a bad back-pass and raced towards goal, but his final shot was charged down by keeper Stevens who was penalised for handling the effort outside his box. Geoff Romaine took the resulting free-kick but hit it disappointingly wide.

Advance' s attempts at getting back in front were limited, despite their superior midfield play.

Only Lambert went close again, taking a pass by Trevor McFaul and bearing down on goal before being forced wide and shooting straight at Hammond.

Sheering, however, still had their trump card to play and after twice testing keeper Stevens in as many minutes, eventually grabbed the glory with McHugh the hero with his sharp shot, eight minutes from the end.

Source : Harlow Gazette

SHEERING RESERVES   **ADVANCE POWER SUPPLIES**

LIVELY AWARD CELEBRATIONS

The League celebrated another fine season with their annual Dinner-Dance and presentation of awards. Presenting the awards was League President John Barry. Special guest was Mr Brian Curtis of the Hertfordshire Football Association, who gave a very lively speech to the packed Memorial Hall in Sawbridgeworth.

Source : Harlow Gazette /Herts & Essex Observer

NOT SO SPORTING GET THE CHOP

Chequers Sports have been thrown out of the League. Clubs voted them out at the League's Annual Meeting following a Management Committee recommendation. The Harlow-based side had a disciplinary record described at the meeting by League Secretary, Dave Wingrove, as 'most unacceptable.'

During the season Chequers players had received 16 cautions and two dismissals. Their sportsmanship marking of 28.1% was one of the lowest on League records. 'They are not the type of club we'd wish to continue in this League,' said Mr Wingrove. The League Chairman said a number of clubs and referees had complained about them. Chequers, who had last season finished sixth in Division I, did not attend the meeting. They owe the League £25.

1,069 players were registered for season 1986/87.

There had been 168 cautions and 28 dismissals as at, 19th May 1987.

There were 54 referees (handbook).

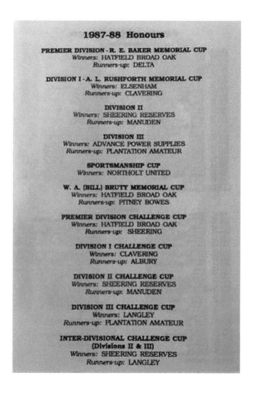

1987-88 Honours

PREMIER DIVISION - R. E. BAKER MEMORIAL CUP
Winners: HATFIELD BROAD OAK
Runners-up: DELTA

DIVISION I - A. L. RUSHFORTH MEMORIAL CUP
Winners: ELSENHAM
Runners-up: CLAVERING

DIVISION II
Winners: SHEERING RESERVES
Runners-up: MANUDEN

DIVISION III
Winners: ADVANCE POWER SUPPLIES
Runners-up: PLANTATION AMATEUR

SPORTSMANSHIP CUP
Winners: NORTHOLT UNITED

W. A. (BILL) BRUTY MEMORIAL CUP
Winners: HATFIELD BROAD OAK
Runners-up: PITNEY BOWES

PREMIER DIVISION CHALLENGE CUP
Winners: HATFIELD BROAD OAK
Runners-up: SHEERING

DIVISION I CHALLENGE CUP
Winners: CLAVERING
Runners-up: ALBURY

DIVISION II CHALLENGE CUP
Winners: SHEERING RESERVES
Runners-up: MANUDEN

DIVISION III CHALLENGE CUP
Winners: LANGLEY
Runners-up: PLANTATION AMATEUR

INTER-DIVISIONAL CHALLENGE CUP
(Divisions II & III)
Winners: SHEERING RESERVES
Runners-up: LANGLEY

W.J. (WALLY) DAY MEMORIAL CUP

Winners : NORTH WEALD Runners-Up : HATFIELD HEATH

Sponsored by Brian Skingle Sports

CHEQUERS SPORTS EXCLUDED

In 1987 Chequers Sports were excluded from the League due to their totally unacceptable disciplinary record.

HEATH HAVE NEW SPONSORS

In September 1987, Hatfield Heath reported to the League that they had sponsorship from Footprint Printers & Stationers Ltd and that their colours were changing from their traditional Gold and Black to Blue Shirts and Black Shorts.

W.A.(WALLY) DAY MEMORIAL CUP FINAL

NORTH WEALD 4 HATFIELD HEATH 3

ALBURY TO CELEBRATE CENTENARY

At a Management Committee meeting in October 1987, Mr Dover reported that Albury FC were founded in 1887 and would be celebrating their 100th season. It was agreed that a celebration match against the League's Representative team should be organised later in the season to commemorate the occasion.

LEAGUE APPOINT NEW SPONSORS

In December 1987, the Honorary General Secretary reported that there had been no replies from Brian Skingle regarding the position of sponsorship. After discussion it was agreed with great reluctance that the League should cease calling itself the Brian Skingle Sports League, in order that alternate sponsorship could be sought for the future.

It was also agreed that Mr Wingrove should write to Mr Skingle informing him of the decision and thanking him for his most valued support in the past.

In 1988 S.C.S. Forklifts became the new sponsors of the League.

In March 1988 Messrs G Banks, G Reed and D Wingrove reported in detail on a meeting held with S.C.S. Forklifts to discuss sponsorship of the League for the 1989/90 season.

Agreement was reached for a five-year sponsorship deal with the terms of payment being reviewed annually. S.C.S. Forklifts also agreed to sponsor the 1988/89 Challenge Cup Finals going halfway towards meeting the cost of the hire of the ground for all six finals.

The Management Committee were unanimous in their approval of the excellent sponsorship agreement and Mr Wingrove confirmed that he had written to the Essex FA seeking permission for the League to be called the S.C.S. Forklifts Bishop's Stortford, Stansted & District Football League from the commencement of the season.

It was agreed to award Albury FC a centenary plaque at the Annual Dinner to commemorate the one hundred years since their foundation.

DIVISION III CHALLENGE CUP FINAL

LANGLEY 2 PLANTATION 1 (AFTER EXTRA-TIME)

Two opportunist goals from Colin Davies helped Langley in the first of their three Cup Final appearances this season at Rhodes Avenue.

The match was made for the cliché 'football was the winner,' because both teams contributed to a contest which was a joy to watch.

They were evenly matched throughout, with neither side able to gain the upper hand for long as play switched quickly and entertainingly from one end to the other.

The spirit shown by both teams was excellent throughout, and it made a refreshing change to see such a final.

The match marked the start of SCS Forklifts' sponsorship of the League, Rod Saunders, a Director and Partner, made the presentations after the game.

Plantation started much the brighter of the sides, and a first minute shot from Steve Monks brought a smart save from Langley keeper Kevin Whitfield – who revived memories of the cloth cap era with a useful display between the posts.

Langley, who won the cup back in 1976, gradually settled with chief striker at the centre of most attacks. After 16 minutes Plantation keeper Bob Linwood mis-handled Simon Bagri's free-kick, but Davies's follow-up effort was headed off the line by influential skipper Pat Crawte.

Four minutes later Plantation's Selwyn Parish gave the ball away to Adam Izzard, but his cross from the right was scooped over by Davies.

Back came Plantation but Roger Tongue blazed Paul Linwood's pass over the bar from close in.

Two minutes later Langley's Noel Roberts beat two men on the edge of the box but fired a shot just too high.

A similar pattern emerged after the break, with Davies again shooting over following Izzard's determined run down the right.

Source : Harlow Gazette

LANGLEY   **PLANTATION**

PREMIER DIVISION CHALLENGE CUP FINAL

HATFIELD BROAD OAK 3 SHEERING 0

Broad Oak demonstrated exactly why they have dominated the League in 90 masterful minutes at Rhodes Avenue.

They scored three times and could have added plenty more as they dictated in all areas against a Sheering side which tried hard but simply could not find the answers to the numerous questions posed by the League champions-elect.

It was Broad Oak's fourth consecutive appearance in the final of the competition and, once they had taken a 36th minute, there was little doubt they would add to their victories of 1985 and 1987.

Broad Oak sounded a warning as early as the fourth minute when Doug Felton – often a central defender but playing midfield this time – fired a first-time drive against the inside of a post.

Sheering continued to live dangerously when Geoff Romaine mis-cued a half-hit Broad Oak's Kevin Field narrowly wide of his own goal.

After that let-off Sheering enjoyed their best spell of the match, and their best effort of the night was a first-time shot by Mark Chisnall from Glenn Thurley's free-kick which went just over.

But Broad Oak replied when Field put Wayne Cracknell through to fire against a post, with Sheering appealing in vain for offside, and two minutes later the League leaders broke the dead-lock.

Kevin Gunn supplied the through ball which sent Field clear to drive a right foot shot past Sheering keeper Paul Smith into the far corner. Field should have added a second just before the break, but his free header from Kevin Gunn's cross was blocked by Smith's legs at point-blank range. Early in the second half Ondre Griggs saved Sheering with a headed goal line clearance from Felton, after Neil Cutmore had denied over Wayne Cracknell's corner.

Broad Oak pressed again and increased their lead in the 56th minute, when Field latched onto Doug Ball's weak back-pass and skipped Smith before scoring – then turned a celebratory somersault for good measure. Dean could have made it a hat-trick of walk-in goals minutes later, but this time keeper Smith managed to stop the effort.

Field and sub Karl Brown both went close before the end as well, but Broad Oak had already done more than enough to retain the cup – leaving Sheering in the same runners-up spot they occupied in 1982.

Source : Harlow Gazette

HATFIELD BROAD OAK **SHEERING**

DIVISION II CHALLENGE CUP FINAL

MANUDEN 0 SHEERING RESERVES 1

Sheering Reserves turned the tables on Manuden to lift the cup at Rhodes Avenue. Manuden ran out winners when the teams contested the Division III Cup Final last season.

But Sheering took the honours this time, with the only goal of the game 15 minutes from the end providing a controversial talking point.

Manuden keeper Mick Buckler ran out to intercept a through pass near the edge of the box but, realising he wouldn't be able to hold the ball and stay inside the penalty, he punched it away from danger.

Referee John McNaughton looked across at his linesman who kept his flag down, then hesitated before awarding Sheering a free-kick for handball just outside the box.

Gary Pullen's kick cannoned off Manuden's defensive wall and fell for Ian Druce – who had just returned to the pitch after treatment for an injury – to fire home a fine shot and decide the match.

Extra-time had looked likely as the two teams, who had been locked in battle for League honours all season, seemed determined to give nothing away.

Manuden had the edge in terms of goal chances created throughout the 90 minutes, but generally both defences looked solid.

Sheering threatened first when Robert Munn set up Druce to shoot just wide. Manuden replied with shots from Peter Pratt, Paul Billings and Pratt again flying wide.

In the 28th minute Sheering keeper Mark Tyne held Andrew Pawsey's shot at point-black range; and at the other end before the break, both Robert Munn and Dave Dobson saw goal bound efforts blocked.

Early in the second half Adam Moulds sent a near-post header inches wide and Manuden substitute Brendan Heath volleyed wide.

Then came Druce's crucial strike – and Sheering might have scored again five minutes from time, but Dobson's shot following Pullen's through pass flew straight at Manuden's keeper Buckler.

Source : Anne Murphy

SHEERING RESERVES

Source : Harlow Gazette

MANUDEN

DIVISION 1 CHALLENGE CUP FINAL

ALBURY 0 CLAVERING 4

Clavering spoiled Albury's centenary celebrations by sweeping them aside at Rhodes Avenue.

Extra experience and sharper firepower saw Clavering to victory, against an Albury side which lacked punch in the penalty area.

Albury defender David Reed made a last ditch attempt to keep the ball out but could only help it over the line.

Within two minutes Albury almost hit back, lively skipper Joel Palmer crossing to Robert Cusick, but the ball took an age to drop and Clavering keeper Richard Cracknell was able to come out and block.

Clavering increased their advantage in the 34th minute when Steve Hagger's in-swinging corner from the left flew straight into the net.

Ironically, the setback spurred Albury on to enjoy their best spell of the match on either side of the break. A goal then would have put the final back in the balance – but Neil Wicks saw a shot parried by Cracknell and Clavering defender Mick O'Connor hooked the loose ball clear, then Wicks was thwarted again by Cracknell, who ran out to hack the ball away.

Clavering regained the initiative and both Kevin Fox and Hagger went close before their side's killer third goal in the 58th minute. Hagger made a strong run down the left and Albury's Darren Wicks turned the ball past his keeper for an unfortunate own goal.

Cusick was denied a consolation goal for Albury by Mattholie's last ditch tackle before Clavering made it 4-0 with four minutes left. Hagger challenged Albury keeper Terry Pomfrett for a through pass, and the ball ran loose for Fox to slot home.

In the final minute Neil Wicks burst through for Albury, but Cracknell maintained his clean sheet with a smart block.

Source : Harlow Gazette

CLAVERING   ALBURY

100 YEARS ON THE DOLE

Albury Football Club are 100 years on the Dole.

That is not a reflection on the players' state of employment, it's how long the club have been playing at their village ground.

They are one of the oldest village sides in Hertfordshire and almost certainly the one of the oldest clubs in the League.

It is unclear how the Dole came to get its name, but the ground was given to the village by the Glyn family, owners of the Albury Hall estate.

The Dole was first used for cricket matches over 100 years ago and from this, stemmed its use as a football pitch.

Sir Francis Glyn, whose father donated the field and was responsible for building a club pavilion in 1913/14, became a President of the club.

It was just after the Second World War that Sir Francis announced that as long as there was football in Albury, The Dole would always be available for use.

He was speaking at the first Annual Meeting of the club, after its re-registration after the war.

Two men responsible for its re-emergence were Horace Dover and George Willett, and their family names have become part of the club's history.

Mr Dover arrived with the army in 1939 and saw The Dole used for matches by Army sides, as well as by the village team.

Now the club's Chairman and Treasurer. He met his wife, Joan, in Albury and has remained there ever since. Their son, Michael, tragically died playing for the club in April 1963.

Another name entwined in Albury Football Club history is that of the Newman family.

Today, Peter Newman (48) manages the team, and he and his three brothers Chris (38), Robert (40) and Trevor (33) – have all turned out in the same side.

Chris, who made a record 25 appearances for the League representative team, hung his boots up two seasons ago.

Peter Newman – who played for the side at school-leaving age and managed the 1975/76 Herts Junior Cup-winning team – also played in the same side as his father, Fred (74), who two seasons ago was the club's Vice-Chairman.

Fred Newman's father, Harry, was also a club official.

Club Secretary, Roy Wicks (45) has been associated with the club since his school days. His sons, Darren and Neil, play for the club, as did his late father, Fred.

There are many other related players in the club's history. Among them, Cecil 'Lew' Dedman, now in his 60's, and his brother, Bertie, who played in goal, are the uncles of former captain, Peter English.

Current centre-half Dave Reed is the son-in-law of Ron Fox, who, with his brother, Eric, are former players.

It is significant that the majority of the club's members live either in Albury or just down the road in Little Hadham.

The highlight of their centenary season was Albury's appearance in the League Division I Cup Final, in which they lost to Clavering.

Albury's most successful spell came in the 1970's when they were the only club from the League to win the Herts Junior Cup. They were Premier Division champions four times

(1970/71, 1971/72, 1972/73 and 1978/79) and were runners-up five times. They also won the League's Premier Division Cup four times (1973/74, 1974/75, 1976/77 and 1978/79) and were also runners-up three times. They were also the first ever winners of the W.J. (Wally) Day Memorial Cup in 1977/78.

INTER-DIVISIONAL CHALLENGE CUP FINAL

LANGLEY 0 SHEERING RESERVES 3

Sheering Reserves completed a hat-trick of wins in the League's Inter-Divisional Cup for their third trophy of the season.

The Division II champions and cup winners had to wait until the 50th minute to open the scoring against plucky Langley, who have already won the Division III cup and finished as runners-up in the Saffron Walden Reserves Cup.

Dave Dobson drove in the opening goal from six yards and 20 minutes later Ian Druce made it 2-0 to finish a goalmouth scramble. Sheering, beaten only once in the League, scored their third in the 89th minute when substitute Dave Smith found the net directly from a corner.

Source : Herts & Essex Observer

SHEERING RESERVES   LANGLEY

W.A. (BILL) BRUTY MEMORIAL CUP FINAL

HATFIELD BROAD OAK 2 PITNEY BOWES 1

Controversy surrounded Hatfield Broad Oak's fifth successive win in the Bill Bruty Memorial Cup.

The winner came in the 85th minute when Broad Oak were awarded an indirect free-kick six yards out in front of the Pitney Bowes goal.

Play was within the centre circle at the time but referee Christopher Deane-Bowers awarded the kick for dissent by Pitney Bowes 'keeper Bruce Grove and the ball was touched aside for Kevin Field to drill past a pack of defenders for his second goal of the night.

The final, at the George Wilson Stadium, hadn't been easy one for Hatfield Broad Oak, who have now completed a remarkable unbeaten season in which they have also won the Premier Division Championship and Cup, and the West Essex Border Charity Cup. Pitney Bowes, runners-up last year and the only other side to have won the Cup, had the better of the first half, with Mark Riggall slotting them into 25TH minute lead.

Broad Oak came back in the second half with Field chesting in a 70th minute equaliser after his shot rebounded off Grove but extra-time looked likely before the free-kick.

League Chairman George Banks presented the Cup.

Source : Harlow Gazette

HATFIELD BROAD OAK   **PITNEY BOWES**

CLAVERING MISSING THE BALL

Source : Herts & Essex Observer

Trophies, shields and medals went like hot cakes as the Memorial Hall in Sawbridgeworth played host to the League's annual awards ceremony

The divisional champions and runners-up were presented with their trophies and medals – all that is, bar Division I runners-up Clavering.

The club was not represented so the League's Management Committee hopes to hand over the trophy and 14 medals at its Annual General Meeting.

Special presentations were made to Albury FC – 100 years old this year – and Sheering Reserves for their third successive Interdivisional Cup success.

Long service awards went to Ken French, League Match Secretary for 13 years; Sheering's Ken Street, in recognition of his 24 years on the League's Management Committee; and to Grange Park's Jim O'Connor, who has completed 12 years as an Officer and Committee member.

Source : Harlow Gazette

Advance Power Supplies, Division III Champions, were all smiles at the League's presentation Dinner.

S C S FORKLISTS FORTHCOMING SPONSORSHIP

At the Annual General Meeting the Chairman, Mr L G Banks, expressed the disappointment of his and fellow Officers to the absence of 12 clubs from the Annual Dinner without even an apology in the case of 9 of them.

Mr Banks recommended to the Meeting that Messrs, K H French, E J O'Connor and E R Street be made Vice-Presidents in recognition of their past services, along with the new League sponsors Messrs. R W Saunders and S C Saunders. This was agreed unanimously. At this point Mr Banks thanked S C S Forklifts for their forthcoming sponsorship and hoped the clubs appreciated the help this would give the League in terms of keeping subscriptions down and being able to give footballs for sportsmanship as happened at this year's Annual Dinner.

Mr A E Dimond was presented with a League tie in recognition of his services to the League as a County Officer.

1,012 players registered, 14 transfers and 10 registrations cancelled.

There had been 32 dismissals and 115 cautions.

There were 54 referees (handbook).

W.J. (WALLY) DAY MEMORIAL CUP

Winners : SHEERING RESERVES Runners-Up : MANUDEN

Sponsored by S.C.S. Forklifts

W.A. (WALLY) DAY MEMORIAL CUP FINAL

SHEERING RESERVES 4 MANUDEN 3

DEATHS OF JOHN SIVYER AND LEN REED ANNOUNCED

In 1989 the tragic death of ex N.A.L.G.O. and League Representative goalkeeper John Sivyer was announced. Also, the death of Mr Len Reed of Farnham FC was announced.

In January 1989, the League Management Committee decided to organize further fixtures for Division 3 teams. It was agreed to play off in 2 groups with the eventual finalists playing for the W.A. (Wally) Day Memorial Cup, as it was the turn of Division 3 to play for the trophy in this season.

The teams will play each other once in their group and then the winners of Group A would play the runners-up in Group B and the Winners of Group B would play the runners-up of Group A in the Semi-Finals.

It was further agreed, in April 1989, to leave the Final of the competition until the traditional opening match for the 1989/90 season at a venue to be decided.

DIVISION III CHALLENGE CUP FINAL

LANGLEY 1 NORTHOLT UNITED RESERVES 3

'We lost to the best team on the night,' admitted Langley Manager Kelvin Whitfield after his team conceded the cup which they won last year. It was also their first defeat of the season. But he promised Northolt a better contest in the W.A. (Wally) Day Memorial Cup.

It was a sporting reaction to a result which denied his side the League and cup double.

But on the night it was the pacy, adventurous men from divisional runners-up Northolt who deservedly picked up the silverware to Manager Steve Godsave's delight.

They had players in Jamie Page and Ian Darkins, along with Peter Laycell and Dean Turner, who had the better of Langley for pace in one-on-one positions.

And they must have sensed an edginess in Langley's defence because they frequently put them under pressure with long through-balls and speculative long-range shots.

The lively Page was a constant handful who couldn't be brought to book.

His 11th minute lob was fingertipped by Langley's keeper Eliot Crace who had to race back to his line to stop a goal.

In the 17th minute Colin Davies got in a threatening header and was denied the opening goal when Dave Henderson blocked at his feet. Davies sustained a dislocated finger.

Then came the inevitable breakthrough in the 32nd minute.

Although the stadium public address system credited Jamie Page, the player himself couldn't claim such an obvious own goal.

The unfortunate culprit was Langley's stalwart defender Gary Cooper who, under pressure from Page, sent a header over Crace into the left hand corner.

But Cooper didn't take long to redeem himself, repeating the feat four minutes later, this time in the correct goal.

A free-kick from the right was allowed to bounce in the heart of the Northolt defence and Cooper glided in at the back to prod the header home.

It was the best moment of the night for the loyal club servant making a record fifth Cup Final appearance in Langley's colours.

Early in the second half Langley enjoyed their best spell, coming close again through Cooper who seemed to have got a taste for pushing forward.

But Northolt regained their momentum and it was a moment of electrifying pace which proved decisive. Dean Taylor was first to a Langley clearance and as the defence was pushing out, he hared around to the by-line before teeing up Page for an open goal finish.

Langley put on Ben Green and Tim Monk in a bid to save the cup but in the 81st minute the game was beyond them.

Page sent a long ball down the left and Ian Darkins planted a perfect 25-yerd lob which bounced once and rose into the top right hand corner.

NORTHOLT UNITED RESERVES   **LANGLEY**

DIVISION II CHALLENGE CUP FINAL

SPARTAK 78 YOUTH 0 HEATH ROVERS RESERVES 2

It was a family affair for Heath Rovers Reserves, as an uncle and nephew goalscoring combination sealed victory in this stimulating final.

For striker Mark Saunders (22) broke the deadlock with a coolly converted spot kick in the 63rd minute.

And uncle Chris, 15 years his senior, made the game safe tucking the ball home when he broke through four minutes later.

The pair are the club's top scorers this season.

To cap it all, the team is managed by another member of the family, Rod, who is Mark's father and Chris's brother. And Rod is the owner of League sponsors SCS Forklifts.

After the game, Rod Saunders was elated. He said : 'It's a great end to a hard season. I was worried it might be a scrappy game, but it wasn't. Far from it.'

In a lively, highly entertaining match these two mid-table teams showed lots of heart and plenty of adventure going forward – they obviously enjoyed their football.

There was an almost constant flow of end-to-end attacking play, laced with some superb passing.

In such an atmosphere, midfield players and attackers stood out. Paul Marsh was particularly effective for Rovers.

He always seemed to have time on the ball and stroked some superb passes around.

Most receptive to this supply was winger Mark Saunders, whose and dribbling skills were a constant threat to Spartak.

Spartak, in turn, had their own playmaker in player/manager Mark Gale, who showed great composure throughout, and a lively front duo in Ashley Bower and Keith Grant.

In an eventful opening 15 minutes, the best of several good chances fell to Spartak skipper Don Martin who moved up from the back for a corner. The kick dropped to him in the box and he was annoyed at himself for stabbing the ball over the top.

On the half-hour mark a lovely move involving Spartak's Gale, Martin Pledger and Grant saw Grant cross from the left for striker Simon Mattson to head just wide.

In the 34th minute, Spartak again went close when Andy Bonham sent a great ball down the right to Bower whose shot on the run beat Rovers keeper Adrian Service but flashed past the foot of the post.

Two minutes later Rovers skipper Peter Hanks joined the attack and did well to turn in the box, but his shot went into the side netting.

Early in the second half Chris Saunders sent an overhead kick just wide of the Spartak goal. A Spartak corner from the right was missed by Service, but Grant's half volley hit the side netting.

The stream of chances had surely to yield a goal. In the end it came from a penalty, resulting from defensive confusion.

Spartak never really cleared their lines from a left-sided corner-kick and play hovered around the edge of their box until Cliff Peddle, for Rovers, jinked into the danger area.

He was just a couple of yards inside the 18-yard line when fouled. Mark Saunders placed the kick well wide of David Pledger.

Four minutes later a superb through ball by Marsh found Chris Saunders galloping through and he finished cleanly.

Spartak battled on gamely and still created enough chances to save the game. Martin swapped positions with Mattson, and substitutes Ian Rooke and Steven Wren came on for Bower and Grant. But it just wasn't their lucky night.

Martin saw a half volley spin just wide of the Rovers post; Rooke caught Pledger out with a lob which carried just over the bar; and Pledger saved well from Gavin Walter.

But Rovers mounted counters in between and could have added more through Mark Saunders, whose shot was saved, and substitute Kevin Neeve, who was narrowly off target in the final minute.

Source : Harlow Gazette

HEATH ROVERS RESERVES   **SPARTAK 78 YOUTH**

PREMIER DIVISION CHALLENGE CUP FINAL

ALEMITE ATHLETIC 2 HATFIELD BROAD OAK 1

Alemite turned the tables on their rivals with a display which deserved a bigger winning margin.

In truth, Alemite's lightning fast wingers made enough openings for them to wrap up the game by half-time.

But they had to survive a late surge of pressure from the League leaders to deny them their third successive win in the competition.

It was a case of too little too late for Broad Oak on a night when they never really got on top of the game.

This was only their second defeat of the season and gave Alemite revenge for their 0-1 loss when the teams met in the League.

Broad Oak's key striker Kevin Field was strangely subdued and nippy winger Wayne Cracknell ran industriously to little effect.

The night belonged to a lively Alemite inside forward who always seemed to have the edge in pace.

Alemite were gifted an opener in the 11th minute when a harmless looking Gary Dance free-kick from the left was deflected into his own net by Trevor Search.

It was unfortunate for Search who was one of Broad Oak's best players.

Alemite hassled well and broke so fast that Broad Oak never settled in the first half. John Bean and Paul Nichols were constant threats with skilful, powerful runs.

In the 13th minute a brilliant through-ball by Mark Morgan released Nichols and he was hacked down by Broad Oak keeper Paul Smith just outside the box. Smith was rightly booked.

But he made a fair stop seconds later when the free-kick led snap shot by Morgan which Smith did well to parry.

Broad Oak's jittery defence kept playing itself into trouble and it was no surprise when Alemite made it 2-0 on the half-hour.

Chris Webb hit a superb 40 yard cross-field pass into the box and John Bean caught a beautiful half volley which went across Smith into the bottom right hand corner.

Two minutes later it should have been 3-0 when Broad Oak fouled Morgan and referee Dave Sullivan awarded a penalty.

Up stepped the formidable figure of Graham Butterworth, but he failed to convert from the spot.

Source : Martin Morgan

ALEMITE ATHLETIC

Source : Herts & Essex Observer

HATFIELD BROAD OAK

INTER-DIVISIONAL CHALLENGE CUP FINAL

BIRCHANGER RESERVES 2 HATFIELD HEATH RESERVES 1

Source : Herts & Essex Observer

BIRCHANGER RESERVES   **HATFIELD HEATH RESERVES**

W.A (BILL) BRUTY MEMORIAL CUP FINAL

ALEMITE ATHLETIC 4 PITNEY BOWES 0

Alemite turned the screw on poor Pitney Bowes and grabbed their second trophy of the season – the W.A. (Bill) Bruty Memorial Cup.

And more misery for Bowes came when substitute Jeff Riley was sent off for an exchange of elbows in the second half.

Bowes gave their Harlow neighbours a good run for their money in the first half and were only one down at the break.

John Bean opened the scoring in the 28th minute after Gary Dance had beaten two Bowes defenders to get to the by-line and square across the area. Bean pivoted on his heels and managed to shoot the ball home.

But if it wasn't for Alemite keeper Brian Williams, Pitney Bowes could have equalised, if not taken the lead.

His saves weren't exactly acrobatic, just happened to have an excellent sense of positioning.

Dave Brett whipped in a fierce free-kick that Williams tipped over, and the keeper had to block well from Phil Groves in the 40th minute.

Seven minutes later, Groves spun round inside the box and had his shot well palmed past the right post.

A highly competitive second half saw both Ian Hawkins for Bowes and Gary Dance going into referee Patmore's little black book, before the game came to life again with Alemite's second goal.

Perry Chandler leapt at the far post to head home a deep cross, and then skipper Mark Morgan made it three after Dance performed magic on the left and put in an irresponsible cross for the burly midfielder to fire home.

Steve Early was delighted to get onto the score sheet when his low drive sped through a jungle of legs and bodies in the Bowes area for Alemite's fourth.

By then, the crowd were screaming five, six or seven.

Just then, Jeff Riley was given his marching orders after getting involved in a little scuffle and duly went back for an early shower

A little unfair perhaps, because although they seemed to lose their way in midfield, Bowes were still battling ferociously until the final whistle.

In particular, Ray Spencer, captain Mark Thompson and Mick Williams all deserve a mention in dispatches.

As for Alemite, it was a workmanlike performance from a side littered with players with senior football experience.

Source : Harlow Gazette

ALEMITE ATHLETIC   **PITNEY BOWES**

DIVISION I CHALLENGE CUP FINAL

GREAT PARNDON 3 ALBURY 2 (AFTER EXTRA-TIME)

Great Parndon clinched the Division I League and Cup double remaining unbeaten all season against Division I opposition.

The first breakthrough came for Parndon when a header by Steve Shearman took an unfortunate deflection off David Reed's leg for an own goal.

In the 54th minute Albury equalised when Mark Saggers profited from some pinball-style ricochets in the Parndon box to hammer a low drive home.

Early in extra-time Parndon regained the lead.

Peter Mays ended a great run from midfield with a through ball to Marshall O'Neill. His cross put keeper Terry Pomfrett under pressure and Matthew Stretton fired the loose ball home on the turn.

Seven minutes later it was level pegging when Saggers got his second goal with a penalty after Simon Goold was brought down by keeper Knight.

The balance only lasted three minutes before May struck the Parndon winner.

Source : Harlow Citizen   Source : Harlow Gazette

GREAT PARNDON   **ALBURY**

At a Management Committee meeting in May 1989, it was reported that, despite it being agreed in the Minutes of the meeting held in May 1987 that Officers should be allowed travelling expenses, the Honorary Auditor wished it to be minuted that Mr Wingrove had charged £48.00 for carrying out League duties over the past season.

She also wished that the agreements on expenses for the following season 1989/90, which included payment form full telephone rental and expenses for journeys backwards and forwards on League business be minuted.

At the League Annual General Meeting the Chairman, Mr L G Banks asked the Meeting to be upstanding in observing a short silence following the recent and untimely deaths of Mr Len Reed of Farnham FC and Mr Ron Hoad of Potter Street FC.

It was unanimously agreed to accept the proposition of Mr G Reed that Mr A E Dimond be elected as a Vice-President of the League. Mr Dimond made a suitable reply of thanks.

Mr L G Banks expressed his desire to make the forthcoming season his last as Chairman.

Mr Wingrove confirmed that he did not wish to seek re-election as Honorary General Secretary for the coming season. Northolt United requested clarification as to whether his resignation as Secretary had any connection to the Minute of the Management Committee Meeting held on 16th May 1989 which referred to his expenses.

Mr Wingrove explained he gave notice four months previously that he would not be seeking re-election, but the Management Committee made an offer regarding expenses following which he decided to stay on. Further to this the Honorary Treasurer requested that on the

Auditors instructions, expenses of £48 incurred by the Honorary General Secretary in travelling for the previous season should be minuted. This, Mr Wingrove found totally unacceptable, particularly as it was agreed in principle at the Management Committee Meeting held on 19th May 1987.

Mr Reed responded by confirming the Honorary Auditor had queried the £48 expenses and asked why it had not been minuted. This he felt she had every right to do and when it was suggested at the Meeting on 16th May offence was taken.

Despite requests from the floor for Mr Wingrove to re-consider his decision, he confirmed that as far as he was concerned nothing had changed and had no confidence that the situation would not re-occur in the future.

Mr Barry summed up the situation and as there were no nominations from the floor to fill this vacancy for Honorary Assistant-Secretary, he requested that Mr Wingrove remain in office until a Management Committee Meeting could be called to discuss the positions further. This Mr Wingrove agreed to do.

EVERY ONE'S A WINNER

Brian Curtis of the Hertfordshire Football Association was guest speaker at the League Annual Presentation night and League President, John Barry presented the trophies.

Source : Herts & Essex Observer

Club representatives with their trophies at the League Annual Dinner and Dance.

992 players registered, 22 transfers and 31 registrations cancelled.

There had been 29 dismissals and 82 cautions.

There were 51 referees (handbook).

The League's bank balance stood at £1,413.37.

Coming next

THE STORY OF THE BISHOP'S STORTFORD, STANSTED AND DISTRICT FOOTBALL LEAGUE

VOLUME 2 1990 - 2016

Introduction

Timeline

Covering the seasons 1989/90 to 2015/16

Past Officers of the League

League Honours

The League Tables 1922/23 to 2015/16

Players that progressed to play for Bishop's Stortford FC

League Representative Matches

League Representative Honours

League Representative Side Selection Committee

Other Representative Matches

Other Representative Honours

The Long Established Clubs

Histories of Albury, Birchanger, Burnt Mill, Great Parndon, Hatfield Broad Oak, Hatfield Heath, Heath Rovers, Langley, Manuden, North Weald, Quendon, Sheering and Thaxted Football Clubs

The Clubs that progressed to higher standard football

Histories of Bishop's Stortford Swifts, Sawbridgeworth, Stansted and Takeley Football Clubs

The West Essex Border Cup

The Saffron Walden Rotary Cup

The Saffron Walden Cup

The Saffron Walden Reserve Cup

Referees that progressed to a higher level

Referees from season 1949/50

Other well-known Referees